FUNDAMENTALS OF MODERN MARKETING

EDWARD W. CUNDIFF
University of Texas at Austin

RICHARD R. STILL
University of Georgia

NORMAN A. P. GOVONI
Babson College

FUNDAMENTALS OF

SECOND EDITION

MODERN MARKETING

PRENTICE-HALL, INC., Englewood Cliffs, New Jersey

Library of Congress Cataloging in Publication Data

Cundiff, Edward W.
Fundamentals of modern marketing.

Includes bibliographical references and index.
1. Marketing. I. Still, Richard Ralph,
(date) joint author. II. Govoni, Norman
A. P., joint author. III. Title.
HF5415.C793 1976 658.8 75-41611
ISBN 0-13-341248-2

FUNDAMENTALS OF MODERN MARKETING *second edition*
Edward W. Cundiff / Richard R. Still / Norman A. P. Govoni

Printed in the United States of America

10 9 8 7 6 5 4 3 2

PRENTICE-HALL INTERNATIONAL, INC., *London*

PRENTICE-HALL OF AUSTRALIA PTY. LIMITED, *Sydney*

PRENTICE-HALL OF CANADA, LTD., *Toronto*

PRENTICE-HALL OF INDIA PRIVATE LIMITED, *New Delhi*

PRENTICE-HALL OF JAPAN, INC., *Tokyo*

PRENTICE-HALL OF SOUTHEAST ASIA PTE. LTD., *Singapore*

CONTENTS

PART THREE
PRODUCTS

PART FOUR
DISTRIBUTION

PART SEVEN
OVERALL MARKETING STRATEGY

PREFACE

This is the second edition of *Fundamentals of Modern Marketing*, an introductory marketing text emphasizing key concepts and issues underlying the modern practice of marketing. Although the basic format of the generally very well-received first edition has been retained, in this edition—in keeping with the title—certain changes have been made. Statistical data have been updated wherever possible, and new materials, such as that on marketing by nonprofit organizations, have been added consistent with the dynamic character of modern marketing.

This text is designed to meet the needs both of students taking only the introductory marketing course and of those planning to take more advanced courses in the field. We hope that both groups will find that this book provides a clear understanding of marketing's role in modern business and society. Even more fundamentally, we hope, too, that readers will conclude that marketing is a highly interesting subject, extremely important not only to the world of business but also to each individual as a consumer and citizen.

The plan of presentation is straightforward. Part One, the general introduction, is a survey of the general nature of marketing, markets, the marketing concept, buyer behavior, the marketing process, and marketing organization. Part Two is an overview of marketing information systems and marketing research. Parts Three through Six are descriptions and analyses of the four main decision areas in marketing—products, distribution, promotion, and pricing. Part Seven, the conclusion, gives special emphasis to the interactions of marketing and society and provides an integrated view of overall marketing strategy.

Each chapter's content has been planned to constitute a unit of understanding. Each opens with a statement of learning objectives, proceeds with descriptions and analyses of key concepts and issues, and closes with a highlight of the chapter's coverage. We have sought, in other words, to adhere closely to the time-tested pedagogical formula of "telling them what you're going to tell them, tell them, and telling them what you've told them." In addition, being strong believers in the discussion method, we have included for each chapter a wide variety of questions, problems, and short cases aimed at provoking interesting and meaningful discussion.

For successful completion of this book, we owe a great deal to a great many people. For providing us with rather definite notions on what should and should *not* be included in an introductory marketing text, our greatest debt is to our present and former students. For candid appraisals and helpful suggestions made at various stages in the development of the manuscript, we are indebted to numerous reviewers and users of the first edition. For contributing frank criticism and advice—most of it informally—we owe considerable thanks to numerous present and former members of the marketing staffs at the University of Georgia, The University of Texas at Austin, and Babson College, as well as to our ex-colleagues at Syracuse University, Cornell University, The University of Missouri at Columbia, and Bowling Green State University. For providing continual help and encouragement we are deeply indebted to the following Prentice-Hall personnel: Garret White, Assistant Vice-President; Judith L. Rothman, Editor–Marketing; and Maureen Wilson, College Book Editorial-Production Department. Last but by no means least, for consistently aiding us through their sympathetic understanding, we are indebted to our wives and families. For all of this assistance—both that acknowledged here and throughout the book, as well as that received from business executives and others—we express our sincere thanks. However, as usual, we accept full responsibility for any and all deficiencies.

EDWARD W. CUNDIFF
RICHARD R. STILL
NORMAN A. P. GOVONI

PART ONE

MARKETING AND THE BUSINESS ENVIRONMENT

When you have mastered the contents of this chapter, you should be able to:

1. Explain the basic role of marketing in different kinds of profit-seeking and nonprofit organizations.
2. Define marketing in terms of product-market interrelationships and ownership transfers.
3. Identify the different environmental factors influencing marketing decisions and activities.
4. Define the concept of a "market."
5. Explain how the consumer market differs from the industrial market.
6. Explain the concept of "market segmentation."
7. Name and illustrate the various bases used for segmenting consumer and industrial markets.

CHAPTER 1

INTRODUCTION

This opening chapter is designed to provide you with an understanding of marketing and its role in business organizations and society. Discussion focuses first on the various kinds of marketing activities performed by different organizations. Then marketing is formally defined and analyzed with respect to its relationship to production—the other main business function—and its relationship to the environment. Next, the concept of a market is clarified and the concept of market segmentation explained. Finally, various forms of market segmentation are examined.

What Does Marketing Do?

Marketing basically involves relating the needs and desires of the market with the performer's products or services in order to achieve transfers of ownership. A manufacturer of shoes, for example, expects its marketing function or subsystem to: provide information on consumer preferences with respect to shoes and on size and location of markets and the nature of competition; make potential consumers aware of and informed about their product; make the product available at places and times convenient to prospective buyers; and participate in the determination of prices that will both be acceptable to potential buyers and yield profits to the company. Marketing plays the same basic role for all producers of goods, whether they produce steel for industry buyers, penny candies for school children, or fresh fruits and vegetables for ultimate consumers.

Marketing also plays a similar role in connection with the distribution of services. A life insurance company (which basically sells the service of protection), for instance, expects its marketing staff to: provide information about its markets and the kinds of insurance service they need and want; provide channels through which these services are made available to prospective buyers; make potential buyers aware of the types and nature of services offered; and participate in the determination of prices (rates) that will both be acceptable to potential buyers and yield profits to the company. Whether the service is dancing instruction, travel advice, or hair styling, marketing is responsible for the ultimate delivery of the service to buyers and for the inward flow of income to the organization.[1]

Marketing is a vital function in both profit-seeking and not-for-profit organizations. Marketing as a management practice has traditionally been analyzed from the viewpoint of profit-seeking institutions and it has been only recently that the marketing-type problems of not-for-profit institutions have been given more than scant attention.[2] Perhaps because marketing is so closely associated with the production of income (and profit) in the profit-seeking organization, nonprofit types of institutions (such as community chests and charitable foundations) are often reluctant to identify the marketing activities which they must carry on as marketing. Thus, for example, the marketing executive of a nonprofit institution may be called the director of public relations or business manager. Nevertheless, the top management of a symphony orchestra needs very nearly the same kind of help as a profit-making recording company with respect to: identifying its market and its preferences in music; providing channels to make the music available to prospective patrons; informing them about and stimulating an interest in the music offered; and establishing a price that will optimize customer patronage and income to defray expenses. Similar marketing activities are essential, whether the nonprofit institution is a hospital, a university or school, or an art museum. Unfortunately, in the past, this reluctance to recognize marketing as a necessary and integral part of the nonprofit institution's total function has resulted in marketing ineptitude and operating inefficiency.

Definition of Marketing

Marketing activities are those most directly concerned with the demand-stimulating and demand-fulfilling efforts of the enterprise.

[1] A notable description and analysis of service marketing may be seen in John M. Rathmell, *Marketing in the Service Sector* (Cambridge, Mass.: Winthrop Publishers, Inc., 1974).

[2] See, for example, Frederick E. Webster, Jr., *Social Aspects of Marketing* (Englewood Cliffs, N.J.: Prentice-Hall, Inc., 1974), pp. 73–92; and Philip Kotler, *Marketing for Nonprofit Organizations* (Englewood Cliffs, N.J.: Prentice-Hall, Inc., 1975).

These activities interlock and interact with one another as components of the total system—by which a company develops and makes its products available, distributes them through marketing channels, promotes them, and prices them. Specifically, then, we define *marketing* as the managerial process by which products are matched with markets and through which transfers of ownership are effected.[3]

Marketing

Product

It should be noted that *product* as used in the above definition is an all-inclusive term which includes services as well as products of a physical nature. In this sense, then, piano lessons are just as much a product as the piano itself. The matching of services with markets to effect transfers of ownership is also marketing.

PRODUCT-MARKET INTERRELATIONSHIP

Our definition states, in part, that "marketing is the managerial process by which products are matched with markets." Marketing and production activities are interlocked—we can only market products that can be produced, and we should only produce those that can be marketed. Thus, it is logical to think of marketing as the business process by which specific products are matched up with specific markets and to think of production as the business process concerned with manufacturing these products.

Matching products with markets is both a marketing and a production problem. It involves selecting, manufacturing, and marketing products that possess as many as possible of the characteristics desired by those who make up the markets while at the same time attempting to achieve maximum progress in reaching the company's overall goals. While top management bears the ultimate responsibility for satisfactorily solving these problems, marketing management plays a highly important role.

Consider, for instance, how products are matched with markets. In some cases, marketing research first uncovers the product characteristics wanted by final buyers, then top management (working with both production and marketing executives) translates these wants into product specifications. In other cases, the products are initiated through technical research carried on within the company, and marketing research focuses on finding and measuring potential

[3] The American Marketing Association defines marketing as consisting "of the performance of business activities that direct the flow of goods and services from producer to consumer or user." See Committee on Definitions, *Marketing Definitions* (Chicago: American Marketing Association, 1960), p. 15. There are two main reasons why we have chosen to use our own definition rather than the "official AMA" definition: (1) we believe that the interrelatedness of *product* and *market* is an essential idea and should be explicitly included in a definition of marketing, and (2) since there can be no marketing unless transfers of ownership occur, we believe also that this point should be explicitly included in a definition of marketing.

markets. In all cases, if management decides to go ahead and market the product, marketing management is responsible for applying certain marketing controllables (personal selling, advertising, other promotion, distribution policy, and price) to gain and hold market favor. In addition, marketing management is responsible for the continual adjustment of marketing controllables for the company's products already on the market, while production management, of course, is responsible for making them. Thus, modern management regards marketing and production as interdependent subsystems—marketing as the subsystem by which specific products are matched up with specific markets and production as the subsystem charged with manufacturing these products.

OWNERSHIP TRANSFERS

Ownership transfers occur repeatedly as products flow from producers to final buyers. For instance, a manufacturer may sell its output to wholesalers who, in turn, resell it to retailers who, again in turn, resell it to consumers. In this instance, every unit of the manufacturer's product that is finally purchased by a consumer has had its ownership transferred three times (from manufacturer to wholesaler, from wholesaler to retailer, and from retailer to consumer). Of course, for an ownership transfer to take place, buying as well as selling is necessary and, in moving a product to market, the producer only sells. The resellers (wholesalers and retailers) both buy and sell, and the consumer only buys. Consumers are the "targets" of marketing activities—the whole movement of products from producers to consumers anticipates this final buying action by consumers. There can be no marketing, then, unless ownership transfers are effected.

Marketing's Environment

Marketing decisions and activities are strongly influenced by environmental factors beyond the control of the producer or the consumer alone. Figure 1–1 illustrates this relationship of internal and external factors affecting marketing. Within the circle are the decision areas controlled by marketing management, each of which is discussed in detail in later chapters. Around the rim of the figure are the various factors which clearly affect marketing decisions and strategy but which marketing management cannot control directly. Thus, management in making decisions on and taking action on the controllables must necessarily take these environmental (uncontrollable) factors into account.

One of these factors—availability of resources (financial, physical, and human)—clearly limits the range and variety of decisions marketing management can make. Resources may be available to the company but not available to marketing management, i.e., when top

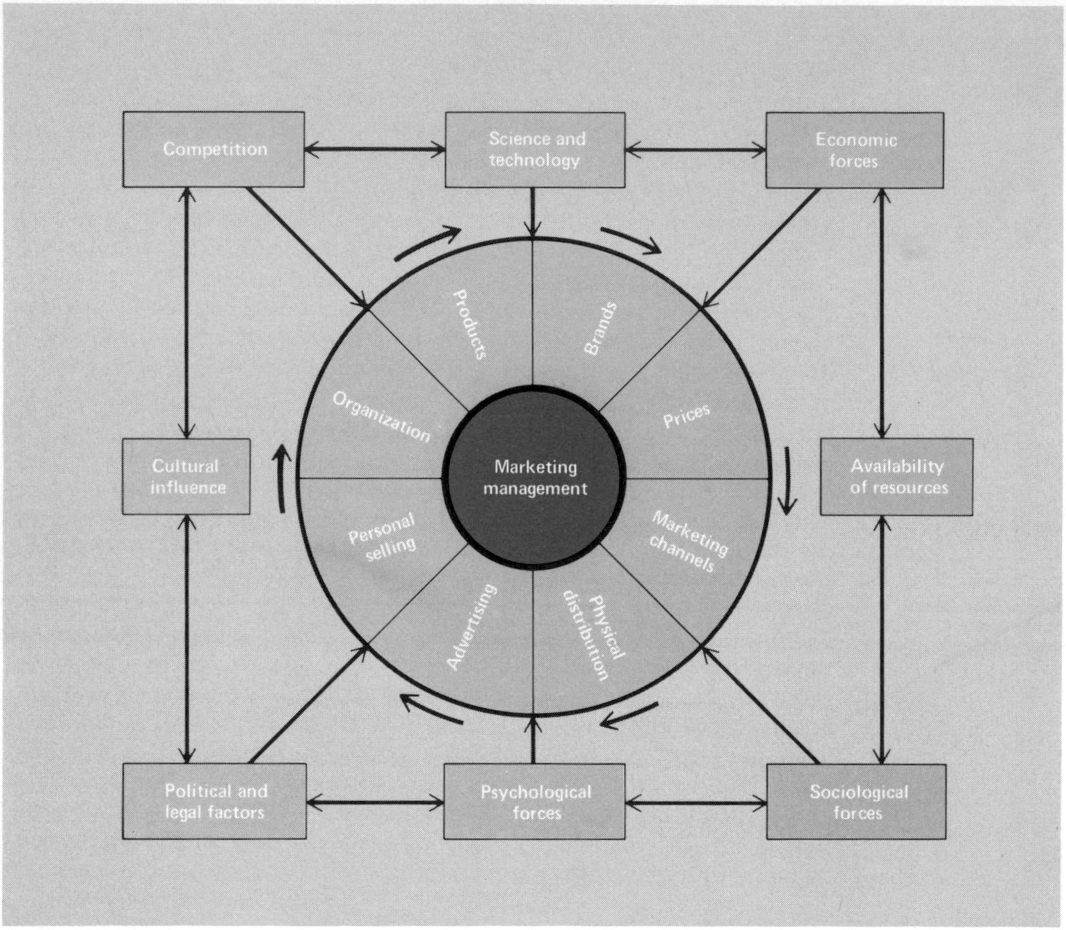

Figure 1–1
Marketing and its environment

management assigns higher priorities to nonmarketing activities in allocating resources.

Three types of external factors—competition, political and legal, and science and technology—directly restrain management's freedom to make marketing decisions and to formulate marketing strategy. No marketing decision of major importance should be made without giving consideration to competition. When contemplating any marketing action, management must be ever aware that there is some chance that competitors will react in ways that may have adverse effects on the company; similarly, each company's management must be prepared to evaluate and possibly counteract the marketing moves of competitors. Likewise, both existing legislation (and its interpretation) and the political climate limit management's freedom to make marketing decisions; for example, even though there are not many laws prohibiting environmental pollution through packaging (as through using "throwaway packages"), the climate of public opinion is such that management must examine all proposed marketing changes carefully to determine whether or not they might produce adverse ecological effects. Similarly, the current state of science and technology has limiting effects on the range of possible marketing moves; for instance, science and technology have not yet progressed to the point where it is possible to make a self-loading automatic dishwasher that will also clear dishes from the table.

The other four types of external factors—psychological, cultural, sociological, and economic—indirectly restrain management's freedom to make marketing decisions through the influences they exert on buying behavior. Psychological forces internal to the individual, such as physiological needs and the needs for self-esteem and the esteem of others, influence all human behavior including buying behavior. Cultural factors help explain why U.S. consumers eat very little rice and Japanese consumers use rice as a main staple in their diet—thus, the problem of increasing rice consumption is different in the United States than it is in Japan. Sociological factors, such as the preferences of an individual's close friends and associates as well as the influences they exert on him or her, strongly affect the individual's behavior in buying clothes, automobiles, houses, and numerous other products. Diverse economic forces, such as the present size of a consumer's income and his or her future income expectations, are basic to his or her decision to buy or not to buy many products. Because these four types of external factors influence the behavior of potential buyers, they limit management's range of appropriate marketing decisions (appropriate in the sense that possible decisions will produce desired results).

Markets and Market Segmentation

Market

The concept of a *market* is extremely important in marketing. The American Marketing Association defines a market as the aggregate demand of the potential buyers for a product.[4] An aggregate demand is a composite of the individual demands of all potential buyers of a product. Thus, the U.S. market for bicycles consists of the total of all the demands for bicycles by all those people in the United States who are potential buyers of bicycles. If a person is considered as a prospective bicycle buyer, he or she is included in the total which makes up the aggregate demand for bicycles. But an aggregate demand, or total market, also consists of the sum of the demands of different *market segments,* each containing a group of buyers or buying units, who share qualities that render the segment distinct and make it of significance to marketing. For example, the total market for bicycles is made up of many market segments, one of which is children. Chil-

[4] *Ibid.,* p. 15.

dren constitute a distinct market segment for bicycles, with respect both to product preferences and buying patterns. Recently, children exhibited strong preferences for the "Sting Ray" or banana seat type of bicycle, and bicycle purchases by children, in most cases, are influenced or made by parents. Other bicycle market segments include: hobbyists, who prefer racing models; health faddists, who want bicycles for exercising; and adults, who want bicycles simply to use for transportation—a rapidly growing segment. Thus, a market is not only an aggregate demand for a product but the sum of the demands of different market segments.

Market Segment

A *market segment,* then, is a group of buyers who share qualities that make the segment distinct and of marketing significance. Existence of a group of individuals with common characteristics does not in itself constitute a market segment. Only when they have common characteristics as *buyers* do they form a market segment. For example, to the extent that teenagers as consumer-buyers behave differently than do other age groups, a teenage market segment exists. The distinctive marketing characteristics of each such market segment make it productive for the marketer to adapt its product and marketing program to meet the needs of each. Thus, modern marketers devote considerable attention to the identification and study of the various market segments for their products.

THE CONSUMER MARKET AND THE INDUSTRIAL MARKET

Ultimate Consumer

Industrial User

The broadest market division is that separating the consumer from the industrial market. This division, so broad that each part is too extensive to consider as a market segment, separates potential buyers into two categories: ultimate consumers and industrial users. *Ultimate consumers* buy either for their own or for their families' personal consumption. *Industrial users* buy to further the operation of businesses or other institutions.

There are striking differences between ultimate consumers and industrial users, because their ways and means of purchasing differ considerably. Obviously, ultimate consumers buy in much smaller quantities and generally for consumption over much shorter periods than do industrial buyers. More important, ultimate consumers are not usually so systematic in their buying as are industrial users. Some industrial users are business enterprises that exist to make profits, which encourages them to adopt systematic purchasing procedures. Other industrial users are nonprofit institutions (such as governmental agencies, schools, and hospitals) whose operations are audited and reviewed by outside authorities, which also encourages systematic purchasing procedures.

Another important difference is that ultimate consumers spend only part of their time buying, whereas the industrial user employs professionals who devote all of their time and effort to purchasing.

Furthermore, the ultimate consumer spreads all his or her buying skill over a wide range of goods and services, whereas the professional tends to specialize and, therefore, has more opportunity to perfect purchasing skills. These are only a few of the many differences between ultimate consumers and industrial users, but they indicate that marketers must use significantly different approaches in marketing to the two broad types of markets.

MARKET SEGMENTATION

Market Segmentation

Market segmentation has existed since the beginning of marketing. The concept of *market segmentation* is based on the fact that markets, rather than being homogeneous, are really heterogeneous. No two buyers or potential buyers of a product, in other words, are ever identical in all respects. However, large groups of potential buyers share certain characteristics of distinctive significance to marketing, and each such group constitutes a market segment. When we consider the market for automobiles, for example, we think of a most heterogeneous group of buyers—buyers representing every income group, every age group, every section of the country, both sexes, married and single people, and so on. And of course industrial buyers, such as the business firm buying a fleet of automobiles for its salesmen, increases further the heterogeneity. If we segment the automobile market by income groups—for example, into lower-, middle-, and high-income groups—we achieve some homogeneity. If, next, we segment each of these income groups into further subsegments—for example, into such subsegments as the Eastern urban, age 30–39, middle-income group—we gain still more homogeneity among buyers within each subsegment. Through the segmentation of markets, management improves its ability to tailor marketing programs uniquely fitted for each segment. Continual refinement and increased sophistication in market segmentation are required on the part of management.

Knowing the market, then, is important to a marketer's success. Knowing the market, however, means knowing the different market segments which make up the total market. Alternatively put, it is essential for the marketer not only to know "who buys the product" but to recognize that not all buy for the same reasons. Only if they have this knowledge are marketers in position to design optimal marketing strategies.[5]

Segmenting the Consumer Market There are many different groupings that can be used for market segmentation. One writer suggests that, historically, there have been two general approaches: *people*-oriented market segmentation and *product*-oriented market

[5] An excellent overview of market segmentation is provided in J. F. Engel, H. F. Fiorillo, and M. A. Cayley, *Market Segmentation* (New York: Holt, Rinehart, and Winston, Inc., 1972), pp. 1–19.

segmentation. The former uses dimensions such as demographics, social class, stage in the family life cycle, product usage, innovativeness, and psychological characteristics, while the latter uses dimensions such as product benefits, product usage occasions, value, ingredients or taste, perceived attributes, and advertising appeals.[6]

Most major market segments used in analysis of consumer markets result from groupings based on income, age, degree of urbanization, and geographic location. Because income is the main source of consumer purchasing power, market segmentation based solely on income is widely used. An individual's income, in most cases, limits not only how much he or she can buy but also what is bought. The person with low income, for example, is often so hard pressed to pay for such necessities as food, clothing, and shelter that he or she cannot afford to buy tickets for a football game and contents himself or herself with watching it on television at home. Table 1–1 shows the distribution of income among U. S. households in 1973. Nearly 45 percent of U.S. households earned between $10,000 and $24,999, while over half of the households earned $10,000 or more. In 1960, only about 14 percent of the households earned $10,000 or more and, in 1970, approximately 48 percent achieved incomes of $10,000 or more. In the thirteen-year period, there has been roughly a 270 percent increase in the number of households earning $10,000 or more.

Market segmentation on the basis of prospective buyers' ages is important for many products, especially for those designed specifically for certain market segments. For example, some brands of breakfast cereal are "aimed" to suit the tastes of children, while other brands are attractive to consumers within a broader range of ages.

Table 1–1 Number and Percent of American Households by 1973 Household Income

HOUSEHOLD INCOME	HOUSEHOLDS	
	Number (in thousands)	Percent
Total	69,859	100.0
Under $3,000	8,395	12.0
$3,000–$4,999	7,641	10.9
$5,000–$6,999	6,976	10.0
$7,000–$9,999	10,181	14.6
$10,000–$14,999	15,820	22.6
$15,000–$24,999	15,422	22.1
$25,000–and over	5,424	7.8

Source: United States Government, Bureau of the Census.

[6] Discussion of these and other means of market segmentation can be found in Joseph T. Plummer, "The Concept and Application of Life Style Segmentation," *Journal of Marketing*, January 1974, pp. 33–37.

Clothing is another product that benefits from market segmentation by age, since different age groups have different clothing needs and preferences. Table 1–2 shows the age structure of the U.S. population in July, 1973. Nearly three-fifths (58.5 percent) of the population was less than 35 years old.

Market segmentation by stage in the family life cycle adds another dimension to age as a basis for segmentation. Expenditures on selected items vary with the life cycle stage. For example, families with young children typically are very good customers for labor-saving appliances, and families with teenage daughters spend relatively more for women's and girls' clothing. The most commonly used scheme for market segmentation by family life cycle stage has five major classes:[7]

First Stage: Single or married head, under 40, no children
Second Stage: Married head, under 40, young children, with or without older children
Third Stage: Married head, under 40, older children, no young children
Fourth Stage: Married head, 40 or older, no children under 20
Fifth Stage: Head living alone, over 40, no children

Segmentation by degree of urbanization—based on whether buyers live in urban, suburban, or rural areas—differentiates buying behavior for many products. Table 1–3 shows the distribution of population in the United States by location of residence. People in

Table 1–2 Age Structure of the U.S. Population, as of July, 1973

AGE	POPULATION Number (in thousands)	Percent
All ages	210,404	100.0
Under 5 years	16,714	7.9
5–13 years	34,739	16.5
14–17 years	16,746	8.0
18–24 years	26,381	12.5
25–34 years	28,605	13.6
35–44 years	22,807	10.8
45–54 years	23,814	11.3
55–64 years	19,270	9.2
65 years and over	21,329	10.1

Source: United States Government, Bureau of the Census.

[7] For an excellent discussion of the effects of the life cycle on needs and purchase behavior, see C. Glenn Walters, *Consumer Behavior* (Homewood, Ill.: Richard D. Irwin, Inc., 1974), pp. 249–250.

Suburbia

the urban fringe and outside urbanized areas (which together constitute *suburbia*) now comprise the largest population group, and they account for a disproportionally higher share of sales of products such as removable floor coverings, sporting goods, and lawn and garden equipment.

Within different parts of the United States, there are sufficient variations in consumption patterns to justify geographical market segmentation. These variations result from differing cultural heritages, topography, and climates and have significant implications for the marketers of some products. Furniture manufacturers, for example, find that consumer style preferences vary considerably among different geographic sections. The Southern consumer shows a much stronger preference for traditionally styled furniture than does the Midwesterner. Similarly, many a Far Western consumer has a noticeably strong preference for furniture styles that show oriental influences. Other examples of distinctive regional preference are found in food, clothing, floor coverings, paint, and housing.

Some of the more important bases marketers use for segmenting their markets have been discussed above, but there are other segmentation bases available. Factors such as social class, level of education, and sex can be important bases for segmenting markets. In addition, it is sometimes good practice to break market segments down into subsegments by cross-classifying a grouping of market segments in terms of another grouping system. The following table (Table 1–4), for instance, shows how an analyst might break down income market segments into subsegments according to the ages of income recipients, each box representing a subsegment. The box marked X, then, would represent those persons with incomes of $10,000–$14,999 who are in the 18–24 age group.

Essentially the same reasons and bases for market segmentation hold true both for domestic and international marketing. However, market segmentation is even more important to the international

Table 1–3 U.S. Population by Location of Residence, 1970

LOCATION	POPULATION Number (in thousands)	Percent
Total	203,212	100.0
Urban	149,325	73.5
Inside urbanized areas	118,447	58.3
Central cities	63,922	31.5
Urban fringe	54,525	26.8
Outside urbanized areas	30,878	15.2
Rural	53,887	26.5

Source: United States Government, Bureau of the Census.

Table 1–4

	INCOME GROUP				
Age Group	Under $5,000	$5,000–$7,499	$7,500–$9,999	$10,000–$14,999	$15,000 & over
18–24				X	
25–34					
35–44					
45–54					
55 & over					

marketer because it is dealing with several nations, each of which has unique customs, beliefs, value systems, language, religion, race, and the like. The increased number and variety of variables also makes effective market segmentation more difficult to achieve. As a result, international marketing management normally must give extremely close attention to market segmentation.

Segmenting the Industrial Market In terms of dollar value of the goods marketed, the industrial market is nearly as large as the consumer market. The industrial market, like the consumer market, is made up of different market segments. Thus, market segmentation is as appropriate for industrial as for consumer products. Separating industrial users into groups facilitates analysis of the industrial market. Many different bases are used for segmenting the industrial market, the four most important and most used bases being: kind of business or activity, geographical location of the user, usual purchasing procedure, and size of user.

Market segmentation by kind of business is usually approached through use of the U.S. government's Standard Industrial Classification System (known as the S.I.C. system), under which all places of business are classified into one of ten divisions covering the entire field of economic activity. Each of these divisions is, in turn, broken down into several "major groups" representing specific kinds of business, and, again, into still further breakdowns of even more specific kinds of business. Thus, with the use of the S.I.C. system, the industrial market can be divided into relatively small, medium, or large market segments—depending upon the degree of homogeneity desired in the analysis. For instance, manufacturers of furniture and fixtures are classified under S.I.C. #25. Further subclassification is effected through three- and four-digit numbers. Thus, manufacturers of household furniture come under S.I.C. #251, and those of metal household furniture come under S.I.C. #2514.

Such factors as variations in topography, climate, and historical tradition cause considerable variation in the way industrial marketing is conducted in different areas. The topography of an area, for example, affects the types and costs of transportation available for shipping industrial goods. Thus, it often proves more expensive to ship bulky and heavy products across the Rocky Mountains than to ship it an equal distance over the Great Plains. Similarly, variations in climate affect the needs of industrial users for building materials and heating and cooling equipment. In addition, geographical segmentation of the industrial market may exist because some kinds of business and service organizations seem to settle in certain areas—for example, steel producers and auto makers in the Great Lakes region.

Industrial users are generally more systematic buyers than are ultimate consumers. But even among industrial users there is much variation in the amount of consideration given to buying different items. The decision to buy a major installation, such as a blast furnace or cement kiln, nearly always requires extensive market and other technical investigations plus the approval of several high executives in the industrial user's organization. But the same firm may treat the purchase of supplies, such as office stationery or pencils, as a routine procedure of concern only to the purchasing agent. The industrial marketer must apply different selling tactics and strategies to each of these buying situations.

The industrial market is characterized by wide variation in the sizes of customers, and sizes of industrial purchases also vary greatly. Since it is generally more economical to sell in large lots than small, the industrial marketer often quotes lower prices to buyers of large orders. This is often the main reason why marketers use different methods for reaching industrial users who vary greatly in size.

Summary

Marketing is the managerial process by which products are matched with markets and through which ownership transfers are effected. Ownership transfers take place in an environment that affects the manner in which marketing operations can be and are performed. This environment includes not only the availability of resources but competition, political and legal factors, science and technology, and cultural, sociological, psychological, and economic forces affecting consumer behavior.

Among the most basic concepts in marketing are those of market and market segmentation. A *market* is the aggregate demand of the potential buyers of a product. *Market segmentation* refers to the analysis of a total market in terms of its component segments, each being made up of prospective purchasers who share common characteristics as buyers.

QUESTIONS AND PROBLEMS

1. Henry Ford, pioneer automobile manufacturer, once said, "The consumer can choose any color he wants, so long as it's black." Contrast this statement with the modern philosophy of marketing and production.
2. "He who builds a better mousetrap will find the world beating a path to his door." How much truth is there in this age-old saying? Has it ever been true?
3. Economists often define production as "the creation of any good or service that people are willing to pay for." Compare this definition with the concept of production held by businessmen (and by most business students). According to this definition, can marketing be considered a form of production or not? Why?
4. It is a fact that every year total sales in this country exceed the total purchases of goods and services by consumers. What reasons might you advance to explain this?
5. Someone has said that "marketing both begins and ends with the consumer." Explain.
6. Explain why marketing is important in nonprofit institutions as well as in profit-seeking institutions.
7. How does marketing add value to goods? Give a few examples.
8. "Marketing and production activities are interlocked." Discuss.
9. Figure 1–1 illustrates the relationship of internal and external factors affecting marketing. Explain this relationship.
10. Many marketers contend that "the solution to every marketing problem lies with the consumer." Is this contention valid? Why or why not?
11. What reasons are there for believing that marketing will be of increasing importance in the future?
12. "With products being differentiated more and more, markets are certain to become increasingly segmented." Agree or disagree? Why or why not?
13. Of what value is a breakdown of markets by industrial users and ultimate consumers since the same individual, when buying a typewriter for his office, is an industrial user, and when buying a typewriter for his home is an ultimate consumer? Is he really likely to act differently in these two situations?
14. Is market segmentation a concept equally valuable to marketers of all kinds of products? Would it be of much help to a soap producer? An automobile manufacturer? A life insurance company? An airline?
15. If a family's income doubles (increases from $10,000 to $20,000),

what would you expect to happen to its relative expenditures for food? Clothing? Housing?

16. In American society, the housewife has become the primary purchasing agent for the family. Is it probably true that with this greater responsibility for buying has gone an increased authority to make buying decisions?
17. Under what conditions should a manufacturer consider segmenting its market along sexual lines? With such segmentation, what differences would probably be necessary in the two marketing programs?
18. A retired elderly couple with an income of $10,000 a year from retirement benefits and social security may have as much buying power as a couple in their twenties with an income of $15,000 a year. Explain how this might be true. In what different ways would they be likely to spend their income?
19. Explain the marketing significance of market segmentation by stage in the family life cycle.
20. Would you expect the U.S. rural market to be much different from the urban and suburban markets in terms of preferences for clothing, food, and leisure time activities? Are these differences likely to be larger or smaller than regional or geographic differences within like groups, for example, urban dwellers?
21. To what extent do ethnic and racial market segments exist in the United States? Would you anticipate that such segments as now exist will become more pronounced or disappear? Why?
22. Would it be accurate to assume that regional differences in consumer preferences are rapidly disappearing with improved communication and transportation? Explain.
23. Would the Standard Industrial Classification System provide an equally satisfactory basis for segmenting the market for drill presses as for typewriting paper? Why or why not?
24. Why should San Diego, California, prove to be a more promising market for the products of a Seattle, Washington, lumber mill than would Denver, Colorado?
25. If it makes sense to identify different segments of the industrial market as potential purchasers of original equipment and replacements, does it make equally good sense to differentiate these products and use separate salesmen? Explain.

CASE PROBLEM

The Gilmore Company manufactured a limited line of lawn and garden equipment. While the company was small by most standards (a matter of choice by Mr. Robert A. Gilmore, Sr., founder and president), it did enjoy a fine reputation as a producer of quality products that sold primarily in the medium price range.

Although Mr. Gilmore staunchly advocated the practice of manufacturing products only after marketing research first uncovered the specific product characteristics wanted by ultimate consumers (no technical research was carried on within the company), he was seriously pondering a new gadget that his son, Bobby, had developed in the basement of their home. The gadget was an attachment for an oscillating-type lawn sprinkler, which could regulate the spread of water. At the time, the only way to regulate the watering area was to adjust the water pressure at the faucet. Mr. Gilmore believed the new attachment had possibilities and decided to discuss the matter with his marketing manager. He felt it was unnecessary to get the opinion of his production manager since the product had a very simple design and should not pose any production problems.

Evaluate Mr. Gilmore's approach to the situation.

When you have mastered the contents of this chapter, you should be able to:

1. Explain the marketing concept in terms of its essential features.
2. Identify the key environmental factors that influence companies in their decisions to adopt the marketing concept.
3. Identify the organizational conditions that generally precede management's recognition of the necessity for adopting the marketing concept.
4. Illustrate how a company should view its planning and operating activities under the marketing concept.
5. Explain how management should go about implementing the marketing concept.

CHAPTER 2

THE MARKETING CONCEPT

Marketing Concept Basically, the *marketing concept* is a philosophy of management that strongly influences the management of marketing efforts in those companies adopting it. Recent significant changes in markets, in technology, and in the ways available for reaching and communicating with markets have intensified competition. These changes, coupled with the growth in size and complexity of business organizations, have made it increasingly important for companies to move toward adoption of the marketing concept.

The Marketing Concept— A Preliminary View

Figure 2–1 portrays the essential features of the marketing concept. A company operating under this concept takes its principal direction from the marketplace; that is, from its knowledge and understanding of its customers' needs, wants, and desires. This becomes, then, the main basis for organizing operations; not only marketing, but production, financial, and other organizational units are geared toward satisfying customers' needs, wants, and desires. However, the organization of operations also is influenced importantly by the company's overall goals; department heads must recognize what results top management is looking for if they are to manage their departments in ways that not only satisfy customers' needs, wants, and desires but also facilitate achievement of company goals. Thus, the marketing concept has three main features: (1) a market or customer orientation, (2) a subordination of departmental aspirations to company-wide goals, and (3) a unification of company operations.

Environmental Factors Influencing Adoption of the Marketing Concept

Certain key environmental factors provide the setting within which companies adopting the marketing concept can reasonably expect satisfactory results. Consider the consumer market: long-term population and income trends have caused large potential markets to exist for the continual stream of product improvements and new products that have been made possible through advances in technology. These market and product factors have produced a rising crescendo of competitive activity, as more and more marketers seek shares of consumers' buying power. Competitive activity has been further heightened by evolution and change in marketing channels and by development and growth of successive new waves of mass communications media, which make it possible to adjust marketing controllables in new ways.

These environmental changes are causing marketers of consumer products to alter both their marketing philosophy and organization. They are becoming less product-oriented and more market-oriented, gearing their operations primarily to customers' needs, wants, and desires and only secondarily to particular products. Promotional emphasis, at the same time, is shifting away from selling the product *per se* to selling the function that the product can perform for customers; for example, rather than promoting the technical features of a self-cleaning oven, one marketer now advertises "this oven will clean itself, permitting the user to avoid a dirty and time-consuming job."

Marketers of industrial products have been slower in adopting the marketing concept. Nevertheless, developments in the consumer

Figure 2–1
The marketing concept

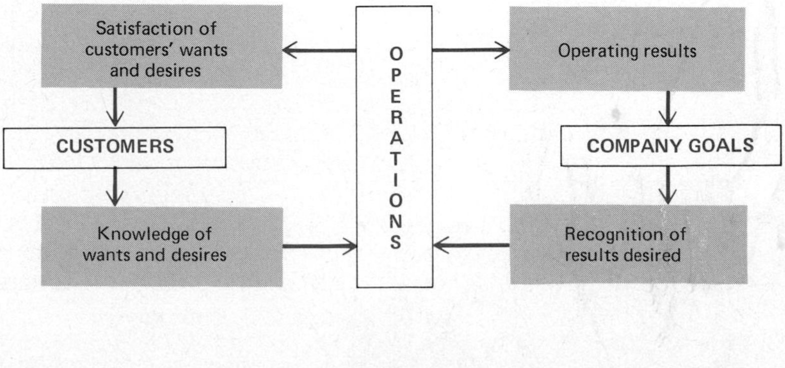

market have "spilled over," and industrial marketers are also adjusting their operations according to the marketing concept. Each of the key environmental factors influencing adoption of the marketing concept, first among consumer goods marketers and then as a spillover among industrial goods marketers, is examined more closely in the following discussion.

CHANGES IN MARKETS

Population Growth Consumer markets are made up of people with money, and the American market has been growing both in population and income. Total U.S. population, as Figure 2–2 shows, has grown from fewer than 100 million people in 1910 to around 206 million in 1975 and the projection for the year 2010 is that population will then exceed 245 million. The American population is growing at a net rate of between 1 and 1.5 million persons a year. Thus, large and growing potential markets exist for the widening stream of new consumer products being introduced to the market.

Growing Number of Households For some products (e.g., household appliances, automobiles, and other consumer durables) market growth is related to the total number of households more closely than it is to the total population. In 1975 the number of house-

Figure 2–2
Population of U.S. 1910–1975 with projections to 2010

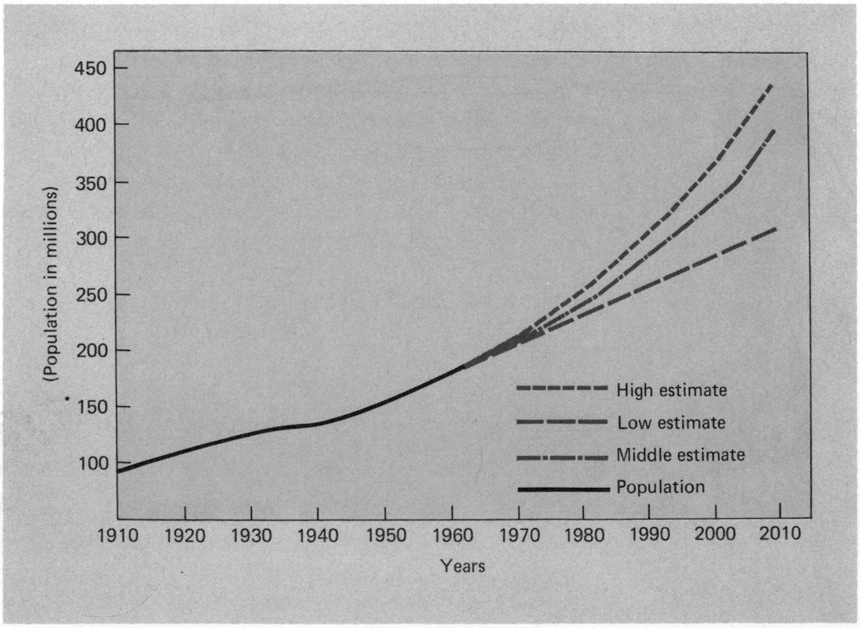

holds approximated 68 million, and even though total population growth is slowing, an average of over 850,000 new households is being added each year. In the near future, the rate of new household formation is expected to accelerate, because the post World War II population bulge will have reached adulthood, and a total of more than 75 million households is predicted by 1985. The number of households is increasing at a faster rate than the total population, and marketers of many consumer durables can look forward to potential markets that grow faster than the consumer market as a whole.

Disposable Personal Income

Growth in Disposable Personal Income Total *disposable personal income* (what people have left to spend or save after paying taxes) rose from a little over $83 billion in 1929 to almost $688 billion in 1970 and was running at an annual rate of over $795 billion in 1972 (in terms of current dollars).[1] However, in 1973 and 1974 the growth leveled off. In terms of purchasing power (i.e., real income), the growth has not been so great, but it is still striking—stated in constant (1958) dollars, the increase was from $150.6 billion in 1929 to $497.5 billion in 1968, a net gain of about 230 percent. However, during 1974 inflation actually decreased total disposable personal income, and it was impossible to predict when it might start to increase again.

In current dollars, per capita disposable income increased from $705 in 1929 to $3,431 in 1968 and is expected to reach $5,760 in 1980. Thus, from 1929 to 1968 the increase was nearly 400 percent and the predicted increase from 1968 to 1980 is an additional 67 percent. The American market has grown increasingly affluent, and the trend is still in that direction.

What has been the impact of rises in the price level on the real purchasing power represented by increasing per capita disposable incomes? Figure 2–3 provides an answer to this question. In this exhibit, per capita disposable income is shown both in 1967 dollars and in dollars reflecting the price level of each year during the period. Thus, in terms of constant (1967) dollars, per capita disposable income rose from under $1,900 in 1950 to about $2,700 in 1967, roughly a 42 percent increase. In spite of rising prices, American consumers have enjoyed continuing increases in the purchasing power at their disposal.

Discretionary Income

Increases in Discretionary Income There is also a trend for households to have increasing amounts of *discretionary income,*

[1]U.S. Department of Commerce, *Statistical Abstract of the United States,* Bureau of the Census, 1974.

which is money left over after buying essential food, clothing, shelter, transportation, and other items a household regards as necessities. Such income may be spent, saved, used for buying non-necessities, or for a combination of these. Experience indicates, however, that a rise in discretionary income usually results in more spending for non-necessities *(discretionary spending).*

Discretionary spending grew, as Figure 2–4 shows, from about $90 billion in 1946 to about $195 billion in 1967. Continuing increases in discretionary purchasing power in consumers' hands have resulted in dramatic expansions in the market potentials for such items as automatic dishwashers, color television sets, and home swimming pools. Moreover, with consumers becoming more affluent, they are also becoming more particular about what they buy and more choosy about what they will accept. Increasing consumer sophistication has led more manufacturers to research consumers' wants and desires more thoroughly and to develop and market products more in line with these findings. Simultaneously, growth in market potentials for non-necessities has encouraged other firms to enter such markets, thus adding to the incentive all competitors have for adjusting their products more closely to what consumers demand.

Leveling Off of Income Distribution Pattern There is also a trend toward a leveling off of income among consumers, a trend which is contributing importantly to growth of mass markets for such luxury items as motorboats which, until recently, only a few

Figure 2–3
Rise in per capita disposable income 1950–1967

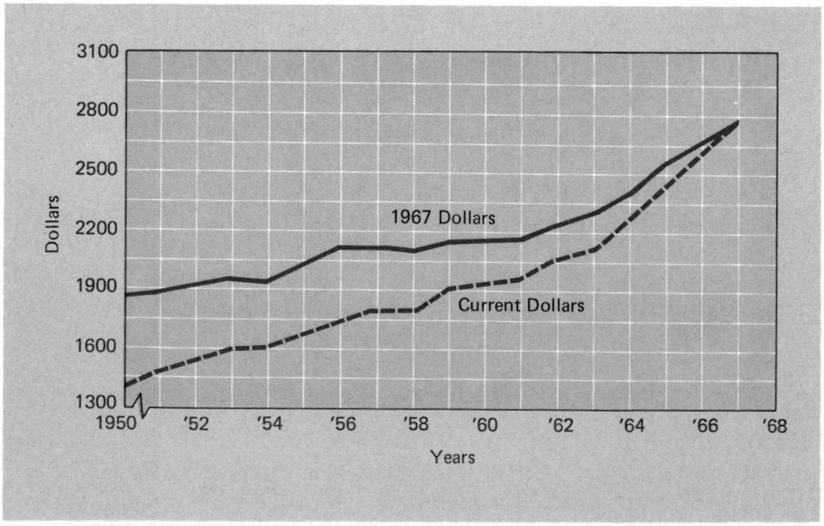

Source: National Industrial Conference Board, Inc., *A Graphic Guide to Consumer Markets: 1963–1969*, p. 26.

could afford. A few generations back, income distribution resembled a pyramid with the vast bulk of the incomes (i.e., the low incomes) at the pyramid base. Today, this distribution more closely approximates a diamond shape, with a large middle-income group positioned between a rich minority above and a poor minority below. Mean average family income reached $9,019 in 1967, with 63 percent of all U.S. families in the middle-income group ($5,000–$15,000), 12 percent in the rich minority (over $15,000), and 25 percent in the poor minority (under $5,000).

Although the rate of rise in discretionary income slowed markedly in 1973 and 1974, still more people tend to have more income, and this is causing new mass markets to develop. More and more products once regarded as luxuries have become necessities. Washing machines, radios, television sets, telephones, and automobiles all have—for ever increasing segments of the population—moved from the luxury class to the necessity class.

New Attitude Toward Debt Ever since the great depression of the 1930s, less and less stigma has been attached to credit buying, and fewer people save in order to pay cash for such products as automobiles, television sets, furniture, and major household appliances. Each year, for instance, more than six in ten new car buyers and five

Figure 2–4 Growth in discretionary spending 1946–1967

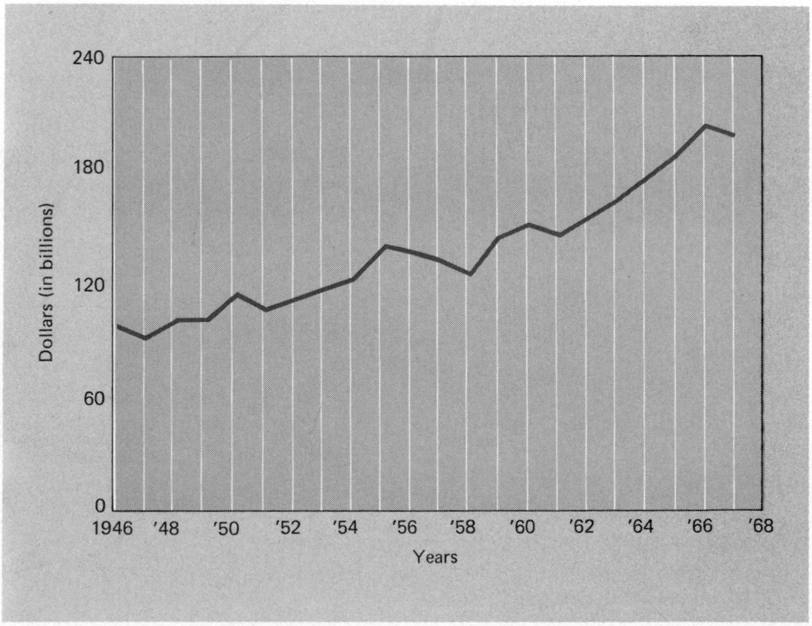

Source: National Industrial Conference Board, Inc., *A Graphic Guide to Consumer Markets: 1968–1969*, p. 30.

in ten used car buyers buy on credit. Many cash buyers borrow from banks, finance companies, and other lenders, so, in effect, they also buy on credit but make their payments to lenders rather than directly to sellers. Credit buying has become a way of life for millions, including many who could pay cash but prefer not to.

The amount of credit a consumer can obtain is related to the size of his or her present income. Marketers of such products as mobile homes, boats, and camping trailers have adopted credit plans to accelerate expansion of their markets; and "Go now—pay later" plans have made international air travel possible for the average person. In addition, the spread of bank-sponsored credit card plans has made it progressively easier to buy on credit even from those retailers who formerly sold for cash only. The changing attitude toward debt and the increasing ability of consumers to obtain credit has added to the intensity of competition for the consumer's dollar.

TECHNOLOGICAL CHANGE

No company has a guarantee that its product will not be made obsolete by some technological advance. Time and again, and with increasing frequency in recent years, technological change has brought overnight obsolescence to products, whole product lines, and even entire industries. At the same time, technology has just as suddenly created vast new markets for other products and industries.

Total expenditures for research and development (R&D) soared from under $2 billion in 1945 to over $31 billion in 1974. The federal government supplied a large portion of these funds to support research in defense and defense-oriented industries as well as for the space exploration program, but private companies also greatly increased their R&D expenditures. One important result of increased R&D spending has been the shortening of product life cycles—time spans from market introductions to market discontinuances—as new products account for an increasing proportion of sales. Another has been that technological developments in one industry often create products sold to markets traditionally supplied by a different industry.

Technological change, then, is a key element in the competitive struggle among companies. An ever-growing number of new products is being introduced to the market each year. Thus, the list of products from which consumers may choose also grows longer.

CHANGES IN MARKETING CHANNELS AND PHYSICAL DISTRIBUTION

Changes in marketing channels have occurred at a more rapid rate, generally speaking, than changes in either markets or technology. At one time, a manufacturer could expect its marketing channels to remain stable and appropriate over a long time. But appearance of new types of distributive institutions, shifts in operating methods of older institutions, and development and change in physical distribution systems have created new distribution problems as well as opportunities.

Many new types of distributive institutions have appeared since the 1930s; the consumer markets for some products have also been invaded by marketers who previously operated elsewhere. Grocery outlets, for example, are stocking traditional drugstore items, such as aspirin and mouthwashes, while druggists retaliate by adding certain food items. Petroleum marketers now sell such items as coffeepots, cameras, and short-wave radios to their credit-card holders by mail. The chains of redemption centers operated by trading stamp companies are important distributors of many products previously sold only through conventional retailers, such as department stores and appliance dealers. Numerous similar examples exist. Thus, the range of distribution options open to the manufacturer has significantly broadened.

Noteworthy improvements in transportation have also been occurring, making it possible to distribute products faster, more economically, and more widely than ever before. Among these are jet air freight, containerized shipping, piggyback, fishy-back, and the unitized train. Technological gains in the design, manufacture, and utilization of transport equipment yet to come will make possible still further gains in the ease with which manufacturers may distribute their products not only nationally but throughout the entire world. Manufacturers who restrict their distribution to certain areas will find themselves confronted by an increasing number of new competitors from elsewhere.

GROWTH OF MASS COMMUNICATIONS MEDIA

With the appearance and growth of successive new waves of mass communications media—newspapers, magazines, AM and FM radio, black-and-white and color television—it has become possible to "spread the word" about new product developments faster, more widely and, for the most part, more effectively than before. They have also made it possible for advertising to play a larger role in marketing. Furthermore, the growth of mass communications media has been further stimulated by the increasing pressures for rapid development of mass markets brought on by the ever-accelerating rate of technological change and by businessmen's efforts to secure the economic advantages of large-scale production. At the same time, communications effectiveness has tended to increase: development and growth of different kinds of mass media have made it possible for marketers to deliver advertising messages in more ways, each medium reinforcing messages delivered by other media and each boosting the combined impact on potential buyers.

SUMMARY OF ENVIRONMENTAL FACTORS INFLUENCING ADOPTION OF THE MARKETING CONCEPT

We can sum up the four main environmental factors helping bring about adoption of the marketing concept as follows:

1. More people have more money although the rate of growth in discretionary income has been slowing.
2. More things are being made – more types of products, more versions of particular products, and closer adaptations of individual product characteristics to the wants and desires of specific market segments.
3. There are more ways to move products to markets, institutionally and physically.
4. Prospective buyers can learn about the products available for sale through more communications media and learn about them more effectively.

Every reason exists for predicting that these trends will continue in the near future. Consumers have an increasing number of ways to spend the incomes they receive. As the growth in incomes slows down, the tempo of competitive activity for the consumer dollar will intensify. Under these environmental conditions, the company following policies consistent with the marketing concept is helping to insure its own survival and is in a good position to capitalize on marketing opportunities as they develop.

Organizational Conditions Preceding Adoption of Marketing Concept

Three organizational conditions, all representing maladjustments to the environmental factors just discussed, generally precede management's recognition of the necessity for adopting the marketing concept.[2]

[2]Many of the ideas in this section trace to ones first put in writing by Theodore Levitt. See his article, "Marketing Myopia," *Harvard Business Review,* July–August 1960, pp. 45–56. This article was reprinted along with further comments by the author in *Harvard Business Review,* September–October 1975, pp. 26ff.

PRODUCT ORIENTATION

The traditional orientation of top management in many companies, particularly those emphasizing mass production, focuses mainly on the product. Such product orientation involves falling in love with the company's own products: concentrating on making them better (technically, mechanically, and aesthetically), improving the production process, bringing down product costs, and the like, while simultaneously neglecting to take into account changes in the market and competitive situation. A product-oriented company expects marketing operations to serve the seller's interests alone and not those of buyers. Focusing on ever-more-efficient manufacturing, top management assigns marketing the task of selling increased outputs—literally, if necessary, of "forcing it down customers' throats." If the fact that the company has a "better mousetrap" does not cause the "world to beat a path to the company's door," the marketing department is expected to go out and sell the output any way it can.

The great danger in the product-oriented company is that top management will not realize what business the company is really in; that is, that it will fail to recognize that it is in business to serve a market and not simply to dispose of a product. The risk is that the market now buying the product will find some more satisfactory way of meeting its needs. Eventually, the owners of horse-drawn buggies nearly all bought automobiles! Where did that leave the makers of buggies? As a pure matter of survival, companies with product orientations must change them in order to stay in business at all.

COMMUNICATIONS PROBLEMS AND UNCOORDINATED PROLIFERATION OF SPECIALISTS

As a company grows, various functions (such as marketing, finance, and production) are split into smaller and smaller parts, each in charge of a specialist. Complexities of administering the growing number of people in the organization also bring into existence a wide range of bureaucratic positions. Thus, with organizational growth, departmental walls tend to rise ever higher, causing some tasks to be duplicated, as department heads and other bureaucrats seek to build their own little empires.

As the number of specialists grows, they tend to lose effectiveness in communicating with others not sharing their specialties. As various technical languages for communicating with others sharing the same specialties develop, overall communications deteriorate because things and events take on a variety of special meanings for different specialists.[3] Additionally, certain specialists feel the need

[3]On this matter, see T. Burns and F. M. Stalker, *The Management of Innovation* (London: Tavistock Publications, Ltd., 1961), p. 155.

for justifying their own positions, and may seek to legitimatize their positions by transforming everyday speech into technical jargon and, in some cases, even into mathematical formulae. Worse yet, in a company where this is going on, management tends to fail to coordinate the proliferation of specialists; so they are inclined to work at cross purposes, and frictions and inefficiencies as well as communications problems permeate the entire organization.

Such difficulties often cause top management to become preoccupied with internal operations. Painfully aware that hoped-for economies of large-scale operations are not being realized, management tends to devote its main efforts toward improving the technical aspects of operations and, likely as not, moves further toward product orientation. Thus, management exhibits a growing inability and unwillingness to see opportunities on the outside caused by market shifts, technological changes, and the like.

CONFLICTS AMONG DEPARTMENTAL GOALS

Also stemming from the strong drives of different specialists to justify their own positions is the conflict among natural departmental goals. In the production department, costs are uppermost in importance. Thus, emphasis is placed on reducing costs in every possible way by minimizing the number of products, standardizing product variety, lengthening the interval between model changes, and maximizing the length of production runs. In the marketing department, everything tends to revolve around sales volume. Hence, sales are pushed by any means available, and pressures are exerted to offer the widest variety of products, to change models at short intervals, to get the products into every conceivable outlet, to promote them continuously and heavily, and to price them at or below competitive levels. Finance specialists also are involved in the effort to justify their own positions—often seeking to maximize short-run returns to stockholders, not only neglecting to consider customers' wants and desires but also opposing research and development projects needed to keep the firm competitive, frustrating the efforts of both production and marketing to install innovations that cost money now but pay off in the long run, and generally trying to minimize costs and maximize revenues at the same time. As each department emphasizes attainment of its own goals, the total enterprise's future potential for serving its markets profitably is reduced. With each department trying to optimize its own performance, the company's overall performance is suboptimized.

Planning and Operating Under the Marketing Concept

Figure 2–5 shows how a company should view its planning and operating activities under the marketing concept. Research and analysis is needed both to identify market needs and to clarify company goals as well as to provide relevant information on both for decision making. Then, management formulates an overall company operating plan—integrating marketing, production, financial, and other plans into a unified whole. After this extensive planning, management initiates the actions needed (i.e., it puts into effect the various actions required to make the plan work). The anticipated results—in the ideal situation—would be both the fulfillment of market needs and the attainment of company goals. Note carefully, how-

Figure 2–5
Planning and operating under the marketing concept

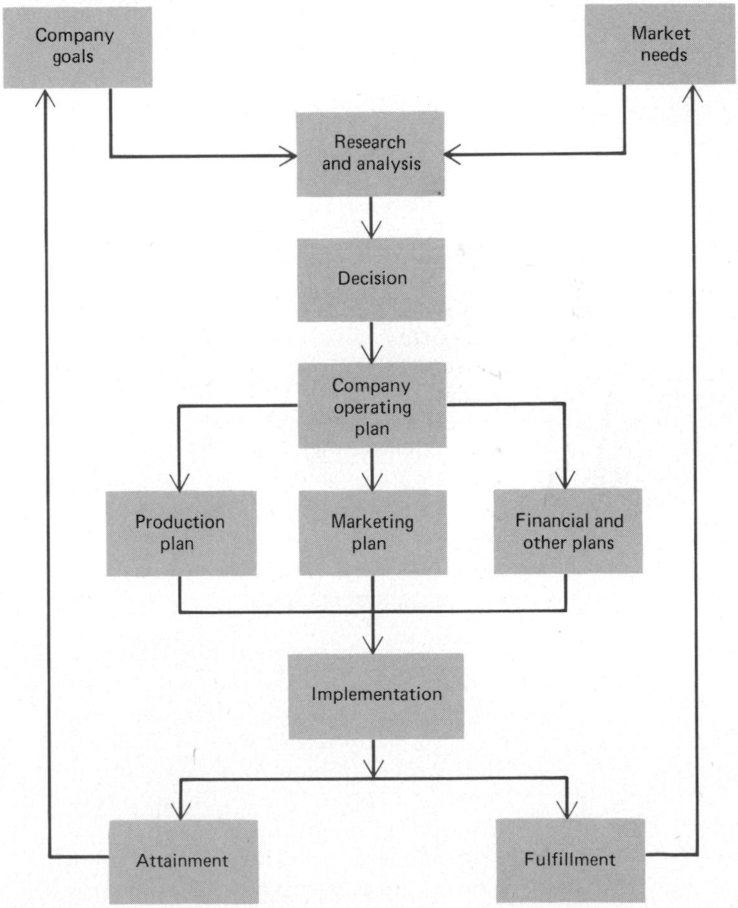

ever, that should the ideal situation not occur, then the entire process recycles—as indicated by the closure arrows (i.e., those running back from attainment to company goals and from fulfillment to market needs).

Implementing the Marketing Concept

Three main features distinguish the company managed according to the marketing concept: (1) adoption of a predominantly market or customer orientation, (2) subordination of departmental goals to a set of company goals, and (3) unification of company operations, both to serve markets effectively and to meet company goals.

MARKET ORIENTATION

In adopting a market orientation, management focuses on the customers' wants and desires primarily and on the product only incidentally. Thus, emphasis is put on using marketing research to keep abreast of market trends and developments and on doing research and development work (even if it results in making present products obsolete). Specifically, management exerts every effort to keep up-to-date on the changing answers to five important questions:

1. What business are we really in?
2. Who are our customers?
3. What do they want and desire?
4. How can we best distribute our products to them?
5. How can we communicate most effectively with them?

FORMULATION OF COMPANY GOALS

Top management formulates a set of company goals to which individual departmental goals are subordinated, thus giving tangible recognition to the fact that the company exists to achieve something as a company rather than as a collection of uncoordinated individual departments. Such total company goals as achieving a given profit level or a certain return on investment become of prime importance. Therefore, in working toward achievement of a given profit level, for instance, the production department is made aware that obtaining low manufacturing costs is not enough. The marketing department is guided toward placing less emphasis on high sales volume and more on making profitable sales. The financial department is alerted to top management's desire not only to provide a satisfactory short-run return for the stockholders but to serve the company's markets profitably over the long run. In other words, a coordinated effort is made to optimize the company's total performance, recognizing that this undoubtedly means suboptimizing the performance of individual departments.

UNIFICATION OF COMPANY OPERATIONS

In seeking to achieve company goals by effectively serving chosen markets, management works continuously to weld the different parts of the organization into an efficient operating system. An orchestration of effort is required to correct such organizational deficiencies as the communications problems among the specialists and the parallel tendency for their proliferation to go uncoordinated. Management strives to secure a synergistic effect—to achieve greater total results than could be obtained by the individual departments working separately and not coordinated with each other. Therefore, a company managed under the marketing concept plans, organizes, coordinates, and controls its entire operation as *one system directed toward achieving a single set of goals applicable to the total organization.*

Summary

This chapter has focused upon what is perhaps the single most important idea in modern marketing—the marketing concept. You should now thoroughly understand both the meaning of this concept and its significance for the management of marketing efforts. You should also know how the critical changes that have been—and are—occurring in markets, in technology, and in the ways available for reaching and communicating with markets have exerted—individually and collectively—increasing pressures on managements to adopt the marketing concept. Similarly, you now should know and understand how the growth in size and complexity of business organizations has made it increasingly important for their managements to adopt the marketing concept. Recognition of these changes and conditions by management leads ultimately to adoption of the marketing concept which requires management to view its planning and operating activities in a new light. In implementing the marketing concept, management must adopt a market orientation, formulate company goals, and unify company operations.

QUESTIONS AND PROBLEMS

1. Why do marketing changes generally seem to appear first in consumer goods markets rather than in industrial goods markets?
2. List five products with markets more closely related to the total number of households than to the total population.
3. Distinguish between disposable income and discretionary income. How closely is discretionary income related to discretionary spending?
4. Analyze the trends existing in the income distribution pattern of the United States. What direction do you expect future trends will take? Why? What will be the significance for marketing?
5. Explain how technological change contributes to the rising tempo of competition.
6. What is "technological forecasting"?
7. Discuss how the growth of different mass media has affected the role of advertising in marketing.
8. What new types of distributive institutions have appeared recently? What niches have they filled?
9. Outline the main environmental factors that have helped bring about adoption of the marketing concept. Do you anticipate that these factors will continue to play an influential role in shaping the nature of marketing in the future? Why or why not?
10. Explain the differences between a company with a product orientation and one with a market orientation.
11. As an enterprise grows, there is a tendency for communications to lose effectiveness. Why? What can be done to improve this condition?
12. How can less than optimal overall performance result in a company when each of its departments emphasizes attainment of its own goals?
13. What businesses are the following concerns really in?
    a. a commercial bank
    b. a city bus system
    c. an electric utility
    d. a hotel
    e. an outdoor movie
14. Explain fully what the marketing concept is all about. How would you convince a skeptical businessman of its value?

CASE PROBLEM

Mr. Winfield Robinson, president of the Longwear Shoe Company, had just concluded his weekly meeting with the production manager, the controller, and the marketing manager. He was deeply concerned with several developments in the meeting that gave indication that the internal operation of the company had lost some of its sense of purpose and unity.

The Longwear Shoe Company manufactured a line of high-quality men's shoes and had experienced rapid growth, more than doubling its sales volume in the past five years. In this period, each department had added several new positions, manpower believed necessary to keep pace with the increasing scale of operations.

During the meeting, the three department heads strongly disagreed with each other on several points, each claiming his department should be given priority because it was the most important in the company. Some significant issues went unresolved because of the failure to reach agreement. In addition, Mr. Robinson was troubled by the fact that several key communications had become distorted as they were fed through the departments.

Recognizing that the meeting was rapidly degenerating into a venture in futility, Mr. Robinson abruptly concluded it with a statement that he did not intend to become preoccupied with internal operations and that the three department heads should come to the next meeting prepared to discuss ways of resolving the internal strife and difficulties that had been brought to the surface.

What issues are involved in this situation and what should Mr. Robinson tell his department heads at their next meeting?

When you have mastered the contents of this chapter, you should be able to:

1. Explain the model of economic man and *evaluate* its usefulness in analyzing buying behavior.
2. Show how conglomerations are turned into assortments as indicated by sorting theory.
3. Identify the more important "uncontrollable" economic factors influencing personal consumption spending.
4. Name the basic factors influencing learning and *explain* how they provide marketers with several keys to understanding consumer behavior.
5. Identify the several contributions made by clinical psychologists to the explanation of buyer behavior.
6. Show how need satisfaction theory helps to explain buyer behavior.
7. Explain how the concepts of self-image and brand image and Festinger's theory of cognitive dissonance help to explain buyer behavior.
8. Explain the following as influences on human (and buying) behavior: reference groups, the individual's concept of social role, the diffusion process, social class, and culture.

CHAPTER 3

BUYER BEHAVIOR

In order to understand marketing, you must also understand buyer behavior. Marketing success, or failure, depends importantly on target customers' individual and group reactions expressed in the form of buying patterns. Analysis in this chapter focuses on the three main approaches to the explanation of buyer behavior: (1) the economic, (2) the psychological, and (3) the sociocultural. Social scientists in each of these fields have attempted to explain why people behave as they do—of particular interest to marketing are their explanations of why people behave as they do as buyers. Such relevance exists in the economist's explanations of consumer motivation, and the relationships of certain economic factors (e.g., income, its distribution, and its characteristics) to buyer behavior. Relevance is also found in the psychologist's explanations of: how people learn about products and services, the motivations that underlie buying behavior, the influences of individual needs and drives on buying behavior, and the perceptions individuals have of themselves and the products they buy. Similar relevance also lies in the explanations advanced by sociologists and cultural anthropologists concerning: the influences of group behavior upon individual behavior, the diffusion of ideas (and new products) among various groups, and the impact of the culture upon its members. You should recognize, of course, that all of these influences interact in highly complex ways, affecting the individual's total pattern of behavior as well as his or her buying behavior.

Buyer behavior may be viewed as *an orderly process whereby the individual interacts with his or her environment for the purpose of making marketplace decisions on products and services.* Every consumer goes through the same decision process, which consists of the following stages: problem recognition, search for information, evaluation of information, purchase decision, postpurchase or postdecision evaluation. The individual's specific behavior in the marketplace is affected by internal factors such as needs, motives, perception, and attitudes, as well as by external or environmental influences such as the family, social groups, culture, economics, and business influences.[1] To achieve a better understanding of the consumer decision process and the factors influencing that process requires an in-depth search of those disciplines which can offer some explanation as to why people behave as they do.

Buyer Behavior— Insights from Economics

ECONOMIC THEORY

Economists were the first to advance formal explanations of buyer behavior. Generally, they visualize the market as made up of homogeneous buyers who act in a predictably similar fashion, and the economic process as the matching of homogeneous segments of supply with homogeneous segments of demand. Economic theory describes man as a rational buyer who has perfect information about the market and uses it to obtain optimum value for his buying effort and money. Price is regarded as his strongest motivation. He compares all competing sellers' offerings and, since all are alike in every respect, he buys the one with the lowest price. Above all, economic man's behavior is rational. Under these circumstances, his buying choices are predictable and yield maximum value.

In some situations the model of economic man helps us understand and even predict consumer buying behavior. It explains why a housewife may select the food store with the most or best "weekend specials" for her Friday shopping trip. It explains why a special price on Brand X may attract a customer who normally buys Brand Y. It also explains why a consumer, having decided to buy a new Ford station wagon, visits several Ford dealerships to get the best trade-in and price.

However, for the most part, decision making by individuals is far too complex to reduce to the simplistic model of economic man. Although this model may explain, for example, why a buyer chooses one Ford dealer over another, it does not explain why the decision was to buy a Ford instead of a Chevrolet, a station wagon instead of a sedan, or a V-8 instead of a six. This suggests, then, that in order to

[1] C. Glenn Walters, *Consumer Behavior* (Homewood, Ill.: Richard D. Irwin, Inc., 1974), pp. 7–17.

analyze buyer behavior, we must consider both economic and noneconomic factors.

Markets Are Heterogeneous In striving for a realistic explanation of buyer behavior, we must discard one assumption that pervades the concept of economic man—that markets are homogeneous. Heterogeneity, not homogeneity, characterizes markets. The entire notion of market segmentation (described in Chapter 1) is based on the realization that not all buyers are alike, that they differ in numerous and distinctive ways. Furthermore, this heterogeneity is evident on both the supply (sellers') and demand (buyers') sides of every market. Essentially, then, the real overall marketing problem of the total economy is to match heterogeneous segments of supply with heterogeneous segments of demand.

One way to explain buying behavior is in terms of what buyers are trying to do. Sorting theory, as shown in Figure 3–1, regards the entire economic process as starting with conglomerations, going through various types of sorting, and ending with assortments. Ultimate consumers, for example, are engaged in building assortments, in replenishing or extending inventories of goods for use by themselves and their families. This means that the consumer buyer enters the market as a problem solver.[2] Solving a problem, on behalf of either a household or a marketing organization, means reaching a decision in the face of uncertainty. In the double search which pervades marketing, the consumer buyer and the marketing executive are opposite numbers. The consumer buyer looks for products in order to complete an assortment, while the marketing executive looks for buyers who need the company's products.

This explanation is consistent with those economic theories that explain competition among sellers by emphasizing innovative competition, product differentiation, and differential advantage. The position occupied by every firm engaged in marketing is in some respects unique. Each firm is differentiated from all others by the characteristics of its products, its services, its geographic location, or its particular combination of these features. Therefore, each firm's survival requires that it present, to some group of buyers, a differential advantage over other suppliers. Any marketing organization makes sales to a core market composed of buyers who prefer this source and to a fringe market made up of buyers who find the source acceptable, at least for occasional purchases.[3] A firm's *hard core market* is that segment composed of brand-loyal buyers. The farther one goes from the core, out to the fringes, the less brand loyalty is shown by buyers, to the point where brand name is of little importance. The

Hard Core Market

[2] See W. Alderson, *Marketing Behavior and Executive Action* (Homewood, Ill.: Richard D. Irwin, 1957), pp. 164–184.

[3] W. Alderson, "The Analytical Framework for Marketing," *Proceedings of the Conference of Marketing Teachers from Far Western States,* ed. D. J. Duncan (Berkeley: University of California, 1958), p. 18.

Figure 3–1
Sorting theory

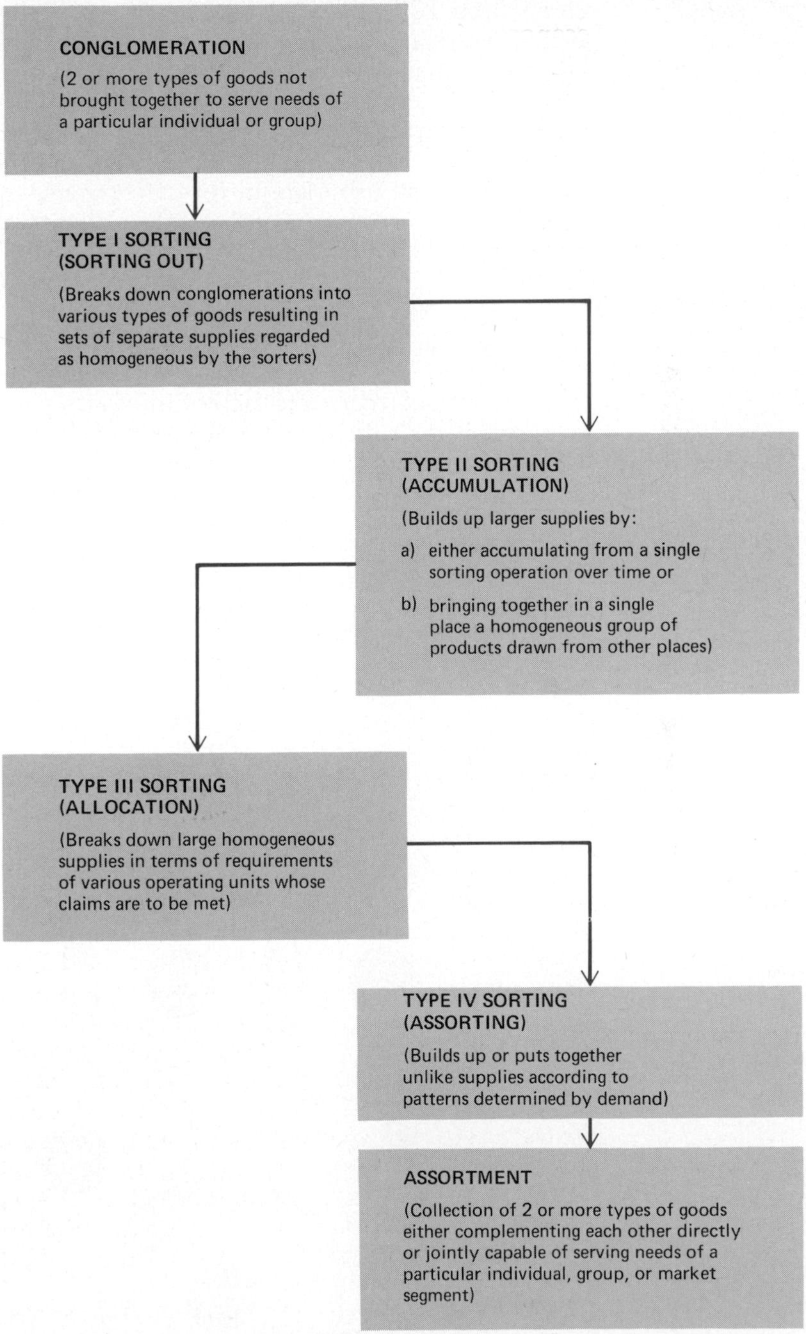
CONGLOMERATION
(2 or more types of goods not brought together to serve needs of a particular individual or group)
TYPE I SORTING (SORTING OUT)
(Breaks down conglomerations into various types of goods resulting in sets of separate supplies regarded as homogeneous by the sorters)
TYPE II SORTING (ACCUMULATION)
(Builds up larger supplies by:
a) either accumulating from a single sorting operation over time or
b) bringing together in a single place a homogeneous group of products drawn from other places)
TYPE III SORTING (ALLOCATION)
(Breaks down large homogeneous supplies in terms of requirements of various operating units whose claims are to be met)
TYPE IV SORTING (ASSORTING)
(Builds up or puts together unlike supplies according to patterns determined by demand)
ASSORTMENT
(Collection of 2 or more types of goods either complementing each other directly or jointly capable of serving needs of a particular individual, group, or market segment)

core market concept has special meaning for the firm that wants to increase its market share, since this normally means that it must concentrate its marketing efforts in areas where its fringe overlaps that of another firm's. Figure 3–2 shows the core market concept, with the overlapping fringe areas. Note that a given firm's fringe area overlaps with varying numbers of other firms' fringes. This connotes the idea that not all firms are in direct competition with one another, even though they are part of the same industry. The key point is that, for a firm to increase its market share, it must expand at the fringes.

INCOME AND PERSONAL CONSUMPTION SPENDING

Uncontrollable Economic Factors

Numerous economic factors influence consumers in the ways they spend their incomes for personal consumption. In this section we examine a few of the more important *uncontrollable economic factors;* that is, those that individual firms cannot influence to any significant extent.

Disposable Personal Income Goods and services are produced for purposes of consumption; purchasing power is used to

Figure 3–2
The core market concept for a specific industry

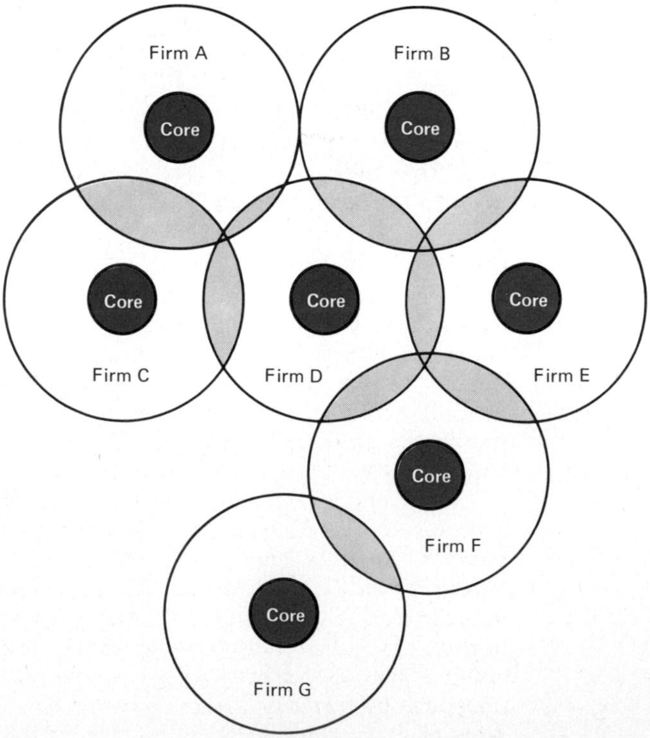

convert production into consumption; and disposable personal income (that is, what people have left to spend or save after they have paid their taxes) represents potential purchasing power in the hands of consumers. In most years, however, people do not spend all of their income. Disposable personal income is used both for personal consumption spending and for saving.

To facilitate analysis of the way people allocate changes in their total incomes between spending and saving, economists have developed two important concepts: the *marginal propensity to consume* and the *marginal propensity to save.* If disposable personal income should rise from $600 billion to $610 billion, businessmen would be interested in learning what proportion of the additional $10 billion consumers might spend and what proportion they might save. Suppose that out of the $10 billion of marginal income, consumers spend $9 billion and save $1 billion. The proportion spent (9 ÷ 10), or 90 percent, is the marginal propensity to consume. The proportion saved (1 ÷ 10), or 10 percent, is the marginal propensity to save.

Marketing analysts are usually more interested – with good reason – in examining the effect of changes in income on spending and saving than they are in the average relationships. Consider what happens to personal consumption spending with a change in income. The percent of disposable personal income used for personal consumption spending rose from 91.15 percent in 1972 to 91.21 percent in 1973, an increase of only six-hundredths of one percentage point. In other words, the average propensities to consume and save changed very little.

But what happened to the marginal propensity to consume? From 1972 to 1973, disposable personal income rose from $797 billion to $882.6 billion, while personal consumption spending went up from $726.5 billion to $805 billion. There was, then, an $85.6 billion increase in income and a $78.5 billion increase in spending. Dividing the change in spending by the change in income (78.5 ÷ 85.6), the marginal propensity to consume was about 92 percent; a similar calculation for the period 1971 to 1972 shows a marginal propensity to consume of over 116 percent – that is, people were spending not only the extra $51 billion in income (income rose from $746 billion in 1971 to $797 billion in 1972) but even more! Thus, while the average propensity to consume changed hardly at all, the marginal propensity to consume rose by 24 percentage points.

Personal consumption spending tends both to rise and fall at a slower rate than does disposable personal income. But in inflationary periods, such as throughout most of the 1960s and into the mid-1970's, spending sometimes rises faster than income. Generally, however, in years of higher income a lower proportion is spent and a higher proportion is saved. In years of lower income, the proportion spent tends to increase while that saved declines. The concepts of marginal propensity to consume and to save take into account the rates of change, and that is why analysts consider them valuable.

Size of Family and Family Income Size of family and size of family income obviously affect spending and saving patterns but, unfortunately, little research has been reported on these relationships, and what studies have been done are relatively old. Two studies are cited here to illustrate the type of research that can provide useful information concerning spending behavior as it relates to size of family and family income.[4] The Wharton study disclosed that in urban families with lower incomes, average personal consumption spending exceeded income. It also showed that the average propensity to consume tended to decline rather rapidly as income rose above the poverty level.

A second study provided some insights on spending behavior relative to household gross income (i.e., income before taxes). It confirmed what businessmen had long assumed: average annual household spending rises with increases in gross income per household; those with above-average incomes are above-average spenders, those with below-average incomes are below-average spenders. But, contrary to what is commonly assumed, this study found that the number of people in a household appears directly related to the size of its annual income. As the numbers of people in a household increase, annual household income rises—perhaps because more members have incomes and/or because people with larger incomes can afford larger families. This study also revealed that high-income households accounted for a disproportionately high share of total spending—53 percent of the households with above-average incomes accounted for 67 percent of total spending.[5]

Findings such as these are important to the marketing analyst. They imply that significant changes occur in a family's spending and saving pattern as it moves from one income bracket to another. They also indicate that changes in the distribution of all the families in a population, relative to income brackets, may bring about significant changes in propensities to consume and to save.

Consumers' Income Expectations The incomes that consumers expect to receive in the future have some bearing on their present spending patterns. In particular, spending for automobiles, furniture, major appliances, and other expensive items tends to be influenced by consumers' optimism or pessimism about future income. This tendency has been confirmed by the annual surveys of consumers' buying plans made by the University of Michigan's Survey Research Center. Consumers' expectations of higher or lower income have a direct effect on spending plans.

Consumers' Liquid Assets Consumer buying plans are influenced, especially those for "big ticket" items, by the size of their

[4] See *Study of Consumer Expenditures, Incomes, and Savings* (Philadelphia: Wharton School of Finance and Commerce, University of Pennsylvania, 1958), Vol. 18; and *Social Indicators*, United States Government, Office of Management Budget, Bureau of Research in Higher and Professional Education, 1973.

[5] *The Life Study of Consumer Expenditures*, Vol. 1 (1957), pp. 18–21.

holdings of liquid assets; that is, cash and other assets readily convertible into cash—for example, balances in checking and savings accounts, shares in savings and loan associations, deposits in credit unions, and holdings of government bonds and readily marketable stocks and bonds. Even though a consumer may actually buy with current income, the freedom with which he or she spends is influenced by his or her accumulation of liquid assets. Retired and unemployed individuals may use liquid assets to buy everyday necessities. Other consumers may use liquid assets to meet major medical bills and other emergencies.

Consumer Credit Availability of consumer credit strongly influences the pattern of consumer spending. Through credit, which allows one to buy now and pay later, a consumer can command more purchasing power than that represented by his or her current income. Thus, availability of credit has been a key factor in the rapid growth of the markets for mobile homes, boats, camping trailers, and the like.

Personal debt includes all short- and intermediate-term consumer debt, other than regular charge (i.e., nonrevolving) accounts, and excludes mortgage and business debt. Personal debt, thus defined, is equivalent to installment credit; that is, the consumer pays off the debt in a number of installments. Generally speaking, more than half of all spending units have such debt. The size of income is directly related to the amount of credit a consumer can obtain; lower income groups tend to have either no debt or smaller debts than higher income groups. Since 1964, the volume of installment consumer credit has been approximately four times that of noninstallment credit.[6]

DISCRETIONARY INCOME

A family with money left over after buying such necessities as food, clothing, shelter, and transportation has discretionary income. During the early 1970s, for example, families with disposable personal incomes under $7,500 generally had little or no discretionary income. But, as families moved above $7,500, there was extra income for other purposes. They could buy better food and drink, or better furniture, or they could take a small flyer in the stock market, or they could spend it all on one big fling, such as a trip to Europe.

By the time families move above the $15,000 income level, about half of their income is discretionary, and the decisions are not between purchasing certain items or others but rather of choosing an entire life style. The skilled laborer with a $15,000 income can choose to live in a working class neighborhood and save a large portion of his income, or he can choose to live like a junior executive. It is estimated that in 1975 roughly half of all disposable income was discretionary.

[6] *Federal Reserve Bulletin,* February 1974, p. A 54.

Even small fluctuations in income cause sharp repercussions in consumers' purchases of durables. This traces partly to the fact that consumers are able to postpone or speed up their purchases of such durables as automobiles, furniture, and major appliances. If a family is temporarily short of income, it can always use the old refrigerator for another year or so. Or, if it finds itself suddenly with more discretionary income, it may decide to replace the refrigerator this year instead of next. The quick response of durable goods expenditures to income changes traces also to the wide use of installment credit in financing such purchases. Consumers are more willing to increase installment debt when income is rising and are more reluctant to incur additional indebtedness when income is declining. Lenders are also more agreeable to debt creation in prosperous times. Purchases of nondurables and services, which are much less postponable than purchases of durables, react far less violently to changes in income.

Buyer Behavior— Insights from Psychology

Social Psychology

There have been three major approaches to the development of a psychological theory of human behavior: the experimental, the clinical, and the Gestalt. Experimental psychology has concentrated upon physiological tensions or body needs as motivational forces and has experimented with both human beings and animals. In clinical psychology, the basic physiological drives are examined as they are modified by social forces. Gestalt psychology, often called *social psychology*, regards the individual and his environment as an indivisible whole and considers individual behavior as being directed toward various goals. Each approach adds to our understanding of human behavior, but thus far no single psychological theory of consumer motivation is completely adequate or satisfactory in explaining buyer behavior. Consequently, marketing has borrowed those theoretical concepts which seem most applicable.

HOW PEOPLE LEARN ABOUT PRODUCTS

Studies of learning and the related areas of recognition, recall, and habitual response have furnished marketers with several keys to understanding consumer behavior. Concepts borrowed from learning theory help in answering such questions as these: How do consumers learn about products offered for sale? How do they learn to recognize and recall these products? By what processes do they develop buying and consuming habits?

The current trend in psychological thinking is to look at the total experience of the individual and to consider learning as a process in which total functions are altered and rearranged to make them more useful to the individual. Particular external stimuli do not always activate predictable responses, because motives and other factors internal to the individual also affect responses. What does this mean for the marketer? Simply that the buyer is influenced not only by external stimuli—for example, the marketer's promotion—but also by internal factors.

The Basic Factors Influencing Learning What are the basic factors influencing learning? One writer answers, "repetition, motivation, conditioning, and relationship and organization."[7]

Repetition

Repetition is necessary for the progressive modification of psychological functions and must be accompanied by attention, interest, and a goal—if it is to be effective. Mere repetition of situations or stimuli does not promote learning; advertisers who depend on repetition alone waste both their efforts and advertising dollars.

Motivation

The individual's *motivation* is the most important factor involved in initiating and governing his or her activities. Activity in harmony with one's motives is satisfying and pleasing; other activity is annoying at best and frustrating at worst. When, in a given situation, an individual has several motives, they may either reinforce each other, which promotes learning, or be in conflict, which hinders learning. Human motivation is a topic of considerable interest to marketing professionals, especially those concerned with preparing advertising and sales presentations. But neither marketers nor the psychologists have thus far been able to reach more than partial agreements about what constitutes even the most common or basic motives.

Conditioning

Conditioning is a way of learning in which a new response to a particular stimulus is developed. For example, seeing just any glass bottle does not evoke any standard response but seeing one particular type of bottle makes most Americans think of Coca-Cola. Through long advertising effort and continual exposure of this symbol, the Coca-Cola Company has conditioned the American public to recognize its bottle. The conditioned response, however, establishes a temporary rather than a permanent behavior pattern and, if it is not frequently reinforced by the original stimulus, the conditioned response eventually disappears. Furthermore, research indicates that all persons do not respond equally well to conditioning, nor are their responses generally predictable.

Relationship and Organization

Relationship and organization are also factors facilitating learning. Or, to put it another way, learning effectiveness is enhanced if the thing to be learned is presented in a familiar environmental setting. Thus, a salesman more effectively demonstrates a vacuum cleaner by using it on the customer's carpet in her home and showing her the dirt it has picked up than by describing its capacity and cleaning power in a store. The housewife is interested in the

[7] O. Mowrer, *Learning Theory and the Symbolic Processes* (New York: John Wiley & Sons, 1963), p. 225.

machine's performance specifications only as they directly relate to the task of cleaning her own carpets. Thus, sales messages should relate the products to the consumer's needs and interests, if they are to attract the consumer's attention and lay the groundwork for purchase.

Retention and Forgetting of Learned Information There is particular significance for the advertiser in the psychological explanation of retention and forgetting. Retention is explained in terms of impressions left in the nervous system as a result of learning. Forgetting, or negative retention, develops with the deterioration of these impressions. The more meaningful the material learned—that is, the more the learner completely understands it—the greater the rate of retention and the lower the rate of forgetting.[8] Retention curves for both meaningful and unmeaningful materials, plotted as functions of time, drop most rapidly immediately after learning and then gradually decline until the material is almost or entirely forgotten. This phenomenon is particularly important with respect to long-run promotion and advertising campaigns. Messages should be spaced closely enough to fortify the learning process. If they are too far apart, information learned from earlier messages will have been forgotten and must be relearned.

EXPLANATIONS OF BUYER BEHAVIOR FROM CLINICAL PSYCHOLOGY

Clinical Psychology

Clinical psychology has evolved from the pioneering work of Sigmund Freud. The principal motivation research techniques used in marketing trace to concepts originally developed by clinical psychologists. Among the most important of these concepts are those of the *unconscious, rationalization, projection,* and *free association.*

The Unconscious This concept was strongly championed by Sigmund Freud, the founder of psychoanalysis. According to Freud, the mind contains ideas and urges—some conscious and some beneath the threshold of consciousness but all influencing behavior. People are not usually consciously aware of all their motives, and this explains why consumers are often unable to articulate their real reasons for buying or not buying. Recognizing the existence of the unconscious mind, motivation researchers use indirect approaches, such as depth interviewing. More conventional research approaches, such as direct questioning, have been unsuccessful in providing data sufficiently reliable to justify predictions of consumer behavior. Practical marketers, of course, have long known that there are often wide discrepancies between what people say they will buy and what they actually do buy.

[8] B. Berelson and G. Steiner, *Human Behavior: An Inventory of Scientific Findings* (New York: Harcourt, Brace & World, 1964), p.102.

Rationalization This concept relates to the mental process of finding reasons to justify an act or opinion that is actually based on other motives or grounds than those stated, although this may or may not be apparent to the rationalizer. In advertising, rationalization may often be capitalized upon by providing readers or listeners with a plausible, acceptable reason for buying in situations where they may be unwilling, consciously or unconsciously, to admit the real reasons. The prevalence of rationalization in our society explains why such direct questions as "Why did you buy this?" or "What were your reasons for buying?" so often fail to uncover the real buying motives. Thus, when it is suspected that rationalizing is a factor in consumer behavior, indirect research approaches, such as depth interviewing, are used.

Projection This concept concerns the reaction that occurs when a person, seeing someone else facing a certain problem or situation, assumes the other person's reactions would be the same as his or her own. In other words, he or she ascribes his or her own motives to the other person. Putting the projection concept to practical use, motivation researchers have designed projective techniques (for example, the stimulus picture) that provide a means for uncovering consumers' hidden or unconscious motives and attitudes.

Free Association The principle of free association, which traces to Freud and is used extensively in psychoanalysis, has also been put to use by motivation researchers in their development of indirect research techniques. As Newman says, "The basic idea is that if a person gives up the usual logical controls he exercises over his thoughts and says whatever comes into his mind at the moment in the presence of a skilled listener, unconscious feelings and thoughts can be discovered.[9] Thus, an application of the principle of free association is found in depth interviewing, many of the techniques of which take the form of word association tests, in which respondents are asked to give the first word that comes to mind for each of a list of unrelated words. Given the word *rain*, for example, the respondent might reply *drip*. Among the many marketing applications of the word association tests are those of screening possible names for new products, measuring the penetration of advertising appeals, and approximating the market shares of different competitors.

NEED SATISFACTION AND BUYER BEHAVIOR

Psychological studies indicate that human activity, including buying behavior, is directed toward satisfying certain basic needs.

[9] J. W. Newman. *Motivation Research and Marketing Management* (Boston: Division of Research, Harvard University Graduate School of Business Administration, 1957), p. 65.

Not every individual acts in the same way in the effort to fulfill these needs; the actions of each not only depend upon the nature of the needs themselves but are modified by the individual's particular environmental and social background. The motivation for any specific action derives from the tensions built up to satisfy basic needs, needs that frequently lie beneath the threshold of consciousness. Whatever action the individual takes is directed toward reducing these tensions.

Although clinical psychologists have not agreed on a single list of basic needs, the different lists available show more agreement than disagreement. In one list, illustrated in Figure 3–3, Maslow enumerates basic needs in their order of importance for most people. According to him, an individual normally tries to satisfy the most basic needs first and, satisfying these, he or she is then free to devote his or her efforts to the next one shown on the list. Each category of need on the Maslow list is described as follows:[10]

Basic Needs

1. *Physiological Needs.* The needs to satisfy hunger, thirst, sleep, and so forth. These are the most basic needs, and until they are satisfied other needs are of no importance.
2. *Safety Needs.* In modern society, these needs are more often for economic and social security rather than for physical safety.
3. *Belongingness and Love Needs.* The need for affectionate relations with individuals and a place in society is so important that its lack is a common cause of maladjustment.
4. *Esteem Needs.* People need both self-esteem, a high evaluation of self, and the esteem of others in our society. Fulfillment provides a feeling

[10] A. H. Maslow, *Motivation and Personality* (New York: Harper & Brothers, 1954), pp. 80–85.

Figure 3–3 Maslow's hierarchy of needs

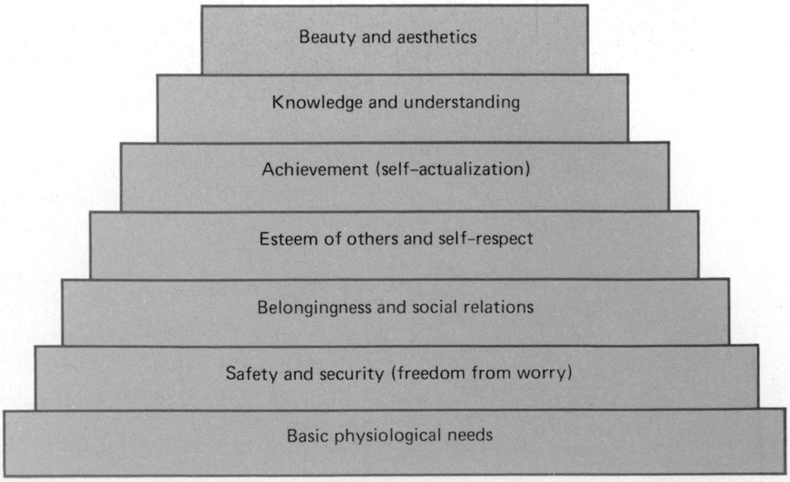

A. H. Maslow, *Motivation and Personality* (New York: Harper & Brothers, 1954), pp. 80–85.

of self-confidence and usefulness; nonfulfillment produces feelings of inferiority and helplessness.

5. *Need for Self-Actualization.* This is the desire to achieve to the maximum of one's capabilities. Although it may be present in everyone, its fulfillment depends upon prior fulfillment of the more basic needs.
6. *Desire to Know and Understand.* These needs refer to the process of searching for meaning in the things around us.
7. *Aesthetic Needs.* These may not appear to be present among many individuals because of their failure to satisfy more basic needs, but among some the need for beauty is strong.

Often the marketing success of a brand depends on its ability to satisfy several needs at once; now that motivation research techniques are available to identify the strength or weakness of a product in terms of the needs it fulfills, the concept of basic needs and the theory that individuals normally try to satisfy them in some order are especially significant.

HOW BUYERS PERCEIVE THEMSELVES AND THE PRODUCTS THEY BUY

Buyers see both themselves and the products they buy in terms of images. These images are the formalized impressions residing, consciously or unconsciously, in the minds of individuals with regard to given subjects. Patterns of buying behavior are influenced by the images consumers have of different products, particular brands, companies, retail outlets, and of themselves. Because images affect consumer buying behavior, marketers take them into account in drafting promotional plans and programs. Differences among individuals, products, brands, and the like result in different images, and motivation research is used not only to identify the nature of images but to detect the implications for marketing action.

Self-Image

Self-Image The *self-image* is the picture a person has of himself—the kind of person he considers himself to be and the kind of person that he imagines others consider him to be. Different people have different kinds of self-image, and this gives rise to market segmentation along psychological lines. For instance, the woman who sees herself primarily as a good housewife and mother exhibits a different total pattern of buying behavior from that shown by the woman who sees herself as a social leader or professional careerist. A basic tenet of motivation research is that in many buying situations an individual prefers to buy those products and brands whose images appear consistent with his or her self-image. However, the power of the self-image as a buying influence varies from individual to individual and even within the same individual as he or she makes different buying decisions at different times.

Brand Image

Brand Image The *brand image*, another stereotype, results from all the impressions consumers receive, from whatever sources, about a particular manufacturer's brand. In the minds of consumers familiar with a particular brand, there tends to be considerable consistency in the brand image or, as it is sometimes called, the *brand personality*. But for competing brands there are usually, in the minds of consumers, distinctive images. Similarly, retail stores exhibit distinct images or personalities, as do corporations.

Consumers' appraisal of the distinctiveness of a brand's physical attributes not only affects the brand image but has important implications for marketing. When consumers believe the brand is physically different from competing brands, the brand image centers on the brand as a specific version of the product. Depending on whether the marketer considers the image favorable or unfavorable, physical attributes of the product may be retained or changed, and marketing strategy may be directed toward reinforcing or altering the image. By contrast, when consumers believe a brand has no differentiating physical attributes, the brand image tends to be associated with the personalities of the people who are thought to buy it.

Through long-continued use of particular advertising and selling appeals, many brands have acquired definite images. In numerous cases, a brand image has developed without the management's intending it. Whether or not a particular brand image was shaped deliberately, management should identify its nature precisely. Otherwise, ignorance of the brand image may result in poorly planned promotional programs. If the image is favorable, for example, inconsistent sales and advertising appeals are likely to be ineffective and may confuse or alienate existing customers. Before introducing a new brand to the market or an established brand to a different market, management should determine the sort of image it wishes to build.

FESTINGER'S THEORY OF COGNITIVE DISSONANCE

According to Festinger, when a person makes a decision, dissonance or discomfort will almost always occur. The reason is that the person making the decision knows that it has certain disadvantages as well as advantages. After making his decision, then, the person tends to expose himself to information that he perceives as likely to support his choice and to avoid information that may favor the rejected alternative(s).[11] Festinger evidently intended his theory to apply only to decisions involving postdecision anxiety, but it seems reasonable that it should also hold for situations involving predecision anxiety: a buyer may panic as the time of decision arrives and either rush into buying as an escape from the problem or delay it because of the difficulty in deciding among alternatives. In marketing, an important goal both of advertising and personal selling is to reduce cognitive dissonance on the part of buyers and pros-

[11] L. Festinger, *A Theory of Cognitive Dissonance* (Evanston, Ill.: Row, Peterson & Company, 1957).

pects. Customers suffering cognitive dissonance may need reassuring that their decisions are or were wise ones. This can be accomplished by providing information that permits them to rationalize their decisions. For example, the owner's manual which accompanies a product when it is purchased usually begins by citing some important reasons why the buyer's decision to buy that product was an excellent choice.

BUYING MOTIVATION OF INDUSTRIAL USERS

Industrial users tend to be more "rational" in their buying than do ultimate consumers. Industrial users buy to fill the needs of their organizations, and these needs normally are of a very practical nature. But it is nonetheless true that organizations are composed of individuals, that one or more individuals do the buying, and that they all have personal needs that sometimes become enmeshed with their roles as buyers.[12] Thus, even industrial purchases may be made on emotional bases, as in the case of the purchasing agent who buys from a certain supplier because the salesman is a good friend.

Buyer Behavior—Insights from Sociology and Anthropology

Sociologists and anthropologists view marketing as involving the activities of groups of people motivated by group pressures as well as by individual desires. Their studies have emphasized the significance of reference groups, the individual's concept of social role, the diffusion process, social class, and culture as influences on human behavior. These studies have demonstrated the importance of social factors in analyzing and influencing consumer behavior.

REFERENCE GROUPS AND THE DIFFUSION PROCESS

The people with whom an individual regularly associates exert strong influences on his or her behavior. He or she must conform at least partially to their standards of behavior to gain group acceptance. An individual's behavior is also influenced by groups with whom he or she has little regular contact but with whom he or she identifies closely. Both types of groups are called reference groups, which include family and peer groups, social groups, and others, such as religious or fraternal organizations.

Reference Groups

[12] For an excellent discussion of this important matter, see Frederick E. Webster, Jr., and Yoram Wind, *Organizational Buying Behavior* (Englewood Cliffs, N.J.: Prentice-Hall, Inc., 1972).

Primary Groups These groups, fundamental in determining the social nature of the individual, are groups of people involved in intimate, face-to-face contact and cooperation. The most pervasive and traditionally the most influential primary group is the family but, with the emergence of the modern small, two-generation family, much of this influence has passed to other primary groups, particularly peer groups. Peer groups are composed of individuals who spend considerable time together and are of fairly common age and social background. Among children, these are often play groups; among adults, they include neighborhood and community groups. Other groups with varying degrees of socializing influence are religious, educational, and political institutions, and work groups.

Each individual may hold membership in several different primary groups. At work one may be a part of a close-knit, friendly group of co-workers. As a church member, one may or may not have close personal contacts with other members. As a member of social or fraternal organizations, one may be a part of still other primary groups. Any of these groups may be classified as peer groups if they are sufficiently homogeneous. Purely social groups are most likely to qualify. The peer group has the greatest influence on the individual as a consumer because the group's general interests and mode of life are most nearly like his or her own.

Significance of Reference Groups to Marketing Knowledge of reference groups and their influences makes it easier to explain why consumers behave in particular ways and—more important to marketers—to predict their behavior. It explains, for example, why two groups of young people in the same community—one, high school seniors, and the other, college freshmen—adopt very different styles of dress or other behavior even though they are nearly the same age and come from similar family backgrounds. Even within a college freshman group, different reference groups dictate wide variations in dress and behavior. Even the same individual behaves differently at different times as he or she identifies with different reference groups. A young executive, for example, may dress and act conservatively when on the job and in other contact with his business associates, but off the job he may be a sports car racing buff and behave and dress very differently.

Individualism and Group Behavior

Individual's Concept of Social Role in Groups The way a person sees his role in the social groups in which he holds membership is important in explaining his motivation. If he is a "rugged individualist," he may enjoy establishing a reputation as one who sets his own patterns of behavior—within existing group norms of acceptable conduct. Individualism was once a common mode of behavior, but it is now rare. Group behavior has since evolved and become more important. The newer mode of behavior requires fairly close conformity to group norms. The group-oriented individual is anxious to fit into the behavior patterns of his peers. What they do, he must do. This does not imply, however, that his pattern of behavior is rigidly frozen. Group norms may change, and he adjusts his behavior accordingly. The group-oriented individual is seldom motivated by the traditional appeals of "being an innovator" or "leading the pack." If he is to be motivated to action, he must first be persuaded that the suggested action is accepted by his peers as the proper thing to do.

Influentials

Influentials An influential is a person who serves as an opinion leader of a group. Such opinion leaders are not confined to any one social class; they are found at all levels of society. Outwardly, influentials and those they influence (i.e., others in the same social groups) are apt to be very much alike—similar incomes, occupations, family backgrounds, and so on. According to one sociologist, an individual's influence is related to: (1) who one is, (2) what one knows, and (3) whom one knows.[13] For example, an unmarried girl may be a fashion leader because of who she is; an older woman her group's cooking expert because of what she knows; and a man his group's political leader because of whom he knows, not only in the group but outside it.

Influentials play key roles in marketing. If an influential tries or uses a product, his or her followers are prone to do the same. Marketers, therefore, often target their promotional efforts to reach influentials and, through them, reach their followers by word-of-mouth or other subtle influences exerted by the influentials.

THE DIFFUSION PROCESS

Diffusion

The social process of spreading information about new products or services to persuade consumers to accept them is known as *diffusion.* Studies of the diffusion process reveal that most users do not adopt an innovation simultaneously. The first group to adopt an innovation is made up of a small number of "innovators." They are soon copied by another group, who, though not venturesome enough to try first, want to be among the early users. Gradually, members of other groups adopt the innovation until it finally reaches market saturation. For a dramatically new product, such as television, the entire process may take ten years or more.

A model of the diffusion process is shown in Figure 3–4. The diffusion process is visualized as a curve approaching a normal distribution, with 16 percent of the consumers in the combined innovator and early adopter groups, 34 percent each in the early and late majority groups, and 16 percent in the laggard group. It is important to identify target market segments at each stage in the diffusion process. In the initial phases of market introduction, for instance,

[13] E. Katz, "The Two-Step Flow of Communication: An Up-to-Date Report on an Hypothesis," *Public Opinion Quarterly*, Spring 1957, pp. 61–78.

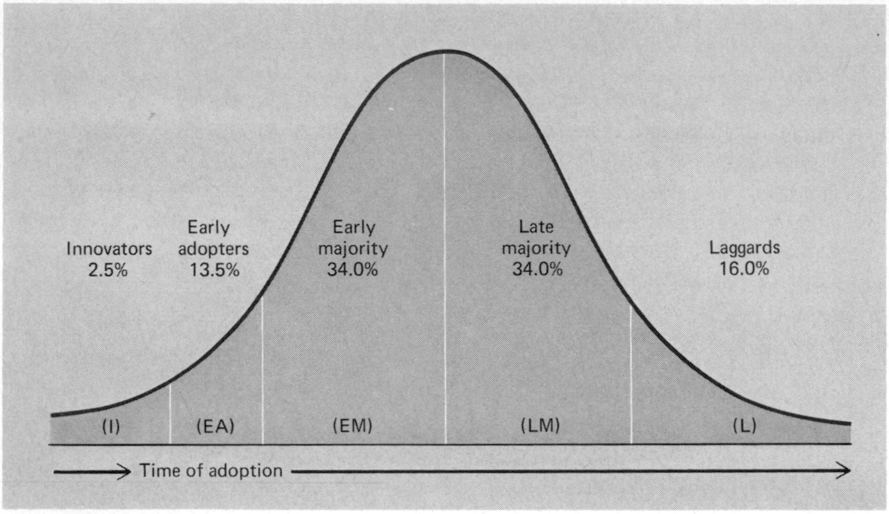

E. M. Rogers, *The Diffusion of Innovations* (New York: The Free Press, 1962), p. 76.

Figure 3–4
Classification of adopter groups

effort and money may be wasted if the marketer tries to cultivate the entire market all at once.

The various adopter groups exhibit marked differences. The innovators are usually the youngest and have the highest social status and wealth; they are frequently cosmopolites and have professional, business and personal contacts outside their own immediate social circles.[14] Those in the early adopter group are generally influentials (i.e., opinion leaders), but their contacts are restricted largely to their own local group;[15] they enjoy high status within their own social groups and are usually younger than those in the groups following. Those in the early majority group are the most deliberate; they will not consider buying a new product until a number of their peers (innovators and early adopters) have done so.[16] Those in the late majority have below-average income and social prestige and are older than members of earlier groups. Laggards have still lower incomes and social status;[17] by the time they buy a new product, the earlier groups are often already trying something newer.

Innovators

Early Adopters

Early Majority

Late Majority

Laggards

SOCIAL CLASSES

Every society classifies its members according to some social hierarchy. All have people who occupy positions of relatively higher

[14] G. Zaltman, *Marketing: Contributions from the Behavioral Sciences* (New York: Harcourt, Brace & World, 1965), p. 150.

[15] R. Cohen, "A Theoretical Model for Consumer Market Prediction," *Sociological Inquiry*, Winter 1962, pp. 43–50.

[16] E. M. Rogers, *The Diffusion of Innovations* (New York: The Free Press, 1962), p. 314.

[17] *Ibid.*

status and power. Most sociologists divide American society into three broad, roughly defined classes: the upper, middle, and lower classes. W. Lloyd Warner, on the basis of studies in three American towns, set up a hierarchy of six social classes: upper upper, lower upper, upper middle, lower middle, upper lower, and lower lower.[18] Under Warner's system the class status of each person is ascertained by asking his equals, his superiors, and his inferiors to rank him. This dependence on the ratings of others has been the main criticism of the Warner system. The ordinary citizen does not think in terms of this complex hierarchy and, when asked to classify his or her fellow citizens into the six groups, he or she shows little agreement with others who are asked to do the same thing.

Status Symbol

Status Symbols Despite difficulties in classifying individuals by social class, most sociologists agree that the twin urges for self-expression and self-betterment take the form of aspiring to higher status. Sociologists explain the so-called *status symbol* by holding that (1) people express their personalities not so much in words as in symbols (for example, mannerisms, dress, ornaments, possessions); and (2) most people are increasingly concerned about their social status. Different products vary in their status symbol value, and these values may change. The automobile was once the major status symbol, but many now assert that it has been replaced by the house and its furnishings. The status symbol concept is a valuable one for the marketer, for when it recognizes that it is selling a symbol as well as a product, it views its product more completely. The marketer should understand not only how the product satisfies certain needs but how it fits into modern culture, because social classes exhibit differences in life style.[19]

CULTURE

Every culture evolves unique patterns of social conduct. Analysis of these patterns helps in explaining the buying behavior of individuals. Many aspects of American culture are unique, including the roles of ethnic groups, religion, women in society, leisure time, and fashion, as well as the population composition itself.

Ethnic Groups The United States is a melting pot of cultures and peoples, but this blending has not been complete. An identifiable American national culture has emerged, but it has not equally permeated all portions of society or all geographic regions. There is, for example, an African influence not only in the Deep South but wherever black people have moved in large numbers, a Mexican influence in much of the Southwest, a Scandinavian influence in

[18] W. L. Warner and P. S. Lunt, *The Status System of a Modern Community* (New Haven: Yale University Press, 1942), pp. 88–91.

[19] Thomas S. Robertson, *Consumer Behavior* (Glenview, Ill.: Scott, Foresman and Company, 1970), pp. 116-129.

Minnesota and the Pacific Northwest, and a Cuban and Puerto Rican influence in such cities as Miami, Chicago, Washington, New York, and Philadelphia. Although ethnic differences decrease with each succeeding generation, their continuing existence helps explain differences in consumer motivation and behavior that would not exist in a country with a population of common cultural heritage.

Religions Whereas the predominant religions in some nations stress passive acceptance of life and man's role, the Christian and Jewish religions, which comprise the basic religious heritage of American society, emphasize the perfectibility of man and his environment and, hence, encourage him to improve himself and his way of life. Therefore, the production and consumption of goods are acceptable activities because they contribute to these goals. Within the American Judaeo-Christian religious pattern, however, there are many individual sects and creeds; and, although they share similar feelings about the overall social roles of production and consumption, consumption patterns of selected foods, beverages, and apparel vary considerably among them.

The Role of Women Roughly one-third of adult American women work and have incomes of their own; labor-saving appliances provide the other two-thirds with more time free from domestic responsibilities and, hence, more time for shopping. American women have either sole or major responsibility for making many kinds of purchases and exert increasing influence on all buying decisions. As the Women's Lib movement has gathered strength, increasing numbers of women take active rather than passive roles in society—this trend has great significance to marketing, especially in the choice of advertising themes.

Leisure Time Increasing numbers of people have greater amounts of leisure time, and this is reflected in changes in values and the way of life. Instead of buying an expensive car to impress his friends, a consumer may economize on his car in order to buy the boat, shop tools, or fishing equipment he wants. New homes are planned to simplify participation in leisure time activities. People have ceased being producers for much of their lives and have become active consumers for the products and services that go along with increasing leisure. The old Puritan dictum that "For Satan finds some mischief still for idle hands to do" is being overthrown, but the Puritan influence still remains. People refer to "active" leisure rather than just "leisure"—the active disassociating leisure from the guilt-loaded idea of loafing.

Fashion The role of fashion in American society has been growing in importance. With widespread ownership of television sets, not to mention rising circulations of magazines and newspapers and the increasing mobility of consumers, fashion news is disseminated in minimum time. The time span covered by the appearance of a new fashion, its adoption by a few pacesetters, its rise to popularity, and its subsequent decline is becoming progressively shorter. At the same time, expansions in discretionary income permit consumers to spend more in their attempts to satisfy the desire for change. Since there are increasing numbers of group-oriented people and fewer individualists, more importance has been placed on conforming to fashion changes. However, the "counterculture," including the "hippies," tends to emphasize noncomformance with fashion (and other) changes made by other segments of society.

Population Composition Most of the population growth in metropolitan areas is in the suburbs rather than in the cities themselves. This trend has marketing significance because the suburbanite often represents a very different market than the city dweller. The suburb retains much of the character of a small town—thus, neighborhood and local social groups strongly influence individual consumption patterns.

The population composition of the central core cities has been changing to a predominately low-income and poverty-level group of consumers. At the same time, an increasing proportion of central city residents are members of minority groups—from 1960 to 1970, for instance, New York's black population doubled. Low-income and ghetto groups are often served by different marketing institutions than those serving others; recent studies have raised questions as to whether such groups are being served adequately.[20] One countertrend should be mentioned: the "back to the city movement," a social phenomenon evident in certain large cities that can be traced to the increased living inconveniences resulting from the extreme sprawling of suburban areas.

Summary

Buyer behavior has been analyzed in this chapter through examining various insights derived from economics and the other behavioral sciences. In classical economic theory, financial self-interest explains buyer behavior; economic man acts rationally to maximize his financial well-being. Unfortunately, this explanation provides little help to businessmen, whose customers confront them daily with apparently irrational behavior. So, searching for a clearer explanation, businessmen next turned to psychology which, in the main, explains individual behavior in terms of basic needs common to all people. Psycho-

[20] For example, see F. D. Sturdivant, *The Ghetto Marketplace* (New York: The Free Press, 1969).

logical explanations of human motivation helped but, from the standpoint of businessmen, fuzzy areas were still left where there were no satisfactory answers. More recently, businessmen, searching for added insights, combed the literature of sociology and anthropology, and now it is recognized that individuals, as social creatures, are strongly influenced in their buying by the social and cultural environments in which they live. Thus, each of the behavioral sciences—economics, psychology, sociology, and cultural anthropology—have helped fill in the missing pieces of what might be called the "jigsaw puzzle of buyer behavior." Yet so complex is human behavior in general and buyer behavior in particular that missing pieces in the jigsaw puzzle still remain; as of now, at least, no general theory of buyer behavior has received widespread acceptance among practical marketers. Nevertheless, if you have mastered the content of this chapter, you have the basic background material on buyer behavior relevant to marketing, which you should now find helpful in analyzing practical marketing situations.

QUESTIONS AND PROBLEMS

1. Show how sorting theory can be used to explain the economic process whereby conglomerations are converted into assortments.
2. Demonstrate how sorting theory might be applied in explaining the buying behavior of consumers.
3. "The survival of a firm requires that it present, to some group of buyers, a differential advantage over all other suppliers." List some forms of differential advantage, and give examples of companies presenting each form.
4. Of the many factors affecting the strength of market demand, why is income considered the most powerful?
5. Discuss the relationships which exist among the following: production, consumption, purchasing power, disposable personal income.
6. Why are marketing analysts usually more interested in the marginal propensity to consume than they are in the average propensity to consume? Would this be as true of the analyst of the market for sports cars as of the analyst of the market for breakfast cereals? Why?
7. What possibilities are there for influencing the propensity to consume through such marketing activities as advertising, personal selling, trading stamp plans, liberal credit terms, and so on?
8. Of what significance, if any, would studies of consumers' income expectations be for: (a) a manufacturer of tape recorders; (b) a mail-

order house specializing in "do-it-yourself" electronic kits; (c) a manufacturer of tires for passenger cars; (d) a manufacturer of photographic equipment and supplies?

9. Of what significance would a forecast of the magnitude and distribution of discretionary income be for: (a) a chain of grocery supermarkets; (b) a manufacturer of patio and outdoor furniture; (c) a major domestic airline; (d) an importer of Scotch and Canadian whiskies; (e) a local transit company?
10. Why do you think a company selling tire-making machines might carry on an advertising program directed not to potential buyers of tire-making machines but to potential buyers of tires? Does this sort of strategy make sense for any company whose product has a derived demand? Why?
11. Why do you suppose many advertisers have relied primarily on repetition to achieve customer recognition of their products, when learning is more easily achieved with proper motivation?
12. Would you say that many consumers have become conditioned to shut out (not see or hear) all advertising to which they are exposed? What are the implications for advertisers?
13. Would it be fair to say that when a conscious and an unconscious motive conflict, the conscious motive will dominate? Through rationalization, the consumer finds a sensible or reasonable excuse for actions motivated by frivolous reasons. What is the implication for marketing?
14. Does the concept of projection help in motivating the consumer, or only in learning what motivates him?
15. Give some examples of how the self-image of a bank teller and a taxi driver might lead them to act differently as consumers, assuming equal incomes.
16. "Once a brand image has developed in the minds of the public, there is little that can be done to change it." Comment on this statement.
17. "In order to develop distinctive brand images, there must be clearly identifiable physical differences in the products involved." Do you agree?
18. Does the failure of psychologists to agree on a common list of basic needs destroy the concepts of such needs as a marketing tool?
19. Under Maslow's classification of basic needs, different individuals have achieved different levels in satisfying their needs. Does this imply that it would be necessary to appeal to different needs to sell the same product to different people?
20. What is Festinger's theory of cognitive dissonance? Cite some instances where you personally experienced cognitive dissonance in buying situations. What, if anything, did the seller do in an attempt to reduce your discomfort?

21. Are psychological and sociological motives within the individual likely to be in conflict at times? If so, how would such conflicts affect the marketer?
22. When an individual is a member of several peer groups, are his or her consuming activities likely to be affected equally by all groups? Explain.
23. Does membership in a peer group result in conformity in the actions of its members? Does this have implications for marketing?
24. What is an *influential*? How would you go about identifying influentials? Who would the influentials likely be in connection with the purchase of the following products? (a) golfing equipment; (b) plants and shrubs for landscaping; (c) musical instruments for teenagers; (d) office typewriters; (c) stereo components.
25. If influentials are found at all levels of society, how would those in the upper and middle classes differ, if at all, from those in the lower class?
26. Explain how a marketer contemplating the introduction of a radically new type of product might use Rogers' model of the diffusion process in planning the marketing strategy.
27. Assume that a particular social group has norms that are strongly in favor of change for change's sake. In such a group, would the influentials then be the innovators? Explain your reasoning.
28. Try to enumerate five products fairly clearly related to the lower class, the middle class, and the upper class, respectively.
29. Do you think that the decline in the importance of the automobile as a status symbol in the United States indicates a decreasing importance attached to status symbols by American society? Discuss.
30. Minority racial and ethnic groups in the United States generally perceive promotion and products in a different light and, thus, require different marketing treatment. Comment on this statement.
31. A marketer comments, "I would like to segment the market for my company's new instant breakfast cereals on the basis of social classes, but I don't know how to do it." What advice would you give this marketer?
32. Individuals with high opportunity costs for leisure offer the best potential market for goods. Please explain.
33. Why do you suppose some products have status connotations and others do not? Which group might be easier to sell?
34. Is it possible for some people to escape completely from the influence of fashion? Justify the position you take.

CASE PROBLEM

Bill Casey, recently married, used the installment plan to buy a new automobile and to furnish his newly purchased home (which was financed through a 30-year mortgage). When Bill told his father about this, the older man was horrified and said, "Your mother and I got where we are today because we saved our money, paid cash for all major purchases, and never paid a dime of interest to an installment seller." Bill replied, "If I waited to pay cash for these things, I would have a long grey beard before I could enjoy them!"

Which side of this argument would you take and why?

When you have mastered the contents of this chapter, you should be able to:

1. Identify examples of marketing activities, given descriptions of situations in which marketing activities are or are not being performed.
2. Name the nine activities generally classified as marketing activities.
3. Give examples of the different ways in which each of the four kinds of merchandising activities may be performed.
4. Explain why performance of the physical distribution activities (storage and transportation) is both necessary and important.
5. Explain why marketers perform (or do not perform) each of the three supporting activities.
6. Explain why no general scheme for classifying marketing activities is universally applicable.
7. Discuss the relationship of the performance of marketing activities to marketing efficiency.

CHAPTER 4
THE MARKETING PROCESS

Marketing, as defined earlier, is the managerial process by which products are matched with markets and through which ownership transfers are effected. Thus, the two general purposes (goals) of marketing are to obtain and to service demand, but each company also has additional and more specific marketing goals whose nature varies both with its own situation and its overall company goals. For example, a company that has a reputation for leadership in product innovation not only attempts to obtain and service demand but continues to work toward furthering its reputation as a leader in product innovation. Both the inputs (marketing activities) and the outputs (marketing goals), then, vary with the company and its overall goals. Specific companies perform and combine different marketing activities in highly individualized ways, not only to obtain and service demand but to work toward other more specific marketing goals.[1]

Identification of Marketing Activities

Identifying marketing activities might seem simple because it would appear necessary only to itemize those steps required to move products and services from producers to final buyers. But the task is complicated by difficulties met in determining just where marketing begins and ends. It is oversimplifying to assume that marketing activities are concerned only with the flow of products and services;

[1]Our thinking on this subject has been strongly influenced by the perceptive article of R. J. Lewis and L. G. Erickson, "Marketing Functions and Marketing Systems: A Synthesis," *Journal of Marketing*, July 1969, pp. 10–14. See also T. L. Sporleder, "Marketing Functions and Marketing Systems: A Synthesis—A Comment," *Journal of Marketing*, July 1970, pp. 63–64.

to achieve marketing efficiency, there must also be a reverse flow of information, from the market to the producer. This information-gathering activity is performed both before the product is planned or produced and after the product is on the market. Conceptually, then, the marketing process both begins and ends with the final buyer, with information flowing back to the producer and products flowing forward to the final buyer.

The marketing activities most easily identified are those concerned with bringing products into contact with markets. Selling is one of these. Buying, the other side of selling, is not so easy to identify as a marketing activity, the ease of identification varying with who is buying. For instance, the buying of merchandise for resale is one of the retailer's most important tasks, for, to achieve his goal of selling goods to consumers, he must buy those things consumers need and want. But is buying as clearly a marketing activity for the manufacturer? In some cases, his buying decision is influenced by the effect his purchase has on his product's marketability; in other cases, it is influenced by the effect on product costs. The selection and purchase of materials for television cabinets mainly affects the finished product's marketability, but the selection and purchase of parts and materials for the receiving equipment itself is largely a production and cost problem. In most instances, both marketing and production needs influence buying decisions. So manufacturers properly look upon buying as a marketing activity whose performance is frequently conditioned by production and cost considerations.

Activities not directly concerned with bringing products into contact with markets are more difficult to identify. For instance, although planning and designing the product may not seem like marketing activities, products should possess those characteristics that final buyers want and desire. These wants and desires must be discovered in an early stage of product development, otherwise the product is destined for marketing failure.

The final buyer often personally performs some marketing activities. Marketers strive to move products and services into the hands of final buyers, but it does not follow that all marketing then ceases. For example, storage is generally classified as a marketing activity. Potatoes, produced seasonally, are held and sold throughout the year by marketing institutions, but sometimes individual consumers take over part of the storage activity—they may buy potatoes by the bushel to store in their homes. The storage activity continues to be performed, but by consumers rather than marketing organizations.

A Classification of Marketing Activities

Classification of marketing activities facilitates analysis of specific situations, but no general classification does or can apply to every marketing situation. Any classification scheme needs some modification to fit the particular analytical requirements imposed by an individual company's marketing circumstances. Keeping this restriction in mind, we classify marketing activities into three general categories containing nine activities in all:

Merchandising Activities
1. product planning and development
2. standardizing and grading
3. buying and assembling
4. selling

Physical Distribution Activities

5. storage
6. transportation

Supporting Activities

7. marketing financing
8. marketing risk bearing
9. obtaining and analyzing marketing information

These activities are arranged in a logical sequence. Merchandising begins with an analysis of market needs and the development or procurement of products to meet these needs, and it ends with the activities involved in stimulating market demand most directly. Physical distribution makes the products available at the times and places final buyers want them. The supporting activities, generally speaking, have the main purpose of improving the effectiveness with which merchandising and physical distribution activities are performed.

MERCHANDISING

Merchandising

Merchandising consists of activities necessary to determine and meet market needs with products or services and to stimulate market demand. Some marketing writers classify standardizing and grading as auxiliary or supportive activities. We include them as merchandising activities chiefly because they involve managing product uniformity and consistency.

Product Planning and Development Most products, to be marketed successfully, must possess characteristics that conform rather closely to buyers' needs, wants, and desires, and this requires frequent product adaptation. In most industries this process is endless—with product improvements flowing from changing technology while shifts in buyer preferences simultaneously create continuing product obsolescence. In a rapidly changing industry such as pharmaceuticals, products developed within the last 20 years normally account for over half the sales and profits of the leading companies. In such industries, the noninnovating company almost certainly faces eventual elimination from the market. In other industries, where rates of product obsolescence are slower, the elimination process takes place over longer time spans.

Growing recognition of the importance of satisfying buyers' changing product preferences is evidenced by the trend among manufacturers toward making the marketing department increasingly responsible for product planning and development. Middlemen have always regarded product planning and development, which for them usually takes the form of changes in products handled or services offered, as crucial to their success.

A grocery wholesaler who begins a cash-and-carry service is engaging in product planning. A men's clothing store that adds a selection of women's clothing or abandons delivery service is also doing product planning. Both retailers and wholesalers call such changes merchandising, but what they are actually doing is comparable to what manufacturers do under the name of product planning and development.

Standardizing and Grading These activities involve establishment of basic measures or limits to which articles must conform.

Standard

A *standard* specifies what basic qualities a product must have to be designated consistent with established characteristics. Standards should be based on the qualities desired by buyers or on the use to which the article is to be put. For example, in clothing manufacturing, it is useful to establish standards of size so that all size 12 dresses will fit the same people.

Grading

Grading is the act of separating or inspecting the goods according to the established specifications. The specifications are set by the standards established and may include size, weight, or quality.

Standardizing and grading are important to efficient marketing. Both make it possible for customers to purchase by description instead of by inspection; for example, to order a ton of steel or coal of a specified grade by mail or by telephone. Both make it possible to merchandise products closer to what customers want. A mixed lot of ungraded fruits is less attractive to prospective customers and commands a lower total price than the same lot after it has been graded and priced by grade.

Grading also helps in streamlining the physical handling of many farm crops because it makes possible the mixing of lots belonging to different owners for storage and transportation. This permits the grain elevator operator to store the crops of different farmers in a single elevator. It also allows the transportation company to mix the same crops in shipment.

Standardization

Standardization, the application of standards, relates mainly to manufactured products. Its first step involves establishing physical standards to which the product should conform. But, prior to selecting the standards, the manufacturer should have assessed the market. Thus, a suit manufacturer can measure the potential market for each suit size and either produce each size in proportion to the probable demand or produce only certain more popular sizes.

Grading refers to the application of basic descriptive standards—such as size, color, or weight—to the products of nature where growers or producers have very limited control over their products' physical specifications. Since the United States Department of Agriculture has set standards for the sizes and grades of oranges, for example, growers sort their crops according to these sizes and end up with oranges in each of several sizes or grades, each of which commands a higher price than ungraded fruit. For grading to be used, all properties to be graded must be measurable. Thus, canned peaches can be graded in terms of properties such as sugar content, color, and size, but they cannot be graded in terms of taste, since there is no objective way to measure differences in individual tastes.

Standardizing is most effective when adopted on an industry-wide basis. Otherwise, a consumer may not confidently expect a size 9 to be the same regardless of the maker. Standardization in each industry is normally voluntary.

Buying

Buying and Assembling *Buying*, as a marketing activity, is the procurement of items for eventual resale to ultimate consumers or industrial users. Most of the items purchased by producers are used in the manufacturing process and generally reach final buyers in a different form as part of finished products. By contrast, the products middlemen buy are resold by them in essentially the same form to other middlemen or to final buyers.

Assembling

Assembling is closely related to buying. It involves bringing together either (1) different quantities of a wide variety of items for resale by a single establishment or (2) a large quantity of similar items for resale in a particular region. The first type of assembling is performed by retailers, such as department stores and supermarkets, who bring together products from many diverse sources, making it possible for consumers to satisfy a variety of wants on a single shopping trip. The second type is illustrated by the operations of centrally located wholesalers of agricultural produce who buy from numerous growers throughout the country and distribute the assembled produce to local wholesalers for eventual resale by retailers. Although the manufacturer's procurement of parts, materials, and the like is considered assembling, most assembling is performed by middlemen.

Successful buying requires an ability to estimate customers' needs weeks and even months in advance. When ordering merchandise that will be delivered and placed on sale two or three months later, retailers, for example, try to anticipate what consumers will do in the future, even though consumers are not sure themselves. It is important to know customers' needs and buying habits to predict their buying actions. A retailer must know the consumers who comprise his market, their income levels, their product preferences, their shopping habits, and so forth. A wholesaler must have just as complete an understanding of his own customers—the retailers—and at least a general knowledge about their customers. Similarly, the manufacturer must be familiar with the buying habits, financial capabilities, promotional policies, and other characteristics of his own immediate customers, and he must also be acquainted with the needs and buying patterns of other marketing intermediaries and of final buyers.

Selling

Selling *Selling*, in its broad sense, has the purpose not only of making sales (i.e., effecting ownership transfers) but of identifying prospective customers, stimulating demand, and providing information and service to buyers. In working toward these goals, the marketer must combine such activities as personal selling, advertising, sales promotion, packaging, and customer service. Management does not usually rely on any one selling activity but tries, through continuous experimentation, to find an effective combination. (A blend of selling activities coordinated into a sales program is called a promotional mix.) Skill is needed not only in planning an optimum promotional mix, but in coordinating the different selling activities.

Personal Selling

1. *Personal Selling*. Personal selling is the chief means through which marketing programs are implemented. The unique strength of personal selling lies in its ability to personalize sales messages for individual customers. Capitalizing fully on this strength, however, requires trained and competent salesmen. Substantial investments must be made in recruiting, training, paying, and supervising salesmen—thus, personal selling is a relatively high-cost selling method. The cost of each advertising message per prospect reached is much lower than the cost of each personal sales contact. But it often takes many advertising messages to move a prospect to buying action, while a single sales presentation may do the job. Generally, management seeks to minimize selling costs through using some combination of personal selling and other sales activities. In theory, all selling activities—personal selling, advertising, and so on—should be used up to the point where their marginal efficiencies are equated.

Advertising

2. *Advertising*. Because advertising generally is a relatively low-cost way to convey selling messages to numerous prospects, it is important in most marketing programs. It is used not only to stimulate demand but for many other purposes. It can secure leads for salesmen and middlemen by convincing readers, listeners, and viewers to request more information and by identifying outlets handling the product. It can force middlemen to stock the product by building consumer interest. It can help train dealers' salesmen in product uses and applications. And it can build dealer and consumer confidence in the company and its products by building familiarity.

Marketing management's most frequent assignment to advertising is to stimulate market demand. By using advertising to presell customers—that is, to arouse and intensify their buying interest in advance—management hopes to facilitate the salesmen's selling task. While sometimes advertising alone may succeed in achieving buyer acceptance, preference, or even demand for the product, seldom can it be solely relied upon. Usually, advertising is most efficiently used with at least one other sales method, such as personal selling or point-of-purchase display, which are generally more effective in directly moving customers to buying action. Effective advertising by a manufacturer, for instance, often arouses a consumer's interest, but it will rarely send him to retail stores actively seeking the product. However, when he is in a store, and an alert clerk or an attractive display calls his attention to the manufacturer's product, the impact of previous advertising often helps in persuading him to buy.

Point-of-Purchase Display

3. *Point-of-Purchase Display.* Point-of-purchase display supplements and coordinates personal selling and advertising, helping to make them more effective. Thus, its main purpose is to impel on-the-spot buying action by prospects. It is used much more extensively in marketing consumer products than in industrial marketing chiefly because ultimate consumers are more susceptible to making impulse purchases. Furthermore, with the spread of self-service retailing, consumers seeking product information have come to depend less on sales clerks and more on such sales promotional devices.

Packaging

4. *Packaging.* Marketing management expects the package to: attract consumers' attention at the point of purchase, furnish them with needed information about the product, and provide the extra push so often required to propel them into buying. With the spread of self-service retailing, packaging—like point-of-purchase display—has risen in importance as a marketing activity. Traditionally, the package was regarded solely as a container for the product, and production departments had exclusive responsibility for packaging.

The package's basic role is still that of a container but today it is also expected to play important marketing roles. In most consumer product marketing programs, for example, the package is designed to relate the product to the manufacturer's advertising, thus improving the chances that consumers will recognize it in retail outlets. In selling through self-service retail outlets, the manufacturer's salesmen are responsible for persuading retailers to stock the product; advertising is responsible for making consumers aware of the product, its uses, and its advantages; and packaging is responsible for tying in the salesmen's efforts and advertising's impact.

Customer Service

5. *Customer Service.* As a selling activity, customer service provides assistance and advice on such things as product installation, operation, maintenance, and repair. For prospective buyers of many products, availability and adequacy of customer service are major factors in the choice among competing sellers. Through providing superior customer service, a seller may obtain the patronage of certain buyers even in the face of strong price competition. As more technical features are added to a product and it becomes more complicated to install, operate, and maintain, customer service gains in importance as an instrument of competition.

PHYSICAL DISTRIBUTION

Storage and transportation are the activities necessary to move products from their times and places of production to their times and places of consumption. In a highly developed and complex economy, such as in the United States, most of each producer's customers are located hundreds and even thousands of miles away, and products must be transported to and stored at points more accessible to them. Furthermore, in developed countries, such as those in Western Europe and North America, most manufacturers produce in anticipation of market demand and hold inventories until orders are received and filled. In developing countries, by contrast, many manufacturers wait for orders before they begin manufacturing and have minimum stocks of finished products, although they do maintain stocks of raw materials. As countries develop and as multinational trade increases, both storage and transportation, as well as inventory management and the processing and handling of customers' orders, increase in importance.

Storage

Storage Because in our complex economic system products are generally produced in anticipation of market demand, storage is necessary and important. Manufacturers, wholesalers, and retailers all hold and manage inventories. When consumers make purchases from retail outlets, retailers' inventories are reduced and are replenished from wholesalers' inventories which, in turn, are replenished from the manufacturer's inventory. Similarly, the consumer's own supply of products is reduced by his own consumption and replenished by his purchases. When a product is purchased at the retail level, stock levels fluctuate all along the line of distribution.

Marketers have three other important reasons for holding products in storage. One is to even out the seasonal factor in production or in sales. A manufacturer of Christmas ornaments, for example, has a market for its products only during the immediate pre-Christmas period, but its costs are lower if production is carried on throughout the year; so it stores its output from one selling season to the next. Similarly, many farm products are harvested in one season but are bought and consumed throughout the year—so growers and middlemen store them from one harvesting season to the next. A second reason for storage is to obtain economies in other business operations: for instance, manufacturers who make products in a large number of sizes, such as nuts and bolts, use the same machines to produce different sizes. It is often more economical to schedule long production runs of several weeks' supply of particular sizes rather than making the total needs of each size weekly. A third reason for storing products is to improve their quality and value—products such as cheese, whisky, and tobacco must be aged or conditioned to improve their flavor and, hence, to increase their value.

Transportation

Transportation Because most markets are geographically separated from production areas, transportation is a necessary and important marketing activity. Many factories are located away from urban areas to avoid population and traffic congestion and high land costs, with the expectation that the lower costs incurred in a nonurban location will more than offset the costs of moving finished products to urban markets. Other factories are separated from their largest markets through historical accident. For instance, many businesses start up in the founder's home town, and as they prosper and grow, the founder seeks ever farther removed markets for the expanding production. Eventually, strong reasons develop for building additional plants nearer the larger and more distant markets, but many manufacturers conclude that lower production costs in a single large plant more than offset transportation costs to distant markets. In some industries, such as lumber and steel, where transportation costs for raw material are higher than for the finished products, manufacturing facilities are located near raw material sources with little regard for market location. Regardless of the location of production facilities, transporting products to markets is an important distributive activity.

SUPPORTING ACTIVITIES

The supporting activities do not relate directly to ownership transfers but support or contribute to other marketing activities. Supporting activities include marketing financing, marketing risk bearing, and obtaining and analyzing marketing information. Because of the relationships these activities bear to the formulation of marketing and other basic business policies, top management often seems to pay closer attention to the activities than it does to others.

Marketing Financing Marketers, both as receivers and sources of credit, are concerned with financing. As receivers, they sometimes use short-term financing to tide their operations over seasonal peaks that require additional inventory investments and higher promotional expenses. Many retailers, for instance, increase their inventories 50 percent or more during the months just before Christmas and increase their sales forces and advertising outlays accordingly; if permanent capital investments were kept at a level high enough to meet these seasonal needs, much money would lie unproductive the rest of the year. Consequently, most businessmen finance seasonal variations in marketing expenses through credit.

Trade Credit

Marketing organizations have two main sources of credit: trade credit and banks. Trade credit, highly important in short-term financing, is extended by suppliers. Manufacturers and middlemen offer their customers credit terms allowing them from as few as 10 to as many as 120 or more days in which to pay. Trade sources are usually willing to assume greater credit risks than are banks, but trade credit also tends to be more expensive, especially when interest is charged on overdue balances.

Installment Credit

Providing credit to customers is essential to the success of most marketers. Most "big ticket" consumer durables, such as automobiles and furniture, are sold on the installment plan; surprisingly few consumers are both able and willing to pay cash for such items, and there is no doubt that installment credit has contributed significantly to the development of mass markets for many consumer durables. Department stores and other retailers use credit (in the form of charge accounts or through honoring various credit cards) as one means of attracting patronage. At the wholesale level, most transactions are on a credit basis. Mercantile credit, which is granted by manufacturers and wholesalers, not only assists in but simplifies ownership transfers. By extending credit to buyers, the seller avoids the undesirable alternatives of having transportation companies make collections on delivery or asking customers to pay at the time of order placement.

Mercantile Credit

Inventory Risk

Marketing Risk Bearing Marketing risks arise from both supply and demand changes and natural hazards. Any institution that carries an inventory takes the risk that supply and demand conditions may change. Thus, marketers who perform the storage activity also perform not only financing (by taking ownership) but risk bearing. Most marketing institutions have the problem of deciding on the proper size of inventories. There is always risk that an inventory will not be sold if it proves too large relative to market demand. But there is also risk that if it proves too small, orders will be lost because they cannot be filled.

Risk Transfer

A marketer may transfer part of its risk burden, eliminating some risks entirely and converting others from unpredictable amounts of potential loss to known items of expense. For example, when a seller agrees to reimburse a buyer for any drop in a product's price that may occur within a given period, the buyer succeeds in transferring the entire risk of a price decline during the period to the seller. *Hedging* provides another way to transfer the risks of price changes in a limited number of items traded on organized commodity exchanges.[2]

Hedging

Risks attached to such natural hazards as fire and floods, deterioration of products in storage, and damage in transit can often be transferred to institutions that specialize in assuming such risks. Insurance companies cover all these risks in return for premium payments. When risks are transferred in this way, unpredictable amounts of potential loss become known amounts of expense.

Risk Reduction

Because many marketing risks cannot be transferred, marketers concentrate on trying to reduce them. Risks of changes in market demand are reduced through accurate sales forecasting and marketing research; for example, while available techniques for market measurement are by no means foolproof, a well-considered sales forecast can help reduce the margin of error in deciding on inventory size. Also, risk of a change in market demand is reducible through aggressive programs of advertising, personal selling, and the like. Reasonably accurate sales forecasting should also help in reducing the supply risk of being out-of-stock and unable to fill customers' orders.

Other risks involved in changing supply conditions, such as the

[2]*Hedging* is a procedure involving simultaneous sales in the futures market when purchases are made in the current (spot) market, and simultaneous purchases in the futures market when sales are made in the current market, so that gains or losses on current transactions are approximately balanced off against the opposite experience in the futures market.

risk that an oversupply will cause competitors to cut prices, may be partially offset by differentiating products so that customers will be reluctant to accept substitutes. To the extent that product differentiation succeeds in building customer loyalty, a marketer gains control over the supply; its customers will not switch to substitutes simply because of small price differentials. In a limited sense, the marketer gains a degree of monopoly control over the product's supply. However; product differentiation only reduces the risk of price competition; it does not eliminate it. Few marketers ever succeed in completely differentiating their products.

Obtaining and Analyzing Marketing Information Both for the sound formulation of marketing programs and for the intelligent direction of marketing activities, management needs to obtain and analyze a great deal of information. The success of a company's marketing operations depends largely upon management's knowledge and appraisal of such important information as the size, location, and characteristics of different markets for the products; the nature of present and prospective customers making up various market segments, their needs and wants, and their buying habits and preferences; competitors' strengths, weaknesses, activities, and plans; and trends in market supply and demand. Management secures these types of marketing information, appraises the significance, and adjusts company operations accordingly.

Marketing Information

Besides the general types of information mentioned above, particular items of market information are often important. For example, the fact that a market glut for lettuce exists in Chicago is important to a Texas lettuce grower planning shipments to that area. Similarly, knowing the extent to which Pacific Coast steel users are buying Japanese-made steel is important information to a domestic steel producer. Likewise, it is important for an upstate New York manufacturer of room air conditioners to learn as soon as possible of a run on its product in Washington, D. C. Such items—which have immediate, though often fleeting, implications—are called *market news* to distinguish them from other pieces of marketing information that generally have longer range and continuing significance.

Market News

Marketing information is gathered in diverse ways. Executives obtain much market news rather informally through casual conversation; from reading business and trade publications, syndicated market news letters, and daily newspapers; from newscasts; and from reports submitted by field sales executives and salesmen. More formal information-gathering methods are used to obtain marketing information of long-range significance. Sales analysis techniques are applied in combing company records for information about customers and markets. Marketing research methods are used in tapping information sources outside the company. Economic and business forecasting techniques are used to secure important information on future market conditions.

Variations in Classification of Marketing Activities

Although availability of a systemized classification of marketing activities assists in studying marketing and its problems, no such classification scheme is universally applicable in analyzing the activities of particular companies or industries. For a cosmetics manufacturer, packaging and advertising may be so important that they deserve classification as separate marketing activities; while storage may be so unimportant as not to deserve separate classification. Each marketer should set up its own classification of marketing activities, emphasizing those important to the operation's success, deemphasizing others. Each company has its own individualized set of company and marketing goals, and the list of marketing activities is simply a compilation of those necessary to achieve these goals.

If the numbers and kinds of marketing activities required vary with the marketer, the product, and the distribution method, we may reasonably ask whether it is meaningful to classify activities performed under diverse circumstances into general groups. Certainly, for example, farmers, unlike manufacturers, cannot change the design of their products. Melon growers know that consumers would prefer seedless watermelons, but they cannot develop them personally. They can only hope that plant scientists will eventually succeed in doing so. Hence, farmers appear naturally to have little practical interest in product design. Despite such variances, different marketers still share enough common goals and activities to justify generalizations about the marketing activities they perform.

Performance of Marketing Activities and Marketing Efficiency

Some marketing critics assert that repetition in performance of marketing activities is a sure sign of inefficiency. In evaluating this criticism, we must admit that some activities are performed at each distribution level—buying and selling, for example, may be performed several times since each middleman, interposed between producer and final buyer, customarily both buys and sells. But, seeing this as further evidence of inefficiency, the critics suggest that marketing costs could be reduced through eliminating certain middlemen. Following this line of reasoning to its logical end, the most efficient marketing system would stress direct sales by producers to final users. In some instances, of course, as in marketing certain industrial products, direct sale is the most efficient marketing system; but, in most situations, direct sale is not very efficient and in marketing many consumer products it is impractical. Agricultural marketing provides numerous examples—direct distribution of potatoes or oranges by thousands of growers would not only be prohibitively expensive but highly inconvenient for consumers, most of whom prefer to buy several food items at once and at a time of their own choosing.

Even with such manufactured products as soap and flour, produced mainly by a few large companies, direct sale is impractical because consumers buy these products frequently and in small quantities so that the amount of money realized from each transaction would be insufficient to cover the costs of reaching the customer. Marketing channels for such products are necessarily complex and long, and individual marketing activities must be performed repeatedly as products move from producers to final buyers. At each distribution level, these activities are performed in specialized ways; under these conditions, shortening the marketing channel often results in increased costs and reduced efficiency.

The question is not which activities have to be performed but rather which combination of marketing institutions can perform them most efficiently. Ultimately, marketing efficiency results from finding the optimum division of responsibility among the institutions performing the activities at different distribution levels.

Summary

Discussion in this chapter has focused on the marketing process and the activities performed during its various phases. While the marketing process, conceptually speaking, both begins and ends with the product's final buyer, specific companies combine and perform different marketing activities (making up the process) in highly individualized ways, not only to obtain and service demand but to achieve other, more specific goals. Thus, no general classification of marketing activities does or can apply to every marketing situation, but individually designed classification schemes do facilitate analysis of specific situations. Consequently, each company needs its own classification scheme, detailing those activities necessary to achieve its own unique set of company and marketing goals. Such goals determine which marketing activities are necessary, and marketing efficiency results ultimately from finding the optimum division of responsibility among different institutions performing them.

QUESTIONS AND PROBLEMS

1. Identification of marketing activities is sometimes a complicated matter. Explain.
2. What department in a company do you feel should bear responsibility for product planning and development? Why?
3. Discuss the reasons why standardizing and grading are important to efficient marketing.
4. In what way is the assembling activity related to buying? Discuss.
5. Selling is the most important marketing activity. Agree or disagree? Justify your position.
6. Explain the importance of storage.

7. The only reason transportation is an important marketing activity is that markets and production sites are geographically separated. Discuss.
8. Assess the role of marketing financing.
9. Marketers attempt to reduce marketing risks that cannot be transferred by a variety of means. Explain.
10. A company's marketing success is directly related to its ability to obtain and analyze marketing information. Explain.
11. Explain why it is impossible to have a single classification of marketing activities which is universally applicable.

CASE PROBLEM

Jerry Seager and Chris Whichard, next-door neighbors in a Pittsburgh suburb, were discussing the role of marketing in a free enterprise economy. In particular, they were discussing whether or not marketing activities were justified.

Jerry, a computer programmer for a large company, complained loudly about prices. "My feeling," said Jerry, "is that if you eliminated the middleman we'd get lower prices and we'd all be better off. In fact, the entire marketing system would function more smoothly and we would all benefit from the increased efficiency by being able to get the same goods at much lower prices we all could afford."

He went on to cite a recent purchase of a refrigerator that cost him \$350. He estimated the cost of manufacturing the refrigerator at around \$200 and suggested that he failed to see how \$150 worth of value was added to the product as it passed through a "totally unnecessary" channel of distribution. "So," Jerry said, "I'm forced to pay \$150 for the mere existence of a bunch of middlemen who don't do anything to the refrigerator except pass it on to the next guy. It just doesn't seem right."

Chris, a local men's clothing store operator, took the position that greater efficiency, not less, resulted from the activities performed by middlemen. "Take my case, for example," said Chris. "Eliminate me. Where does that leave you? I'll tell you—when you want a suit of clothes, rather than hopping into your car and driving the few miles to my store and making your selection from among a wide assortment of brands, you'd have to deal directly with the manufacturer. You might save a few dollars on the price of the suit, but I don't think you'd find it a very desirable situation." Chris said further: "And I'm talking only about a suit of clothes. How about the shirts, ties, socks, belts and other things that go along with it, all of which you can get under my store roof? Do you think you'd like to have to maybe deal with a different manufacturer for all of your clothing needs? And, one other thing—think about it for *all* the products you, your wife, and your kids buy. You're asked to pay for the activities performed by various middlemen, sure, but you never get something of value for nothing, do you? You're able to enjoy your standard of living because of marketing, not despite it. So, be thankful for the middleman—he helps to make it possible for you to live the kind of life you like."

Evaluate the arguments of Jerry Seager and Chris Whichard. With whom do you agree? Why?

When you have mastered the contents of this chapter, you should be able to:

1. Explain the relationship of company goals and the marketing organization.
2. Analyze the impact of the marketing concept on the marketing organization *and* the company organization.
3. Explain why nonmarketing executives should help formulate certain marketing policies and why marketing executives should help formulate certain policies in other functional areas.
4. Outline the conditions under which each of the various bases for dividing marketing line authority is appropriate.
5. Describe the reasons for the creation of product manager positions and the general nature of the product manager's job.
6. Contrast and compare the formal marketing organizational plans of: manufacturers, retailers and wholesalers, and service businesses.

CHAPTER 5
ORGANIZING FOR MARKETING

People, as individuals and as members of groups, do the actual work of marketing. In order to understand how marketing work gets done, then, you must know a good deal about both organization in general and marketing organization in particular.

Organization

An *organization* is the mechanism through which a managerial philosophy is translated into action. As this philosophy changes, organizational goals are revised and basic changes are made in the organization itself. In moving toward the marketing concept, especially significant changes occur in the marketing organization, which is the company's main link with the market. The *marketing organization* provides the vehicle for making decisions on products, marketing channels, physical distribution, promotion, and prices. It is also the vehicle through which these decisions are implemented.

Marketing Organization

Company Goals and the Marketing Organization

The modern view of an organization is that it is a group of people brought together to participate in a common effort to accomplish certain goals. The basic goals of a company, then, indicate, to a large extent, what the company wants to be, since they tend to override and to permeate the rest of its administration. Certain goals have particularly important implications for the marketing organization.

1. *Desired Financial Results.* Traditionally, businesses are intended to be economic institutions. Generally, the organizers anticipate that a com-

pany's operations will generate profits. Once operations are under way, profits must be forthcoming on a sufficiently regular basis to permit the company's continued survival. The company's profit goal is of great importance to the marketing organization. It affects both the amount of sales volume that is sought and the level of costs allowed. Also important is the time allowed for reaching a target profit goal, as this affects management's willingness or unwillingness to trade current profits for potentially greater future profits.

2. *Desired Place in the Industry.* A company defines its desired place in the industry in terms of such variables as size of operation, major function (manufacturing, wholesaling, retailing, etc.), quality and price levels for its products, and specialization or diversification of its activities. Different decisions on these variables result in different marketing organizations. For instance, a company that strives to have the largest sales volume in the industry requires a different marketing organization than one that wants to have the highest quality products.
3. *Disposition Toward Change.* A company's attitude toward change largely determines the type of employees who are attracted to it and the scheme by which they are welded into an organizational framework. Clearly, firms operating under the marketing concept have opted in favor of emphasizing change rather than stability. They recognize the need for making continual adjustments in operations and organizational structure in the process of adapting to changing market requirements and competitive conditions.
4. *Social Philosophy.* The basic goals controlling a company's relationship with the community and governmental units affect the operations of all departments and, most certainly, the marketing department.
5. *Competitive Posture.* A company's posture with respect to its competition has direct implications for the marketing organization, such as whether or not it will incorporate features permitting aggressive selling and advertising.
6. *Desired Customer Service Image.* There is a world of difference between a company seeking long-run customer satisfaction and one emphasizing quick "one-time" sales. This facet of the company image is important to all company departments producing, selling, and servicing the product line.
7. *Relationships with Suppliers.* The nature of a company's desired relationships with suppliers has indirect but important implications for marketing organization, since such relationships affect product quality, availability of repair and replacement parts, pricing practices, and the like.

Marketing Organization and Transition to the Marketing Concept

It is top management that determines how far a company moves toward adopting the marketing concept. Such factors as executives' personalities and experience influence this decision, but perhaps the most critical is top management's appraisal of the current state and probable future intensity of competition. The more directly such environmental trends as those discussed in Chapter 2 impinge upon a company's operations, the more severe is its competition and the more crucial is adoption of the marketing concept to its survival, especially during periods of shortages and inflation such as we have witnessed during the 1970s.

HISTORICAL SHIFTS IN TOP MANAGEMENT'S BUSINESS PHILOSOPHY

Production Emphasis When production problems were of prime importance, top management generally visualized a need for only a skeletal marketing organization. A slow rate of technological change made product changes infrequent; marketing channels were well defined and adhered closely to traditional patterns; little promotion was required due to the absence of strong competition; and pricing was mainly based upon cost plus a desired profit margin. Under these conditions, the marketing organization was little more than an adjunct to the factory—charged with physically distributing its output.

Personal Selling Emphasis As introduction and refinement of mass production techniques caused greatly increased factory outputs, the key problem became that of selling at the highest possible price what the factory was capable of producing. Advertising and other marketing activities were cast in supporting roles, being viewed mainly as the means for making personal selling more effective. Products and quantities manufactured were determined according to what the factory could produce, and the sales force was charged with selling that output. The sales organization often constituted the entire marketing organization or, at least, dominated other marketing activities.

Market Emphasis Top management in a growing number of concerns has recognized that focusing solely on what the factory can produce makes far less sense than determining what consumers want and then designing, manufacturing, and marketing products capable of satisfying those wants. With this shift in orientation, far-sweeping organizational changes have occurred. Marketing information has become an important input of marketing organizations, and it has seen increasing use in improving market knowledge and understanding. Product research and development have gained in organizational stature as consumers become steadily more sophisticated in what they will buy. At the same time, advancing technology makes it possible to tailor product specifications ever more closely to what consumers want. Even though personal selling—and the sales department—continues as the backbone of most marketing organizations, advertising's organizational stature has been elevated, as evolution and expansion of mass media have helped make it a more powerful element in marketing strategy. Recently advertising has focused more on "reason why" advertising, with emphasis placed upon the information value of advertising. This change in emphasis has been in response to the fact that buyers, more than ever before, because of inflation, are looking for wise ways to stretch their dollars. Changes in marketing channels, in operating methods of distributive institutions, and in physical distribution facilities have made channel and distribution decisions more important and have earned a place in many marketing organizations for specialized units dealing with these areas. Finally, in industry after industry, the competitive tempo has risen making pricing decisions more important and sometimes causing reallocations of decision-making authority. Summing up, all types of marketing decisions are rising in importance resulting in changed organizational structures as companies move toward adoption of the marketing concept.

COMPANY ORGANIZATION AND THE MARKETING CONCEPT

Probably the most noteworthy characteristic of modern thought on organizations is that it is based upon a study of the organization as an integrated whole, i.e., a "system." Proper company organization under the marketing concept must result in a total integration and coordination of all organizational units (marketing, research and development, manufacturing, financial, etc.) into a single operating system directed toward achieving company goals and, at the same time, toward effectively serving the market and its changing wants and desires. Neither marketing nor any other organizational unit should dominate. All should be welded into an operating system whose components are so orchestrated that the market is served effectively while company goals are being reached.

The organizational structure of a company operating under the marketing concept is subject to frequent, sometimes drastic, modifications. Shifts in environmental factors, such as technological breakthroughs by competitors or changes in distributive institutions, may require changes in operating strategies that can only be effectuated by changing the organizational structure. Ideally, the organization should have built-in flexibility enabling it to adapt readily to unstable conditions; the hierarchy itself should change with changing conditions, each member performing his or her speciality according to a common understanding of the company's goals.

ORGANIZATIONAL RESPONSIBILITY FOR MARKETING POLICY FORMULATION

As a company reorganizes in line with the marketing concept, a hard look should be taken at the ways in which responsibility is assigned for formulating marketing policies. Traditionally, sales force management, advertising, marketing research, and the management of marketing channels have been recognized as marketing activities. Traditionally, too, marketing executives have been responsible for policy formulation in these areas. But certainly other departments, such as production and finance, have strong interests in how salesmen are trained and operate, in the messages advertising conveys, and in the data the marketing information system gathers. Therefore, in the modern organization, good reasons exist for nonmarketing executives to participate in making policies for these areas of marketing.

Similarly, marketing executives should help make policies in organizational areas where there are important marketing implications. One such area is pricing, which often is the responsibility of the treasurer, controller, production manager, or some combination. Another is the product line, traditionally the province of production or research and development or both. Still another is physical distribution, often either under the production department or segregated into a separate department. Policies on pricing, products, and physical distribution all have important implications for marketing; by their very nature, these are interfunctional activities and, as such, marketing executives should share the responsibility for policy formulation. When a company is in the process of changing to the marketing concept, every effort must be made to pull down the walls between departments. The main way to do this is to discard traditional authority and job-task relationships wherever they prevent or act as deterrents to effective coordination of the organization as an operating system.

INTEGRATION OF MARKETING ACTIVITIES

As marketing receives recognition as a major business function, one requiring coordination of numerous activities, top executives reexamine the ways in which these activities are incorporated in the formal organizational structure. Sales force management, advertising, and marketing research, for instance, have traditionally operated as separate departments reporting directly to top management. Integration, or centralization of these activities under a single high-ranking marketing executive, by improving coordination, generally increases marketing effectiveness. There has been a strong trend in this direction.

Organization of Marketing Responsibilities in the Manufacturing Firm

Executives in small marketing departments must handle all types of problems, but in large departments dividing the work is not only desirable but critical. In a large marketing organization, numerous executives are specialists, with technical knowledge of activities such as advertising, marketing information, and physical distribution. The chief marketing executive is responsible for dividing the work among these specialists and other subordinates.

THE CHIEF MARKETING EXECUTIVE

Chief Marketing Executive

Increasing centralization of marketing responsibilities and growing complexity of the marketing function have led large companies to search for a new "breed" of *chief marketing executive,* whose time is devoted primarily to planning and coordinating all marketing activities. The traditional line marketing responsibility—management of the sales force—is delegated to a subordinate, the general sales manager. Other marketing staff responsibilities—such as advertising, marketing information, and credit management—are moved from various other organizational slots and now come under the direction of the chief marketing executive, enabling him or her to exert a greater total impact on marketing strategy and tactics. Similarly, newly created staff divisions, such as product management and physical distribution, are organizationally located in ways that facilitate their coordination—by the chief marketing executive—with other marketing activities.

DIVIDING MARKETING LINE AUTHORITY

Line Executive

Line executives are those in the direct chain of command whose jobs consist mainly of managing subordinates who directly accomplish the company's goals. In a marketing organization, the chief marketing executive is also its top line executive, and the direct chain of command runs from him or her down through the sales organization (since it is the salesmen who ultimately and directly perform the work leading to company goals). Generally, however, he or she assigns the major responsibility for sales force management to a subordinate—the sales vice-president or general sales manager—who is then regarded as the marketing organization's principal line executive. When the sales force is small, the principal line executive manages it directly. But as the sales force expands line authority is divided.

Geographic Division When a sales force is deployed over a wide area, line authority is often divided geographically. Geographic division of authority is especially appropriate when the market or buyers or both vary in character from region to region; in such instances, each sales region can adapt its selling methods more closely to the needs and customs of local markets. However, the underlying reason for dividing line authority geographically is to improve the sales force's effectiveness by increasing the frequency of executive contacts with salesmen and by simplifying and strengthening their supervision. Subordinate sales managers devote their main efforts to improving the performances of the salesmen under them. Whether they are permanently based in their assigned areas or not makes little difference; increases in the availability and speed of public transportation have all but eliminated the need for this requirement, which once was nearly universal.

Product Division Sometimes a company's products dictate the organization of its sales force. When variations among products require considerably different selling methods and technical know-how from salesmen, line authority may be divided by products and separate sales forces set up for each product or product group. General Electric requires different kinds of salesmen to sell large electrical generators and small household appliances. Generator salesmen need technical training and sometimes must be prepared to wait years for their first order from a utility company; small appliance salesmen need little technical training and perform routine selling work. It would be wasteful to use the more technically trained personnel to sell both types of products so separate selling groups are maintained—each qualified to sell its particular products and each reporting to its own sales executive.

Maintaining separate sales forces for different products is expensive because it frequently results in more than one salesman covering the same geographical areas. Thus, the benefits should clearly outweigh the extra cost. These benefits are greatest for companies selling broadly diversified product lines, for companies reaching different markets with different products, and for companies having individual products with unique selling problems.

Customer or Marketing Channel Division When customers or marketing channels for a product or group of products vary substantially, it may be appropriate to divide line authority on a customer or market basis. A power-saw manufacturer, for example, sells identical products to two very different markets: the lumber industry and the construction industry. These two markets have both different geographical characteristics (lumbering is heavily concentrated in the Northwest and Southeast, whereas construction is broadly distributed relative to population and industrial concentration) and different buying practices. Under these market conditions, separate sales forces are justified.

Many marketers sell the same consumer products through multiple marketing channels. Part of the factory's output may reach consumers through wholesale distributor and independent retailer channels, another part through chain stores buying directly from the factory, and still another part through export middlemen selling to overseas markets. The type of selling required in each case is quite different, and the number and kinds of buyers vary greatly. (It takes, for example, only a few salesmen to reach all chain store buying offices in the United States, but it takes dozens or hundreds to reach all wholesalers.) Marketers using multiple channels often find it advantageous to organize separate sales forces for each channel.

Division on Several Bases Many companies use more than one basis for dividing line authority. Large sales organizations require several levels of management, and different bases of division may be used at different levels. When product differences require division of authority along product lines, the sales force may be organized accordingly, but if further subdivision is needed it may be on a geographic basis. Thus, the resulting organization provides sales specialization in terms of both different product lines and geographical market differences.

DIVISION OF MARKETING STAFF AUTHORITY

Staff Executive

Theoretically, staff people have purely advisory roles with no place in the command structure and without the right to give orders, but this does not exist in practice. The nature of the *staff executive's* work gives him an intimate and broad view of line executives' problems that almost inevitably gives him or her informal authority. Furthermore, with higher management relying increasingly on processed information, the staff authority to advise becomes the authority to screen and, thus, to make decisions. Generally, division and allocation of staff authority is decided according to areas of special competence.

THE PRODUCT MANAGER

Product Manager

The *product manager* does not fit neatly into either the line or staff categories. In large multiproduct companies, product managers are becoming increasingly common and more important. In such companies the chief marketing executive is responsible for all products but neither he nor his staff subordinates may give equal attention to all products in the line. Thus, no individual is specifically responsible for the success or failure of particular products. It is possible for some products to receive too little or too much promotion, for advertising programs for particular products not to be coordinated properly with sales activities, and for changes in consumer wants and competitors' actions with respect to individual products to go unheeded. The product manager's position was created in an attempt to fill such vacuums—in effect, he serves as a deputy marketing director for a particular product or product group. Normally, he concerns himself with all phases of the planning, execution, and control of marketing activities for his assigned products. He is deeply involved with the buying public, distributors, sales force, advertising agencies, product development, marketing research, and other marketing and corporate personnel.[1] Thus, the broad scope of his duties makes him a combination line and staff executive with respect to the products for which he is responsible.

[1] David J. Luck, "Interfaces of a Product Manager," *Journal of Marketing*, October 1969, p. 33.

Another way to view the product manager's organizational status is that he operates on a horizontal plane, in sharp contrast to most marketing personnel who operate primarily on a vertical plane. Since the product manager's specialization is cross functional, with a central focus on a specific product line or brand, his position is somewhat of a major departure that is not easily inserted into and absorbed by the existing organization. As a result, the position of "product manager" is difficult to define, staff, and implement for action. Yet, many companies credit a large measure of their success to the product manager concept.[2]

ORGANIZATION UNDER THE MARKETING CONCEPT

Figure 5–1 shows a typical formal marketing organization for a large manufacturer operating under the marketing concept. The organization is divided into three main parts; marketing services (mainly staff responsibilities), management of personal selling (including the line organization and staff activities closely related to sales force operations), and product management. The subdivisions on the marketing services side illustrate the broad range of staff-type responsibilities. Those under the general sales manager, who here serves as the principal line executive, are: field sales (made up of line executives managing the sales force); sales training (a staff activity concerned with increasing selling efficiency); sales service (a staff activity involving installation, maintenance, and repair services); and physical distribution (concerned with transportation, storage, materials handling, inventory management, and movement of customers' orders). Those under the products manager are in charge of product groups A, B, and C—each product manager being responsible for coordinating all marketing activities (staff as well as line) exerted in behalf of the group's products.

Staff personnel are generally concentrated at the central office because many of their activities are similar for all products, marketing channels, and geographic regions. Centralization allows coordination of efforts and a pooling of financial resources so the best available personnel and equipment can be brought together. Without good staff liaison at headquarters, some divisions might make decisions for their own good rather than for the good of the entire company; for example, long-range research projects might be omitted because of their immediate adverse effect on a division's profits. A strong central staff keeps division executives aware of broad company goals.

In large marketing organizations, it may still be necessary to provide staff assistance in field sales offices. In such instances, it must be decided whether (organizationally) to place these staff field executives under the authority of central office staff executives or

[2] *Ibid.*, p. 33.

Figure 5–1
Organization under the marketing concept

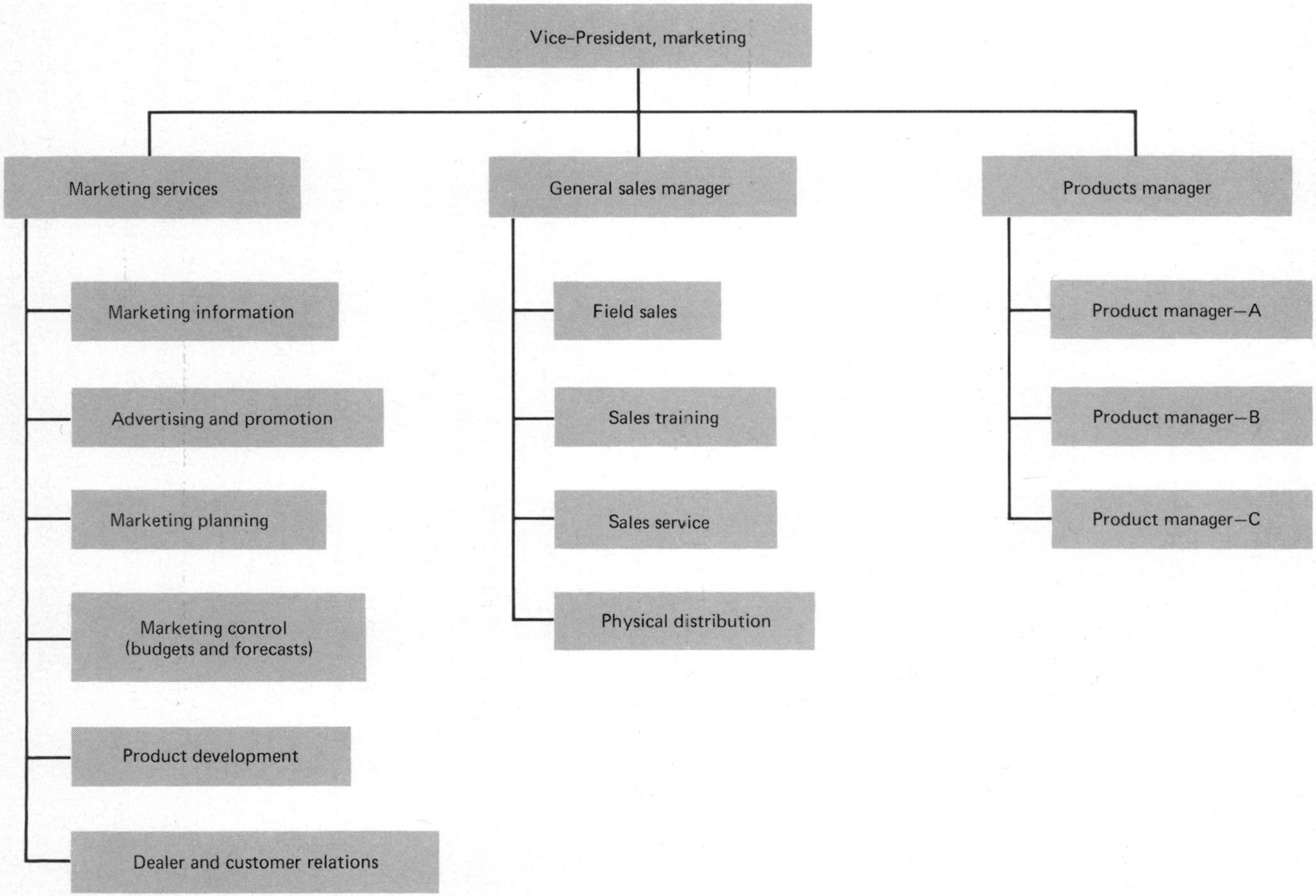

under local line sales executives. As in other organizational decisions, the solution rests in compromise among the authority, communication, coordination, and human relations needs of the individuals and groups involved.

Organization of Marketing Responsibilities in Businesses Engaged Mainly in Marketing-Type Activities

Retailers and wholesalers are specialists in marketing. They are not involved in making products but only in their distribution. They serve as stepping stones in the channels that move goods from producers to the final buyers. While to most manufacturers and other producers the marketing concept is a relatively new idea, most successful retailers and wholesalers long have had strong orientations toward their customers. Marshall Field and Company, a Chicago department store organization, for example, has promoted its slogan "The customer is always right" for nearly a century.

Merchandising

Marketing businesses are organized with merchandising as the primary or line function. *Merchandising* is defined as knowing what the customer wants and making it available at the right time and place for him or her to buy. The senior officer, or president, of most retail or wholesale establishments is generally a merchandiser, having moved up through various merchandising positions in the organization.

Figures 5–2 and 5–3 illustrate the organizational structures of two retailers—a large department store and a retail chain. In each of these institutions merchandising responsibility is assigned to an executive reporting directly to the president. This executive, then, has primary responsibility for the buying of all merchandise for resale. Generally, too, he or she is responsible for the preparation and administration of the merchandise budget, which determines the amount of merchandise which should be bought and on hand. Yet another of his or her primary responsibilities is that of selling the merchandise bought, through personal selling, advertising, and point-of-purchase and window display.

MERCHANDISING

Department stores and independent specialty stores organize the merchandising responsibility in much the same ways. Buying responsibility is divided by groupings of similar merchandise items and assigned to buying executives. In some instances, these buyers are also assigned supervisory responsibility for the sales personnel; in other cases, a sales executive supervises the sales personnel.

Wholesalers and chain organizations normally separate the buying and selling activities and assign responsibility for their per-

Figure 5–2
General organization chart of a department store

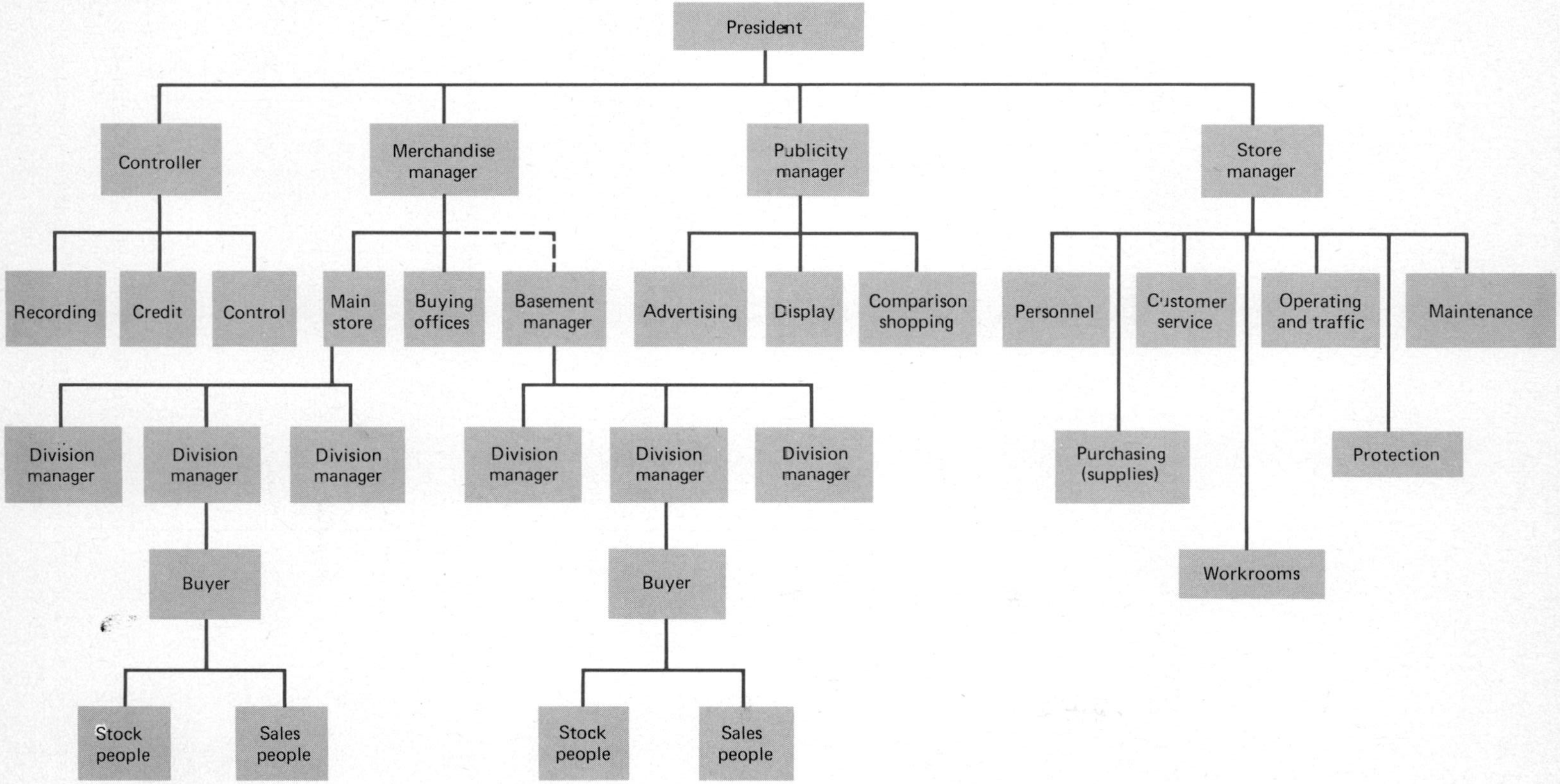

Figure 5–3
Organization chart for a retail chain

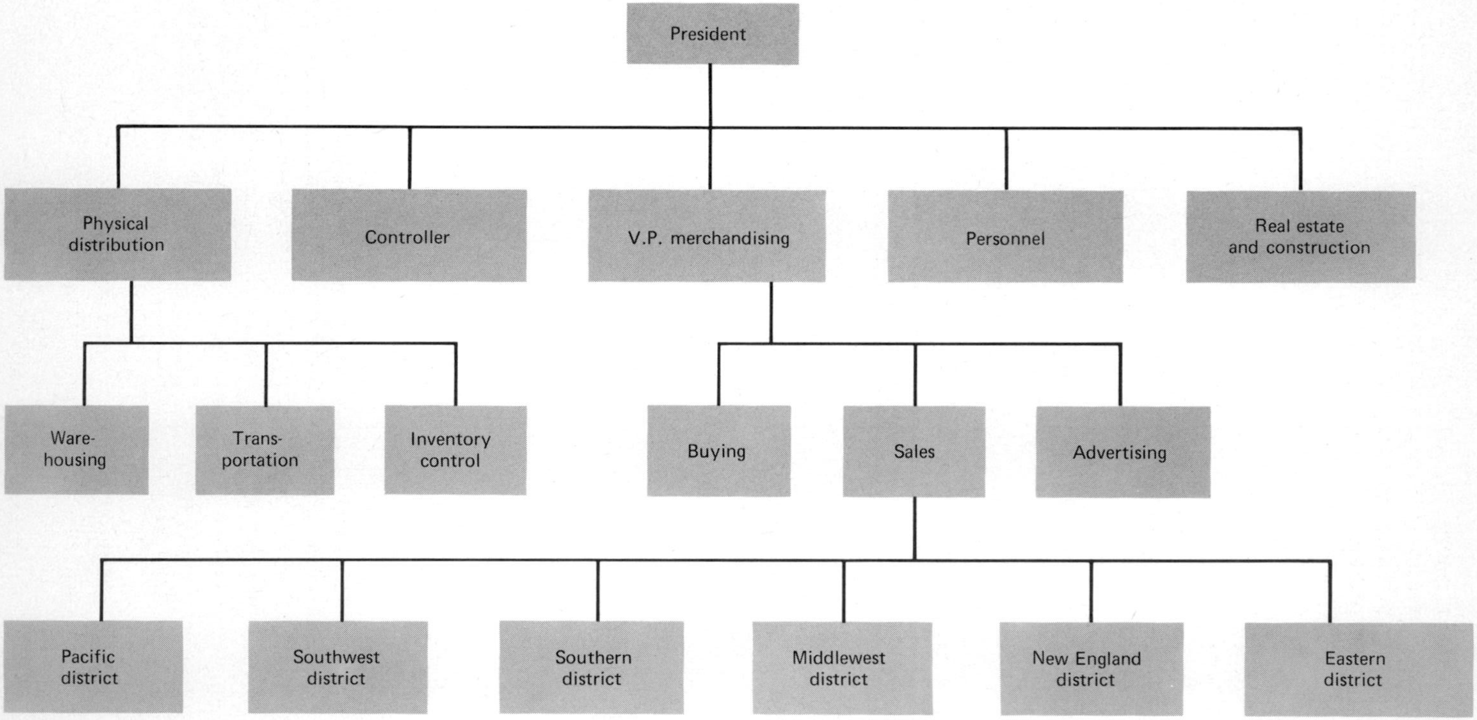

formance to different executives. In chain organizations, buying responsibilities are centralized at the home office, but selling responsibilities are necessarily decentralized to each of the chain's retail outlets.

NONMERCHANDISING ACTIVITIES

Supporting Activities

The supporting, or nonmerchandising, activities common to all marketing institutions are controlling, personnel, and management of the physical plant. Both the wholesaler and the large retailer tend to organize these activities along similar lines. Controlling includes record keeping, control over costs and profits, and credit management—which is very important in many marketing institutions. Personnel activities include, among others: recruitment and selection, training, supervising, and motivating of both selling and nonselling personnel. Management of the physical plant includes receiving and processing merchandise, purchasing of supplies, customer service, maintenance, and protection. A wholesale or retail organization operating only a single establishment generally assigns the responsibility for traffic management and storage to the physical plant manager; but those operating multiple establishments generally have a manager of physical distribution who is responsible for storage, transportation, and inventory control activities. Normally, retail outlets combine another group of activities—advertising, display, and publicity—and assign the responsibility for their performance to a specialized executive.

Organization of Marketing Responsibilities in a Service Business

Businesses that market services rather than products have been slow, generally speaking, in recognizing marketing as a key element in their operations. The same has been true of nonprofit institutions, most of which continue to operate without any marketing personnel.[3] The general tendency among service businesses has been to fragment the responsibility for performing various marketing activities; most, for instance, have no single high-ranking executive, such as a marketing vice-president or marketing manager, who has total responsibility for the marketing function. This is in spite of the fact that the typical service business performs marketing activities very similar to those performed by manufacturers. The failure to recognize marketing as a separate and important function and to organize personnel accordingly often results in ineffective performance of marketing activities.

In some service businesses, however—especially in those primarily engaged in providing advisory services for other businesses—the failure to recognize marketing as a separate and impor-

[3] Philip Kotler, *Marketing for Nonprofit Organizations* (Englewood Cliffs, N.J.: Prentice-Hall, Inc., 1975), p. 229.

tant function is not particularly serious. This category of service businesses includes, among others, advertising agencies, marketing research firms, and management consultants. In this type of service business, generally the head of the organization—the chief executive—personally directs and coordinates the organization's marketing activities and he or she, in addition, is also generally a marketing professional. Responsibility for performance of specific marketing activities, of course, is divided among various groups in the service organization. In the advertising agency, for example, typically the major responsibilities are divided among three groups: (1) the creative people, who develop campaign ideas and themes, write copy, do art work, and design advertising layouts, (2) the account executives, who provide liaison and continuing sales contact with the customers, and (3) the media buyers, who are responsible for determining which advertisements should appear in which media at what times.

COMMERCIAL BANKS

Although a few commercial banks have well-organized and effective marketing operations, the typical bank appears to have given marketing only slight organizational recognition. The typical, traditional-type of bank has an executive, often with the title of vice-president for public relations or vice-president for business development and advertising, who is responsible for selling various banking services such as loans, saving accounts, charge cards, and safety deposit boxes. Generally, this executive is not at the senior vice-presidential level but, rather, reports to an executive on that level, as illustrated in Figure 5–4. Essentially, his or her job is that of a "sales manager" and, as such, he or she rarely plays direct roles in such important marketing activities as market evaluation and measurement, designing service innovations and modifications, or formulating pricing strategy. Thus, in the typical bank, responsibility for performing the marketing function tends to be diffused throughout the organization with no one executive responsible for overall marketing performance. The lack of coordination frequently results in overemphasizing some marketing activities, such as advertising, at the expense of others, such as providing adequate customer service at tellers' windows.

INSURANCE COMPANIES

Again, although there are notable exceptions, the typical insurance company, like the typical bank, appears to lag behind most manufacturers in recognizing the marketing concept philosophy in their organizations. Insurance companies tend toward a strong sales orientation since the services they sell, although certainly necessary ones, rarely sell themselves. Potential policyholders are reluctant to think about disaster and death, so they postpone planning for these

Figure 5–4
Organization of a typical traditional commercial bank

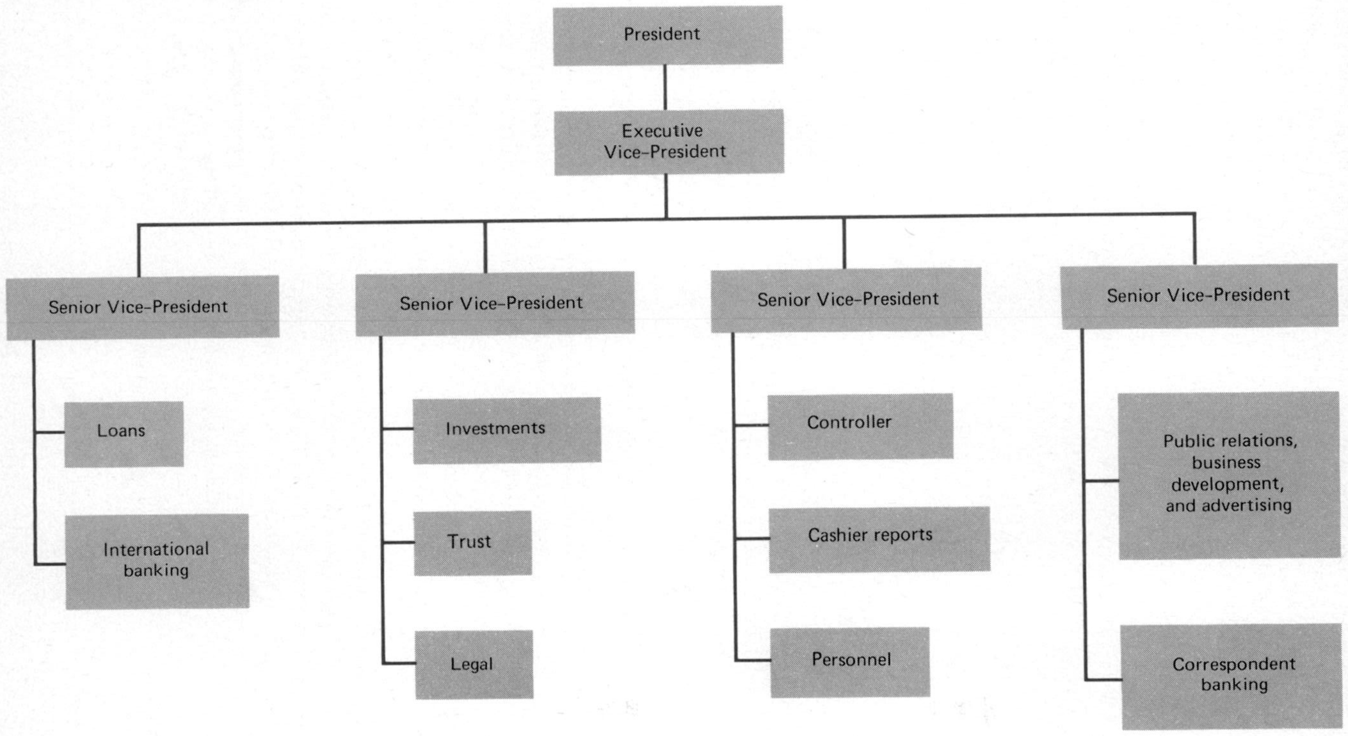

possibilities until they are contacted and influenced by insurance agents. Thus, the insurance company's natural orientation is toward sales, not marketing. Typically, its organization chart shows a sales executive on the same level as others responsible for selection of risks (product planning), policy writing (customer service), rating or actuarial (pricing), and agency management (distribution)—all marketing activities. As is true of most banks, then, the insurance company sales executive has no responsibility for or control over the whole group of marketing activities that make up an integrated marketing strategy.

Summary

You now should have a good understanding of how businesses organize the complex relationships among both people and activities in order to achieve their various goals. Developing an effective marketing organization begins with the identification of overall company goals and determination of their implications for marketing. As the necessity for making the transition to the marketing concept becomes increasingly clear, management looks more and more to its target markets for guidance and seeks to structure the organization so that both the market is served effectively and overall organizational goals are reached. Managerial attitudes toward the marketing concept show up in the ways in which marketing activities are organized in various kinds of enterprises.

Management's approach to total company organization, as well as to marketing organization, should be dynamic. An organization that is satisfactory today may prove inadequate tomorrow. Markets themselves change because of changes in income, shifts in population, changes in tastes and life styles, and the like. Market changes coupled with technological advances result in a flow of new products and the continual modification of old products. Furthermore, important developments in mass communications media and in marketing channels have been occurring and more such changes should be expected. A significant change in any market factor can reduce the effectiveness of an organizational structure not only for serving the market's needs but as a vehicle for achieving the company's goals. Since market factors are forever in a state of change, continual monitoring and regular reappraisal of organizational effectiveness are imperative.

QUESTIONS AND PROBLEMS

1. "Management of an organization largely involves the solution of problems in communication." How does this generalization apply to the management of a marketing organization? Give some examples.

2. What are the implications of the company's profit objective for the marketing organization?
3. Company A wants to have the largest sales volume in its industry. Company B wants to be the first to introduce product innovations in the industry. Assuming that both A and B compete in the same industry, how would these differences in goals likely result in rather different types of marketing organizations?
4. Comment on the various company objectives that have direct implications for a company's marketing organization.
5. Who is responsible for bringing the need for adopting the marketing concept to top management's attention? Why?
6. As more and more "market emphasis" has permeated top management's business philosophy, what changes have come about in marketing organization?
7. Should the marketing function dominate the organization in a company operating under the marketing concept? Why or why not?
8. "Good reasons exist for encouraging nonmarketing executives to participate in making policies for some areas in marketing." To what extent do you agree (disagree) with this statement? Should the marketing executive also be encouraged to participate in making policies in certain areas outside of marketing?
9. What reasons lie behind the trend in U.S. companies toward centralizing such activities as sales force management, advertising, and marketing research under a single high-ranking marketing executive? Is this trend likely to continue?
10. Which type of responsibility, staff (e.g., marketing research manager) or line (e.g., sales manager), is likely to give the best preparation for the new job of chief marketing executive?
11. "Staff executives represent the thinking arm of the organization, and line executives tend to react more automatically on the basis of experience." Evaluate.
12. Would it be proper to say that line marketing responsibilities and authority are described in the formal organization and that staff responsibilities are described in the formal organization, but that staff authority is a part of the informal organization? Which kind of authority is more important?
13. Under what circumstances should a marketing organization divide line authority geographically? By products? By marketing channels? On more than one basis?
14. Why are product managers becoming increasingly common and more important? What does the product manager's job consist of?
15. It has been said that the use of product managers results in conflicting demands on the time of salesmen and excessive intracompany product competition. Comment.

16. "Improved communication between a company's home office and its field salesmen should eliminate the need for district sales managers and supervisors. Comment.
17. The almost continuous change in the structure of many marketing organizations has been explained as resulting from the dynamic character of marketing. Do you agree? Why or why not?
18. The marketing concept is a relatively new idea for most manufacturers; yet most successful wholesalers and retailers have exhibited a strong orientation toward their customers. What do you suppose are the reasons for such circumstances? Explain.
19. Why have most service businesses been rather slow in recognizing marketing as a key element in their operations? Discuss.

CASE PROBLEM

The Neary Manufacturing Company of Topeka, Kansas, manufactured and distributed a line of heavy duty drills. The company very successfully sold its products exclusively to the construction industry. For several months, however, Mr. Raymond Neary, company president, had been considering expanding the distribution of the drills. The evidence uncovered numerous alternatives for expanded distribution and it was decided that the mining industry offered the best possibilities in terms of sales potential. While there was agreement on selling the drills to the mining industry, Mr. Neary and his sales manager were at odds regarding the organization of the sales force under the new distribution plan.

Mr. Neary contended that a separate sales force should be established to call on mining companies. He reasoned that division of marketing line authority on a customer basis would result in a more efficient sales effort. He argued that the construction industry and the mining industry were substantially different and two sales forces would be required.

Mr. Leo LeClaire, sales manager, took the position that a separate sales force was unnecessary and undesirable since the identical products would be sold by each sales force. He also felt that having separate sales forces would double the administrative problems. Finally, Mr. LeClaire argued that the Neary sales force was highly competent and could easily take on new customers.

Should the Neary Manufacturing Company have set up separate sales forces?

PART TWO

MARKETING INFORMATION

When you have mastered the contents of this chapter, you should be able to:

1. Identify the appropriateness of intuition-based decisions or the need for information-based decisions, given descriptions of different marketing problem situations.
2. Explain the nature and purpose of a marketing information system (MIS).
3. Describe how an MIS should be designed.
4. Calculate four different types of operating ratios (gross margin, expense, sales returns and allowances, and net profit), given the data required.
5. Compute three other analytical ratios (markup, markdown, and stockturn rate), given the data required.
6. Explain the nature of sales records and describe how they can be used in making effective marketing decisions.
7. Describe the probable direction of future development of MIS's.

CHAPTER 6

MARKETING INFORMATION SYSTEMS

Key decisions in marketing, as elsewhere, should be based more on factual information than on intuition or "gut feel." Really important marketing problem situations, in other words, should be resolved mainly through analysis of the facts, even though management must resolve the vast bulk of day-to-day marketing problems largely on an intuitive basis. In this chapter analysis focuses on (1) the relationship of marketing information to marketing decisions, (2) marketing information systems, and (3) internal (inside-the-company) sources of marketing information. External sources of marketing information are discussed in Chapter 7 (Marketing Research).

Marketing Information and Marketing Decisions

In guiding an organization's activities toward the achievement of marketing goals, management must (1) recognize problem situations, (2) determine alternative courses of action, (3) appraise the alternatives, and (4) decide on a particular course of action. The heart of decision making, therefore, relates to the choosing of courses of action aimed toward achieving desired outcomes. From management's standpoint, however, different problem situations require that it devote varying amounts of attention to the four decision-making steps. So management makes some decisions with minimal forethought, others only after a great deal of deliberation. Generally, decisions made quickly are intuition-based, while those made after considerable analysis are information-based.

INTUITION-BASED DECISION MAKING

Not every problem situation in marketing is sufficiently important to justify decisions based on rigorous and time-consuming factual analysis. A supermarket manager, for example, cannot afford to spend much time deciding whether to stock one or two dozen crates of tomatoes for the weekend trade. And some situations are so serious as to require immediate decisions—before the situations worsen. Even if a marketing executive could consider all problems before they became serious, their sheer number would still force him or her to make most decisions intuitively.

In making intuitive decisions, however, executives generally draw on more than just their intuition. Usually, they draw on their previous experience and their knowledge of similar problem situations, combining common sense and judgment. Only when they have no information whatever are their decisions truly intuitive.

While time and expense considerations force marketing managers to make most decisions intuitively, they should confine intuitive decision making to relatively minor problems. Such problem situations are alike in that their possible consequences, financial and otherwise, are not particularly serious, and decisions on them are relatively easy to change if that becomes necessary. Therefore, the marketing manager requires skill in discriminating between major and minor problem situations. Such skill involves the development of mental processes calling for considerable judgment and keen insight.

INFORMATION-BASED DECISION MAKING

Major problem situations in marketing deserve information-based decision making. Major marketing problems have two characteristics: (1) they arise at irregular intervals so decisions on them do not have to be made frequently; and (2) they have important consequences which must be lived with for a long time as it is extremely difficult and awkward to change such decisions once they are made. Examples of major marketing problems include those involving the introduction of new products, opening up new markets, changing the basic structure of sales organizations, choosing marketing channels, or determining the types and amount of personal selling and advertising and other elements in promotional mixes. Because decisions on such matters are critical to marketing success they should be reached only after thorough analyses of relevant information. Their possible consequences are of such high and far-reaching importance that a marketing executive should not risk making them intuitively. He or she should take whatever steps are necessary to assure the availability of sufficient marketing information to permit information-based decisions on all major marketing problems.

Marketing Information Systems

MIS For the company operating under the marketing concept, a clear need exists for coordinated, systematic, and continuous information gathering. Meeting this need is the main purpose of a *marketing information system* (MIS), which is an organized set of procedures, information-handling routines, and reporting techniques designed to provide the information required for making marketing decisions. An effective MIS makes it possible to reduce the volume of intuition-based decisions, since it makes available to decision makers relevant and usable information from both internal and external sources. Another important, though secondary, purpose of an effective MIS should be mentioned—it provides a mechanism for reducing the often overwhelming flood of available marketing information to pertinent, usable amounts.

Ultimate responsibility for the effectiveness of a company's MIS rests with the top marketing executive. He or she, along with subordinates, must provide the MIS's designers with clear-cut statements of their needs with respect to the supply and flow of marketing information. The design and operation of the actual MIS is delegated to specialists (systems analysts) thoroughly acquainted with the MIS's various objectives (provided by the marketing executives) and highly skilled in information-gathering and information-handling techniques capable of meeting these objectives. Generally, the systems analysts are assisted by an advisory group made up of representatives from marketing, finance and accounting, operations research, data processing, and other organizational units. The advisory group helps not only in the initial design but later on as the MIS becomes a functioning reality. The group then maintains continual surveillance over the MIS, suggesting modifications to meet the company's marketing information needs as they evolve.

DESIRED INFORMATION OUTPUTS

Identifying the desired information outputs is the most critical aspect of MIS design. Since the basic purpose is to make possible more and better information-based decisions, system designers should focus their efforts on the decisions each executive in the marketing organization must make to perform his or her job effectively. Analysis of each executive's decision-making responsibilities, in other words, should clarify his or her marketing information requirements, thereby identifying the information outputs that the MIS should provide him or her. The composite of the marketing information requirements for the entire organization thus identifies the variety and nature of specific information outputs that the MIS should provide. While differences among organizations cause them to have varying information requirements, one expert says that "whether the products involved are building materials, breadsticks, or bonds," marketing managers want the kinds of information required to answer questions such as those in Figure 6–1.

Another important aspect of MIS design relates to tailoring information outputs to fit each executive's individual information needs. Each executive wants complete and accurate information received on a timely basis, yet not provided (routinely) in overwhelmingly and confusingly large quantities. It is ironic that while organizations generate increasingly massive volumes of data, many executives continue to voice complaints that available information is too incomplete and not sufficiently relevant or timely to use as a basis for marketing decisions. The MIS should have the built-in capability of extracting from the data bank timely items of information relevant for each executive's use in decision making.

Marketing executives generally want to receive certain information outputs on a regularly scheduled basis. The top marketing executive, for example, may want a daily report on sales by main classes of products and by marketing areas, while the chief sales executive may want a daily report on each salesman's performance. It is doubtful, however, that either of these executives could afford the time required to evaluate the totality of marketing performance information that could be made available daily. Most marketing executives have relatively small needs for information provided on a daily basis; for most, it is sufficient to provide (depending on the specific information output) reports on a weekly, monthly, or annual basis. The top marketing executive, for instance, may want a detailed analysis of

Figure 6–1
Examples of questions most marketing managers want answered

CUSTOMER INFORMATION
- Where is volume concentrated?
- Who are specific major customers, both present and potential?
- What are their needs for products?
- What are their needs for sales coverage and service?
- What order activity and volume are expected?
- What are the differences in profitability between types and classes of customers?
- Where is performance significantly short of expectations?

PRODUCT INFORMATION
- What are the relative profitabilities of products at the gross margin level? After direct marketing expenses?
- Which elements of variable product cost are influenced by marketing decisions? What is the current cost structure?
- Which products tend to respond most favorably to sales promotion at the wholesale, retail, and consumer levels?
- What are the major advantages and disadvantages of current products in the eyes of consumers, relative to competitive products?
- What factors have the greatest influence on sales volume?
- What is the status of volume and profitability relative to objectives?

SALES FORCE INFORMATION
- What area and which customers are assigned?
- What call activity is required, both for protection of present volume and development of new business?
- Do current compensation systems motivate the desired mix of salesmen's activity?
- What is current performance relative to objectives?

Source: N. Doppelt, "Down-to-Earth Marketing Information Systems," *Management Adviser*, Sept.–Oct., 1971, pp. 19–26.

each product's gross margin and profit contribution only once a year, while certain of his or her subordinates may want similar analyses monthly.

Some executives need certain kinds of information only when a given situation shifts outside a range of acceptable normalcy. In one company, for example, the general sales manager does not concern himself with individual salesmen's day-to-day performances, leaving that responsibility to his subordinates. He does, however, want to know whenever any salesman's performance increases or decreases by as much as 25 percent in a month's time. Effective MIS's are capable of providing such "exception reports" to those executives who should receive them.

Exception Reports

The real challenge in designing an MIS lies in determining what kind and how much information is required how often by each executive in the marketing organization. Modern data processing equipment and techniques make it possible to provide total information daily on certain facets of the marketing operation, but executives can neither cope with nor digest and use total information. An MIS makes its most significant contributions through evaluating information needs and uses and through providing information output accordingly.

INFORMATION INPUTS

The MIS's information inputs come from diverse sources, both within and outside the organization. Internal sources provide the major information flows of a routine and continuous nature. Such information sources include the controller, research and development department, long-range corporate planning unit, the legal department, economic research groups, and, of course, the sales department.

Information Retrieval

An important problem in MIS design is that of making internally generated information easily retrievable for use by marketing executives. Sales invoices, for example, have historically flowed into the accounting department and, after providing needed data for accounting purposes, have been buried in that department's files. But sales invoices constitute a valuable source of such kinds of marketing information as sales performance by product line, by type of customer, or by market area. Even some companies with highly developed data processing systems are guilty of storing information from sales invoices so that it is either impossible or prohibitively expensive (in terms of computer time) to retrieve for nonaccounting uses. Consequently, all data that might provide useful input for marketing decisions should be stored in as disaggregated (i.e., broken down) a form as possible, making it easy and economical to retrieve for diverse uses.

External sources also provide information inputs to the MIS. One class of information from external sources is known collectively

Marketing Intelligence

as *marketing intelligence*, which includes raw data, summary statistics, qualitative inferences, expert and lay opinions, impressions, and even rumors. Sources of marketing intelligence pervade the organization's entire operating environment, including the competitors (whose marketing plans and strategies have obvious intelligence value). For maximum utility, the MIS must provide for the routing of each item of marketing intelligence to that executive who is in the best position to assess its impact on the organization's current or future operations. Likewise, all bits of marketing intelligence must be fed into the MIS routinely and without delay.

Other information from external sources is gathered through marketing research on both a routine and a nonroutine basis. Routine information, for example, might be a monthly report on sales of competitive products in selected retail outlets. On a nonroutine basis, management, for instance, may want to learn more about its customers: Who buys the product? How do buyers differ from nonbuyers? What do buyers like and dislike about the products? Or management may desire to test the market for a new product and to determine and measure the reactions of final buyers and middlemen. Information from marketing research studies provides important inputs to an MIS but usually a separate organization unit, the marketing research department, or, in some cases, an independent marketing research firm, is responsible for its generation. The main reason for this arrangement is that marketing research requires specialized skills and rather unique methodologies. While the marketing research director may report directly to the MIS director, more usually he or she reports to the top marketing executive.

Operating Data as an Internal Source of Marketing Information

No other type of marketing information sees more frequent or varied use in marketing decision making than operating data. Almost daily, the marketing executive uses such data to help him or her throughout the entire range of decision-making steps: recognizing problems, developing alternative solutions, appraising them, and deciding courses of action. The company's own financial, accounting, sales, and production records are the sources of operating data. The marketing executive needs to know not only the types of operating data that are or can be made available but also how to use them in decision making.

THE OPERATING STATEMENT

Profit-and-Loss Statement

The operating, or profit-and-loss, statement is the most used internal source of marketing information. By definition, it is a financial summary of operating results for some period—usually a month, a quarter, or a year. It shows whether the firm operated at a profit or a loss and explains how that profit or loss resulted from the quantitative relationships that existed between sales and cost of goods sold and expenses. *Cost of goods sold* represents the total cost value of the goods actually sold during the period and not the value of the goods on hand at any particular time. *Expenses* are the total of the marketing, general, and administrative costs incurred during the operating period. If sales income exceeds the total cost of goods sold and expenses, then the statement shows a net profit. If sales income is smaller than the total of cost of goods sold and expenses, the statement shows a net loss. These relationships, then, are:

Cost of Goods Sold

Expenses

	Sales
Minus:	Cost of Goods Sold
Equals:	Gross Margin (or Gross Profit)
Minus:	Expenses
Equals:	Net Profit (or Net Loss)

This skeleton operating statement portrays only the relationships among the major operating items—sales, cost of goods sold, and expenses. Each major item is, in its turn, the result of a set of relationships existing among more detailed items of financial operating data. Figure 6–2, an operating statement shown in considerable detail, illustrates these several sets of relationships as well as the interrelationships among the major operating items.

The "Cost of Goods Sold" section in the operating statement in Figure 6–2 illustrates the way a retailer or wholesaler would determine this amount. Such middlemen are buy-and-sell businesses. By contrast, manufacturers are make-and-sell businesses; hence, their operating statements substitute a "Cost of Goods Manufactured" subsection for the "Purchases" subsection used by retailers and wholesalers.

OPERATING RATIOS

The "Percentages" column in Figure 6–2 expresses the relationships between net sales and several important items in the operating statement. These ratios are expressed as a percentage of net sales with net sales equal to 100 percent. The rationale for computing all operating ratios with net sales as the base—that is, the denominator or 100 percent—is that all costs, expenses, and profits (if any) must come out of the proceeds of net sales. Thus, when a businessman says his net profit is 5 percent, he means 5 percent of net sales. Similarly, when he says that his gross margin is 39 percent, he means 39 percent of net sales.

Gross Margin Ratio

Gross Margin Ratio *Gross margin* is the difference between sales and cost of goods sold. Expressing this amount as a percentage of net sales allows comparison with previous operating periods or with competitors' figures. The ratio may be increased or decreased in two ways—by changing the selling price per unit or by changing the cost per unit. When a marketing executive believes his gross margin ratio is high or low relative either to his own past performance or to competitors' experience, he may try to change his prices, reduce his costs, or both. Thus, a retailer alerted by an abnormally low gross margin ratio might reevaluate his buying procedure to find more economical sources of supply, improve his working capital position to take advantage of cash discounts, improve his traffic control to decrease freight costs, or improve his merchandise selection to command higher markups. In the same manner, a manufacturer might be alerted to reduce its production costs or improve its product to command a higher markup. Without this analytical tool such inefficiency might go unnoticed.

Figure 6–2
Operating statement for the year ending December 31, 197–

				PERCENTAGES
Gross Sales			$1,050,000	105.0%
Less: Returns & Allowances			50,000	5.0
Net Sales			$1,000,000	100.0%
Cost of Goods Sold:				
Opening Inventory @ Cost		$100,000		
Purchases @ Billed Cost	$650,000			
Less: Purchase Discounts	15,000			
Net Cost of Purchases	$635,000			
Plus: Freight-In	40,000			
Net Cost of Purchases Delivered		675,000		
Cost of Goods Handled		$775,000		
Less: Closing Inventory @ Cost		165,000		
Cost of Goods Sold			610,000	61.0
Gross Margin (Or Gross Profit)			$ 390,000	39.0%
Expenses:				
Advertising	$ 40,000			
Sales Salaries & Commissions	105,000			
Warehousing & Delivery	90,000			
Administrative	40,000			
General & Other	60,000			
Total Expenses			335,000	33.5
Net Profit on Operations (before income taxes)			$ 55,000	5.5%

Expense Ratio

Expense Ratio The *expense ratio* provides the basis for evaluation of the relationship between sales, gross margin, expenses, and profit. It is not concerned with a breakdown analysis of individual expense categories but with a comparison of total expenses with other figures on the operating statement. The ratio of expense to sales may vary considerably between companies, even in the same industry. A company that attracts its customers mainly on the basis of low prices will natu· ılly spend less on selling and will, thus, have a low expense ratio. Another that emphasizes promotion rather than prices to attract patronage will have a high expense ratio. For this reason, expense comparisons between companies must be made with caution.

Sales Returns and Allowances Ratio

Sales Returns and Allowances Ratio This ratio, like other operating ratios, is expressed as a percent of net sales, even though sales returns and allowances are subtracted from gross sales to arrive at net sales. Analysis of sales returns and allowances ratios helps management to determine whether these figures represent normal or abnormal experience. A certain number of returns and allowances is to be expected because of human error and product failings, but excessive returns and allowances may reflect bad merchandise or overselling.

Net Profit Ratio

Net Profit Ratio This operating ratio relates most directly to the profit objective but, used alone, it has limited value. A profit decline may alert management to possible trouble, but since profit results from a combination of sales, gross margin, and expense, evaluations of all three ratios are necessary to pinpoint the problems. Likewise, if management wishes to increase profits, proposed operational changes should be considered in light of other operating ratios. For example, a retailer may want to estimate the effects on net profit of an anticipated increase in "store traffic." "Supposing," he says, "that increased store traffic causes a 60 percent rise in sales but requires the hiring of two additional clerks thus raising weekly expenses by $188." "I would expect," he continues, "that the percentage relationship of cost of goods sold to sales would be unchanged." The weekly operating statement of the retailer's store together with the expected operating statement for the next week based on his assumption are as follows:

	PRESENT SITUATION		CONTEMPLATED SITUATION	
	$	Percent	$	Percent
Sales	$1,000	100%	$1,600	100%
Cost of goods sold	670	67	1,072	67
Gross margin	$ 330	33%	$ 528	33%
Expenses	300	30	488	30.5%
Net profit	$ 30	3%	$ 40	2.5%

This analysis indicates that the retailer's dollar profits will rise from \$30 to \$40 a week, but the net profit percentage (profit as a percent of sales) will fall from 3 to 2.5 percent. It is quite possible, then, for a change in operations to produce more net profit dollars but a smaller net profit percentage. This, of course, does not always happen, but it does happen often enough that businessmen should be aware of the possibility. Marketing executives agree that the dollar payoff is the most important item to consider, but they also agree that percentage relationships are helpful in making comparisons.

OTHER ANALYTICAL RATIOS AND THEIR USES IN DECISION MAKING

Certain analytical ratios serve as everyday aids in decision making. Included are the markup, the markdown, and the rate of stockturn. These ratios are so well known, in such wide usage, and so basic to marketing decision making that they are the main subject matter of "marketing arithmetic."

One preliminary word of caution: The following discussion uses retailing-type situations to illustrate the ratios and their uses. Wholesalers use the same ratios, the methods of calculation are identical, and there is no need for duplicate illustrations. These particular ratios do not apply directly to the operations of manufacturing firms but apply instead to the operations of middlemen handling the products of manufacturers. Marketing executives in manufacturing firms not only should know how middlemen use these ratios but should use them themselves in planning marketing and promotional programs.

Markup

Markup The amount by which an item's intended selling price exceeds its cost to the seller is known as the *markup*. When a discount house pays \$15 for a transistor radio and prices it at \$20, the \$5 difference is the markup. Out of the total of all such markups placed on all of the items it sells, the discount house seeks to cover its expenses and earn a net profit.

A businessman thinks of a markup not only as so many dollars and cents but also as some percentage, either of original selling price or of cost. He often uses the markup concept, in other words, as an analytical ratio to express the relation between dollar markup and original dollar selling price or dollar cost. If an automobile dealer pays the manufacturer \$2,400 for a vehicle and prices it at \$3,000, his markup percentage is 20 percent (i.e., $\frac{\$600}{\$3,000}$) on the original selling price.

Most sellers use original selling price rather than cost as the base, and whenever we speak of markup as a percentage we will mean markup as a percentage of original selling price. Keep in mind, however, that under either system of computing markup percentages, you are dealing with the same dollar markup, as illustrated in Figure 6–3.

Laymen often get confused when a retailer says that he decides on an item's selling price by marking it up by some percentage of the selling price. When asked how he can apply a percentage markup to a selling price which he does not even know yet, but which he is trying to determine, the retailer answers: "Very simple. All I do is divide the dollar cost by the cost percentage." What the retailer does is shown more clearly in Figure 6–3. The auto dealer knows the dollar cost ($2,400) and if his desired markup percentage on the selling price is 20 percent, he can simply subtract this from the selling price percentage (100 percent) to determine the cost percentage of 80 percent. Then, dividing the $2,400 dollar cost by the 80 percent expressed as a decimal, he arrives at the selling price of $3,000. Or, shown in equation form:

$$\frac{\$2{,}400 \text{ (Dollar Cost)}}{.80 \text{ (Cost \% expressed as a decimal)}} = \$3{,}000 \text{ (Selling Price)}$$

Markdown Merchandise does not always sell at the original selling price placed on it and a seller may, in an effort to make it move, mark down, or reduce, the price. When a gift shop proprietor, for example, concludes that a fancy ashtray is not going to sell at the $10.00 price he put on it in the beginning, he may mark it down to $7.50, at which price a customer finally buys it. The difference between the original selling price and the actual selling price is called the *markdown*. The dollar markdown, then, is $2.50 in the ashtray example. Customarily, retailers compute markdown percentages using actual selling price as the base.[1] So when an item is marked down

Markdown

[1] The opposite seems to be the widespread practice in Puerto Rico and Latin America. Retailers there claim that by computing markdown percentages from original selling price they can recognize more readily the actual price markdown that was required in order to make the actual sale.

Figure 6–3

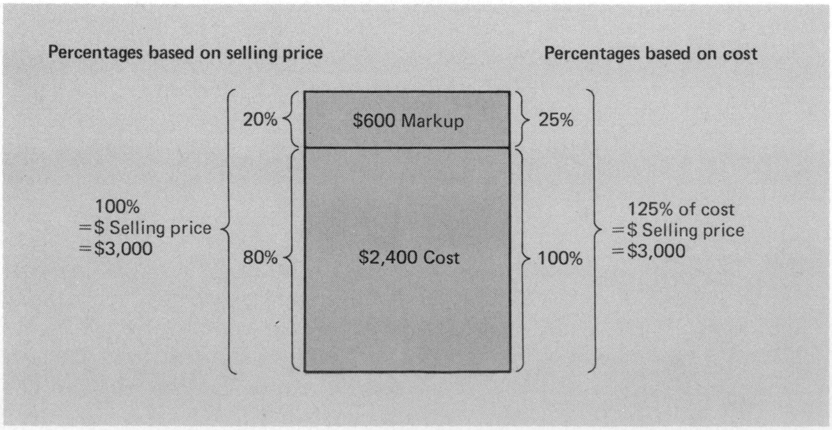

from \$10.00 to \$7.50, the \$2.50 price reduction is a 33 1/3 percent markdown (i.e., \$2.50/\$7.50). The above type of markdown does not appear on the operating statement, since the first item on the statement is gross sales, and markdowns occur before sales are made. However, "Allowances to Customers" does appear on the operating statement, and such allowances are also properly viewed as markdowns. Most markdowns occur before sales are made, but some keep sales from becoming unmade! To illustrate this point, say the ashtray sold at the \$10.00 price, but the customer became dissatisfied with the purchase and brought it back to the store. The proprietor, seeking not only to keep the sale from coming undone but wanting to keep the customer's goodwill, might say, "Keep the ashtray and I'll grant you a \$2.50 allowance." If the customer agrees, the accounting system will show \$10.00 as the original sale, \$2.50 as the allowance to the customer, and \$7.50 as the net amount of the transaction. Because markdowns and allowances to customers are both downward adjustments in price, merchants ordinarily lump both together in calculating the markdown ratio for the operating period.

Merchants recognize that every item in their stocks carries some possibility of having to be marked down. Such markdowns can occur either before or after sales are made. Both types should be considered in setting original selling prices, for the total of original markups should be sufficiently high that subsequent markdowns will not reduce sales below the total of cost of goods sold and expenses. The formula, then, for computing the markdown ratio is:

$$\text{Markdown \%} = \frac{\text{\$ Allowances to Customers} + \text{\$ Markdowns}}{\text{\$ Net Sales}}$$

The markdown ratio provides information needed in planning original markups. Its existence serves as a reminder to price setters that prices have to be set (sooner or later) at levels customers are able and willing to pay. If the original markup is too high to satisfy the market, markdowns are inevitable.

The markdown ratio is used, too, as a measure of the efficiency of store buyers and retail sales personnel. Reasonably low markdowns are an indication of effective buying, realistic pricing, and good selling. When using the markdown ratio as a performance measure, management should define what it considers a desirable markdown ratio. Such standard markdown ratios are derived either through studies of store markdown ratios over past periods or from reports of trade associations.

Stockturn Rate

Stockturn Rate The *stockturn rate* is an analytical tool used for measuring operating efficiency. It indicates the speed at which the inventory "turns over"—the number of times the average inventory is sold during an operating period. If a retailer, for instance, starts the year with an inventory having a cost of \$20,000 and ends the year with a \$30,000 inventory at cost, the average inventory at cost has been \$25,000. If the cost of goods sold during the year amounted to \$100,000, the business had a stockturn rate of four, calculated as follows:

$$\text{Stockturn Rate} = \frac{\text{Cost of Goods Sold}}{\text{Average Inventory at Cost}} =$$

$$\frac{\$100{,}000}{\tfrac{1}{2}\ (\$20{,}000 + \$30{,}000)} = 4$$

This retailer, in other words, sold his average inventory four times during the year, or once every three months. If he makes a net profit of three cents every time he sells something costing him a dollar, we can say he had a return of twelve cents (3 cents × 4) on each dollar invested in inventory.

We computed the stockturn rate above by the method most commonly used. Both the numerator and denominator in the formula were cost figures, readily available from accounting records. There are, however, some businesses that value their inventories in terms of selling prices rather than in terms of costs, and they are said to use the retail method of inventory valuation. In such businesses, the following formula is used for computing the stockturn rate:

$$\text{Stockturn Rate} = \frac{\text{Net Sales (\$)}}{\text{Average Inventory at Selling Price}}$$

Thus, a department store using the retail method of inventory valuation might start the year with a \$100,000 inventory at retail and end it with an inventory of \$80,000 at retail, or an average of \$90,000. If net sales during the year were \$720,000, the stockturn rate would be eight (i.e., \$720,000/\$90,000). Notice that the only real difference between this formula and the earlier one is that here we express the numerator and denominator in terms of selling price rather than of cost.

The stockturn rate provides a yardstick for measuring operating efficiency. An increase in the rate of turnover of capital invested in inventory will normally increase total profits, unless the net profit ratio is decreased proportionally. Thus, a higher stockturn is a much-sought-after goal.

The stockturn rate is also used as a basis for comparing the effectiveness of branches or different outlets. The unit with the highest stockturn rate may be the most efficiently managed, but not always. Where, for instance, are the two units located? The store with the fastest turnover rate might be across the street from the factory with the opportunity to replenish inventory daily, while the other might be 3,000 air miles away with the necessity of maintaining a large reserve inventory. Also, one store may cater to only a small market segment—for example, men only—while the other may serve the whole family, necessitating a much larger basic stock. Or, perhaps, the store with the high turnover handles only low-priced, low-margin lines.

These and similar considerations should cause us to be cautious in drawing conclusions based solely on differences in stockturn rates among stores. Of course, such considerations are less likely to be important when the stockturn rate is used for comparing the same store's operating efficiency during two different periods.

Analysis of Sales Records

Analysis of a company's sales records, generally with the aid of a computer, makes it possible to detect various marketing strengths and weaknesses. Although sales records are regularly summarized in the "sales" section of the operating statement, such summaries reveal little about strong or weak features of the company's marketing efforts. Through periodic computer-assisted sales analysis, management seeks insight on such matters as strong and weak sales territories, high-volume and low-volume products, and the types of customers providing the most and least satisfactory sales volume. This type of analysis, then, is used to uncover significant details which otherwise lie hidden in the sales records. It provides information that management needs to allocate future marketing efforts more effectively.

Sales Analysis

MISDIRECTED MARKETING EFFORT

In most businesses, a large percentage of the customers, territories, orders, or products bring in only a small percentage of the sales. One sales executive, using a diagram (Figure 6–4) to illustrate this, said, "The column on the left represents our total number of dealers, and the column on the right our total dollar sales volume. The diagonal indicates that 80 percent of our customers give us only

80–20 Principle

Figure 6–4

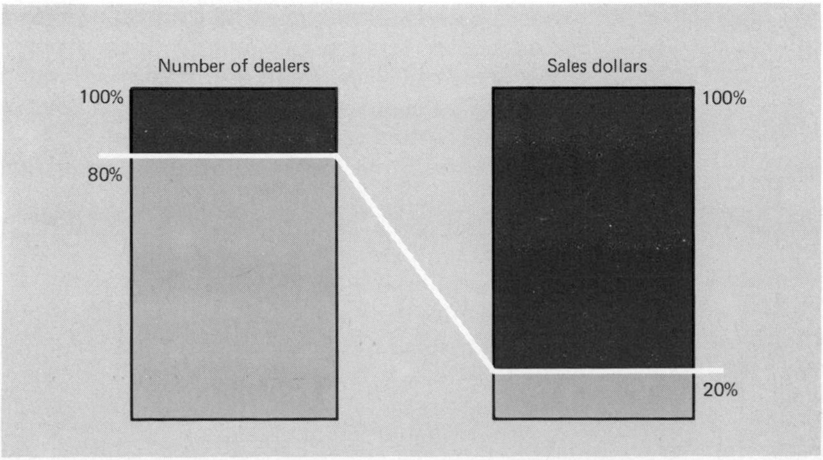

20 percent of our volume." Similar situations exist in most companies, a large percentage of the customers accounting for a small percentage of the total sales and, conversely, a small percentage of customers accounting for a high percentage of total sales. And comparable situations are found where a large percentage of the sales territories, products, and orders bring in only a small percentage of total sales. Sometimes such situations are referred to as examples of the "80–20" principle.

Such sales patterns do not always result in unprofitable operations, but operations are often less profitable than they should be. Why is this so? Simply because marketing efforts and, hence, marketing costs all too frequently are divided on the basis of customers, territories, products, orders, and so forth, rather than on a basis of actual or potential dollar sales. It usually costs, for example, just as much to maintain a salesman in a bad territory as in a good one, almost as much to promote a product that sells slowly or not at all as one that sells in large volume, and as much to have a salesman call on and service a customer who orders in small quantities as another who gives the company large orders. It is not uncommon for a large proportion of the total marketing efforts to result in only a very small proportion of the total sales and profits. Detecting such situations is the important task of sales analysis, since it may identify customers, products, or territories that are actually unprofitable. Abandonment of these losers would reduce expenses more than it reduced sales and would increase total profit.

NATURE OF SALES RECORDS

Companies vary greatly in the type and form of information they have available on sales. At one extreme, some have none, other than accountants' records of sales that are made, and carbons of customers' sales invoices. At the opposite extreme, some firms, when extracting necessary accounting information from sales invoices, also record highly detailed marketing information on computer tapes so that it is readily available in usable form for making sales analyses by individual salesmen, types of products, classes of customers, sizes of orders, and other pertinent breakdowns.

Generally, the most important sources of data useful in sales analysis are customers' sales invoices, which contain two types of information, both essential for sales analysis. Each identifies and describes the customer (e.g., the name and geographical location), and each contains data on the specific transaction (e.g., the date of the order, the products sold and the quantities, the price per unit, total dollar sales per product, and total amount of the order). Companies with highly developed systems of sales analysis organize these basic items of sales information systematically—that is, in ways which facilitate analysis.

SPECIFIC PURPOSES OF MAIN TYPES OF SALES ANALYSES

The purpose of sales analysis is to detect marketing strengths and weaknesses. Each main type of sales analysis sheds light on a different aspect of these strengths and weaknesses. Analysis of sales by territories answers the question of how much is being sold *where*. Analysis of sales by products answers how much of *what* is being sold. Analysis of sales by customers answers the question of *who* is buying how much. All types of sales analyses relate to the question of *how much* is being sold, but each answers in a different way. Although sales analyses can identify marketing strengths and weaknesses, they cannot explain *why* they exist. Answering the "why" question is management's task.

Simulations of Marketing Decisions in Information Systems

Marketing information systems are made up of a number of subsystems, each providing information for a particular problem, or, ideally, providing an automatic decision. If the system analysts who design the system are to prepare a system to aid in decision making, they must start with theoretical foundations. Consequently, decision makers must tell the systems analyst the kind and amount of data that constitute the theory or model on which they base their decisions and the structural relationship of the variables—how they are interrelated and fit together. This forces the decision maker to think through his or her decision process in great detail. This may be the first time he or she has ever tried to analyze his or her own process of decision making, and that step alone may improve his or her future decisions.

The ultimate goal in developing each subsystem is a situation in which the computer is fed current information, and it selects from predetermined alternatives a course of action, informing the decision maker only when the predetermined alternatives do not provide an adequate solution to the problem. It is rarely possible to develop such an ideal, automatically functioning subsystem on anything but the simplest kinds of decisions, either because the decision maker is unable to reduce his or her decision process to a formal model, or because it is not possible to obtain all the necessary information in a sufficiently accurate form. Nevertheless, the long-term goal of the designers of marketing information systems is to simulate reality to the extent of providing automated responses in as many subsystems as possible. Until such a goal is reached, the information system will serve the narrower function of providing the optimum amount of information useful to management in making each decision as it arises.

Summary

You should now have a good understanding of the role of marketing information in the making of marketing decisions and the systems necessary for accumulating and processing such information. Many routine or unimportant decisions are necessarily made upon an intuitive basis, relying upon past experience and accumulated information. However, important decisions should be supported by information in as much detail as can be made available, and the marketing information system is designed to provide such data. Marketing information comes from both internal and external sources. Internal sources are more readily available and more accurate, and they include financial statements and ratios, other analytical ratios, data from analysis of sales records, and simulations developed from historical data. External sources include marketing intelligence and marketing research (which is covered in the following chapter). Finally, you should now have a good idea how the marketing executive uses operating data as an important internal source of information.

QUESTIONS AND PROBLEMS

1. Clearly distinguish between intuition-based decision making and information-based decision making.
2. What is the importance of marketing information systems? Discuss.
3. Who should be responsible for initiating development of a marketing information system? Explain.
4. What are the characteristics of a good marketing information system? Discuss.
5. Distinguish between:
   a. gross margin ratio and net profit ratio
   b. markup and markdown
   c. markup on selling price and markup on cost
6. Define the following terms:
   a. operating statement
   b. stockturn rate
   c. sales analysis
   d. misdirected marketing effort
7. What reasoning lies behind the fact that operating ratios are usually expressed as percentages of net sales?
8. How would you account for a situation in which two companies, both in the same industry and with comparable products, had different expense ratios?
9. What are the main causes of markdowns? Why is it that *all* markdowns do not appear on the operating statement? Should a

retailer strive to eliminate markdowns completely? Why? What corrective measures would you suggest to a retailer who says that his markdowns are too high?

10. Under what conditions are stockturn rates appropriate as measures of operating efficiency? What are the reasons why different businesses have different stockturn rates?
11. Summarize the various ways a marketing manager might use sales analysis.
12. Find the missing figures in the following table:

COST	MARKUP PERCENT ON COST	MARKUP	MARKUP PERCENT ON SELLING PRICE	SELLING PRICE
$8.00		$1.00		
$1.50			25%	
	75%	$2.00		
			10%	$15.00
$0.75	40%			
		$5.00		$25.00

13. Find the missing figures in the following table:

MARKUP PERCENT ON COST	MARKUP PERCENT ON SELLING PRICE
20%	
	35%
67%	
	17½%
200%	
	23%
100%	
	60%

14. A retailer purchased an item for $1.50, originally priced it at $1.95, and finally sold it at $1.69. What was the markdown percentage?
15. On the basis of the following operating data, calculate the 1975 opening inventory at cost:

1975 cost of goods sold	$120,000
1975 stockturn rate	4
1975 closing inventory at cost	$10,000

16. Last month, Retailer A had gross sales of $12,000, sales returns and allowances of $500, opening inventory at cost of $2,500, purchases at cost of $4,000, closing inventory at cost of $1,500, and expenses of $2,000. What was A's net profit? Gross margin?
17. Last month, Retailer B had cost of goods sold of $3,000, expenses of $2,000, and a gross margin of $2,500. What was B's net profit? Net sales?
18. Last month, Retailer C had an opening inventory at cost of $2,200, closing inventory at cost of $3,200, and cost of goods sold of $10,000. Find C's purchases at cost.
19. A wholesaler is planning his operations for the coming year. After analyzing company records, he estimates that during the coming year expenses will amount to $19,900 and gross margin will be $27,000. The wholesaler says he will be satisfied with a net profit of 4 percent on sales. What sales volume goal should he set for the coming year?
20. On the basis of the following operating data, compute stockturn rates (a) using cost figures, and (b) using selling price figures:

Net Sales	$19,500
Markdowns	250
Allowances to Customers	250
Cost of Goods Sold	10,000
Opening Inventory at Cost	3,000
Opening Inventory at Selling Price	6,000
Closing Inventory at Cost	2,000
Closing Inventory at Selling Price	4,000

How do you explain the difference between the two stockturn rates?

21. A retailer currently has monthly sales of $100,000 and an average inventory of $25,000 at selling price. He wants to increase his stockturn rate from four to four and a half. Explain at least two different alternatives he might consider in working toward this target stockturn rate of four and a half.
22. In analyzing the operations of a supermarket, an investigator obtained the following data:

DEPARTMENT	PERCENT OF STORE SALES	PERCENT OF STORE GROSS MARGIN	SALES PER SQUARE FOOT	GROSS MARGIN PER SQUARE FOOT
Grocery	38.65%	31.04%	$1.66	$0.24
Meat	34.39	38.49	3.00	0.61
Produce	10.71	15.78	1.70	0.46
Dairy	9.10	6.92	4.47	0.62
Bakery	4.97	5.47	1.33	0.27
Frozen Food	2.18	2.30	1.20	0.23
	100.00%	100.00%		

a. Suppose you are the owner of this supermarket. How might you go about analyzing the above data?

b. How might various suppliers of supermarkets make use of this information?

c. What is the significance of the sales per square foot figure? The gross margin per square foot figure?

CASE PROBLEM

The Cranston Company manufactured industrial products, which it sold to mill supply houses through five salesmen, each serving a separate territory.* Total net sales in a given year amounted to $1,193,000. Compensation and expenses of the salesmen came to $99,000. This yielded a direct selling expense ratio of 8.3 percent. While management found this information interesting, it desired further details and, as a result, the following two tables were prepared. Scrutinize the data in these two tables and make whatever recommendations to management you think might be appropriate.

*Adapted from C. H. Sevin, *Analyzing Your Cost of Marketing* (Washington, D.C.: Small Business Administration, June 1957).

Comparative Performance of Salesmen

SALES AREA	TOTAL CALLS	TOTAL ORDERS	SALES/CALL RATIO	SALES BY SALESMAN	AVERAGE SALESMAN ORDER	TOTAL CUSTOMERS
A	1,900	1,140	60.0%	$ 456,000	$400	195
B	1,500	1,000	66.7	360,000	360	160
C	1,400	700	50.0	280,000	400	140
D	1,030	279	27.1	66,000	239	60
E	820	165	20.1	31,000	187	50
	6,650	3,784	44.8%	$1,193,000	$317	605

Comparative Cost of Salesmen

SALES AREA	ANNUAL COMPENSATION	EXPENSE PAYMENTS	TOTAL SALESMAN COST	SALES PRODUCED	COST/SALES RATIO
A	$11,400	$ 5,600	$17,000	$ 456,000	3.7%
B	10,800	7,200	18,000	360,000	5.0
C	10,200	5,800	16,000	280,000	5.7
D	9,600	12,400	22,000	66,000	33.3
E	10,000	16,000	26,000	31,000	83.8
	$52,000	$47,000	$99,000	$1,193,000	8.3%

When you have mastered the contents of this chapter, you should be able to:

1. Explain the relationship of marketing research to the various stages of the decision-making process.
2. Describe the nature and purposes of: market measurement studies, studies of influences of the controllables, studies of the competitive situation, and studies of influences of the uncontrollables.
3. Explain the general nature of marketing research procedure.
4. Identify and illustrate the key decisions involved in planning a marketing research project.
5. Compare the different research methods used in marketing research.
6. Define the following terms: probability sample, nonprobability sample, sampling error, nonsampling error.
7. Discuss the problem of balancing the value of having information against the costs of obtaining it.

CHAPTER 7

MARKETING RESEARCH

Marketing research, broadly defined, is the systematic gathering, recording, and analyzing of data about marketing problems to facilitate decision making. The information inputs for a marketing information system (MIS), as brought out in the previous chapter, come from diverse sources, both within and outside the organization. Generally, marketing research studies tap external sources of information and focus on the relation of the firm to its environment and particularly to its markets.

Marketing Research and the Marketing Information System

Marketing Research

Marketing research is a vital component in the marketing mix, providing a foundation for the planning and execution of marketing programs. The importance of marketing research is borne out in a recent study of over 1,100 companies, conducted by the American Marketing Association.[1] The results showed a steady growth in the total number of marketing research departments in both industrial goods and consumer goods companies and an increase in the number of marketing research directors reporting to top management. Marketing research, as an integral part of a marketing information system, should provide a flow of information inputs, mainly from external sources, useful in marketing decision making. A logical place to start,

[1] Dik W. Twedt, *A Survey of Marketing Research* (Chicago: American Marketing Association, 1974).

then, in understanding marketing research's role is with the decision-making process itself. Figure 7–1 shows how marketing research, through systematic gathering and analysis of information, should assist in answering questions that management must resolve at each stage in the decision-making process.

Figure 7–1
The decision-making process

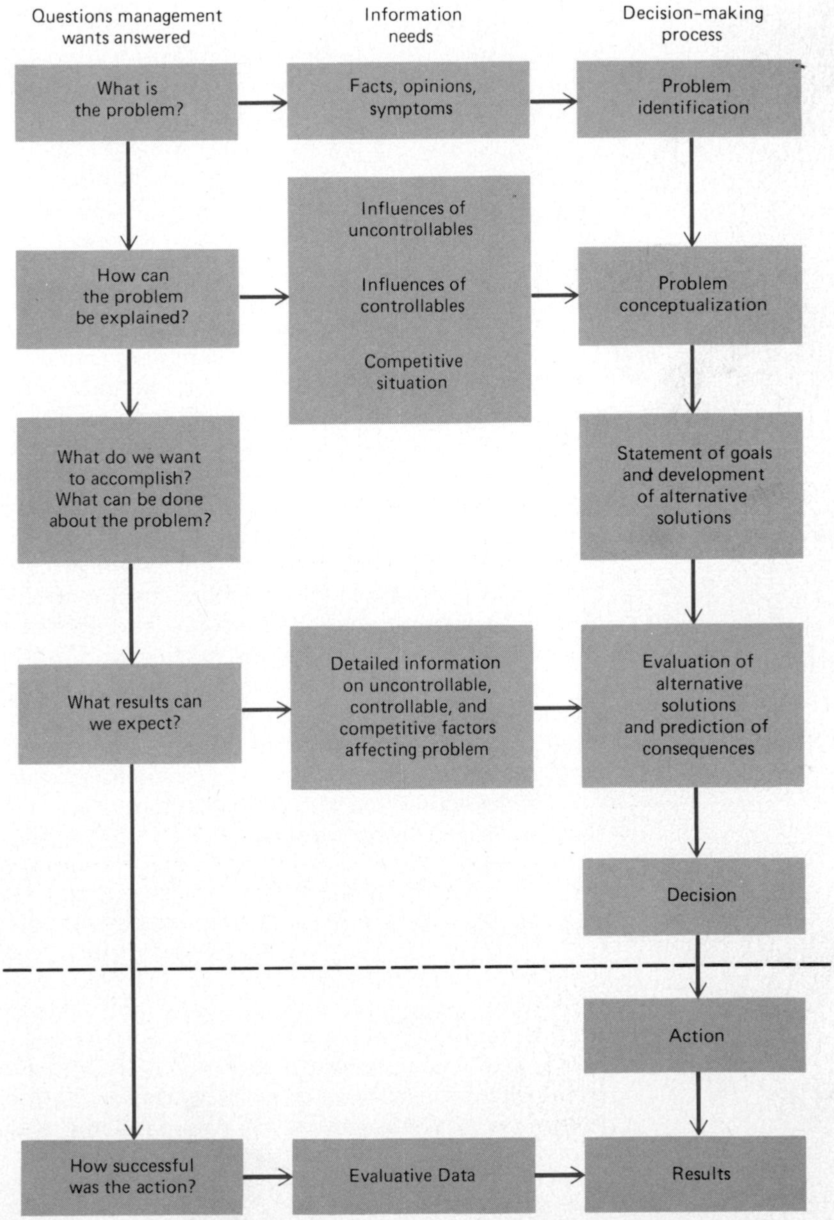

Starting with the problem identification stage, marketing research gathers facts, opinions, and symptoms to help marketing management in recognizing the problem situation. Problem identification phases naturally into problem conceptualization where marketing research, through providing information inputs on the influences of uncontrollables (psychological, cultural, social, and economic factors) and controllables (products, distribution, promotion, and pricing) and the competitive situation, helps management explain the problem situation. At this stage of decision making, marketing research analyzes information drawn, of course, from both internal and external sources. Marketing researchers refer to this aspect of their work as preliminary exploration.

Marketing management, at the next stage, seeks to answer the questions "What do we want to accomplish?" and "What can be done about the problem?" As Figure 7–1 indicates, these are questions management pretty well has to answer for itself, but even here marketing research can make a contribution. It can help, for instance, in the creative thinking involved in developing alternative solutions to the problem. Before marketing research can make this contribution, however, marketing management must make clear what it wants to accomplish—formulating the statement of goals, in other words, is marketing management's responsibility.

Next comes the evaluation of alternative solutions and the prediction of their consequences. Answering management's question "What results can we expect?" often requires that marketing research gather and analyze additional and detailed information on the factors affecting the problem—the uncontrollables, controllables, and the competitive situation. This added information may be gathered through various research methods and techniques—for example, consumer surveys, test market studies, and motivation research.

After considering all this information (tempering it with previous experience, judgment, and imagination), marketing management reaches its decision and takes whatever actions are required to carry out the decision. Later, as management wonders how successful was the action, marketing research may be called upon to provide the necessary evaluative data.

Scope of Marketing Research

Marketing research has a broad scope, embracing numerous types of studies, tapping diverse information sources. For purposes of the following discussion, marketing research studies are divided into four major categories: (1) market measurement studies, (2) studies of influences of controllables, (3) studies of the competitive situation, and (4) studies of uncontrollables.

MARKET MEASUREMENT STUDIES

Market measurement studies are aimed toward obtaining quantitative data on potential demand. These data indicate how much of a particular product can be sold to individual market segments over some future period, assuming the application of appropriate marketing methods. These data relate to market potential, sales potential, or both. Measurement of market potential involves determining for particular market segments the maximum possible sales opportunities open to all sellers of a good or service during a stated future period. Measurement of sales potential involves determining for particular market segments the maximum possible sales opportunities open to a specified company selling a good or service during a stated future period. To illustrate, consider the sales opportunities for 19-inch portable color television sets in Dade County, Florida, during the coming year—the market potential for the television set industry is a somewhat higher figure than the sales potential available to a particular manufacturer, such as to the Zenith Radio Corporation.

Market measurement data are particularly helpful in planning overall marketing strategy. In evaluating a proposed new product, for example, management must estimate its probable marketing success. Analysis of market measurement data provides valuable insights as to whether a potential market exists and, if so, its likely size. If management decides to add the new product, market measurement data are again helpful in determining the geographical sequence of market introduction. In addition, breakdowns of potentials by types of customers make it possible for management to ascertain which groups should be the targets for promotional efforts of varying amounts, and in what order. Management makes similar use of market measurement data in resolving questions regarding dropping certain products from the line, or deemphasizing their promotion to particular market segments.

STUDIES OF INFLUENCES OF CONTROLLABLES

The widest variety of marketing research studies focus on the influences of controllables—products, distribution, promotion, and price. Management can manipulate the controllables, and studies of them provide needed decision-making guidance. Management also uses studies of controllables to appraise the effectiveness of current product, distribution, promotion, and pricing policies and practices. Thus, for example, many companies make frequent studies of the effectiveness of advertising and other promotional devices, individual salesmen, existing sales methods, and sales compensation plans. Formal studies of this sort often draw management's attention to situations requiring changes in policies and practices. Management can manipulate controllables without such formal studies, but manipulation is more effective with the added insight gained from special studies.

STUDIES OF THE COMPETITIVE SITUATION

Many companies emphasize studies of the competitive position of their own products more than they do studies of the nature and impact of their competitors' activities. Specifically, a study measuring the share-of-the-market owned by a company's product is much more common than one appraising the marketing strengths and weaknesses of a competitor's products, evaluating the marketing effects of a competitor's product improvement, measuring the impact of a competitor's price change, or appraising the effects of a competitor's change in advertising approach. The most likely reason is that share-of-the-market information is often obtainable through outside research organizations, generally on a subscription basis.[2] Companies also find it easy to estimate share-of-the-market percentages for their own products, especially if industry sales figures are gathered and distributed by trade associations.

Most companies could benefit significantly if they would do more intelligence type studies—studies specifically designed to delve into competitors' marketing practices and policies. Management needs this information to understand how competitors' actions affect the company's marketing situation. Only if management has such intelligence can it do a really effective job in plotting marketing strategy and counterstrategy.

STUDIES OF INFLUENCES OF UNCONTROLLABLES

Relatively few marketing research studies focus directly on the influences of uncontrollables. This is probably because most executives feel that they can obtain the needed information in the course of their regular business reading. Published information is readily available on such uncontrollables as the level of consumer credit, business expansion plans, age- and income-distribution trends, and consumer buying intentions. Federal government publications such as the *Statistical Abstract of the United States,* the *County and City Data Book,* the *Survey of Current Business,* and the *Federal Reserve Bulletin* are rich sources of quantitative data on the uncontrollables and, in

[2] The A. C. Nielsen Company, for example, provides a number of information services widely used by manufacturers. One of these services—the Nielsen Retail Index—provides continuous factual marketing data on foods, drugs, pharmaceuticals, toiletries, cosmetics, confectionery, tobacco, photographic, and other products. For the food industry, for instance, Nielsen provides its subscribers with reports on sales to consumers measured at the point of sale, sales of competitors' products made to consumers, breakdowns of sales figures to consumers nationally or by the manufacturer's sales territories and by size and/or type of stores.

addition, often provide analyses of trends in income distribution, population growth and shifts, and consumer installment credit. The U.S. Department of Commerce's Office of Business Economics gathers and publishes data on the national economic situation and outlook and the balance of international payments. The Department of Commerce also maintains field offices to help businessmen looking for specific types of information. Considerable information on the uncontrollables also appears in such publications as *Business Week, Forbes, Dun's Review, Advertising Age, The Wall Street Journal, Nation's Business,* and *Sales Management.*

Even though executives obtain much information on the uncontrollables from their regular business reading, they seldom have the time required to organize data gathered from numerous sources and to analyze the results in terms of their own company's marketing problems. Marketing researchers, however, when assigned the task of studying the uncontrollables, can expertly assemble and analyze data, putting it into a perspective more useful to decision makers.

The motivation research studies, which probe psychological and sociological variables affecting buying behavior, are in a class by themselves. Research has indicated that relatively few companies conduct this type of study. Why do so many companies fail to do motivation research? Part of the answer is that doing and interpreting motivation research requires trained specialists—psychologists and sociologists skilled in the research methods of their own fields. Few companies employ such people, and most motivation research is handled by outside consultants. Then, too, motivation research is still comparatively new, and many executives not only doubt its value but are suspicious of many of its findings.

Marketing Research Procedure

While the marketing manager need not be a qualified researcher, he or she should understand general marketing research procedure. The marketing manager, in other words, is primarily a user of marketing research, not a researcher. Regardless of whether a company does its own research or uses an outside agency, the marketing manager must know enough about marketing research procedure to be able to at least evaluate research findings. Table 7–1 shows the largest marketing research companies in the United States, by estimated research volume in dollars.

The marketing manager, as well as the researcher, must bear in mind the current business environment, because the effectiveness of marketing research, in part, depends upon responsiveness to trends in the economy.[3] For example, one basic change in the business envi-

[3]David K. Hardin, "Lower Profits Put Pinch on Researcher," *Advertising Age,* July 15, 1974, p. 26.

ronment has been the shift from a concept of virtually unlimited growth to a more deliberate, planned growth in light of shortages of materials and the resulting limited product availability. The marketing research procedure, therefore, should reflect a consideration of such trends.

PROBLEM IDENTIFICATION AND MARKETING RESEARCH

Even though marketing management may have already identified the problem to be investigated, it must make certain that the researcher understands its precise nature. The marketing researcher, like the marketing decision maker, looks upon problem identification as a basic first step in his or her work. Only if he or she knows what problem management is trying to solve can he or she do an effective job in designing a research project that will provide the needed information. Only if he or she has the problem clearly in mind can he or she be expected to intelligently direct the resulting project—to steer it as directly as possible to predetermined informational goals (set by the nature of the problem itself) and to keep it from going off course on the way to those goals. A competent marketing researcher, therefore, does not undertake any study until he or she is certain that the executive making the request has some problem already "pinned down" and until that executive has communicated the problem's nature clearly. All too frequently, executives

Table 7–1 Largest Marketing Research Companies in the United States, by estimated dollar volume, 1973

COMPANY	RESEARCH VOLUME Estimated (in millions)
A. C. Nielsen Co.	$117.7
IMS International	33.5
Selling Areas Marketing (SAMI)	18.5
American Research Bureau	16.0
Market Facts	14.5
Burke International Research	12.0
Audits & Surveys	10.0
Inmarco, Inc.	8.0
Daniel Yankelovich, Inc.	4.9
National Analysts	4.9
Opinion Research Corp.	4.9

Source: Jack J. Honomichl, "Research Top Ten: Who They Are and What They Do," *Advertising Age*, July 15, 1974, p. 24. Other large research companies include: Chilton Research Services, Starch INRA Hooper, Inc., Market Research Corp. of America, Louis Harris and Associates, Market Opinion Research, National Family Opinion, Inc., Marketing and Research Counselors, Inc., Haug Associates, Inc., Marketing Evaluations, Inc., and Oxtoby-Smith, Inc.

originate requests for studies that subsequently prove of little value simply because they had not probed deeply enough to identify the basic problem. In one such case—where management asked for a study of advertising effectiveness—further probing by an alert researcher revealed that a sales decline was not a result of ineffective advertising, but could be traced directly to the effects of a newly inaugurated distribution policy that was slowing up deliveries to retail outlets thus causing them to be out of stock frequently.

PRELIMINARY EXPLORATION AND THE "SITUATION ANALYSIS"

In the course of identifying the problem, marketing researchers begin preliminary exploration of data sources which, they hope, will help them gain insights into the problem's nature. Because the specific problem is not yet identified, they are required to do a certain amount of groping around for information. Therefore, the preliminary exploration is an informal and, to a large extent, unplanned investigation.

In doing a preliminary exploration, researchers tap as many sources of readily available data as time permits. They examine company records (sales, financial, production, and others) that might shed some light on the problem. They skim trade and professional publications for reports on similar situations encountered and/or researched by others. And they study their own company's reports of previous investigations of similar and related situations. Thus, they build background for their own thinking. Marketing researchers refer to this phase of preliminary exploration as the *situation analysis*.

Situation Analysis

PROJECT PLANNING FOR MARKETING RESEARCH

Basically, a marketing research project is a planned search for information. Time spent in project planning should not only reduce the time required to conduct the project but also ultimately result in securing more reliable and meaningful information. When project planning is neglected, marketing researchers flit aimlessly from one information source to the next, choose research methods and approaches at random, and have only vague notions of the specific information needed. The earmarks of project planning in marketing research, as elsewhere, are well-defined goals, an organized effort, and a step-by-step schedule—all aimed at uncovering, reporting, and analyzing as reliable and meaningful information as it is possible to obtain in the available time.

Planning a marketing research project involves making decisions on (1) research objectives, (2) specific information needed to achieve these objectives, (3) sources to tap in seeking the information, and (4) research methods to employ in collecting the information.

Deciding on Research Objectives After the marketing problem has been identified and the preliminary exploration finished, the first key project-planning decision relates to the setting of research objectives. The preliminary exploration should have clarified the purposes for any subsequent formal research. In studying how the company spends its advertising appropriation, for instance, the researcher may have concluded tentatively that less money should be devoted to newspaper advertisements and more to radio. Thus, the purpose of formal research might be to test two hypotheses:

1. The company should spend less on newspaper advertising.
2. The company should spend more on radio commercials.

The statement of research objectives should, whenever possible, be limited to a small number of hypotheses to test or questions to answer. The number must be small because no project can produce timely and reliable information for managerial decision if it is directed toward obtaining too many facts. In pruning the list of objectives, the researcher should consider two questions about each tentative objective:

1. If we succeed in obtaining this information, of what value will it be to the decision maker?
2. If this information is of possible value, is it valuable enough to justify the cost of obtaining it?

Deciding on Information Needed The second key project-planning decision is to determine the specific information needed to achieve the research objectives. The researcher considers the different types of information that seem pertinent to achieving the objectives and ascertains that each bit of specific information finally decided upon is relevant to achieving them. Suppose, for example, that the project being planned has the objective of answering a business executive's question, "Should I open a self-service shoe store in Middletown, Pennsylvania?" What kinds of information are necessary to answer this question? The researcher should search out, as a minimum, the following:

1. Number of Middletown residents who are potential customers for this type of store.
2. Probable frequency and intensity of patronage. (How often and how much will members of different market segments patronize this store?)
3. Competing stores, their relative advantages, and their comparative costs.
4. Amount, kinds, and costs of persuasion (advertising and so forth) needed to move Middletown residents to patronize the store.

Deciding on Information Sources The third key decision is to identify the sources for the different items of information. For this purpose, it is helpful to classify information sources as primary or secondary. A primary source is one from which information is obtained directly as, for example, through questionnaires and interviews. Primary sources include consumers and buyers, middlemen, salesmen, trade association executives, and others. Secondary data sources are mostly published materials, such as government census publications and *Sales Management's Survey of Buying Power.* Sometimes another type of secondary source (such as company files of marketing research and other reports) contains the desired information, although this may not be known to the decision maker needing it. Secondary data sources, in other words, are repositories not of items of information gathered specifically to achieve the objectives of the research project being planned, but rather of material assembled for other purposes.

The researcher should always look to the secondary sources first, for if the needed information is already available, the time and expense of gathering it from primary sources is saved. Usually, however, some information can be gleaned from secondary sources (for example, population and income statistics) but more crucial data (for example, the disposition of consumers to buy a given product under certain marketing conditions) must be obtained from primary sources. In the Middletown study on opening a self-service shoe store, for example, census publications (a secondary source) should reveal the number of residents who are potential users, and city directories (another secondary source) could be consulted to identify competitors selling shoes in the trading area. But, to obtain other desired items of information, primary sources (namely, the potential consumers) would have to be tapped.

Deciding on Research Methods If all the needed information is obtainable from secondary sources, no decision on research methods is required; if, as is more likely, however, primary sources must be used, a fourth key decision—on research methods—is required.

The Survey Method In the survey method, information is obtained directly from individual respondents either through personal interviews or through mail questionnaires or telephone interviews. Questionnaires are used either to obtain specific responses to direct questions or to secure more general responses to open-end questions. A direct type of question is designed to force the respondent to choose among a limited number of answers as, for example, in the question: "How do you feel about the styling of this new cordless electric shaver? Do you rate it as EXCELLENT ______, GOOD ______, FAIR ______, or POOR ______?" This question contrasts sharply with the open-end question: "What do you think about the styling of this new cordless electric shaver?" The open-end question permits respondents to formulate their own answers.

The survey method has three main uses: (1) to gather facts from respondents, (2) to report their opinions, or (3) to probe the interpretations they give to various matters. The survey method's accuracy and reliability varies in each application. Generally, it is most accurate and reliable when used to gather factual data, less so when used to record opinions, and least so when used to gain insight into respondents' interpretations.

Factual Survey

In the *factual survey,* respondents are asked to report actual facts, as exemplified by questions such as: "What brand of cigarettes do you smoke?" "Where do you do most of your shopping for groceries?" "How many persons live at this address?" Even the answers to factual questions are subject to error because some respondents have faulty memories, are unable to generalize about personal experiences, or may give answers they believe interviewers want to obtain.

Opinion Survey

The *opinion survey* is designed to gather expressions of personal opinions, to record evaluations of different things, or to report thinking on particular matters. Opinion surveys share the potential errors of factual surveys and, in addition, by forcing immediate answers to questions on subjects that the respondents have not thought about lately, may produce answers not accurately reflecting real opinions.

Interpretive Survey

In the *interpretive survey,* the respondent acts as an interpreter as well as a reporter. Interpretative data are gathered by using such questions as "Why do you use Brand X spray deodorant?" and "What feature of the new *Thunderbird* appeals to you most?" A limitation of the interpretive survey is that respondents' answers often reflect an inability to consciously interpret personal feelings, motives, and attitudes.

The Experimental Method Patterned after the procedure used in scientific research, the experimental method as used in marketing research involves carrying out of a small-scale trial solution to a problem while simultaneously attempting to control all relevant factors except the one being studied. An advertiser, for example, may run two versions of a proposed advertisement (ad A and ad B) in a city newspaper, with half of the copies of the issue carrying ad A and the other half ad B. This experiment, called a *split-run test,* might be used to determine the most effective advertisement in one or more market areas, which might then be placed in newspapers in other markets or in national media.

Split-Run Test

The main assumption in the experimental method is that the test conditions are essentially the same as those that will be encountered when conclusions derived from the experiment are applied to a broader marketing area. Of course, test conditions are never quite the same as parallel conditions in the broader market. Nevertheless, a well-designed experiment, even though it cannot replicate total market conditions, can provide guidance and information for decision making.

The Observational Method Here, marketing research data are gathered not through direct questioning of respondents, but by observing and recording consumers' actions in a marketing situation.

So, for example, in studying the impact of a department store's mass display of shelving paper, observers, stationed unobtrusively, record the total number of people passing by a display, the number stopping, the number picking up and examining the product, and the number making purchases. In another study, whose purpose was to determine which types of consumers bought what brands of home remedies, researchers made inventories of the contents of household medicine cabinets. In a third study, researchers used concealed tape recorders and posed as customers as part of a project to evaluate selling techniques used in florist shops.

The main advantage of the observational method is that it records respondents' expressed actions and behavior patterns. Its principal shortcoming is that its design does not provide for detection of buying motives and other psychological factors since, in its pure form, at least, this method involves simply watching or listening or both, with no attempt being made to probe the reasons lying behind actions and behavior patterns.

GATHERING PRIMARY DATA THROUGH SAMPLING

Sample

In gathering data from primary sources, most marketing research projects make use of sampling. A sample is, by definition, only a portion of the "universe" from which it is drawn; therefore, studying the characteristics and attitudes of the members of a sample, rather than of all members of the relevant universe, not only makes possible completion of a study in less time but results in lower research costs. Limitations of time and money are the main reasons that marketing research usually studies samples rather than whole universes.

Data obtained through sampling may contain fewer errors than data gathered through a complete census. For instance, when the universe size is very large and scientific sample selection methods are used, there is a strong possibility that sampling will result in fewer errors. The possibility is even stronger when, as often happens in marketing research, limited funds are available for the study. With limited funds, making a census requires that expenditures be spread thin; by contrast, restricting the size of the field operation (through sampling) makes relatively larger amounts available, both for better control of data collection processes and for using higher caliber interviewing and other research personnel.[4]

Marketing research uses sampling extensively and, since research results are important ingredients for decision making, marketing managers should know enough about sampling to allow them to evaluate the data they use. More specifically, they should know the

[4] C. R. Wasson, "Common Sense in Sampling," *Harvard Business Review*, January–February 1963, p. 110.

inherent advantages and limitations of samples selected by different methods, and they should understand how sample size affects the amount of error present in research results.

However, a word of caution is necessary. Even though management wants to avoid basing decisions on erroneous data, it also wants to avoid demanding such error-free data that inordinate amounts of time and money are spent on the study. Greater expense and longer periods of investigation, in other words, are the price of reductions in errors in marketing research. If, for management's purpose, accuracy within 10 percent of the true picture is sufficient, aiming for accuracy that is within 5 percent wastes both research time and money.

Classes of Samples All marketing research samples fall into one of two classes: probability and nonprobability. The fundamental distinction between these two classes lies in the way items are selected for inclusion in the resulting samples. Probability samples result from a process of random selection whereby each member of a universe has a known chance of being selected for the sample. Nonprobability samples result from a process in which judgment (and, therefore, bias) enters into the selection of the members of a universe included in the sample. Judgment is also involved in using probability samples (in deciding, for instance, on a particular sample design), but the actual selection of the individual items for inclusion is made solely through a probability mechanism as, for example, a table of random numbers (eliminating the human bias otherwise entering into the selection).

Probability Samples

Nonprobability Samples

This difference as to the extent to which judgment enters into selection of the sample may be illustrated as follows: In a "quota" sample, one type of nonprobability sample, interviewers may be given quotas specifying that they are to select for interviewing a certain number of people who possess given characteristics: one such quota might specify, "Interview 20 women in the 35 to 45 age bracket, half of whom have full- or part-time jobs and half of whom are not employed outside the home." If the same study were to be made using a probability sample, the probability mechanism itself would be relied on to select representative proportions of people with the given characteristics, and the interviewer would play no part whatever in the actual selection of respondents.

Errors There are two kinds of errors in samples: nonsampling and sampling. Samples contain both kinds of errors, whereas complete censuses contain only nonsampling errors. This, however, does not mean that census results are necessarily any more error-free than sample results. It means only that there is one kind of error in a census and two kinds in a sample.

Nonsampling Errors

Nonsampling errors are the accidental (or deliberate) mistakes or errors that can happen during any of the stages of data collection, recording, and enumeration. Here are some examples: a field worker checks off a wrong answer; a respondent misinterprets a question; an interviewer misinterprets an answer; a field worker selects a wrong respondent; a field worker falsifies an interview; a clerk tabulates some data incorrectly; an interviewer biases respondents' answers by the way he or she asks questions; a poorly designed question elicits erroneous responses. Nonsampling errors, in other words, are blunders, and they occur both in complete censuses and in samples. Nonsampling errors cannot be measured (as can sampling errors) and taken into account in evaluating study results. Thoroughness in project planning and careful control over all phases of the subsequent study are the only ways to minimize these errors.

Sampling Errors

Sampling errors trace to the sample itself, causing it not to be completely representative of the universe from which it is drawn. The measurements produced by samples (statisticians call these measurements *statistics*) are really estimates of the true parameters. Statisticians, in evaluating a sample, use the term *accuracy* to refer to the difference between a sample result and the real statistic, and the term *precision* to refer to the difference between a sample result and the result of a complete count (parameter). Although it is virtually impossible to measure the accuracy of sample results, precision is statistically measurable but only for probability samples.[5] Measures of sampling error (i.e., standard error measures)[6] can be computed for such values as arithmetic means and percentages pertaining to probability sample results. Because it is not essential to our discussion to go into the calculation methods, and because marketing research texts explain these calculations in detail, we need not go into them here.[7] It is sufficient to keep in mind the fact that it is possible to calculate the sampling error present in probability samples.

Sample Size Common sense tells us that the larger a sample, the greater are the chances that research results will be reliable. Sampling errors are the only errors that can be reduced by increasing sample size. And, because the statistical formulas for computing sampling errors apply solely to probability samples, only in their case can we obtain measures of the adequacy of sample size. The amount of sampling error considered acceptable in each situation (and, hence, the acceptable sample size) depends mainly on management's willingness to assume risk (i.e., to risk making a bad decision

[5] The statistical sampling error of probability sample results is a measure of precision and not of accuracy.

[6] The measure of sampling error is known technically as the "standard error of the sampling estimate," and is defined as "a measure of the variability inherent in a sample value, due only to the sampling process (sampling error); (it) may be computed for almost any mathematically determined value obtained from a probability sample." See K. P. Uhl and B. Schoner, *Marketing Research: Information Systems and Decision Making* (New York: John Wiley & Sons, Inc., 1969), p. 121.

[7] See P. E. Green and D. S. Tull, *Research for Marketing Decisions*, 3rd ed. (Englewood Cliffs, N.J.: Prentice-Hall, Inc., 1975), pp. 244 ff.

because of erroneous data) and on the amount of money available for the project. In other words, "once the sample attains a certain size," as two prominent statisticians say, "additional observations will not reduce the *sampling error*, that is, the allowance for sampling variability in the conclusions, enough to be worth the additional cost."[8]

Costs of Marketing Research

While most companies engage in some type of marketing research, few spend as much on it as they should. One study of annual expenditures on marketing research by nearly 250 firms revealed that 90 percent of them spend less than 1 percent of their annual sales on marketing research.[9] This contrasts sharply with expenditures on product research and development (R&D), where budgets often amount to 10 percent of sales or more. Although there is wide variation among companies with respect to how much is spent on marketing research, three factors appear to influence budget size: the company's size, nature of operations, and aspirations for market leadership. Generally, the bigger the company, the more complex, widespread, and intricate its operations; and the higher its aims for a market leadership position, the greater the size of its marketing research budget.

Individual marketing research projects vary considerably in cost. Those requiring nothing more than the tapping of secondary sources of information incur only the costs for the time of research and support personnel assigned to the project, perhaps a few thousand dollars at most. Others, such as nationwide surveys utilizing a large number of personal interviews, can easily cost from $10,000 to well over $100,000.

VALUE AND COST OF HAVING INFORMATION

To the question of "How much should a particular marketing research project cost?" the theoretical answer is, "Something less than the value the decision maker places on the information produced by the research." Both amounts—the should cost and the value of having the information—are difficult to estimate. Not only is it hard to put a dollar tag on the worth of specific items of information, it is at least as hard to say how much should be spent on obtaining that information.

[8]W. A. Wallis and H. V. Roberts, *Statistics: A New Approach* (New York: The Free Press, 1956), p. 127.

[9]L. W. Forman and E. L. Bailey, *The Role and Organization of Marketing Research,* Experiences in Marketing Management No. 20 (New York: National Industrial Conference Board, 1969), p. 8.

But, in spite of these difficulties, we can say a few things about the costs of individual marketing research projects. For one thing, it is never worthwhile to launch an investigation seeking all the possible items of information about a particular decision situation; we can never get all the information anyway because decisions are made for the future and there are always some uncertainties about the future. Research information can help reduce these uncertainties, but it cannot eliminate them entirely. We can also say that the cost of a project is related to the degree of precision management expects the research results to have—increased precision is bought at the price of higher project costs and greater amounts of time spent in processing the results. Another way of making the same point: the more confidence management wants to be able to put in the results, the larger and more expensive the sample and the more costly the research techniques that are needed to obtain data with the desired level of precision.

Summary

You should now understand marketing research's relationship to marketing decision making. Marketing research, through systematic gathering and analysis of information, should assist management in answering questions that must be resolved at each stage in the decision-making process. Marketing research has potentials for furnishing data on diverse factors affecting marketing decisions—market measurement data, influences of controllables, the competitive situation, and influences of uncontrollables. The starting point of any marketing research project should be mutual agreement on the identity of the problem (by management and the researcher), because both research time and money are wasted if the problem is not clearly defined. Each project should be truly a planned search for information, directed toward obtaining as reliable information as is possible to obtain within the limits of time and money available. Both with respect to total marketing research expenditures and the costs of individual projects, management must try to balance the costs of obtaining information against its value for decision-making purposes.

QUESTIONS AND PROBLEMS

1. "By contributing toward reductions in the cost of distributing goods from producer to consumer, marketing research makes it possible for the consumer to enjoy better products at lower prices than would otherwise be possible. By thus enabling each dollar to buy more, the entire standard of living of the people is raised to higher levels." Arthur C. Nielsen, Sr., in "Marketing Research—Past, Present and Future," *Nineteenth Charles Coolidge Parlin Memorial Lecture,*

Philadelphia Chapter, American Marketing Association, May 21, 1963. Do you agree with Mr. Nielsen's contention? Why or why not?

2. In what way does the systems approach to marketing management change the traditional role of marketing research? Does it increase or decrease the role of research in marketing management? Explain.
3. Discuss the potential contributions marketing research can make during each of the several stages in the decision-making process. Analyze the relationship of internal and external studies to marketing decision making.
4. Comment on the following two statements:
   a. "To manage a business well is to manage its future; and to manage the future is to manage information."
   b. "It is equally important for management to know when not to use research as to know when to use it."
5. Refer to the major types of marketing research performed by American companies, and answer the following questions:
   a. What information of value to decision makers might each type of study provide?
   b. Why is it that so few marketing research studies focus directly on the influences of uncontrollables?
   c. Why do so many focus on the influence of controllables?
6. Who should identify the problems to be studied—the marketing researcher or the marketing decision maker? Justify the position you take.
7. Explain the meaning of each of the following:
   a. preliminary exploration
   b. situation analysis
   c. permissible sampling error
8. Differentiate:
   a. primary and secondary data sources
   b. factual, opinion, and interpretative surveys
   c. experimental method and observational method
   d. universe and sample
   e. probability and nonprobability samples
   f. nonsampling error and sampling error
9. "Bad research is the cause of many marketing failures. Polling is the greatest contributor to marketing failure because it is conducted on the assumption that people can or will tell you why they buy a product." To what extent is this statement true? False?
10. Why should a marketing research project be a planned search for information? In planning a marketing research project, what types of decisions are required? Who should make them? Why?
11. What problems are involved in relating research objectives to the amount of money available for marketing research? Who should resolve these problems? Why?
12. Discuss the various criteria for choosing the research method(s) to be used in carrying out particular marketing research projects.

13. Explain how statisticians use the terms "accuracy" and "precision" in referring to samples.
14. How is sample size related to errors in sample results? When is a sample "the right size"? What does the decision maker's willingness to assume risk have to do with sample size?
15. Compare and contrast the relative merits and limitations of probability and nonprobability samples. Who should specify the type of sample—the marketing researcher or the decision maker? Justify the position you take.
16. How do you explain the fact that the size of the marketing research budget varies greatly from company to company and from industry to industry?
17. How should the decision be made on the amount of money to invest in a particular marketing research project? Who should make this decision? Why?
18. Discuss the various controls over marketing research expenditures that management might set up.
19. Under what conditions might the manager of a marketing research department ask that a "reserve for contingencies" be included in the budget for his department?
20. You have just been hired by a medium-sized manufacturer of dog food to set up and manage a marketing research department. You are to report directly to the vice-president in charge of marketing but, since the company has not previously had a formally organized marketing research department, there is no clear-cut statement of departmental objectives and you have no job description as yet. Formulate a statement of department objectives and write a job description for your position as department head.

CASE PROBLEM

The Catskill Toy Manufacturing Company with annual sales of $2,500,000 sells its line of wooden toys mainly to schools and church organizations, but some mail-order business has been transacted with parents and other consumers. Even though the number of school-age children has grown significantly over the last decade, Catskill's unit volume has remained relatively stable with dollar sales increases being largely accounted for by price rises. The line of products ranges from building blocks sold in $1, $5, and $10 sets to large wooden playground equipment priced as high as $225. The company employs no salesmen but sells its products through school supply houses and manufacturers' agents, by means of a catalog distributed on request to interested parties. As the newly appointed marketing vice-president of this concern, you have an advertising manager and a sales manager reporting to you and you have just been authorized to add a marketing research man to your staff.

Outline the procedure you would follow in recruiting and selecting this new man. What kinds of studies would you want the new marketing research man to conduct and in what priority?

PART THREE

PRODUCTS

When you have mastered the contents of this chapter, you should be able to:

1. Explain what is meant by "a product."
2. Distinguish consumers' goods from industrial goods.
3. Discuss the marketing characteristics of the three classes of consumers' goods.
4. Discuss the marketing characteristics of the four major categories of industrial goods and give examples of the types of goods included in each.
5. Discuss the marketing significance of each of the four stages of the product life cycle.
6. Illustrate how and explain why different kinds of products have different types of life cycle curves.
7. Justify the need for product objectives and product policies.
8. Explain the nature of each of the three major phases in new product planning.

CHAPTER 8

PRODUCTS:
MARKETING CHARACTERISTICS, LIFE CYCLES, AND INNOVATION

Successful marketing programs are built around two essential elements—products and markets. The essence of marketing, in other words, is the bringing together of products possessing want-satisfying capabilities with markets made up of potential customers having particular wants. Discussion in this and the following chapter focuses on the marketing significance of key aspects of product management.

What Is a Product?

Product

A *product* is both what a seller has to sell and what a buyer has to buy. Thus, any enterprise that has something to sell, tangible goods or not, is selling products. A laundry, for instance, sells the service of cleaning clothes and is just as surely engaged in selling a product as the retail stores that originally sold the clothes it cleans. Any firm that has something to sell, in fact, sells services as part of that something, even though we may think of it as dealing in tangible goods rather than services *per se*. Furthermore, what a buyer buys is a mixture not of goods and services but, rather, of expected physical and psychological satisfactions. In other words, the buyer buys a total product, not merely the physical product itself.

Formally defined, then, *a product is a bundle of utilities consisting of various product features and accompanying services.*[1] The bundle of

[1] Wroe Alderson, *Marketing Behavior and Executive Action* (Homewood, Ill.: Richard D. Irwin, Inc., 1957), p. 274.

utilities (i.e., the physical and psychological satisfactions that the buyer receives) is provided by the seller when he sells a particular combination of product features and associated services. When a man buys a suit from a clothing store, for example, he buys not only the garment itself but the clerk's assistance and advice, the store's alteration service, the prestige of the store's and maker's labels, perhaps charge and delivery services, and the privilege of returning the item for refund or allowance should it not yield the expected satisfaction. The clothing store sells not only men's suits but related services that customers regard as bundles providing both physical and psychological satisfactions during consumption.

In marketing, the term "good" is used as a synonym for "product." This is in line both with long-standing business usage and well-established academic practice. In the following discussion, as throughout this entire book, "good" and "product" are used interchangeably.

Consumers' Goods

Industrial Goods

Depending upon the use for which it is destined, each good is classed as either a consumer or an industrial good. Consumers' goods are destined for final consumption by individuals (ultimate consumers) and households. Television sets, perfume and lipsticks, and boxed candy are all consumers' goods. Industrial goods are destined for use in the commercial production of other goods or in connection with carrying on some business or institutional activity. Iron ore, machine tools, and electronic computers are all industrial goods.

Actually, not many goods can be classified exclusively as consumer goods or industrial goods. Typing paper, for example, is used both for business and personal correspondence and, therefore, is both a consumer and an industrial good. Depending upon the circumstances surrounding its use, the same article can be either a consumer or an industrial good.

Why is this apparently artificial distinction important? Because consumers' and industrial goods are bought not only for different purposes but—of greater marketing significance—characteristically, their purchasers take different approaches in making buying decisions. Consequently, the nature of marketing problems and appropriate marketing strategies also varies, depending upon whether the product is marketed as a consumer or an industrial good.

Consumers' Goods

The variety of consumers' goods is almost endless, literally ranging from A to Z—apples to zippers—and including such diverse items as candy bars, home swimming pools, grand pianos, and frozen TV dinners. There are so many different consumers' goods that it is clearly impractical to analyze each individually. Several classification systems have been devised to facilitate marketing analysis, but the traditional classification presented below is the most widely used.

TRADITIONAL CLASSIFICATION OF CONSUMERS' GOODS

Sometime prior to 1923, Professor Melvin T. Copeland of the Harvard Business School, a pioneer marketing teacher, set up what is now known as the traditional system for classifying consumers' goods. Copeland based his classifications on differences in consumer buying attitudes and behavior. Under his system, three classes of consumers' goods are identified: convenience, shopping, and specialty.

Convenience Goods

Convenience Goods Items the consumer buys frequently, immediately, and with minimum shopping effort are *convenience goods.* Examples include cigarettes, candy and chewing gum, magazines and newspapers, gasoline, drugs, and most grocery items. Note that these are all nondurables; that is, they are consumed or used up rapidly. Hence, consumers buy them frequently and normally neither postpone their purchases nor make them much in advance of the consumption time. Note, too, that, in buying convenience goods, habit dominates the consumer's behavior. Through force of habit it is easy for the consumer to make buying decisions. In buying cigarettes and gasoline, for example, consumers know which brands they prefer, and they know the retail outlets where they generally buy them. Little or no conscious deliberation is required to decide each individual purchase. The typical consumer minimizes the time and effort devoted to buying convenience goods.

In buying most convenience goods, the consumer rarely bothers to compare competing offerings on the bases of price and quality. "It isn't worth shopping around for" expresses the typical consumer's attitude. However, if the item represents an important item in the consumer's budget, he or she may be willing to spend considerable time or effort getting the best buy. For example, a housewife may have a favorite brand of coffee and buy it habitually, but she may watch for "specials" and try to buy it then; she may even visit a store not usually patronized if it advertises a special price on her favorite brand. Also, if the price or quality of a convenience good, such as of a favorite brand of bread, gets too far out of line with competing brands, many consumers revise their buying decisions. The consumer's possible gains in such situations outweigh the costs in time and effort.

Seeking to minimize shopping time and effort, the consumer buys convenience goods at convenient locations. A convenient location may be near the consumer's home, on the way to work, or near the place of work. Recognizing that consumers will not go far out of their way to buy, marketers of convenience goods make them available for sale in numerous and diverse outlets.

Shopping Goods

Shopping Goods Items the consumer selects and buys after making comparisons on such bases as suitability, quality, price, and style are *shopping goods.* Whenever a substantial number of consumers habitually make such shopping comparisons before they select and buy an item, it is considered a shopping good. Examples of goods that most consumers appear to buy in this way include furniture, rugs, dress goods, women's ready-to-wear and shoes, and household appliances. Before buying these items, consumers shop around and compare different stores' offerings. Notice that the typical shopping good is bought infrequently, is "used up" slowly, and that consumers often are in positions to defer or advance the purchase date. Thus, they can afford to devote considerable time and effort to the buying decision. In other words, consumers believe that the possible gains from making shopping comparisons exceed the costs in terms of time and effort.

Not every consumer uses the same bases of comparison in buying shopping goods. In some cases, a consumer shops primarily to find something suitable—for example, the person who looks for drapes to match a particular carpet or upholstery fabric. In shopping for clothing, some women consider style the most important factor, whereas others are mainly "price shoppers." In shopping for childrens' shoes, these same women may consider quality the most important basis for comparison. The bases of comparison and their relative importance vary both with the product and the shopper, but the key word in identifying shopping goods is comparison.

Branding is much less important for shopping goods than for convenience goods. In some instances, the consumer undoubtedly is willing to pay more for a branded shopping good. For example, some women prefer certain brands of dresses, not because of styling or design characteristics, but merely because they have found they fit them with little alteration. But, in most cases, if the product is truly a shopping good, the consumer is unwilling to pay for the possible prestige of the brand name.

Because, typically, consumers devote considerable time and effort to the buying of shopping goods, shopping goods marketers can manage with fewer retail outlets than can convenience goods marketers. The shopping goods marketer places great emphasis on having its goods for sale in outlets where consumers are likely to look for such items rather than on having them available in every store.

Specialty Goods

Specialty Goods Items for which significant numbers of consumers are habitually willing to make a special purchasing effort are known as *specialty goods.* Items in this category must possess unique characteristics or have a degree of brand identification or both. Examples of items usually bought as specialty goods are stereo components, fancy foods, stamps and coins for collectors, and prestige brands of men's suits. Consumers already know the product or brand they want; they are willing to make a special purchasing effort to find the outlet handling it. In reaching the buying decision, consumers do not compare the desired specialty good with others, as in the case of shopping goods. However, as specialty goods are often in the luxury price class, consumers may take considerable time in deciding to start the special search required.

Specialty goods are found in low as well as high price ranges. For instance, to obtain a stamp collection's missing stamp worth a dime or quarter may require nearly as much purchasing effort as to locate the rarity worth hundreds of dollars. Although less money is involved in one case than in the other, both prices are high relative to those of other articles without such unique characteristics. Consumers exert special purchasing efforts to locate such items, and prices are secondary considerations in buying decisions.

However, an item does not have to be difficult to locate to make it a specialty good. The consumer who wants to buy Bayer Aspirin and will not accept a substitute can find the brand in nearly all drugstores and most grocery stores. An item is a specialty good if many buyers are willing to make a special purchasing effort, not that they always have to. Marketing practices of many manufacturers of specialty goods make it unnecessary for consumers to exert special purchasing efforts. They make their brands easy to locate, thus easy for consumers to buy.

Industrial Goods

Industrial users exhibit more uniform patterns of buying behavior than do ultimate consumers. Different industrial buyers are remarkably alike in the ways they go about making buying decisions for similar products. The automobile manufacturer's approach to the buying of machine tools, for example, closely resembles those taken not only by its competitors but by other buyers of machine tools. Industrial goods, therefore, readily lend themselves to a classification system based on the uses to which they are to be put. There are four major categories: (1) production facilities and equipment, (2) production materials, (3) production supplies, and (4) management materials.

PRODUCTION FACILITIES AND EQUIPMENT

This category includes installations, minor equipment, and plants and buildings.

Installations These are major items of capital equipment (such as factory turret lathes and commercial laundry dryers) essential to an industrial user's operations. Buying an installation involves investment of a comparatively large sum, so buying decisions generally require approval of both top management and the department head concerned. Because of this multiple influence on purchase decisions, salesmen of installations commonly must convince several individ-

Multiple Purchase Influence

uals before they actually get the orders, the negotiating periods often extending over considerable time. Some installations are designed and manufactured especially to buyers' specifications—for example, installations used in cane sugar processing and refining; salesmen selling such items need technical background or training or both. Because of the characteristically high unit value, most installations are sold directly to industrial users by the manufacturers.

Minor Equipment This subcategory includes pieces of equipment (such as work benches, lift trucks, and hand tools) that the industrial user utilizes in producing its product or service. Buying procedures are routine; ordinarily the industrial user's purchasing executive orders according to specifications set by the department requesting the item. Because of the relatively high purchase frequency, marketers of minor equipment make certain that their salesmen call frequently on prospects. Listing in industrial catalogs, trade journal advertising, and direct-mail promotion make up the usual program for maintaining representation at the buyer's plant between salesmen's calls.

Plants and Buildings These are necessary to an industrial user's operation and represent sizable capital investments. Thus, the plants and buildings subcategory somewhat resembles the installations subcategory; however, it also resembles the minor equipment subcategory since plants and buildings are supplementary to, rather than directly used in, the production of the industrial user's output. Plants and buildings are not usually marketed as complete units, though some construction engineering firms specialize in such products. In all major respects, industrial users approach the buying (or constructing) of plants or buildings in the same way that they go about buying installations.

PRODUCTION MATERIALS

This category includes raw materials, semimanufactured goods, and fabricating parts.

Raw Materials These are the basic products of farms, mines, fisheries, and forests that enter into the production of manufactured goods. Buying procedures for raw materials vary, depending upon the proportion their costs bear to total production costs and upon market conditions. If raw materials cost represents only a small part of total production costs, the suppliers are middlemen and the buying procedures routine. But when raw material cost accounts for a large part of a finished good's total cost, high-ranking purchasing executives deal directly with raw material producers. Similarly, if a raw material's market is characterized by stable supply and price conditions, relatively low-level executives use routine purchasing procedures. But, when raw material supplies and prices vary erratically, highly skilled and high-ranking executives do the buying and seek to adapt procurement procedures to changing market conditions.

Semimanufactured Goods These are items—such as steel, glass, and lumber—that are one industry's end product and another's basic manufacturing material. Compared with raw material prices, semimanufactured good prices are relatively stable, so their purchase is more routine. Since most producers of semimanufactured goods are large companies, they sell direct to large industrial users. Where semimanufactured goods are also sold to numerous small industrial users, marketing channels contain one or more levels of middlemen.

Fabricating Parts These are manufactured goods which, without any substantial change in form, are incorporated into or assembled into a more complex and finished product. Storage batteries, spark plugs, and tires for an automobile are examples. Industrial users buy fabricating parts, made to their own specifications, directly from the manufacturers. Single sales contracts are negotiated for periods of several months to a year, and the relationship between seller and buyer is generally a long-term one. These negotiations are directed by high executives of both buying and selling companies.

PRODUCTION SUPPLIES

These products are essential to industrial users' business operations but do not become part of finished products. Included are such items as fuel oil, coal, sweeping compound, and wiping cloths. Purchase of production supplies is a routine responsibility of industrial users' purchasing executives, and they usually buy them through middlemen rather than directly from makers. But when an item is used in large quantities, as a public utility uses coal in steam-plant generation of electricity, long-term purchase contracts, similar to those used in buying fabricating parts, are directly negotiated by top-ranking executives of buying and selling firms.

MANAGEMENT MATERIALS

This category covers office equipment and supplies. Pieces of office equipment of high value, such as electronic computers and data processing systems, are usually leased rather than bought outright but, in either case, decisions are reached in essentially the same way as those on production installations. Purchase or lease of major office equipment items involves substantial sums; hence, decisions require approval of both top management and the department head concerned, and the purchasing department merely handles the needed paper work.

Typewriters, desk calculators, and similar pieces of equipment are bought by the purchasing department as needed, on requisitions originating in the using departments, often with brands and models being determined by preferences of typists and clerks. Pencil sharpeners, staplers, and other low-unit value articles of office equipment—as well as such office supplies as stationery and typewriter ribbons—are bought routinely, the purchasing department taking the initiative in ordering and generally carrying a stock on hand.

Product Life Cycles

All products, like people, have a certain length of life during which they pass through certain identifiable stages. From the time a product idea is conceived, during its development and up to its market introduction, a product is in various prenatal stages (i.e., it is going through various product development phases). Its life begins with its market introduction, it then goes through a period during which its market grows rapidly, eventually it reaches market maturity, afterwards its market declines, and finally its life ends.

Figure 8–1 is a visualization of a product life cycle for an industry (i.e., firms marketing directly competing items). Three curves are shown: (1) total market sales (this is the "industry product life cycle"), (2) total market profit (notice how this declines while sales are still rising, and (3) the relative number of competitors (notice how this continues to go up for a time after profits have turned down).

The exact path traced by the product life cycle varies. For some, like the "hula hoop," the product proves a fad and has a short life cycle, perhaps only a month or so. For others, such as plumbing fixtures, life cycles span decades. In between are most products with life cycles ranging from a few months (e.g., fashion apparel) to several years (e.g., washing machines and home freezers). All products are at some stage in their life cycles at any particular moment in time.

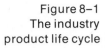

Figure 8–1
The industry product life cycle

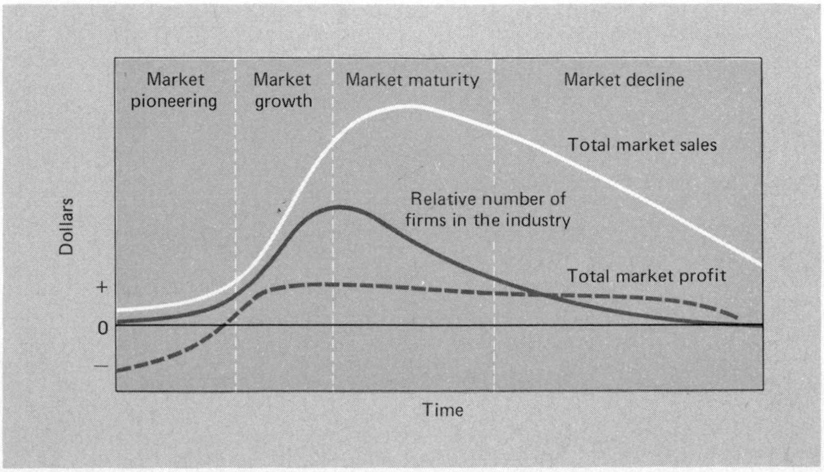

Life cycle curves also exist for each company's individual products. Figure 8–2 shows a life cycle curve for a product's sales by the company doing the innovating. During the market pioneering stage of the industry product life cycle, one company—the innovator—may be the whole industry. But, by the "market growth" stage, the innovator shares the market with several competitors. Only coincidentally does the shape of an individual company's product life cycle resemble that of the entire industry, since after the market pioneering stage the industry cycle is a composite of several companies' experiences. Furthermore, managerial action can cause a particular company's product life cycle to vary from that of the typical company in the industry—for example, management may drop a product at any time, thus terminating its life cycle insofar as that company is concerned. The product life cycle concept can be a major factor in successful and profitable product management, from new product introduction to old product disposal.[2]

MARKET PIONEERING

The market pioneering stage is one of heavy promotion, of securing initial distribution, and of identifying and eliminating product weaknesses. Insofar as possible, marketing channels are kept adequately stocked with the product. But, if the product is destined for success, the innovator generally finds in this stage that demand exceeds what it can bring to market.

MARKET GROWTH

During the market growth stage, competition increases rapidly, and manufacturing and distribution efficiency are important keys to

[2] For an excellent discussion, complete with several illustrations, on the use of the product life cycle in marketing strategy planning, see John E. Smallwood, "The Product Life Cycle: A Key to Strategic Marketing Planning," *MSU Business Topics*, Winter 1973, pp. 29–35.

Figure 8–2
Product life cycle—innovating company

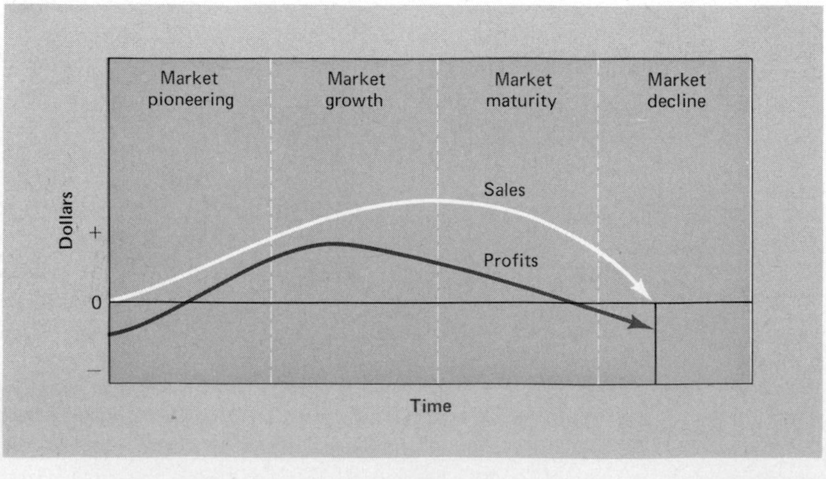

marketing success. Competing firms use selective demand advertising, each emphasizing its own brand's advantages. At first, personal selling is directed toward getting new outlets and keeping them stocked but later shifts to selling against the competition. Ultimately, competition becomes severe enough that if buyers cannot easily find favored brands they can readily be persuaded to accept substitutes.

MARKET MATURITY

During the market maturity stage, stiffening competition forces profits lower: prices come down and marketing expenditures rise. Sales continue to increase for a while but at a decreasing rate, eventually leveling off with market saturation. Supply exceeds demand for the first time, making demand stimulation essential, and competitors heavily promote their brands, emphasizing subtle differences. Because of the squeeze on profits and growing similarity of competing brands, dealer support becomes increasingly critical while most dealers now refuse to stock more than a few brands. During later phases of this stage for durable goods, replacement sales dominate the market. Industry sales tend to stabilize, causing the competitive structure to solidify.

The duration of the market maturity stage varies for different kinds of products. While the product life cycle shown in Figure 8–1 indicates that sales generally drop off right after the market saturation point, this is not always what happens. Actually, in the cases of some convenience goods which consumers buy frequently and rapidly consume (nondurables), total market sales may level out, stabilizing there for several months or even years. Or, total market sales may slowly rise, reflecting perhaps the growth rate of the total population, as illustrated in Figure 8–3, which is a visualization of the life cycles typical of various broad categories of breakfast cereals and hand soaps.

Products characterized by long consumption lives after purchase (i.e., durable goods) have still a different type of life cycle curve. Shortly after passing through the market growth stage, the life

Figure 8–3
Industry product life cycle for product quickly consumed and repurchased

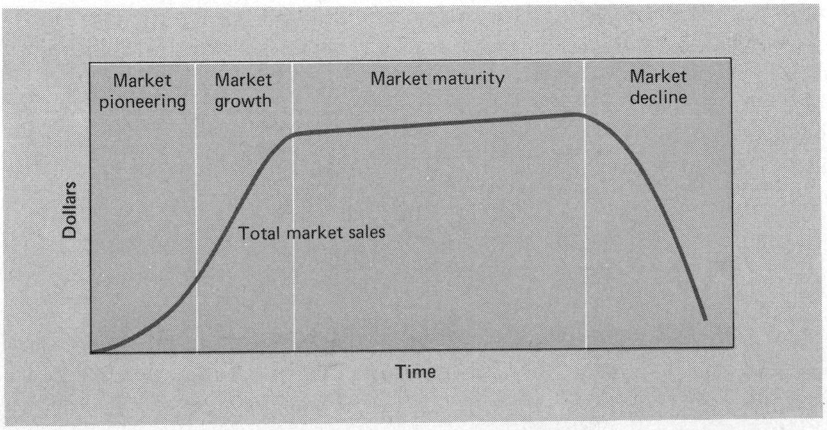

cycle for such products reaches a temporary market saturation point when everyone who would likely buy has already bought, and total market sales rapidly fall off for a while. But, as units of the product in the possession of consumers begin to wear out and people start buying replacements, total market sales again stabilize, perhaps staying at that lower level for a long period or even resuming a slow rate of growth. Figure 8–4 illustrates this type of product life cycle, typical, for example, of appliances such as refrigerators or dishwashers. Notice that the market decline stage for this type of product starts only after market sales begin to fall off permanently.

MARKET DECLINE

The market decline stage is characterized by either the product's gradual displacement by some new innovation or by an evolving change in consumer buying behavior. Industry sales drop off and the number of competitors shrinks. With production overcapacity, price becomes the main competitive weapon, and drastic reductions occur in advertising and other promotional expenditures. Under these conditions, most managements shift their attention to other products, gradually phasing out the declining product as its outlook grows increasingly bleak.

Product Innovation

Throughout modern industry, product innovation receives increasing emphasis and attention. The underlying reason is that markets are highly dynamic. What was a profitable product yesterday may not be tomorrow. Furthermore, successful new products command substantially higher profit margins than mature or declining products. Successful new products are profitable—at least for a while—mainly because it takes time for competitors to come up with their

Figure 8–4 Industry product life cycle for a durable consumer good

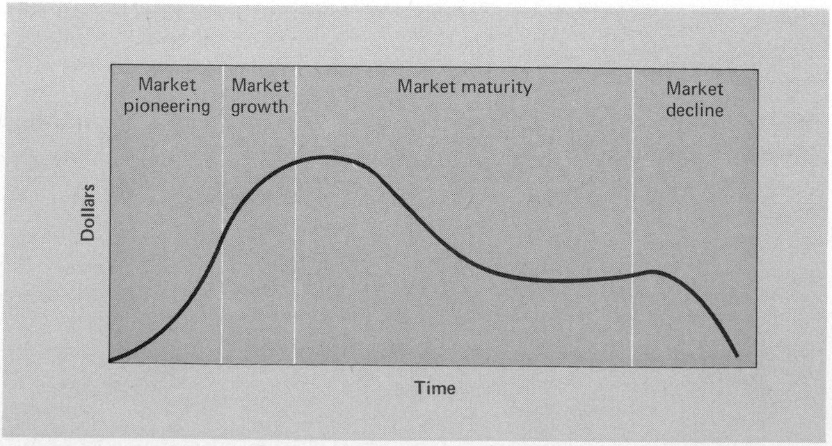

own versions, enter the market, and eventually compete on a price basis.

Most companies face the inevitable choice of product innovation and improvement or of gradually fading from the market. Most wagon and buggy manufacturers saw their market disappear as the automobile replaced the horse. Yet Studebaker, a wagon maker, recognized the need for change and successfully shifted to auto manufacturing and, much later, finding itself no longer able to compete profitably in the automobile market, moved into other product fields.

NEED FOR PRODUCT OBJECTIVES

Product Objectives

A company advances toward its overall objectives mainly through achieving acceptance of its products in the marketplace. Therefore, product objectives, derived directly from the company objectives, give direction to product innovation. They summarize the characteristics products should have in order that the company will actually be in the business it wants to be in. Yet, at the same time, they should not be so narrow or restrictive as to prevent adjustment to changes in the market. Product objectives, of course, apply to all products, both new and old, regardless of stage in the product life cycle.

Relation to the Marketing Concept

Under the marketing concept, a company's product objectives are oriented toward the customers and their wants. They state explicitly that the company is engaged in servicing certain needs of specific types of customers. For example, one product objective reads, "To develop, manufacture, and market products meeting the heating and cooling needs of industrial and commercial establishments of all sizes." With this objective, note carefully, the company does not limit itself to specific products; rather, it limits its market to given types of customers with particular needs. As the market and its needs change, the company adjusts its products accordingly. Actually, of course, most firms are somewhat constrained in their choice of products by their capabilities in research and development, manufacturing, and marketing. However, unused capabilities may lead to development of products that may or may not be compatible with present markets.

For each major company objective, there should be a parallel product objective. Furthermore,.all product objectives should be consistent with other components of marketing strategy—marketing channels and distribution, promotion, and price. When either company objectives or marketing strategy change, product objectives require reappraisal.

NEED FOR PRODUCT POLICIES

Product Policies

Product policies are the general rules management sets up to guide itself in making product decisions. They should derive directly from, and be wholly consistent with, product objectives. If a product objective, for example, states that "this company desires to make and market products requiring only a minimum of service after their purchase by consumers," then a product policy (or policies) is needed to spell out how this objective will be attained. Generally, product policies take the form of a series either of short definitions or of questions arranged as a check list.

PLANNING NEW PRODUCTS

While the details of new product planning vary with the company, generally they cover three major phases.

New Product Ideas

Phase one involves creation of new product ideas. The planners evaluate the extent and importance of identified market needs (determined perhaps through marketing research and analysis of buyer behavior) and appraise the extent to which present products fulfill them. They also evaluate the company's capabilities with respect to scientific knowledge and technological skills in terms of possible new products.

Product Idea Evaluation

Phase two focuses on more thoroughly investigating the competitive market situation and company resources with respect to each product idea developed in Phase one. Market research is critical during this phase since market potentials and competitive marketing methods can reveal, among other things, the size and type of marketing organization required. Analysis of company resources indicates the adequacy of plant capacity, product service facilities, marketing channels, engineering abilities, and other human resources. This phase ends with selection among alternative product candidates, based on comparisons of each against specific product objectives, such as relative profitability, target market segment, and opportunity to attain product leadership.

New Product Development

Phase three relates to actual development of the new product. A program is put together for management and execution of the development project. This includes, among other aspects, an overall plan for the product's eventual marketing.

Summary

Discussion in this chapter has focused on the product's critical roles in marketing, since all businesses that have something to sell sell a product of some sort. We have analyzed different kinds of products—emphasizing mainly the way in which buyers' attitudes, behavioral patterns, and buying procedures vary from one product category to another. We have also explored the product life cycle concept, indicating that products, like people, have a certain length of "marketing life," during which they pass through various identifiable stages, the cycle's nature varying somewhat for different kinds of products. Recognition of the existence of product life cycles underscores the need that marketers have for continuous programs of product innovation, thus providing replacements for dying products as well as opportunities for business growth.

QUESTIONS AND PROBLEMS

1. Describe the nature of the products sold by each of the following businesses: a commercial bank, an automobile insurance company, an architectural firm, a management consulting organization, a news magazine such as *Newsweek* or *Time*.
2. What is the main basis used for distinguishing between a consumers' good and an industrial good? Why is the distinction important?
3. Fully evaluate the "traditional" system for classifying consumers' goods.
4. Explain how cigarettes might be bought as convenience goods, as shopping goods, and as specialty goods by different consumers. Does this lack of uniformity in the classification of goods destroy the usefulness of classifying? Explain.
5. Would you recommend using the same kind of salesman to sell installations as to sell minor equipment? Why or why not? Describe a typical sales presentation for each kind of product.
6. How might the buying procedures differ for a steel fabricating plant buying sheet steel and a shoe manufacturer buying processed hides? In which company would the buying responsibility probably be more important? How would the marketing programs of a company selling sheet steel and a seller of processed hides differ?
7. The marketer of a fabricating part, such as automobile tires, often sells both to the OEM (original equipment market) and to the replacement market. Does such a marketer really sell the same product to both markets? Explain.
8. Compare the behavior of industrial users in buying production supplies with their behavior in buying each of the two main types of management materials.
9. How do you account for the fact that the rate of product change (i.e., the speed of product innovation) varies so much from industry to industry? Why has it taken longer to approach market saturation with sewing machines than with television sets?

10. What is the difference between a commodity and a product? Give some examples of products that may be in danger of becoming commodities.
11. Explain how fashion accelerates the speed with which markets change.
12. Give some examples of changes in technology which (1) broadened the market for an old product; (2) brought into existence an entirely new market.
13. To what extent does product innovation provide an escape from price competition?
14. What is the purpose of a product objective? Of a product policy? How do they differ?
15. Refer to Chapter 5 on the marketing organization. Visualize a particular company serving a specific market and show how each company objective (that has marketing significance) could be the source of one or more product objectives.
16. Is it possible for a new product to be too new? Would this hold for all market segments? Support your position fully.
17. How can a company tell what bases of competition to expect for a new product?
18. Give some examples of products you regard as being in the market pioneering stage of their life cycles.
19. In what respects does an industry product life cycle differ from the life cycles for the individual products of competitors in the industry?
20. Name some products that are in the market decline stage. Do you believe the decline is irreversible? If you believe the decline is only temporary, what action would you recommend for rejuvenation?
21. Appraise the product life cycle concept relative to its use in forward planning.

CASE PROBLEM

The Martin Plastics Company, a medium-sized plastics fabricator, had been quite successful in a very competitive industry. While the company was not known for its emphasis on new products, preferring instead to concentrate on a relatively few plastics products, it did enjoy a good reputation as a quality manufacturer. Competitive pressures were such, however, that it was apparent that Martin Plastics would have to develop some new products in order to maintain its position in the industry.

Previously, Martin Plastics had confined its operations to producing special packages for grocery and drug manufacturers, parts (such as handles) for makers of small appliances, and small components for computer makers.

In an effort to put more emphasis on new products, Mr. David Martin, company president, hired Mr. Thomas Caragliano to head the newly formed New Product Planning Division of the firm. One of Mr. Caragliano's first responsibilities was to submit to the new product screening committee a proposal for new products which might be considered as additions to the existing product line.

Assume you are Mr. Caragliano, the head of product research and development for Martin Plastics Company. Prepare a list of possible sources of new product ideas and rate them, giving reasons for each evaluation.

When you have mastered the contents of this chapter, you should be able to:

1. Draw a grid illustrating the nine different product-market strategies aimed at improving a company's profitability.
2. Explain the meanings of: product design simplification, greater integration, and reverse integration.
3. Identify the chief forms of remerchandising.
4. Discuss the factors management should consider in deciding to use: (a) family brands or individual brands, (b) multiple brands for identical items, (c) private branding.
5. Explain how a marketer should go about searching for new users and new uses.
6. Describe the three versions of the "product change—no market change" strategy.
7. Explain how a product customization strategy differs from a product systems strategy.
8. Differentiate trading up from trading down.
9. Outline the conditions under which a product replacement strategy is appropriate.
10. Explain the meanings of: product line extension, diversification into related product lines, and product mix diversification.

CHAPTER 9

PRODUCT-MARKET STRATEGIES

Highly significant interacting relationships exist between products and their markets. Every product is aimed at some market, and its marketing success depends importantly on its "fit" with that market. Most companies are in business to make profits. They accomplish this through utilizing marketing's skills in matching products with markets and in effecting ownership transfers. In this chapter, we consider how companies use different product-market strategies in attempts to improve their profitability.

There are two main ways to increase a company's profits: (1) through increasing its sales volume, and (2) through reducing its costs. Newly organized firms generally seek to increase profits through growth in sales. As a company grows—or as its size tends to stabilize—its management devotes increasing attention to the search for greater profits, not only through further sales growth but also through improving marketing effectiveness and reducing costs. Therefore, management must continually strive to improve the effectiveness and profitability of its product policies and strategies and, as uncertain economic conditions prevail, new complexities account for higher risks in product management and strategy.[1]

Figure 9–1 shows different combinations of product-market strategies that a company might use to improve its profitability. Notice that each product strategy is associated with some market strategy and that each has important implications for the other. Dis-

[1] Thomas A. Staudt, "Higher Management Risks in Product Strategy," *Journal of Marketing*, January 1973, p. 4.

cussion in this chapter focuses on interactions of each product strategy with each market strategy, a total of nine different combinations. As you study this chapter, it is helpful to refer frequently to this figure.

No Product Change—No Market Change

This is the least complex product-market strategy. There are two main versions: (1) simplifying the product's design, and (2) altering the amount of integration in the product's manufacturing and/or marketing. Both seek to improve profitability mainly through cost reduction, and both involve selling essentially the same product to the same market.

PRODUCT DESIGN SIMPLIFICATION

Product Design Simplification

Simplifying a product's design may lower its manufacturing costs, thus contributing to greater profits. *Product design simplification,* strictly speaking, does not improve the product (from the user's standpoint) but makes the product simpler and cheaper to make. If a design simplification effort results in an improved design in the eyes of prospective buyers, then, of course, the product is no longer the same but now reflects product change in such terms as being easier to maintain or performing better. Improved designs, in other words, become easier to sell, while simplified designs remain unchanged both as to basic product features and salability.

Product Features Among the most important product features is product size. The chief consideration in determining product size is consumer need. Thus, when aspirin was first put on the market, tablet size was based on normal dosages, minimum dosages, and a size small enough to achieve these dosages with multiples of a single tablet. Furthermore, each basis of market segmentation may affect size requirements: for example, when baby aspirin was introduced (to reach that age market segment), marketers offered a smaller size of tablet.

Size range and variation are also affected by inventory costs and stockturn, both for middlemen and for the manufacturer. This is especially evident with products such as clothing, where the range of possible sizes is very large. Although consumers' needs may dictate a large range of sizes, the costs of maintaining inventories and the low stockturn of the more extreme sizes may make it advisable to restrict the offering to sizes in the middle range.

In industries where standardized product size specifications have been established, most firms find it advantageous to adhere to the standards because of the favorable effects on consumers and mid-

Figure 9–1
Grid of possible combinations of product-market strategies to improve profitability

Market strategy / Product strategy	No product change	Product change	New product
No market change	Design simplification . . . . Greater integration – marketing, production, etc. – or "reverse integration"	Product line simplification and product discontinuance . . . . New models . . . . Planned obsolescence	Replacement of old product
Improved market	Remerchandising (e.g., branding change, change in guarantee, change in service policy, packaging change, etc.	Product customization . . . . Product systems	Product-line extension . . . . Diversification (related fields)
New market	New uses . . . . New users	Market extension (e.g., trading-up or trading-down)	Product-mix diversification (unrelated fields)

dlemen. The consumer's buying job and the middleman's buying and selling jobs are both simplified if they know, for example, that all size 10 men's socks are exactly the same and need not be measured or tried on. Against these favorable effects must be weighed the possible disadvantages of reduced product differentiation and increased substitutability of competitive products.

Other product features—such as basic weights and measures, performance requirements, and chemical or technical properties—are determined in essentially the same manner as size. Each decision results from an evaluation of consumer needs, the effect on middlemen, comparative costs, and industry practice.

GREATER INTEGRATION OR REVERSE INTEGRATION

Greater Integration

Sometimes it is possible to reduce the costs (thereby increasing profits) of making and/or marketing a product through *greater integration* (i.e., by adding functions formerly purchased from others). An appliance manufacturer, for example, that formerly purchased plastic handles and other plastic components established its own plastic manufacturing operation, thus reducing manufacturing costs. Another manufacturer reduced its marketing costs by switching from distribution through wholesalers to direct distribution to retailers.

Reverse Integration

In other situations, costs are reducible through *reverse integration* (i.e., by purchasing functions from others that were formerly performed by the company). Thus, a supermarket chain discontinued its integrated bakery operation and contracted with a large commercial baker for its requirements, thereby reducing the costs of supplying its stores with bakery products. And a large grocery products manufacturer cut its marketing costs by switching from direct distribution to retailers to an indirect system utilizing specialty wholesalers.

Decisions to change the degree of integration of manufacturing and/or marketing operations require thorough analyses of numerous factors. Among these are the relative costs, probable future sales, impact on product quality, the importance of secrecy, availability of needed resources and skills, and the likely reactions of middlemen and final buyers. Alternative courses of action should be carefully evaluated, in other words, for their effects on all aspects of the business. Whenever the potential gains from capturing a bigger slice of the gross margin outweigh the associated disadvantages, greater integration may pay off. However, sometimes costs can be reduced by "farming out" more of the manufacturing and/or marketing operation—thus, reverse integration is also worth considering, but only after evaluating the possible total impact on the business.

No Product Change – Improved Market

Remerchandising

This strategy aims to improve the product's market and profitability by increasing sales to present markets. This process of *remerchandising* is directed toward making the product more salable. Remerchandising, in other words, leaves basic features of the physical product unchanged but makes changes in the accompanying services. The following discussion analyzes the chief forms of remerchandising, proceeding generally from the more elementary to the highly sophisticated forms.

PRODUCT QUALITY

Different kinds of marketers have varying degrees of latitude in determining product quality. Marketers of the products of farms, forests, fisheries, and mines can exert little control over quality, defining it mainly through grading. Even for some manufacturers the limits of quality control are narrow: a chemical company, for example, cannot change basic compounds; it can affect quality only in terms of absences of foreign elements – that is, purity. But for most manufacturers a broad spectrum exists within which management can set and enforce standards over product quality – durability, uniformity, reliability, and similar characteristics.

Effective standardization of product quality provides the consistency and predictability in product performance so essential to building consumer brand preference. Buyers have a right to expect that all units of a product under a particular brand name will be alike. Consistency and predictability in product performance mean that more buyers who try the brand, if satisfied, will become steady customers. This indicates, then, that a manufacturer should assess market needs and preferences before it sets quality standards for its product. Generally, effective standardization of product quality is also a prerequisite to the profitable use of branding.

PRODUCT SERVICE

For many industrial products, service policies are indispensable; for some consumer products, they are important elements in marketing programs. For complex industrial products, such as computers, it is necessary to provide not only installation and repair services but, in most cases, training for customers' personnel. In fact, in industrial markets, product service is often the most critical factor that a buyer uses in selecting a vendor. For many products, though, especially consumer items, the need for service is not so clear-cut. Nevertheless, if an item is a consumer durable or semidurable with a comparatively high price and a relatively low purchase frequency, it may be difficult to consummate sales unless the manufacturer or dealer, or both, provide service.

Manufacturers, however, sometimes overestimate the importance of offering certain services. Appliance makers, for example, at first were reluctant to sell through discount houses, mainly because these retailers did not provide repair and installation services. When these manufacturers learned, to their surprise, that many consumers were willing and able to handle both installation and servicing, their opposition to discount house distribution faded. The decision on what product services to offer customers should flow from an appraisal of their needs and expectations.

Appropriate service policies and practices not only facilitate initial sales but also help in keeping products sold, stimulating repeat sales, and building customer goodwill. There is no place in a marketing program for policies that fail to accomplish these aims. Each product service offered (e.g., product installation, advice on operation, maintenance, and repair) should be evaluated against two criteria: the extent to which it accomplishes desired merchandising aims and whether it contributes to net profit.

PRODUCT GUARANTEES

Guarantees, express or implied, are promises made by a seller to buyers assuring them that they will receive certain services or satisfactions. Thus, a guarantee is part of the bundle of satisfactions a buyer receives when buying a product. The manufacturer expects its guarantee to serve one of two purposes: (1) to protect against abuses of the service policy, or (2) to provide an additional promotional element for selling against the competition. For remerchandising, the promotional guarantee is of the most interest; and, in evaluating a proposed promotional guarantee, management should consider both the benefits and the costs. If the estimated increases in sales are greater than the added costs involved, a promotional guarantee increases net profits. Promotional guarantees are most effective in stimulating sales when:

Protective Guarantees

Promotional Guarantees

1. The product has a high retail price, and prospective buyers want assurance that it will perform as represented.
2. The product has a long useful life, and prospective buyers are concerned about the risk of product failure.
3. Buyers visualize the product as complex and costly to repair.
4. The product is not well known, and consumers need assurance to help them overcome uncertainty about it.[2]

PACKAGING

Packaging

Packaging changes are often key elements in remerchandising. There are many reasons for packaging a product—to protect it, to dif-

[2] J. G. Udell and E. E. Anderson, "The Product Warranty as an Element of Competitive Strategy," *Journal of Marketing*, October 1968, p. 7.

ferentiate and identify it, to make it more salable, to allow greater ease in handling, to give greater convenience in use, or to provide information which helps the consumer make a purchase decision. Coal needs no protection against damage from the elements and handling, whereas photographic film needs protection from exposure to light; these are extremes, but the need for protective packaging of almost any product is usually just as clear.

If a product is packaged for brand differentiation and identification, it should remain packaged until purchased by the final buyer. Bulk packaging, removable before the final buyer buys, is for protection or handling convenience. Five-pound bags of sugar, for example, reach the supermarket inside a large paper bag—the small bags are for brand differentiation and identification, the large bag for protection and handling convenience.

When the brand name can be placed directly on the product, as with appliances, packaging for brand identification is not needed. But, if a product is hard to differentiate, as with nails, packaging may be the only way to differentiate it and secure, perhaps, some brand identification. For most consumer products, however, packaging is the main way to identify the brand at the point of purchase. The package, like a promotional display, relates the product to the producer's advertising and makes consumers aware of its availability in retail outlets. Beyond this, marketing executives expect the package to furnish consumers with needed product information and to provide the extra push so often required to propel consumers into buying.

Package Design When packaging is primarily protective, design decisions are technical and involve comparative strengths, costs of materials, and shapes. When a package is primarily a promotional device, its elements must attract consumers' attention, hold their interest, and build their desire to buy. Package color, size, and shape are all important promotionally so decisions on these elements should reflect the target market segment's preferences. With more and more products being sold through self-service outlets, the promotional aspect of package design becomes increasingly important, since in these stores the package carries the promotional burden it formerly shared with sales clerks. So much promotional emphasis, in fact, is placed upon the package that it is often referred to as the "silent salesman."

Package design must also consider convenience in product handling by both middlemen and consumers. The shape should permit easy display on retail store fixtures. It should make it easy for the consumer to take the product home and to store it. In addition, package design must permit convenience in use and reuse.

Package Size The package-size decision evolves from appraisals of several factors but the most important are the consuming unit and the rate of consumption. Cigarettes, candy bars, and toothbrushes are consumed by individuals and are packaged in units for individual rather than group consumption. Cake mixes and gelatin desserts are consumed by household or family units and are packaged for group consumption. Dry breakfast cereals are packaged both ways: in family boxes and individual-serving packs.

Findings on the consumption unit and rate of consumption sometimes have to be modified when custom or habit strongly influences package size. For example, the housewife is so used to buying margarine in one-pound (453.6 grams) units that it would be difficult to change to an unrelated unit, such as the pint or quart. She has learned to compare prices and to measure recipes on the basis of pounds and ounces of margarine and would resist buying in an unrelated unit of measure.

Package size sometimes affects total consumption. When consumers have plentiful supplies of a product on hand, they may consume more than if they have to make special buying trips to obtain it. The six-pack carton for soft drinks has demonstrated the success of this approach. So important is the package-size/consumption-rate relationship that a major base for market segmentation is that of product usage which, of course, has special meaning for package size. For example, it is often useful to segment markets on the basis of heavy, moderate, or light user characteristics, and to develop package sizes accordingly.

Package Cost The protection needed to deliver the item to the user in good condition determines the package's minimum cost, but consumer preference and convenience often make it advisable to exceed this minimum. A metal container may be less expensive but, because of strong consumer preference, the marketer may use a glass container for certain products, such as jellies. Likewise, a reclosable package, although more expensive than a throwaway, allows the customer to store the product easily until it is entirely consumed without having to transfer it to another container. Each such addition to the minimum cost should be justifiable in terms of its beneficial effect upon demand.

When a package is aimed at achieving brand identification or other promotional goals, its cost is usually higher than if it is solely for product protection. Nevertheless, most marketers of consumer items expect their packages to help in promotion and see cost differences as worthwhile. At a bare minimum, the package must carry the brand name, the marketer's name, a description of the contents, and other descriptive material (e.g., how to use the product). Once the cost of designing an attractive promotional label has been amortized, the cost per package may be no more than that of a purely protective-type container.

As the discussion has indicated, packaging must perform different functions and must meet diverse requirements. More specifically, the same consumer package must perform different functions and satisfy varied requirements and must do so in different environments. Whenever a single element has so many functions to perform and demands to meet, the possibility of conflict emerges. So it is with packaging. To construct a package which satisfies everyone who comes into contact with it is a most difficult task. Consider the following, said many years ago, but very true today:

> All packages have the opportunity to perform, at least partially, each of these functions. But it is the unusual package that performs each to the same degree. That the package gives superior performance of one function does not necessarily mean that it will give a superior performance of another. Because he needs to choose a package, the packager, whether he recognizes it or not, must assign priorities to the value of each of these functions to further his product's sale and use.[3]

The marketer must recognize the potential conflicts among package functions and resolve them in a way which provides both consumer satisfaction and profits. For example, consider the product protection and salability functions. Thin plastic film is used to package apples, since consumers like to see what they are buying (salability). A package made of cardboard, while more protective, would prohibit or make more difficult visual inspection of the apples. Hence, a compromise is struck in the form of the thin plastic film which provides both salability and protection, although each function is performed adequately, rather than to its fullest degree.

BRANDING

Branding

The relative significance of *branding* as a means for enhancing a product's salability varies with the product and company. The truck farmer raising fresh peas competes for sales almost solely on a price basis, since buyers neither know nor care who grew the peas they buy. Yet the food processor, canning or freezing the same peas, can build consumer preference for its brand through differentiating and promoting it, convincing buyers of its superiority.

Brand Identification

Branding's function is to bridge the gap between the manufacturer's promotional program and consummation of sales to final buyers. Brand identification, then, is essential for the firm wanting to differentiate its product, giving the company some degree of control over the product's resale by middlemen, and at the same time enhancing promotional effectiveness. Through brand identification, a company prepares itself to compete on a nonprice basis.

Brand Differentiation

Some products lend themselves less readily to brand differentiation than others. Many products of farms, fisheries, forests, and mines are difficult to differentiate because of their unprocessed form

[3] William R. Mason, "A Theory of Packaging in the Marketing Mix," *Business Horizons,* Summer 1958, p. 92.

but, even here, brand identification coupled with imaginative packaging and promotion frequently achieves some product differentiation, thus insulating the marketer from the full force of price competition. Swift and Company, for instance, achieved this with its "Premium Butterball Turkeys." Product differentiation through brand identification and promotion is easier to obtain for consumer than for industrial products; highly standardized industrial items, such as sheet steel, can be identified by brand name but appear impossible to differentiate effectively.

The branding decision is especially important for products where the potential effectiveness of brand identification to secure product differentiation is unclear. A few years ago, for instance, experts contended that branding women's dresses was of minimal value because women bought according to criteria unrelated to brand—such as color, design, styling, and fit. Today the dress industry not only uses brand names but promotes them heavily. Manufacturers learned, among other things, that variations in women's sizes and shapes, not provided for by differences in standard dress sizes, provided opportunities for real product differentiation and profitable branding. Brand identification has the highest potential payoff where it is possible to differentiate the product effectively in terms of features consumers consider important. But it also has payoff potentials where present products have features shoppers look for—brand identification reduces the searching time shoppers have to spend in finding products with the desired features.

Family Brands Versus Individual Brands When a company sells more than one product it must decide whether to sell each under a separate brand or to use a family brand. Many situations exist where greater returns can be realized through making one choice rather than the other. Such decisions require evaluation of three factors: nature of the product line, promotional policy, and desired market penetration.

Family Branding

The nature of the product line is the most important. Similar products naturally related in consumers' minds, such as sheets and towels, benefit particularly from family branding. Favorable reaction to one item often leads buyers to buy others in the line. But this halo effect can also detract from a marketer's reputation, if unfavorable experiences with one item turns consumers against the entire line. Particular care must be taken that all items carrying the family brand conform to consumers' standards of acceptance.

Individual Branding

Products lacking common marketing attributes are usually best marketed under individual names, since little benefit comes from jointly associating them. There may even be adverse sales reactions from family branding; for example, associating a food item with a soap product may handicap sales of the food since many consumers associate soap with an unpleasant taste.

All products do not lend themselves to sale under a family

brand. The quality of family-brand products should be very nearly similar so that no single item in the line can lower the quality reputation of others. The products should also be fairly compatible: A housewife may prefer a particular brand of soap, but she will probably not be at all interested in a new perfume carrying the same name because she is not convinced that experience in soap making will carry over to perfume making. However, some perfume manufacturers have been successful in selling soap under their labels, because of the use of similar scents coupled with skillful promotion. The products should also be sold to the same markets: little is gained from applying a family brand to one item sold to industrial users and to a second sold to ultimate consumers.

Promotional Policy and Branding

Promotional policy is important because using a family brand, rather than individual brands, usually makes possible a smaller total promotional budget. Under a family brand, much promotion can be directed toward the entire line, and even promotion emphasizing a single item tends to increase recognition and demand for the entire line. With individual brands, separate and often duplicating promotional efforts are required. Thus, a family-brand policy permits the most effective use of limited promotional funds for similar products, yet family-brand promotional programs restrict opportunities for emphasizing individual differences in items.

Desired Market Penetration

The desired market penetration is important, because individual items in a product line face varying degrees of competition. A maker of kitchen and laundry appliances, for example, may meet only mild competition on dishwashers and electric ranges, but a competitor may make only washing machines and, through aggressive promotion, may have captured a large market share and be extremely difficult to displace. In such instances, where the same degree of market penetration is not possible for all items in the line, individual branding allows greater promotional flexibility. Items facing the strongest competition may be given larger shares of the promotional budget so that optimum market penetration can be achieved for each item in the line. This makes it easier to draw buyers' attention to changes and improvements in particular items. Individual branding also allows a producer to achieve greater market penetration by marketing similar but differentiated products appealing to different market segments.

Multiple Branding

Multiple Brands for Identical Items Makers of specialty goods often sell through a limited number of selected retail outlets to gain their dealers' cooperation in aggressively promoting the products. This has the effect of limiting the total sales potential because in any one market no single retailer or small group of retailers is normally in a position to attract all potential buyers. In such cases, market penetration may be increased by offering identical merchandise under a different brand name to a second group of selected retailers.

Frequently, mergers result in the use of multiple brands. The decision to retain the separate brands or to change to a single brand may depend on whether the different brands have developed dissimilar images that appeal to different market segments or on whether they have developed strength in different regional markets with well-known names that management is reluctant to abandon.

Private Branding

Private Branding Private brands are those owned and controlled by middlemen rather than by manufacturers. Both manufacturers and middlemen face policy decisions on private branding. Manufacturers must decide whether to sell their products to middlemen for private branding. And middlemen must decide whether they can benefit from their own brands. The manufacturer's decision on the acceptance of private-brand orders should depend on the probable effect on the sales of its own brand, if it has one. A middleman's decision to promote private brands of its own should be based on the expectation of greater profits and/or greater control over the market.

No Product Change—New Market

This product-market strategy is particularly significant for companies with products already in, or about to enter, the market maturity stage in the life cycle. During this stage, industry sales tend to reach a plateau and then gradually fall off, but some companies explore the possibility of rejuvenating the product's sales and profit growth rates through finding new markets. In searching for new markets for a product that is approaching, or has already reached, the saturation level in its present market, management should consider both (1) possible new users, and (2) possible new uses.

NEW USERS

Search for New Market Segments

The search for possible new users involves finding and evaluating yet untapped market segments. Management should start by reviewing the nature of the product's present market. One maker of crystal glassware, for instance, had for years focused its marketing efforts on the bride-to-be market, but its sales had topped out. After studying the market more closely, management concluded that there were actually three market segments: (1) the bride-to-be, (2) the matron (women who had been unable to afford crystal at the time of marriage but could now), and (3) the "rich aunt" (the affluent relative who buys gifts for brides). Marketing efforts were redirected to tap the new market segments, and company sales and profits resumed their growth.[4]

[4] W. J. Talley, Jr., *The Profitable Product* (Englewood Cliffs, N.J.: Prentice-Hall, Inc., 1965), pp. 93–94.

Management should also evaluate other groups of possible new users. Perhaps the most obvious is the different geographic market segment—that is, potential users outside the present market area. Products at near-saturation levels in industrial market segments sometimes find new markets among ultimate consumers (e.g., small power tools). Products used traditionally by men (e.g., cigarettes) sometimes have been marketed successfully to women, and the reverse has also happened (e.g., hair spray). Products initially aimed at one age group may be redirected to appeal to a different age group (e.g., baby foods for the elderly). Many other possibilities exist, each involving a particular basis for market segmentation.

NEW USES

Detection and exploitation of new uses is a way to stretch a product's life. Fruit and vegetable processors, for instance, were found using small sewage pumps, originally developed for home use, to move items, such as peaches, along special water troughs during processing—thus preventing bruises and other damage.[5] Such unusual applications are difficult to anticipate and sometimes are discovered by accident (e.g., a producer of lighter fluid accidentally found its product being used to remove road film from automobiles). However, management should keep abreast of how its products are being used: salesmen should ask dealers who is buying the product and for what purposes; marketing research should periodically survey buyers for the same reason.

Product Change—No Market Change

The three versions of this strategy are (1) product line simplification and product discontinuance, (2) new models, and (3) planned obsolescence. Strategies involving product line simplification and product discontinuance envision profit increases through cost reductions. Those involving either new models or planned obsolescence seek profit increases through growth in sales volume.

PRODUCT LINE SIMPLIFICATION AND PRODUCT DISCONTINUANCE

Reducing the number of models and/or products in a product line often affords opportunities for increasing profits. Proliferation in a product line frequently traces to efforts to match every item offered by competitors or to satisfy salesmen's and dealers' pleas for more variety. This can develop to the point where the product line con-

[5] Uncommon Markets: Sales Windfalls from Offbeat Product Uses," *Management Review*, November 1962, p. 57.

tains many tired products and models, slow movers draining off working capital and profits.[6]

Product Proliferation

Product proliferation is partially preventable through high selectivity in adding new products and models, but pressures always exist to offer greater variety. Marketing executives, in particular, push for more complete lines and more models, as this helps them to satisfy widely varying market preferences. Production executives fight to keep product lines narrow and the number of models minimal, as this helps them hold manufacturing costs down and simplifies production scheduling.

Under increasingly competitive conditions, market pressures force manufacturers to offer greater and greater product variety; increasing consumer sophistication and increasing market segmentation also contribute to product proliferation. Well-designed procedures for screening new product ideas improve the chances that additions will be profitable but do not insure against product failures. Furthermore, today's successes become tomorrow's failures—products are born, grow, mature, and die, as the product life cycle concept indicates. Market and organizational pressures push in the direction of product proliferation; counterpressures are needed both to control new additions and to weed out tired products and models.

Product Line Simplification

Product line simplification requires continual review of the line and the discontinuation of items not contributing directly (in their own right) or indirectly (e.g., as a repair part) to profits. However, simplification involves more than merely determining present profitability. Sometimes a change in price, promotion, or marketing channels can make a currently unprofitable item profitable. At other times, dealers and customers expect, even demand, a full-line offering, preventing the weeding out of all unprofitable items. Some items, such as repair and replacement parts, may be unprofitable in their own right, yet have selling value and should be retained. Other unprofitable items must be kept in order to sell profitable items (e.g., when buyers regard a group of items as a "product system," as they do razors and blades).

Product Discontinuation

Under some conditions, too, it is desirable to drop a profitable product. Management might discontinue an item, for instance, if the same resources would yield more profit if used in behalf of another item with a brighter future. Likewise, a profitable item might be dropped if it causes salesmen and/or dealers to divert their efforts from still more profitable items. In general, then, any item is a likely candidate for discontinuation if the company does not have the needed resources and/or talents to capitalize fully on its potential profitability.[7]

[6] J. T. Cannon, *Business Strategy and Policy* (New York: Harcourt, Brace & World, 1968), p. 117.

[7] For an excellent discussion and evaluation of various approaches to product abandonment decisions, see Paul W. Hamelman and Edward M. Mazze, "Improving Product Abandonment Decisions," *Journal of Marketing*, April 1972, pp. 20–26.

NEW MODELS

Through introducing new models of old products, management seeks increased profits by stimulating sales volume. New models are not, strictly speaking, new products but rather variations of established products—new sizes, colors, designs, and the like. Management's hope in bringing out a new model generally is that it will come closer to fitting what present buyers really prefer.

Introducing new models is a regular feature of product strategy for many producers, the regularity and frequency of model switching varying among industries and individual firms. Some switch models only when justified by significant product improvements. Others introduce new models on a regular, periodic basis even though changes are superficial. In competing with the American automobile industry, strongly committed to annual model changes, the *Volkswagen* has been marketed successfully under a strategy of changing the model only when technological improvements justify it.

PLANNED OBSOLESCENCE

Product Improvement

Product improvement, whether real or contrived, provides a means for accelerating the rate of obsolescence of products in consumers' possession. This is most important in mature industries whose markets have reached, or are approaching, saturation. In these industries, a manufacturer competes not only with other manufacturers, but with the products all have sold in the past. If a particular competitor depends solely on physical obsolescence, gradual wear, and deterioration, its prospects for sales and profits are limited.

Products in consumers' possession can be made obsolete in two ways: by improving performance characteristics of new models and by altering consumers' concepts of the acceptability of models they already own. The auto industry's introduction of automatic transmissions exemplifies the first type of created obsolescence, and the annual change in auto body style is an example of the second. The term *planned obsolescence* describes both types.

Planned Obsolescence

Planned obsolescence of the second type is highly controversial. Some writers charge that it is economically wasteful,[8] and many business executives call it wasteful and contrary to the country's best interests. Proponents defend it as a necessary support to a high-level economy and point out that the criticisms are based on the moral judgment that a desire for the latest thing is socially bad. Supporters feel that wanting something new and different is socially good. From the consumer's standpoint, creation of obsolescence through real product improvements is generally acceptable, but shifts in stan-

[8] See J. K. Galbraith, *The Affluent Society* (Boston: Houghton-Mifflin Company, 1958), and V. Packard, *The Waste Makers* (New York: D. McKay Co., 1960).

dards of acceptability (as in appearance) are more controversial. Yet fashion, having been part of western culture for centuries, is not the creation of marketers.

Product Change—Improved Market

The two main types of this strategy are (1) product customization and (2) product systems. Both aim to improve profitability through increasing sales volume.

PRODUCT CUSTOMIZATION

Product Customization

Product customization involves tailoring product specifications very closely to buyers' needs in order to make profitable sales to those who would otherwise not buy. The mildest form is to offer a wide choice of models to make it easier for buyers to decide in favor of some model made by the company rather than by its competitors; this form of customization is often used in shopping goods' situations, such as with ladies' shoes or men's shirts. A stronger form of customization involves offering a basic line of standard products but allowing customers to write their own specifications for certain product features; this is common, for example, in marketing grinding wheels to industrial users and in selling custom-designed insurance policies to business buyers. The most extreme product customization occurs in situations where labor looms very large in total production costs, and unusual craftsmanship and scarce technical skills can command premium selling prices. Thus, small firms, such as custom tailors, turn out products more or less meeting customers' exact specifications, while large firms, such as the aerospace companies, turn out items, such as moon vehicles, meeting buyers' specifications within extremely close limits.

PRODUCT SYSTEMS

Product Systems

Product systems strategies seek greater profitability through increasing the utility of products to buyers, thus stimulating sales volume. The automatic washing machine is an example of a product system that combines functions formerly performed by hand and by a washboard, pails, tubs, a scrub brush, a hand wringer, and so on. By combining these functions, it solves more of a household's washing problems than any of the items it replaced and is worth more (i.e., has greater utility) to the household since it also provides greater convenience, eliminates unpleasant tasks, and saves time. Product systems sold to industrial markets, such as the baggage-handling systems used in airports, like those sold to consumer markets, provide added utility to users by relating and automating various necessary tasks formerly performed separately. Generally, too, they provide cost savings and accomplish the entire task more effectively.

Product Change – New Market

This strategy seeks increased profitability through additional sales volume generated by changing certain features of the product and selling it to a new market segment. Very few products wholly satisfy the needs of more than one market segment, so companies often must change certain product features to match them better with the individualized needs of new target market segments. Trading up and trading down are the main forms of this strategy.

TRADING UP AND TRADING DOWN

Both *trading up* and *trading down* involve bringing out changed versions of a product and altering the nature and direction of promotion. Generally, companies trading up or down do one or the other, but not both at the same time.

Trading Up

A company trades up when it adds a higher priced, more prestigious product version with the main goal of increasing sales of a present lower priced version. Thus, while trading up involves cultivating a new market segment, the emphasis is on increasing sales to an old market segment; nevertheless, trading up involves two target market segments – an old one and a new one. Ford Motor Company, for example, introduced the Thunderbird (a prestigious, relatively high-priced car) hoping to increase sales of the lower priced Ford. Thunderbird was promoted separately but in ways that made certain that prospective buyers of lower priced cars would know it was Ford-made. Companies trading up anticipate that a halo effect will carry over from the new prestige item to the older lower priced and less prestigious item.

Trading Down

A company trades down when it adds a lower priced product version in the hope that buyers who would not, or could not, buy a higher priced version will now buy the new version because it carries some of the same prestige. In trading down, then, emphasis is on tapping a new market segment, one not tapped effectively earlier because the original version had too high a price. For example, Ford Motor Company, after successfully trading up with the Thunderbird, saw an opportunity to tap a market segment of "people who would have liked to have a Thunderbird but could not afford it." The traded-down version was the Mustang, a car resembling the Thunderbird but much lower priced, which became an outstanding success.

New Product—No Market Change

This strategy seeks increased profitability through selling a new product to the same market segment, the new product replacing an older product sold for the same general purpose. Thus, product replacement strategy aims at retaining the level of sales now coming from a particular market segment where an older product's sales are being endangered by competitors' new products serving the same uses. Examples of new products that replaced old ones are numerous; a few of them are: automobiles replaced carriages, diesel locomotives replaced steam locomotives, jet planes replaced piston-driven aircraft, the transistor is replacing the vacuum tube, and the ballpoint pen nearly replaced the fountain pen. For companies having products in the market maturity stage, new products should be waiting in the wings, ready for market introduction at the proper times.

New Product—Improved Market

This strategy aims to increase profitability through adding sales volume gained from new products sold to the same market segments. Often the new products are extensions of the present product line; for example, the ready-to-eat cereal added to a line of regular cereals. Sometimes the new products are members of related product lines sold to the same market segments as present products; for example, the pet food added by a marketer of breakfast cereals.

PRODUCT LINE EXTENSION

When final buyers regard several products as a related group or line, management must decide whether to produce a partial or complete line. Consumers, for example, buy both kitchen and laundry appliances in the same retail outlets and sometimes shop for several appliances at the same time. The manufacturer's decision to extend its offerings within a product line should result from evaluation of several factors. It must be financially able to add new items. Management should analyze the likely effect of adding to the line on the profits of existing line members. If management finds that numerous buyers prefer to buy two or more products at the same time (as often happens with matching appliances), a more complete line may increase sales of present products. Similarly, as a company extends its line, each item's marketing costs should be reduced, since little more promotion or selling effort is needed to sell the line than to sell an individual item.

Against these potential gains should be balanced the new

items' probabilities of success. Does the company have the production, engineering, and general management knowhow to develop and produce new products as good as its present products? Management must also evaluate the effect of the proposed additions on the reputations of present products; if buyers consider a new item inferior to those already in the line, the entire line's reputation may suffer.

DIVERSIFICATION INTO RELATED PRODUCT LINES

Companies add related product lines for two main reasons: (1) to capitalize further on company knowhow in serving particular market segments, and (2) to reduce the risk of obsolescence in the present product line. Market segments do not disappear suddenly, but demand for a product line sometimes does.

How far a company should diversify into related product lines depends on various considerations. Will related product diversification reduce unit sales and distribution costs? Can the sales force sell the related line effectively? What promotional expenses are required? Who are the new competitors, what strategies do they employ, and what advantages do they have? Will a beneficial halo effect from the present line carry over to the related line? Can the items in the new line actually be developed, produced at reasonable cost, and differentiated in ways attractive to potential buyers? This type of analysis should permit management to estimate the profitability of adding a related product line.

New Product—New Market

This strategy seeks to increase profitability through greater sales volumes obtained from selling new products in new markets. Thus, it involves product-mix diversification—selling unrelated product lines to entirely different markets. Companies adopt this strategy for reasons such as unexpected research breakthroughs or discoveries of profitable opportunities to develop products for new markets.

This strategy involves considerably greater risk than any other product-market strategy. Both the product and the market are totally new to the company, so proposals for unrelated product diversification merit the most careful investigation. Generally, a company is well advised first to fill out its present line, then diversify into related lines sold to the same markets, and finally (after other profit-increasing possibilities are exhausted) to diversify into new markets with new products.

A final note pertaining to all new product strategies is appropriate. In a competitive economy, in some industries, new product introductions are necessary for a firm's survival. In such cases, there should be a comprehensive method for analysis of the new product introduction program. In addition to the traditional economic criteria (profitability, sales volume, product line compatibility, etc.), the evaluation procedure should include social and environmental factors. Such factors include: environmental and production compatibility, environmental and user compatibility (in use and after use), recycling potential, and social and moral impact.[9]

Summary

Analysis in this chapter has focused on the nine different combinations of product-market strategies and their main forms. Each form of each product-market strategy represents a potential opportunity for improving profitability. Most product-market strategies (all but pure product design simplification, and product line simplification and product discontinuance) seek to increase profitability mainly through increasing sales volume. But achieving increased profits through increased sales involves more than simply deciding on a product-market strategy. As Figure 9–2 shows, the particular product-market

[9] Dale L. Varble, "Social and Environmental Considerations in New Product Development," *Journal of Marketing*, October 1972, pp. 11–15.

Figure 9–2
Product-market strategy and overall marketing strategy

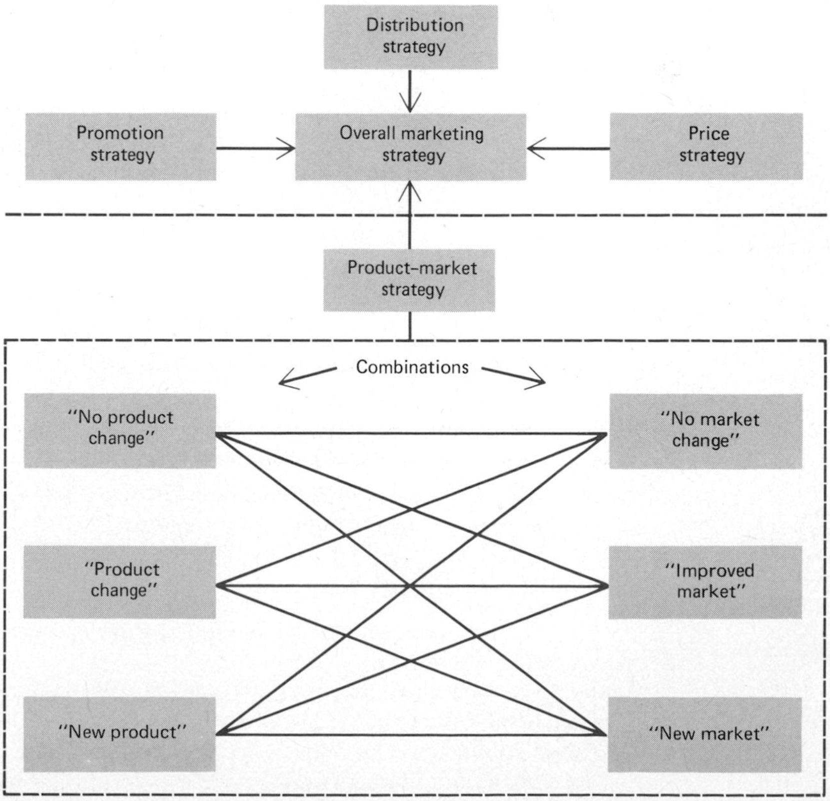

strategy chosen requires integration with appropriate distribution, promotion, and price strategies into an overall marketing strategy. Matching products with markets is essential to marketing, but so is effecting ownership transfers (i.e., making sales). While well-chosen product-market strategies can help in making sales by making a product more salable, to capitalize on potentially profitable product-market opportunities management must also formulate and implement parallel distribution, promotion, and price strategies.

You now have the needed background on the marketing significance of key aspects of product management. From Chapter 8, you have gained understanding of how products vary in their marketing characteristics, how they move through life cycles, and the need marketers have for continuous programs of product innovation. From Chapter 9, you have gained understanding of how companies use different product-market strategies in efforts to improve their profitability. Thus, we are now ready to consider the next major component of overall marketing strategy—distribution.

QUESTIONS AND PROBLEMS

1. Explain: (a) how a newly organized company generally tries to increase its profits; (b) how a longer established company seeks to increase its profitability. In which situation is marketing skill most important? Why?
2. What factors should each of the following organizations consider in determining the sizes in which they should offer their products?
   a. a maker of prefabricated swimming pools for in-ground installation
   b. a perfume manufacturer
   c. a packer of frozen dietary foods
   d. a manufacturer of photographic film
3. Is it possible that industry-wide standardization of certain product features, such as size, may cause the products involved to become commodities?
4. Under what circumstances will increased profitability result from greater integration? From reverse integration?
5. "The make-or-buy decision simply involves determining the cheaper alternative." Agree or disagree? Why?
6. Contrast the make-or-buy decision with that concerning the optimum degree of integration of marketing functions.
7. What are the meaning and marketing significance of each of the following terms?
   a. remerchandising
   b. standardizing
   c. grading

d. customer service
e. guarantee

8. How would you answer the argument that it is to the individual producer's advantage to avoid standardization in the product and its parts so that buyers are forced to return to the producer for repairs and servicing?
9. Comment on the following guarantees with respect to their likely promotional effectiveness:

   For a tape recorder: This is a quality product and fully guaranteed against defective materials and workmanship for a period of 90 days from date of purchase. This guarantee does not cover abuse, neglect, tampering by unauthorized personnel, or damage inadvertently caused by the user.

   For a mattress: We guarantee that the bedding described here will be satisfactory to the original purchaser. If the bedding should be defective due to faulty workmanship or structural defects, during the first year after purchase, we will either replace or rebuild the items involved at our cost. Should the bedding be defective, for the same causes as above, during the 20-year period after purchase, we will, upon payment by purchaser of an adjustment charge for each year or fraction of use, either (a) replace the item involved or (b) rebuild the item involved (excluding exterior covering). Guarantee does not apply to the covering. Guarantee applies only if both mattress and foundation are bought at the same time as a set.

   For a bathroom scale: Should this scale become inaccurate at any time, return it to the Scale Division of the XYZ Corporation (use convenient shipping label attached and enclose this warranty certificate with the scale). Any inaccuracy will be corrected for a minimum packing and handling charge of 50 cents and scale returned parcel post C.O.D. plus postal charges. If scale has been tampered with or subject to abuses (such as dropping on floor), the warranty does not apply. In such cases, a nominal charge will be made for parts replaced in addition to the service fee mentioned above.
10. Can packages be used effectively to differentiate products not otherwise differentiatable? Why or why not?
11. What relationships, if any, exist between packaging decisions and the choice of marketing channels?
12. Would it be sensible to use a rule of thumb that no package is justifiable if it increases the cost of the product by more than 10 percent? Why?
13. Today, canned and frozen foods commonly are put up in standard sizes, but package sizes for detergents and soaps show little standardization. How would soap and detergent makers benefit, and how would they lose from package-size standardization?

14. "The advantages of using a family brand clearly outweigh those of using individual brands on different products." Agree or disagree?
15. Multiple brands for identical products are often used to implement a highly selective distribution policy. Would it be fair to say that this is a compromise that doesn't really benefit anyone – manufacturer, retailer, or consumer?
16. "A contract to make private brands should be at a sufficiently high price that an allocated share of total costs is covered; otherwise, there is no long-range justification for accepting such business." Comment.
17. Which, if any, of the following companies might find it profitable to use branding in combination with consumer advertising?
    a. A maker of prescription drugs
    b. A manufacturer of picture tubes for television receivers
    c. A maker of small gasoline engines used in assembling lawn mowers, snow blowers, and other home lawn care appliances
    d. A producer of fabrics used in apparel manufacturing
18. Which, if any, of the following companies might find it profitable to assist their dealers in financing sales to final buyers?
    a. A producer of small airplanes for sale to private pilots
    b. A manufacturer of mobile homes
    c. A producer of photographic equipment purchased mainly by hobbyists
    d. An appliance maker
19. How would you recommend that each of the following organizations should go about finding new users for their products?
    a. A manufacturer of small, hand-operated paper cutters and hole punchers
    b. A producer of talcum powder for babies
    c. A manufacturer of office furniture
    d. A maker of pots and pans for restaurants and institutions
20. What possible new uses might be found for each of the following products?
    a. pipe cleaners
    b. automatic timing devices for electrical appliances
    c. carpeting
    d. frozen orange juice
21. "A company operating under the marketing concept must let its products proliferate. Otherwise how can it provide all dealers and customers with what they want?" Agree or disagree? State your reasoning fully.
22. "The way to control product proliferation is not to let it happen; kill off most proposed new additions before they are born." How much truth is there in this generalization?

23. Under what conditions should a company consider discontinuing unprofitable products? Profitable products?
24. How can you tell the difference between a new model and a new product? Is it possible that the same item might be regarded as a new model by one company, and as a new product by another? Why or why not?
25. What were the flaws in Henry Ford's reasoning that if you build a basically good product like the Model T, people will continue to buy it? Does the same reasoning apply to the Rolls Royce automobile?
26. What explains Volkswagen's success in departing from U.S. auto industry practice with respect to making annual model changes? Does the Volkswagen actually have planned obsolescence? Explain.
27. To what extent do you believe planned obsolescence is present in each of the following products? State your reasons in each case.
    a. electric razors
    b. men's neckwear
    c. cameras
    d. telephones
    e. jet aircraft
    f. textbooks
28. Under what circumstances might a product customization strategy evolve into product proliferation?
29. Discuss and compare the three main forms of product customization strategy.
30. Do you regard each of the following items as a "product system"? Why or why not?
    a. frozen "TV Dinners"
    b. a refrigerator with a built-in automatic ice-maker
    c. a combination can opener and knife sharpener
    d. a portable electric vacuum sweeper with attachments for spray painting, deodorizing, etc.
    e. a dining room table with matching chairs and buffet
31. What reasons would companies with large market shares, such as Coca-Cola and Pepsi-Cola in the cola market, have for entering new markets with changed products? For example, why did these two companies enter the market for dietary soft drinks?
32. Name some companies, other than those in the auto industry, that have used trading-up or trading-down strategies. Have these strategies been successful?
33. "Trading up should be used only when the economy is booming and trading down only during downswings in the business cycle." Agree or disagree?
34. Would you recommend that the following seriously consider

adopting a "new product—no market change" strategy?
a. a maker of blackboards for school use
b. a producer of hand-operated calculating machines
c. a cigarette manufacturer
d. A grower of pole string beans who has just read that people are eating more artichokes and fewer string beans. His land is suitable for growing either.

35. Why might a company decide to diversify into related product lines rather than extending its present product line?
36. The "new product—new market" strategy involves considerably greater risk than any other product-market strategy. Why?
37. Prepare a list of all the product-market strategies discussed in this chapter, including major variations of each strategy. Then identify those that seek increased profitability through (1) cost reduction, (2) increased sales, (3) both cost reduction and increased sales, and (4) some other means.

CASE PROBLEM

For several months, Mark Scott, Inc., a small manufacturer of personal grooming supplies for men and women, had received scattered complaints about the packaging of several of its products. Moreover, the complaints were coming from both retailers and consumers.

The retailers' complaints centered around the difficulty of physically handling the consumer unit packages, especially the inefficiencies that resulted when trying to arrange an attractive shelf display. Consumers complained specifically about the inconvenience in opening some of the packages, often being forced to tear them apart.

Although the number of complaints about the packaging was not large, and no loss of business could as yet be attributed directly to the packaging, Mr. Fred Taylor, marketing manager of Mark Scott, was very concerned that the complaints might be an indication of a more widespread dissatisfaction with the company's packaging. Consequently, he ordered an evaluation of the entire packaging program at Mark Scott.

If you were Mr. Taylor, where would you begin in evaluating the Mark Scott, Inc., packaging program?

PART FOUR

DISTRIBUTION

When you have mastered the contents of this chapter, you should be able to:

1. Define the following terms: marketing channel, middleman, merchant, agent, retailer, wholesaler, retailing, wholesaling.
2. Discuss the relative power different kinds of producers have in influencing the total sequence of transactions involved in marketing their products.
3. Explain the operating nature of the producers' cooperative marketing association.
4. Contrast the marketing roles played by: general merchandise wholesalers, general line wholesalers, and specialty wholesalers.
5. Compare the operating methods of the service wholesaler and the different kinds of limited-function wholesalers.
6. Compare the operating methods of the main types of agent wholesalers.
7. Outline the circumstances under which producers should include each type of wholesaler in their marketing channels.

CHAPTER 10

DISTRIBUTION: ROLES OF PRODUCERS AND WHOLESALERS

Distribution

Distribution is concerned with the activities involved in transferring goods from producers to final buyers and users. It includes not only physical activities, such as transporting and storing goods, but also the legal, promotional, and financial activities performed in the course of transferring ownership. Since a succession of enterprises is generally involved in the distribution process leading to the final sale to the consumer or user, to understand distribution one must analyze both the different kinds of marketing institutions and the marketing channels in which they operate. Your overall learning objective, then, in this and the following four chapters (all of Part Four) is to gain this broad understanding of distribution.

In Part Four, analysis focuses first on the various types of distributive institutions that bring products into contact with markets and effect ownership transfers, second, on marketing channels and channels policy, and third, on the actual physical distribution of products from producers to final buyers. A *marketing channel,* or channel of distribution, is defined as a path traced in the direct or indirect transfer of ownership to a product, as it moves from a producer to ultimate consumers or industrial users. Every marketing channel contains one or more transfer points, at each of which there is either an institution or a final buyer; during marketing, in other words, legal ownership of the product changes hands at least once. (This bare minimum occurs in situations where producers deal directly with final buyers and there are no intervening middlemen.) Generally, legal title to the product passes from the producer to and through a series of middlemen (distributive institutions) before the

Marketing Channel

consumer or industrial user finally takes possession. Transfer of ownership may be direct, as when the producer sells the product outright to a wholesaler or retailer, or it may be indirect, as when an agent middleman does not take legal title but simply negotiates its transfer. From the producer's standpoint, such a network of institutions used for reaching a market is a marketing channel. We think it logical to examine the building blocks—that is, the institutions—before we look at the different ways they can be joined together in marketing channels.

Some Basic Definitions[1]

MIDDLEMEN

Middleman

Middlemen specialize in performing activities that are directly involved in the purchase and sale of goods in the process of their flow from producers to final buyers. As the name "middleman" suggests, such institutions are situated in marketing channels at points between producers and final buyers. Producers regard middlemen as extensions of their own marketing organizations, because if there were no middlemen their own organizations would have to carry on all negotiations leading up to sales to final buyers. Final buyers—ultimate consumers and industrial users—consider middlemen as sources of supply and points of contact with producers.

MERCHANTS AND AGENTS

Merchant

Agent

Middlemen fall into two broad classifications: merchants and agents. A *merchant* takes title to (that is, buys) and resells merchandise. An *agent* negotiates purchases or sales or both, but does not take title to the goods in which it deals. Thus, the chief distinguishing characteristic relates to whether the middleman takes title to the goods it handles. If it does, it is a merchant. If it does not, it is an agent. Also, the merchant always both buys and resells, whereas the agent may specialize in negotiating only buying or only selling transactions.

RETAILERS AND WHOLESALERS

Middlemen may also be separated into two other major categories: retailers and wholesalers. The principal basis for distinguishing retailers and wholesalers relates to whether the business sells in significant amounts to ultimate consumers. If it does, it is a retailer. If it does not, it is a wholesaler.

[1] Unless noted otherwise, the definitions in this section and the remainder of Part Four are those compiled by the Committee on Definitions of the American Marketing Association. See Definitions Committee, *Marketing Definitions* (Chicago: American Marketing Association, 1960).

Retailer

A *retailer* is a merchant, or occasionally an agent, whose main business is selling directly to ultimate consumers. A retailer is distinguished by the nature of its sales rather than by the way it acquires the goods in which it deals. It usually sells in small lots, but this condition is not essential. The dealer who sells the furniture and floor covering for the initial outfitting of a large home, for instance, may make a sale of several thousand dollars, but it is still a retail sale if the buyer (that is, the homeowner) is an ultimate consumer.

Wholesaler

Wholesalers buy and resell merchandise to retailers and other merchants and to industrial, institutional, and commercial users, but do not sell in significant amounts to ultimate consumers. Notice that this definition does not specify that wholesalers must deal in large-size lots, nor does it require that they habitually make sales for purposes of resale. Most wholesalers do sell in large lots, but many do not. Similarly, most wholesalers do sell for purposes of resale, but there are also many who sell directly to industrial users. The one essential distinguishing feature of the wholesaler is that it must be a middleman who usually does not sell to ultimate consumers.

RETAILING AND WHOLESALING[2]

Retailing

Retailing consists of the activities involved in selling directly to the ultimate consumer. It makes no difference who does the selling; but, to be classified as retailing, selling activities must be direct to the ultimate consumer. Retailers, of course, are engaged in retailing, but so is any other institution that sells directly to ultimate consumers. Manufacturers engage in retailing when they make direct-to-consumer sales through their own stores, by house-to-house canvass, or by mail order. Even a wholesaler engages in retailing when it sells directly to an ultimate consumer, although its main business may still be wholesaling. If the buyer in a transaction is an ultimate consumer, the seller in the same transaction is engaged in retailing.

Wholesaling

Wholesaling involves selling to buyers other than ultimate consumers. These buyers may be wholesalers and retailers who buy to resell. They may be industrial users (manufacturers, mining concerns, or firms in other extractive industries), institutional users (schools, prisons, or mental hospitals), commercial users (restaurants, hotels, or factory lunchrooms), government agencies, or farmers buying items for their agricultural operations. Wholesaling is carried on not only by wholesalers but by manufacturers, other producers, and other business units that make sales to buyers who are not ultimate consumers. If the buyer in a transaction is buying for resale or to further its business or other operations, the seller in that transaction is engaged in wholesaling. All sales not made to ultimate consumers are wholesale sales.

[2] The Committee on Definitions of the American Marketing Association does not provide a definition for "wholesaling."

Producers

Producer

In any marketing channel, the *producer* is the seller in the first of the sequence of marketing transactions that occur as the product moves toward its market. Such producers include enterprises engaged in manufacturing, in mining and the extractive industries, and in farming. Of these, manufacturers normally have the most power to influence the total sequence of transactions involving their products.

MANUFACTURERS

How much power a given manufacturer has to influence the sequence of transactions depends on how much opportunity it has for differentiating its product from those of competitors and on its success in capitalizing on the opportunity. If its product can be differentiated and it can convince final buyers (ultimate consumers or industrial users) that differentiating features make the item a better buy than competing items, the manufacturer has the power to gain a significant marketing advantage. The automobile manufacturer, for example, has considerable opportunity to differentiate its product in appearance, performance, and operating characteristics. The manufacturer of common nails, by contrast, has little opportunity to make the product much different from those of competitors.

Capitalizing on a product differentiation opportunity requires more than simply convincing final buyers of the superiority of the manufacturer's product. It must be possible for them to obtain the product from suppliers at prices they are able and willing to pay. Different middlemen vary in their willingness to support the manufacturer in terms of stocking, promoting, and actively selling the product. Middlemen also vary as to what it costs the manufacturer to use them as components in the marketing channel; and this affects the price that final buyers ultimately have to pay. Balancing the need for support with the costs involved, the manufacturer tries to put together a distributive network that gives final buyers ready access to outlets handling the product at prices they consider reasonable. If the product can be differentiated in ways important to final buyers, the manufacturer can exercise considerable discretion in selecting members for its "channel team"; that is, it has considerable power to control the sequence of transactions involving the product as it moves to market. If little opportunity exists for product differentiation, the manufacturer has little power to control this sequence of transactions, and the sequence may instead be controlled by middlemen or by final buyers. The manufacturer which is attempting to control the marketing channel for its product usually devotes its primary attention to the market—the final buyers of its product. Starting with the market, the manufacturer attempts to detail the sequence of steps required to supply prospective buyers with its product. Even before this, however, the manufacturer should have identified and evaluated final buyers' needs and the strength of market demand and, in its research and product development effort, should have designed a product that meets these needs.

The sequence of steps required for moving the product to market, of course, may or may not call for the services of middlemen at one or more distribution levels. Even after deciding on this sequence—that is, the marketing channel—the manufacturer often devotes considerable effort to assuring that the planned series of transactions takes place. Through its advertising and other promotional activities, for instance, the manufacturer may work to build demand to the point where final buyers insist that suppliers stock and sell the product. Or, as another example, the manufacturer may use advertising to final buyers as a vehicle for directing prospective customers to outlets where the product is on sale. In these and similar ways, the manufacturer seeks to assure that its distribution network functions according to plan.

OTHER PRODUCERS

Enterprises not engaged in manufacturing, such as mining concerns and farmers, have less power to exert significant influences over the total sequence of marketing transactions involving their products. Usually, they can do very little about differentiating their products to meet final buyers' needs more closely. Furthermore, those engaged in nonmanufacturing activities generally find it very difficult to stimulate demand. Demand for the mining company's output, for instance, derives from the demand for products manufactured by its customers. Demand for aluminum, in other words, depends upon the demand for products fabricated by customers of aluminum mining companies; that is, products such as aluminum beach chairs, pots and pans, golf carts, and siding and sash used in building construction. It might seem logical, then, for the mining company to direct its efforts toward stimulating the demand for its customers' products. Individual mining companies, however, are often too small to finance and mount promotional programs of the required magnitude.

Derived Demand

The situation of the farmer is similar to that of the mining company for, unless they sell their crops through cooperatives, they are generally unable to support the extensive promotion needed to exert significant influences on their products' demand. Moreover, the demand for farm products commonly derives from the demand for products of processors of agricultural commodities. When certain food processors, for instance, began making oleomargarine out of "100 percent pure corn oil" and successfully promoted the new product's health benefits to consumers, increases in demand for corn followed increases in demand for corn oil margarine. Furthermore, unlike most manufacturers, who find it relatively easy to drop or add products as demand conditions change, many farmers—such as orchardists, cattlemen, and grain farmers—are limited to a single crop by virtue of their land, equipment, and experience. Thus, they are unable to do much about adjusting the nature of their outputs to fit the market's changing needs and preferences.

Different types of producers enjoy different degrees of power in controlling the flow of their product through marketing channels to final markets. In general, manufacturers have the most power and are able (within certain limits) to use channels containing the type and number of transfer points that they regard as most appropriate for the product and market. Farmers and producers in the extractive industries cannot direct the flow of their products to market. But their products do eventually get to market even though the flow is generally more involved and roundabout than with most manufactured products. Marketing channels serving the extractive industries tend to develop in an unplanned way, the way a river cuts its own course.

PRODUCERS' COOPERATIVE MARKETING ASSOCIATIONS

Producers' Cooperative Marketing Associations

Hoping to improve the efficiency with which their output is marketed, some groups of producers, chiefly in agriculture but sometimes in other extractive industries, organize and operate *producers' cooperative marketing associations.* These associations represent the collective effort of small producers who desire to gain more control over the distribution of their output in the hope of reducing distribution costs and exerting favorable influences on demand. Such cooperative endeavors tend to put their members more on a par with manufacturers so far as control over marketing channels is concerned.

The agricultural cooperative marketing association, with its relatively large size and the specialized attention its management can give to marketing activities, can, if it chooses, bypass one or more levels of middlemen present in more conventional marketing channels. Some cooperatives succeed in eliminating only the assembler or broker of agricultural products, but others extend their marketing operations even to such activities as maintaining sales offices in important marketing areas—as is done by Sunkist Growers, Inc., a cooperative marketer of California and Arizona citrus fruits. Most agricultural cooperative marketing associations are set up primarily to handle the packing and grading of their members' crops, usually managing to perform these activities at lower costs than members would incur individually. Some, such as Sunkist Growers, go so far as to affix brands to the product and to conduct massive promotional programs designed to build and maintain consumer recognition for the brand and to expand its demand. Thus, the cooperative marketing association fairly often succeeds in providing its members with enhanced power in controlling the flow of their products through marketing channels to final markets.

Pooling

Use of Pooling One operating practice unique to cooperative marketing associations is called *pooling*. This is the practice of mixing the outputs of members and, after deducting average expenses, paying them the average price received during the marketing season, usually on the basis of established grades. Among the arguments advanced in support of pooling are that (1) it is difficult or impractical to keep each member's output segregated in storage and en route to market; (2) shipments are made at different times during the marketing season at different prices for comparable qualities and grades of produce.

Cash Advances

Use of Cash Advances Typically, the producers' cooperative marketing association provides its members with *cash advances* when they deliver their crops to the packing house. As sales are made, members receive further advances. Final distribution of the remaining proceeds of sales are often delayed until six to nine months after closing the pool. Some cooperatives do not use cash advances, instead issuing warehouse receipts to members; these can be used as collateral for loans from commercial banks.

Formal Membership Contract

Formal Membership Contracts Most cooperative marketing associations evidently believe it necessary to require members to execute written *formal membership contracts.* The feeling is that this helps to assure the association of a continuous volume of business and enables management to draft firmer plans for future operations, especially when such plans involve financial commitments. At one time provisions of membership contracts were very stringent, often giving the association the right to enforce specific performance by injunction. In recent years the trend has been toward more liberal contracts as, increasingly, associations rely on their own satisfactory performance to hold members' loyalty.

Purchasing Services Many producers' cooperative marketing associations offer their members purchasing services. Many buy such items as seed, fertilizers, tools and implements, and gasoline and oil for resale to members, and a few also deal in various consumer goods. Some, such as AgWay, not only market crops grown by their farmer-members but also operate stores to supply members and others with items used on farms, as well as such diverse goods as grass seed, lawn mowers, automobile tires, and food for wild birds.

Wholesaling

Wholesaling is a very large business, both in terms of the total number of establishments and of their total sales volume. In the United States, as Table 10–1 shows, over 300,000 wholesale establishments transact over $450 billion in sales annually. During the period 1948 to 1967 (the latest date for which data are available), as this table also shows, the number of wholesale establishments rose by almost 50 percent. In the same period, wholesale sales made by wholesale establishments increased even more spectacularly, rising by more than 250 percent.

Table 10–1 U.S. Wholesalers: Number of Establishments and Total Sales—Selected Years

YEAR	NUMBER OF ESTABLISHMENTS	SALES (in Billions of Dollars)
1967	311,000	459.5
1963	308,000	358.4
1958	287,000	285.7
1954	250,000	234.0
1948	216,000	180.6

Source: *Statistical Abstract of the U.S., 1973*, p. 750.

Table 10–2 indicates the relative importance of various types of wholesalers. By far the most important, both in terms of total number of establishments and total sales volume, are the merchant wholesalers, even though as a group they tend to have higher operating expenses than other types of wholesalers. Manufacturers' sales branches and offices, which are separately identifiable wholesaling establishments owned and operated by manufacturers and functioning in ways similar to independently owned establishments, are the second most important type. Agents and brokers (i.e., agent middlemen), the third most important type, negotiate over $60 billion in sales (and purchases) annually for the principals they represent. The two remaining major categories of wholesale establishment are rather specialized operations: petroleum bulk stations and terminals are mainly refiner-owned wholesaling units, while assemblers of farm products include country grain elevators, cream and produce stations, fruit and vegetable packing houses, livestock concentration yards, and other establishments primarily engaged in purchasing from farmers and assembling and marketing farm products.

Several interesting conclusions can be drawn from the data presented in Table 10–2. Manufacturers' sales branches and offices are far more important than their numbers indicate—although they account for only 10 percent of the establishments, they transact 34 percent of the total sales volume. Somewhat less spectacularly, the agent middlemen are also more important than their numbers indicate—with less than 9 percent of the total establishments they negotiate roughly 13 percent of the total dollar sales. By contrast, merchant wholesalers account for over 68 percent of the wholesale establishments but transact only about 45 percent of the total dollar sales. Even though this means that merchant wholesalers, on the

Table 10–2 Total U.S. Wholesale Trade, by Type of Operation—1967

TYPE OF OPERATION	NUMBER OF ESTABLISHMENTS (to Nearest 1,000)	1967 SALES (in Billions of Dollars)*	OPERATING EXPENSES (As Percent of Sales)**
Merchant Wholesalers	213	$206.055	13.8
Wholesale Merchants	205	181.776	14.8
Importers	5	10.353	10.3
Exporters	2	9.508	4.1
Terminal Grain Elevators	1	4.417	4.5
Manufacturers' Sales Branches & Offices	31	157.097	7.2
Sales Branches	17	67.175	11.3
Sales Offices	14	89.922	4.1
Agents & Brokers	26	61.347	4.0
Auction Companies	2	4.792	2.9
Brokers	4	14.030	3.2
Commission Houses	5	14.068	3.4
Import Agents	..	1.790	2.2
Export Agents	1	3.372	1.9
Manufacturers' Agents	12	15.257	6.4
Selling Agents	2	6.890	4.2
Purchasing Agents & Resident Buyers	..	1.147	3.6
Petroleum Bulk Stations & Terminals	30	24.822	0.3
Assemblers of Farm Products	11	10.156	8.6
Country Grain Elevators	6	5.591	7.1
Other Assemblers	5	4.565	10.4

*Entries for agents and brokers represent the gross sales (or purchase) value of the goods in the transactions negotiated.
**Entries for agents and brokers represent brokerage or commission received.

Source: 1967 Census of Business-Wholesale Trade.

average, have lower sales volumes than either of the other major types of wholesale operation, they are the most important single type in terms of total dollar sales. You should also notice that operating expenses as a percent of sales ranges all the way from 0.3 percent (petroleum bulk stations and terminals) to 14.8 percent (wholesale merchants), reflecting differences both in the nature of operations and in efficiency as well as in the average size of wholesale establishments.

Merchant Wholesalers

Merchant Wholesaler

Merchant wholesalers, by definition, buy and resell goods on their own account; that is, they take title to the products they handle and convey title directly to those with whom they deal. In consumer goods marketing, their principal customers are retailers, but they also sell to industrial users and to institutional and commercial users.

Merchant wholesalers are also active in industrial marketing, serving as intermediaries between the supplying manufacturers and the industrial users; here they are known by such names as mill supply houses, mining supply distributors, machinery dealers, and oil well equipment houses.

Table 10–3 shows the sales of merchant wholesalers for 1964 to 1973. Over the ten-year period, total sales increased by nearly 90 percent, with durable goods sales increasing by 121.5 percent and nondurable goods sales by 65.5 percent. Table 10–4 shows sales of merchant wholesalers by kind of business for 1973. Three categories accounted for over half (56.7 percent) of durable goods sales by merchant wholesalers: machinery, equipment, supplies (24.9 percent), motor vehicles, automotive equipment (18.4 percent), and electrical goods (13.4 percent). In the nondurable goods category, groceries and related products accounted for 41.7 percent of the total, with beer, wine, and distilled alcoholic beverages, dry goods and apparel, and drugs, chemicals, and allied products accounting for 9.7 percent, 8.6 percent, and 8.0 percent of the total, respectively.

There are two main ways of classifying merchant wholesalers. First, according to the range of merchandising they handle, there are (1) general merchandise wholesalers, (2) general line wholesalers, and (3) specialty wholesalers. Second, according to method of operation, there are (1) service wholesalers and (2) limited-function wholesalers.

Table 10–3 Sales of Merchant Wholesalers, Durable Goods and Nondurable Goods (excluding farm products, raw materials)—1964–1973 (millions of dollars)

YEAR	DURABLE GOODS	NONDURABLE GOODS	TOTAL
1964	$ 75,722	$ 98,607	$ 174,329
1965	82,691	104,450	187,141
1966	91,026	112,724	203,751
1967	90,447	114,740	205,187
1968	100,012	119,930	219,943
1969	109,578	127,130	236,708
1970	111,778	134,865	246,643
1971	122,420	144,937	267,357
1972	138,446	159,753	298,199
1973	167,713	163,231	330,944

Source: *Survey of Current Business*, 1973, p. 58.

CLASSIFICATION BY RANGE OF MERCHANDISE HANDLED

General Merchandise Wholesaler

General Merchandise Wholesalers A *general merchandise wholesaler* is a merchant wholesaler who carries a general assortment of products in two or more distinct and unrelated merchandise lines. For instance, such a wholesaler may stock and sell dry goods, hard-

Table 10-4 Sales of Merchant Wholesalers by Kind of Business—1973

KIND OF BUSINESS	SALES (Millions of Dollars)
Total Sales (excluding farm products, raw materials)	$ 330,944
Durable Goods, Total	167,713
Motor vehicles, automotive equipment	30,891
Electrical goods	22,475
Furniture, home furnishings	6,891
Hardware, plumbing, heating equipment, supplies	15,696
Lumber, construction materials	18,813
Machinery, equipment, supplies	41,921
Metals, metalwork (except scrap)	19,268
Scrap, waste materials	8,736
Nondurable Goods, Total	163,231
Groceries and related products	68,124
Beer, wine, distilled alcoholic beverages	15,762
Drugs, chemicals, allied products	13,081
Tobacco, tobacco products	7,168
Dry goods, apparel	14,035
Paper, paper products	9,546
Other nondurable goods	35,515
Farm products (raw materials)	33,914
Merchant Wholesalers, Grand Total	$ 364,858

Source: Department of Commerce, Bureau of the Census, *Monthly Wholesale Trade Report*, January 1974, p. 2.

ware, furniture, farm implements, electrical equipment, sporting goods, and household appliances. During the heyday of the retail general store, staple groceries were the main stock in trade. But with the rise of large cities, growth of population, and development of new types of retail institutions more appropriate to the times, the retail general store declined in importance, and with its gradual disappearance came a decline in the importance of general merchandise wholesalers till today there are comparatively few left. However, particularly in predominantly rural sections of the West and South, general merchandise wholesalers still serve as suppliers to hardware stores, electrical supply stores, auto accessory dealers, drugstores, and smaller department stores. General merchandise wholesalers are much less important in terms of both number of establishments and sales volume than either general line or specialty wholesalers.

General Line Wholesaler

General Line Wholesalers A *general line wholesaler* carries a broad assortment of goods within a single merchandise line, but it may also handle limited stocks of goods in closely related lines. Thus, a general line grocery wholesaler usually carries not only a broad stock of canned fruits and vegetables, cereals, tea and coffee, but also razor blades, soaps and detergents, toothpaste, school supplies, and other items commonly sold in retail grocery stores. Measured in terms of total volume of sales, general line wholesalers are more important than either general merchandise wholesalers or specialty wholesalers. General line wholesalers are important distributors of groceries, drugs, and hardware to independent retailers in these fields. General line wholesalers also sell such industrial goods lines as electrical, plumbing, and heating equipment and supplies to both large and small industrial users.

The importance of the general line wholesaler in consumer goods marketing has declined somewhat with the rise of corporate chains and other mass retailers that prefer to buy directly from producers. Similarly, there is a trend among industrial users toward direct buying from producers, and this is reducing operations of general line wholesalers of industrial goods. But, since small-scale independent retailers continue to exist, and because industrial users continue to need some items in quantities too small to justify direct purchase, general line wholesalers remain important marketing intermediaries in both consumer and industrial goods markets.

Specialty Wholesaler

Specialty Wholesalers A *specialty wholesaler* carries only part of a merchandise line but, within its restricted range of offerings, it has a very complete assortment. In the wholesale grocery trade, for instance, specialty wholesalers specialize in such partial lines as: canned foods; coffee, tea, and spices; dairy products; frosted and frozen foods; or soft drinks. The specialty wholesaler represents an advanced step in what seems to be a universal trend among merchant wholesalers to restrict merchandise offerings.

Specialty wholesalers generally pride themselves on the strong promotional support they provide for the restricted number of manufacturers' brands they handle. They can provide this strong support because they concentrate on relatively few items. It is possible for the specialty grocery wholesaler's salesmen, for instance, in the routine performance of their duties to push every item handled on every sales call and to perform on behalf of manufacturers' brands such promotional activities as erecting special displays, handling in-store product demonstrations, and arranging for the distribution of samples. Salesmen working for general line grocery wholesalers, by contrast, find it impossible to give special push to more than a handful of the many thousands of items in stock or to any one manufacturer's brand.

However, the narrowness of the specialty wholesaler's merchandising offering, together with the importance of providing strong promotional support for all items handled, causes it to concentrate on market areas where there are large numbers of retail outlets. Selling only a few items and strongly promoting each one, it can make economical use of salesmen only where there are numerous retailers to call on and relatively little travel time is involved between stops. The specialty wholesaler's salesmen make frequent calls on retailers but, because this makes it possible for retailers to carry smaller stocks, the average size of orders is small. Specialty wholesalers are concentrated in the heavily industrialized and thickly populated parts of New England, the Middle Atlantic states, the Midwest, and the Pacific Coast. In other areas (such as most of the Rocky Mountain states and much of the South), where population is sparse, cities and towns are far apart, and retail outlets are widely scattered and few in number, relatively few specialty wholesalers exist.

CLASSIFICATION BY METHOD OF OPERATION

Service Wholesaler

Limited-Function Wholesaler

Merchant wholesalers perform many marketing activities for their suppliers and customers. Those who perform all or most of the activities generally associated with wholesale trade are *service wholesalers.* (These activities are buying and assembling, selling, storage, transportation, marketing risk bearing, marketing financing, and marketing information.) General merchandise and general line wholesalers perform these activities and, therefore, are also service wholesalers. Some specialty wholesalers perform only a few of these activities; others perform more. Depending on the extent of its service, a specialty wholesaler may be classed either as a service wholesaler or as a limited-function wholesaler who performs only a few of the activities normally associated with wholesaling operations. Remember, however, that all merchant wholesalers—limited-function as well as service wholesalers—take title to the goods they handle and resell to those with whom they deal. Thus, all perform the buying and assembling and selling activities. The main types of limited-function wholesalers are discussed below.

Truck Wholesaler

Truck Wholesalers Combining selling, delivery, and collection in one operation, *truck wholesalers* (also known as "wagon jobbers") carry only a limited range of stock, although the selection within that range may be very complete. Thus, the nature of a truck wholesaler's merchandise offering also makes it a specialty wholesaler. Truck wholesalers call mainly on retailers although some, such as those in the grocery trade, also sell to restaurants, hotels, and other food service establishments. Because the items they handle are often perishables or semiperishables, truck wholesalers make frequent calls on customers. Their ability to make fast and frequent deliveries is their main appeal to both their customers and the manufacturers they represent.

Rack Jobber

Rack Jobbers A *rack jobber* markets specialized lines of merchandise to retail stores and provides certain special services. The merchandising policies of most rack jobbers cause them also to be specialty wholesalers. The original rack jobbers evolved after World War II to serve the special needs of supermarkets which, in increasing numbers, were adding nonfood lines.

Rack jobbers serving supermarkets and other grocery retailers usually specialize in one or both of two lines—toiletries and housewares. Managers of retail stores served by rack jobbers are relieved of the merchandising problems involved in handling what are for them sundry items, and are left free to concentrate their merchandising efforts on their major lines. The rack jobber may or may not furnish its own display racks but, basically, all that it requires of the retailer is some selling space, which the rack jobber stocks with a selection of items priced for immediate sale. Occasional rack jobbers supply merchandise on consignment: that is, they retain legal title to the merchandise up to the time the retailer sells it, the retailer paying only for the goods sold (and, incidentally, for shoplifted items) and retaining a portion of the profit for itself. Through aggressive merchandising and effective use of displays, rack jobbers have built up large volumes of nonfood sales in grocery stores. Manufacturers of nonfood lines find that rack jobbers provide an effective means of achieving low-cost distribution through retail food stores.

Cash-and-Carry Wholesaler

Cash-and-Carry Wholesalers *Cash-and-carry wholesalers* pursue at the wholesale level the same sort of service policy that characterizes cash-and-carry retail operations. Whereas service wholesalers send their salesmen to retailers to solicit orders, later deliver these orders, and grant credit to retailers, allowing them to pay at later dates, cash-and-carry wholesalers require retailers to come to the wholesale warehouse, pick their own orders, pay cash, and carry away their own purchases. By restricting the services it performs and lowering its operating costs, the cash-and-carry wholesaler is able to price its goods lower than those of service wholesalers. Price, then, is what attracts retailers to the cash-and-carry wholesaler. But, because retailers must perform additional services for themselves, they often find that by the time the order gets to the store its cost is every bit as high as if it were purchased from a service wholesaler. However, cash-and-carry departments do provide an economical means for service wholesalers to use in reaching many small retailers who customarily buy in lots too small to justify the wholesaler's sending salesmen, providing delivery, and extending credit.

Drop Shipment Wholesaler

Drop Shipment Wholesalers A *drop shipment wholesaler* does not physically handle the goods it sells but leaves the performance of storage and transportation activities to the manufacturers whom it represents. When goods are ordered, the manufacturer ships them directly to the retailer but bills the drop shipper at factory prices. Subsequently, the drop shipper collects from the retailer. This distribution system makes possible reductions in transportation and storage costs. It eliminates the necessity for double hauling (that is, from the factory to the wholesaler and then on to the retailer), and no costs are incurred for handling the goods in a wholesaler's warehouse.

However, customers buying through drop shippers often order in comparatively small lot sizes and, because freight rates are higher for small lots than for large lots, some of the savings from eliminating double hauling are offset by higher freight rates.

The retailer, to make economical use of drop shipments, must both order in larger than normal quantities and adjust its operations to allow for longer periods during which the goods are in transit. These adjustments are necessary inasmuch as most retailers are located farther from the manufacturers' plants than from the wholesalers serving as alternative supply points. The need for ordering in larger than normal quantities also forces the retailer to invest additional funds in inventory. Despite these unattractive features, however, retailers often find cost savings sufficient to justify drop shipments. This is especially true with standard, fast-selling items that sell regardless of season and that offer little risk that the retailer will be unable to resell the merchandise.

Drop shipment wholesalers are also much used in industrial marketing. They are important distributors of such items as sand, clay, coal, and lumber—all commodities of low value, relative to transportation costs incurred in their distribution, and all involving situations where any interruption of deliveries, causing breaks in customers' production operations, may lead to significant cost increases. Industrial users purchase these items in such large quantities and with such great regularity that it pays them to have several shipments in transit at any one time, each spaced to arrive before it is needed and always allowing some margin of safety for late arriving shipments. Thus, the industrial user manages to work around the long period during which drop shipments are in transit. Furthermore, customers generally buy these commodities in lots large enough to gain freight rates as low as those a service wholesaler might secure.

Mail-Order Wholesaler

Mail-Order Wholesalers A *mail-order wholesaler* substitutes mail-order catalogs and order forms for a sales force and passes on to retailers some of the savings in the form of lower prices. This limited-function wholesaler is mainly active in selling such staple consumer items as hardware and dry goods. With successive improvements in transportation and communication services, the importance of mail-order wholesalers has sharply declined. One basic weakness of this type of operation is that it does not provide a really adequate substitute for strong promotional push by salesmen. Moreover, its success rests on the willingness of retailers to take the initiative in placing orders, something that cannot always be counted on, especially when competitors' salesmen make personal calls on retailers.

Agent Middlemen

Agent Middleman

Agent middlemen—most of whom engage in wholesaling rather than in retailing—assist in negotiating sales or purchases or both on behalf of their principals (buyers or sellers or both). Usually, the agent does not represent both buyers and sellers in the same transaction, and it is ordinarily paid by commission or fee. Agent wholesalers differ from merchant wholesalers in that they do not take title to the merchandise and generally perform only a few wholesaling activities.

Agent wholesalers as a group operate in many fields, but individual agents customarily concentrate on such lines as foods, grain, copper, steel, machinery, electronic supplies, or textiles. The main types of agent wholesalers are brokers, commission houses, manufacturers' agents, selling agents, resident buyers, and auction companies.

BROKERS

Broker

A *broker* is an agent who represents either buyer or seller in negotiating purchases or sales without physically handling the goods involved. The broker is more often the agent of the owner of goods seeking a buyer than of a buyer searching for a source of supply. Each broker tends to specialize in arranging transactions for a limited number of products, and this causes the broker to be well informed concerning conditions in these particular markets.

Acting strictly as an intermediary, the broker has limited powers as to prices and terms of sale, and possesses little or no authority to bargain on behalf of its principal. The broker's main service is to bring buyer and seller together. Representing either the seller or the buyer (but not usually both in the same transaction), the broker relays the buyer's offer to the seller and the seller's counteroffer to the buyer, and continues this process until the terms are satisfactory to both parties, at which time the exchange takes place. The broker never has direct physical control over the goods but sells by description or sample. Whenever the broker arranges a sale, the seller ships the goods directly to the buyer. The broker receives its commission from the principal who sought its services.

Brokers are most used by producers who sell their products at infrequent intervals and find it uneconomical to establish standing sales forces of their own or even to establish long-term relationships with other types of agent wholesalers. Although an individual producer may use the same broker year after year, each transaction is considered completely apart from every other. There is no obligation on the part of either the broker or the seller to maintain this relationship in future transactions. Small canners, whose outputs are too small to justify developing and promoting brands of their own and whose entire pack may be put up in two or three months, often rely solely on brokers. Similarly, farmers harvesting one major crop a year often find it economical to use brokers.

Sometimes brokers are used by larger manufacturers who want to extend the distribution of their products. In such instances, brokers serve as the key middlemen in arranging initial distribution of the product among other types of middlemen. Thus, a broker may be instrumental in opening up a new market for the producer or in gaining access to outlets that have previously not stocked the product.

COMMISSION HOUSES

Commission House

A *commission house* is an agent who customarily exercises physical control over and negotiates the sale of goods belonging to principals. The commission house usually enjoys broad powers as to prices, methods, and terms of sale, although it must also obey its principals' instructions. Generally, it arranges delivery, extends necessary credit, collects, deducts its fees, and remits the balance to its principal. Thus, except for the fact that it does not take title, the commission house performs activities very similar to those of service merchant wholesalers—more so, in fact, than any other agent wholesaler.

Most commission houses are engaged in the distribution of fresh fruit and produce. The relationship of the commission house and its principals generally covers a harvest and marketing season. A truck farmer, for instance, signs a seasonal agreement with a commission house situated in a market center; as the crop is harvested, it is shipped to the commission house. The commission house is authorized to sell each shipment on arrival at the best price obtainable without checking back with the farmer. Although legal title to the goods never passes to the house, it sells in its own name, bills buyers, extends credit, makes collections, deducts its fees, and remits the balance to the truck farmer. The farmer might prefer to hold his product off the market at times and bargain for higher prices, but the factor of perishability makes any delays in selling costly. The commission house's operation is especially geared for rapid sale of perishable commodities, and this is the main reason this type of agent is important in agricultural marketing.

MANUFACTURERS' AGENTS

Manufacturers' Agent

Four main features characterize the operations of a *manufacturers' agent:* (1) it has an extended contractual relationship with its principals; (2) it handles sales for each of its principals within an exclusive territory; (3) it represents manufacturers of noncompeting but related lines of goods; (4) it possesses limited authority with regard to prices and terms of sale. Some manufacturers' agents have physical control over an inventory but most do not. Ordinarily, the manufacturers' agent arranges for shipments to be sent directly from the factory to the buyer. Because its principal activity is selling, the agent maintains a sales staff large enough to provide adequate coverage of its market area. It sells at prices, or within a price range, stipulated by its principal and receives a percentage commission based on sales.

Manufacturers' agents are generally used either when a manufacturer finds it uneconomical to have its own salesmen or when it is financially unable to do so. Some manufacturers, for instance, find that certain market areas do not provide enough business to justify assigning their own salesmen to them. Yet manufacturers' agents, each representing several principals, operate profitably in the same areas. Thus, it is common for manufacturers to use their own salesmen in areas with large potential sales and to use manufacturers' agents elsewhere. Other manufacturers use agents to open up new market areas, then replace them with their own salesmen as the sales volume grows. Still other manufacturers, particularly those who are small and have narrow product lines, use a network of manufacturers' agents to avoid altogether the problems and expenses of maintaining their own sales forces.

Manufacturers' agents are most important in the marketing of industrial goods and such consumer durables as furniture and hardware. In industrial goods marketing, such as in the marketing of electronic components, agents employ salesmen who have considerable technical competence and who contact industrial users directly. In marketing consumer durables, salesmen employed by manufacturers' agents generally call on and sell to retailers. Numerous furniture manufacturers rely on manufacturers' agents to sell their entire outputs. In many cases, in both industrial and consumer goods marketing, the manufacturers' agent can, because of its intimate contact with the market, offer advice to the manufacturer on a wide variety of matters, including styling, design, and pricing.

SELLING AGENTS

Selling Agent

A *selling agent* operates on an extended contractual basis, negotiates all sales of a specified line of merchandise or the entire output of its principal, and usually has full authority with regard to prices, terms, and other conditions of sale. Thus, it differs from the manufacturers' agent in that it is ordinarily not confined to operating within a given market area, has much more authority to set prices and terms of sale, and is the sole selling agent for the lines it represents.

Some selling agents render financial assistance to their principals. This practice traces back to early selling agents who were usually much stronger financially than their principals. Many textile mills, for instance, were originally started with the financial backing of selling agents, who saw this as a way to increase their own business volumes and, hence, their commissions. Today, selling agents generally do not provide investment capital for their principals, but many help their principals in financing current operations. Because many modern-day selling agents continue to have higher credit ratings than their principals, it is fairly common for them to endorse their principals' short-term notes at banks and other lending institutions. Occasionally, too, a selling agent assists its principal financially either by making direct loans on accounts receivable or by guaranteeing these accounts so that a lender will advance needed funds to the principal. There is, however, a trend away from this type of financing activity by selling agents. The trend has accelerated with the growth of financial institutions known as "factors," who specialize in discounting accounts receivable—that is, in making short-term loans with accounts receivable as the collateral.

The manufacturer who uses a selling agent, in effect, shifts most of the marketing task to an outside organization. This frees the manufacturer to concentrate on production and other nonmarketing problems. In addition, because the selling agent is in close contact with buyers, often it is in a position to guide the manufacturer on styling, design, and pricing matters. Fairly often, it assists the principal with or takes over sales promotion and advertising. Sometimes the selling agent, as is true of some in the textile and apparel trades, even specifies the features that the principal should build into the product and how much to manufacture. Since the selling agent works for a straight commission, the principal's selling costs vary proportionately with sales made, and no fixed selling costs are incurred. For all these reasons, it is easy to see why small manufacturers with neither the managerial talent nor the financial strength to market their own products use selling agents.

The manufacturer who uses a selling agent should realize, however, that it is "placing all its marketing eggs in one basket." Because the selling agent is the manufacturer's only contact with the market, the bulk of the bargaining power rests with the agent, not the manufacturer. Recognizing this, selling agents may be tempted to resort to price cutting instead of exerting a reasonable amount of selling effort to sell the manufacturer's output. In such situations, the manufacturer, cut off from the buyers by the selling agent and having dealt with them only through this intermediary, is literally "over the barrel." If it is weak financially and needs loans that cannot be obtained without the selling agent's help, it may not even be able to break with the selling agent in order to obtain another agent. The moral is clear: If the manufacturer is going to use a selling agent, its first choice should be a good one.

RESIDENT BUYERS

Resident Buyer

A *resident buyer* differs from most other agent middlemen in that it represents buyers only. Specializing in buying for retailers, it receives its compensation on a fee or commission basis. The resident buyer operates most often in lines of trade, such as furniture and apparel, where there are well-defined market centers to which retailers ordinarily travel to make their selections. Resident buyers maintain their offices in such market centers and, whenever retailers are unable to make the trip to market in person, they serve as retailers' contacts with the sources of supply.

Resident buyers are completely independent of their principals. They should not be confused with the resident buying offices, maintained in such market centers as New York, which are owned by out-of-town stores. Nor should they be confused with the central buying offices maintained by chain-store organizations. The resident buyer is purely and simply an independent agent specializing in buying for principals who are retailers.

AUCTION COMPANIES

Auction Company

As its name indicates, an *auction company* uses the auction method of catalogs and competitive bidding by prospective buyers in order to sell its principals' products. Auction companies are particularly important in selling products of varying quality and those that cannot be efficiently graded – situations frequent in agricultural marketing. In the fresh fruit and vegetable trade, auction companies are located in central markets – that is, in cities that are important distributing points for such items. In the marketing of livestock and of agricultural crops such as leaf tobacco, auction companies are located in principal producing areas and at shipping points. An auction company has physical control over the lots consigned to it, arranges for their display, conducts the auction, makes collections from the buyers, and remits the proceeds, less its commissions, to the principals.

The auction method of selling leaf tobacco dates back to Civil War days. Until then tobacco leaf was spread on sidewalks for display, and growers usually had no option whatever but to accept the prices offered by buyers. This exploitation of the growers caused the Virginia legislature to give some attention to the marketing situation, resulting first in provisions whereby tobacco was graded by professionals on the basis of intrinsic value and later in the establishment of warehouses using the auction method of selling.

OTHER AGENTS

Other types of agent middlemen have evolved to serve special marketing needs. It appears that whenever a large enough group of buyers or sellers needs some special marketing service, there are always enterprising individuals who will set up in business to provide it. For instance, there are export and import agents in leading port cities who serve the needs of principals seeking foreign markets or overseas sources of supply. And there are purchasing agents, which are independent businesses, specializing in locating sources of supply for buyers of industrial goods. But they all have the same basic economic purpose – they all help to bring buyers and sellers together in return for fees or commissions.

Summary

Producers and wholesalers play important roles in distribution. In any marketing channel, the producer is the seller in the first of the sequence of ownership transfers that occur as the product moves toward its market. If the producer can differentiate its product in ways important to final buyers, it has considerable power to control the entire sequence of ownership transfers; but if it has little opportunity for product differentiation, it has little power to control this sequence and instead middlemen or final buyers may control it. Manufacturers, in general, have more power than other kinds of producers and are more able to use marketing channels containing the type and number of transfer points that they desire.

Wholesalers occupy positions in marketing channels somewhere between producers and final buyers. Merchant wholesalers, the most numerous type, take title to the products they handle and convey title directly to their customers, who may be (depending on the situation) retailers, industrial users, or institutional and commercial users. Merchant wholesalers differentiate their operations both as to the type and range of merchandise handled and the nature of services provided—both for the producers who supply them and for the customers they serve. Agent middlemen, who assist in negotiating ownership transfers without actually taking title themselves, take many different forms, tailoring their operations to meet the needs of the principals they represent (sellers, buyers, or both). Generally, too, agent middlemen perform fewer wholesaling activities than do merchant wholesalers.

You should now, therefore, be thoroughly familiar with the first two building blocks in marketing channels—producers and wholesalers. You should know the definitions of the basic distribution terms: middleman, merchant, agent, retailer, wholesaler, retailing, wholesaling, and marketing channel. You should have a good knowledge of the numerous different types of merchant wholesalers and agent middlemen, particularly with respect to the ways they differentiate their operations and the services they provide. If you know all of these things well, you understand "wholesale distribution."

QUESTIONS AND PROBLEMS

1. Distinguish among the following:
   a. middleman
   b. merchant
   c. agent
   d. retailer
   e. wholesaler
   f. retailing
   g. wholesaling

2. "The middleman can be eliminated, but its functions cannot." Discuss.
3. What is the value of trying to differentiate between wholesalers and retailers, when a great many institutions are carrying on both wholesaling and retailing activities? Has this distinction become artificial?
4. Which of the following are engaged in wholesaling? In retailing?
   a. A manufacturer of power saws who sells to building contractors and homeowners
   b. A dairy farmer who sells to schools and restaurants
   c. A clothing manufacturer who sells through a catalog to ultimate consumers
   d. A retail sporting goods store that sells to the athletic departments of high schools and colleges.
   e. A hardware wholesaler who sells to retail hardware outlets
   f. A tire manufacturer who sells through its own retail stores
   g. A furniture wholesaler who sells to homeowners
5. The Warren Company distributes a line of picnic tables. While approximately 70 percent of Warren sales volume is accounted for by ultimate consumers, the company advertises heavily to—and its small sales force calls on—municipalities, state parks, schools, and hospitals, and these customers account for 30 percent of sales volume. Sales to ultimate consumers are transacted by mail order (the picnic tables are shipped direct to the ultimate consumers from the Warren warehouse) and sales to the other customers are handled by the salesmen.
   Is the Warren Company a wholesaler or a retailer?
6. Producers who can differentiate their products have greater control over the channel through which their products are sold, but is there any real advantage in such control? Would not the traditional channel ordinarily be the best? Discuss.
7. Analyze the factors which determine the extent of a manufacturer's power and influence in the channel of distribution.
8. "The longer the channel the greater the inefficiency." Agree or disagree? Why?
9. Would you think that the greatest strength of a producers' cooperative lies in the economies of size or in its greater ability to differentiate its products? Explain.
10. Define the following:
    a. general merchandise wholesaler - two or more unrelated
    b. general line wholesaler - assortment
    c. specialty wholesaler
    d. truck wholesaler
    e. rack jobber
    f. cash-and-carry wholesaler
    g. drop shipment wholesaler
    h. mail-order wholesaler

11. General merchandise wholesalers have, to a large extent, faded from the American scene, but general line wholesalers have retained a fairly important role. Why do you suppose this has happened?
12. What particular advantages are offered by specialty wholesalers? Explain.
13. Shouldn't it be to the advantage of a retailer to deal only with a very limited number of general line wholesalers instead of a much larger number of specialty wholesalers? If so, how can you explain the greater growth of specialty wholesalers?
14. Discuss the major differences which distinguish service wholesalers from limited-function wholesalers.
15. Limited service retailers have captured an increasingly important share of the market in recent years. Why, then, haven't limited-function wholesalers managed to do the same thing at the wholesale level?
16. Would it be proper to say that the primary appeal of the truck wholesaler is that it allows the retailer to reduce merchandise turnover? Explain.
17. Wouldn't it seem logical that, if a rack jobber can sell sundry items at a profit in food stores, the management of large food chains should be able to do the same job as profitably? Why, then, do many of these chains use rack jobbers?
18. Would you be likely to find cash-and-carry wholesalers in the same general locations as service wholesalers? Explain.
19. Is there likely to be any real advantage in using drop shipment wholesalers, if the retailer finds it necessary to buy in larger than normal quantities so as to keep transportation costs in line?
20. Would it be a fair assessment to say that the primary cause for the lack of success of mail-order wholesalers is laziness on the part of retail buyers? Comment.
21. Explain the major differences between agent wholesalers and merchant wholesalers.
22. Describe the basic operations of a broker.
23. Do you regard brokers as essential to the marketing process or are they collectively just another example of the excess in middlemen who do little, if anything, toward increasing a product's value as it travels through the distribution channel? Explain.
24. The choice as to whether a farmer is more likely to use a broker or a commission house to sell his product will depend primarily on the length of his harvest season and the perishability of his product. Do you agree?
25. How do selling agents differ from manufacturers' agents?
26. Would you agree that a manufacturer should normally look on the manufacturers' agent as a temporary distributor, to be used only until it can be replaced by the company's own salesmen?

27. Explain the conditions most likely to surround a manufacturer's decision to use a manufacturers' agent instead of its own sales force.
28. "The manufacturer who uses a selling agent, in effect, shifts most of the marketing task to an outside organization." Discuss.
29. What is a resident buyer? In what respects is its operation unique?
30. "Purchasing through an auction company is an inefficient method of procurement." Comment on this statement.
31. What type of agent middleman would be most appropriate for the following situations?
    a. A small manufacturer of golf clubs
    b. A manufacturer of a limited line of high-quality men's clothing
    c. A small manufacturer of household cleaning brushes to be distributed through supermarkets
    d. A manufacturer of industrial equipment (for which it has its own sales force) which is adding a line of home swimming pools
    e. A small manufacturer of unbranded men's work clothes

CASE PROBLEM

For ten years, R. F. Barker, Inc., had manufactured a narrow line of motors for industrial equipment. The company was small and employed a field sales force of six men who sold to industrial users in eight Midwestern states. Mr. Ray Barker, president of the company, along with his marketing director, Mr. Robert Gould, felt there was an attractive potential market for motors to be used in lawn mowers, snow throwers, and snowmobiles, to mention a few. A recent marketing research project gave them sufficient reason for this belief.

The company had the plans, facilities, and technical competence to begin production of the motors in a matter of months. The single biggest problem centered around the sales force. Both Mr. Barker and Mr. Gould felt the company was financially unable to support the development and maintenance of a sales force for the new motors. In addition, they both felt that the existing sales force was already handling as much work as it could and that it would be still more inappropriate to use the same sales force since the new motors would serve a different market.

The decision to produce the new motors could not be made until the selling problem was resolved.

Are there any feasible alternatives open to R. F. Barker, Inc., or should the company abandon its plans until such time as it would be financially able to use its own sales force?

When you have mastered the contents of this chapter, you should be able to:

1. Discuss house-to-house selling as a retailing method.
2. Compare the different types of independent stores with respect to their operating methods and competitive advantages and disadvantages.
3. Explain the three main ways in which retail institutions grow.
4. Compare three types of large-scale integrated retailers (mail-order houses, department stores, and chain-store systems) with respect to their development, operating methods, and competitive advantages and disadvantages.
5. Outline the circumstances under which producers should include each class of retailer (discussed in this chapter) in their marketing channels.

CHAP-TER 11

DISTRIBUTION: RETAILING AND MAJOR CLASSES OF RETAILERS

Retailing

Retailing occurs in all marketing channels for consumer goods because, by definition, it consists of the activities involved in selling directly to ultimate consumers. While a few producers of consumer products handle their own retail distribution, most rely on separately owned retail institutions to distribute their outputs to ultimate consumers. Although you, as a consumer, already know a great deal about retailers, to understand retail distribution you must know more, especially about the operating methods of various retail institutions. Discussion in this chapter focuses on (1) the retail field in general, (2) house-to-house selling, (3) small and large independent retailers, and (4) large-scale integrated retailers (mail-order houses, department stores, and chain-store systems).

Marketers and consumers view the roles of retailers somewhat differently. Producers and wholesalers regard retailers as intermediaries providing contacts with target consumer market segments, while consumers think of them as sources of supply for all types of products. Actually, retailers serve both roles—they buy and assemble consumer products (either directly from producers or through wholesalers) and resell them to ultimate consumers. Because both roles are so basic, retailers are the most numerous of all marketing institutions—wherever there is more than a handful of people, there are retailers.

There are many different ways for retailers to play their basic roles. Each adjusts to the expectations of both its suppliers and its customers through the merchandise selection it handles, the size of its operation, its pricing, its location, and its selling methods—as well as through other operating policies and practices. Because of the many choices of this sort open to retailers there is tremendous variety among retail institutions. Retailers range all the way from the roadside fruit stand to the multibillion dollar corporate chain.

While we tend to think of retailing as being confined to fixed retail locations, it may take place wherever an ultimate consumer and seller get together. In fact, fixed retail locations are a relatively recent development. Retailing in ancient times was carried on mostly by traveling peddlers or from temporary stalls situtated in town or village markets. The outdoor public market is still a feature of the retailing system (though a relatively unimportant one), and the peddler has evolved into the house-to-house selling organization.

The Retail Field: Size and Importance

Retailing is a very large business, both in total establishments and sales volume. In the United States, as Table 11–1 shows, about 1,810,000 retail establishments transact over $500 billion in sales annually. In the 25 years from 1948 to 1973, the number of retail establishments grew fairly modestly (up by 40,000), but retail sales increased by over three and one-half times. The average yearly sales per establishment was $278,000 in 1973. Despite the relatively small average yearly sales of retail stores, there are some giant retail organizations, as shown in Table 11–2. Notice that these large retailers had higher profits as a percent of their invested capital than as a percent of sales—the same thing holds true for nearly all retail businesses, small or large.

Figure 11–1 shows the relative importance of different lines of retail trade. Retailers in the food group (grocery stores, meat and seafood markets, and bakery products stores) transact the largest volume of sales, annually accounting for over $105 billion. Automotive group retailers (automobile dealers and tires, batteries, and accessories dealers) rank second to the food group retailers with just over $100

Table 11–1 Retailers: Number of Establishments and Total Sales—Selected Years

YEAR	NUMBER OF ESTABLISHMENTS	SALES (in Billions of Dollars)
1973 (estimated)	1,810,000	503.3
1967	1,763,000	310.2
1963	1,708,000	244.2
1958	1,795,000	200.4
1954	1,722,000	170.0
1948	1,770,000	130.5

Source: *Statistical Abstract of the United States, 1971*, and Department of Commerce, Bureau of the Census.

Table 11–2 The Ten Largest U.S. Retailers in 1973

RETAILER	SALES (000)*	PROFIT	
		As Percent of Sales	As Percent of Invested Capital
1. Sears, Roebuck	12,306,229	5.5	13.6
2. Safeway Stores	6,773,687	1.3	13.1
3. Great Atlantic & Pacific Tea	6,747,689	0.2	2.0
4. J.C. Penney	6,243,677	3.0	14.1
5. S.S. Kresge	4,702,504	2.9	15.0
6. Kroger	4,204,677	0.7	7.6
7. Marcor (includes Montgomery Ward)	4,077,415	2.4	9.4
8. F.W. Woolworth	3,722,107	2.5	10.2
9. Federated Department Stores	2,966,176	3.8	12.8
10. Rapid American	2,341,028	1.3	13.3

*Net sales, including all operating revenues. For companies not on a calendar year, the 1973 figures are for any fiscal year ending no later than March 2, 1974. Sales of subsidiaries are included when they are consolidated.

Source: By courtesy of *Fortune*, July 1974, pp. 120–21.

billion sales, followed by general merchandise retailers (including department stores, variety stores, and mail-order houses), who have nearly $85 billion sales. Together, in 1973, these three groups accounted for over 57 percent of all retail sales in the United States, exactly the same percentage as in 1970.

Figure 11–2 shows per capita expenditures in the various lines of retail trade in 1973. On the average, each individual spent nearly $510 in food group stores, almost $490 in automotive group stores, and about $400 in general merchandise group retail stores. In each case, more dollars per capita were spent in 1973 than in 1972.

House-to-House Selling

House-to-House Selling

Modern house-to-house salespeople are descended from the "Yankee peddlers" who, on foot, on horseback, and then in wagons, traveled from farm to farm and from settlement to settlement, selling various manufactured articles to pioneers and frontiersmen.[1] Today's house-to-house salespeople differ from the peddler in two important ways. First, they are seldom the completely independent operators that their predecessors were. Most house-to-house salespeople are

[1] A fine historical account of house-to-house selling may be seen in: Harry Golden, *Forgotten Pioneers* (Cleveland: World Publishing Company, 1963).

either semi-independent agents or employees of large manufacturers or distributors utilizing this retailing method. Among these large concerns are such well-known organizations as Avon Products (cosmetics and toilet articles), Wearever Aluminum (cooking utensils), Tupperware (plastic housewares), and The Fuller Brush Company (cleaning and household articles). Second, today's house-to-house salespeople tend to restrict their offerings to a small number of articles within a single merchandise line. They may specialize in encyclopedias, lawn and garden stock, vacuum cleaners, china, cosmetics, or household cleaning materials. The salespeople employed by the large house-to-house organizations are almost equally divided between men and women, more than half working part time. Thus, it is not unusual for a direct-selling company to have from 5,000 to 10,000 salespeople, nearly all working on a commission basis. Avon Products has more than 350,000 people, mainly women, selling part time in its world-wide operation.

House-to-house selling eliminates the expenses of retail store operation, but it is by no means a low-cost retailing method. It requires travel and personal contact, and substantial costs are involved in recruiting, maintaining, and managing sales staffs large enough to transact a profitable sales volume. These cost conditions affect the operating methods of direct-selling companies. Many handle either fairly high-priced items or items sold in assortments, in both cases to build up the average order size. Some, such as Avon Products, strive to make more effective use of salespeople's time by establishing steady customers. Others, such as Tupperware, Incorpo-

Figure 11–1
Sales by lines of
retail trade

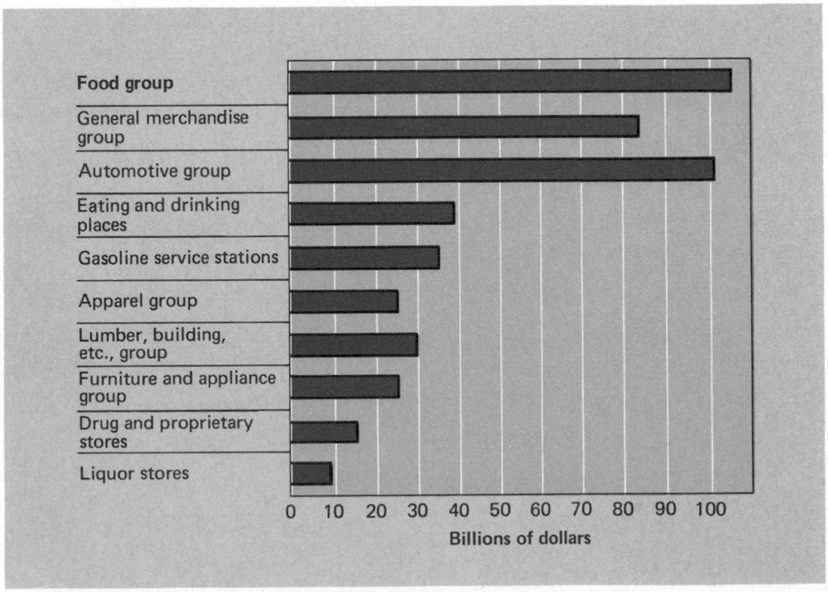

Source: 1973 Department of Commerce, Bureau of the Census.

Figure 11–2
Per capita sales of selected kinds of business of all retail stores in the United States: 1973 and 1972

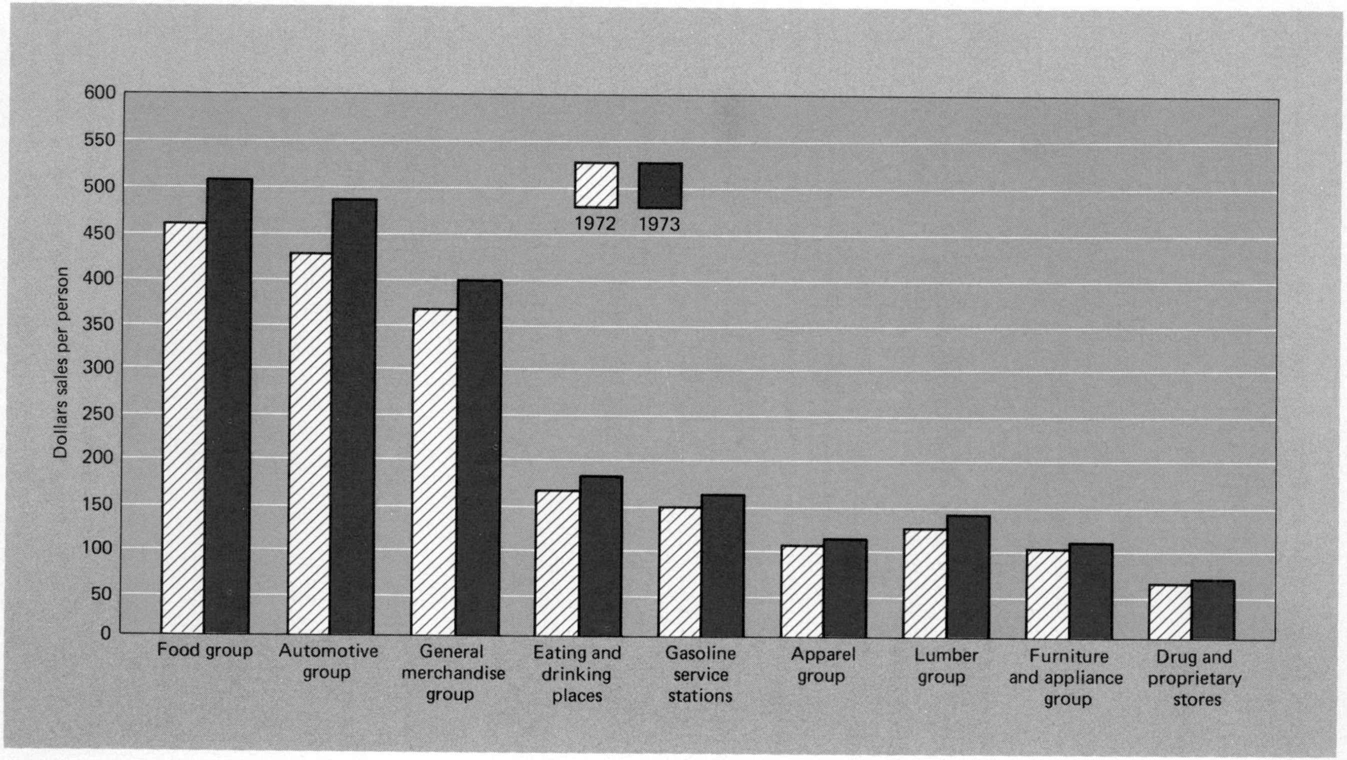

Source: Department of Commerce, Bureau of the Census.

Party Plan Selling

rated, use *party plan selling,* in which a group of potential buyers are brought together in one of their homes for a product demonstration; several orders often result at one time. The commissions paid to house-to-house salespeople usually range from 25 to 40 percent of the amount of the sale.

The total costs of house-to-house selling run to approximately 60 percent of sales. This includes not only salespeople's commissions but costs of supervision and administration, clerical work, shipping, credit, and promotion and advertising. This may appear high, and it is for retailing. But companies using house-to-house selling normally do not have to allow for wholesalers' and retailers' margins, nor do they generally have large fixed selling and administrative expenses. Whether house-to-house selling is an expensive distribution method depends on the manufacturer's alternatives. If they involve the use of wholesalers and retailers and the maintenance of a full-time permanent staff of salaried salesmen, it may well be that house-to-house selling is economical in comparison.

House-to-house selling sometimes is the best solution to a manufacturer's retail distribution problems. This may be the only way that a radically different new product can be introduced, particularly by a company with limited finances. For example, the early manufacturers of vacuum cleaners found it almost impossible to secure distribution among conventional retailers because retailers had difficulties in convincing consumers of the merits of the product. The manufacturers discovered that by demonstrating their cleaner's superior cleaning power in the home on the housewives' own carpets, it was easy to overcome sales resistance. Once vacuum cleaners had been generally accepted by consumers, it was possible to abandon house-to-house selling for regular retailers. However, two successful manufacturers, Electrolux and Kirby, have never abandoned this method of selling their vacuum cleaners. Certain other products, too, such as sewing machines and rug cleaners, seem to sell more easily when demonstrated in the home. Still others, such as encyclopedias and Bibles, appear to be ones that most consumers will not shop for in retail stores but that they will buy if approached in their own homes.

Independent Stores

Independent Store

An *independent store* is a retailing business unit controlled by its own individual ownership or management. Although there are both large and small independent stores, most large-scale independently owned stores are classified under such other headings as supermarkets, department stores, and discount houses. In our discussion, we consider an independent store as any individually owned or managed retail business unit, small or large, which cannot be readily classified as a supermarket, department store, or discount house. We use this working definition to sidestep the academic problem of distinguishing small-scale from large-scale retailers. How does one, after all, decide where small ends and large begins? The sales volume yardstick is the one most used but number of employees, square feet of floor space, and inventory dollar size have all been tried. One big difficulty with all these measures is that the dividing line must still be chosen arbitrarily; furthermore, the idea of just what large means keeps changing. In the 1950s a grocery store with $500,000 in annual sales was considered rather large, but by the 1970s a store in that same range was considered small. Thus, the criteria for largeness are constantly being revised upward. But, because at any given time some retailers are smaller than others, in the following discussion we refer to independent retailers as being relatively small or large.

THE GENERAL STORE

General Store

The *general store* is one of the oldest types of independent retailers. It is a relatively small business, not departmentalized, usually located in a rural or isolated community, and primarily engaged in selling a general assortment of merchandise—of which the most important line is food. Its more important subsidiary lines are notions, apparel, farm supplies, and gasoline. These stores were important in farming and frontier sections until, in the 1920s, the spread of other types of retailing and widespread ownership of automobiles gave consumers greater shopping mobility, causing general stores gradually to decline. Some general stores, however, still operate in sparsely populated areas, especially in the West and South.

OTHER SMALL INDEPENDENT RETAILERS

Today, most small independent stores are concentrated in fields where it is relatively easy to set up in business. Usually, this means that no great amount of capital is needed or that easy financing is available. Probably, this is the main reason why there have been so many small independent grocery retailers until recently[2]—a fairly small investment in inventory turned over rapidly results in a sales figure many times the value of the inventory. Gasoline retailing operates on the same principle, with the bonus that many petroleum refiners offer generous financial assistance to individuals who want to open their own stations. Many small retailers, of course, are well financed, but they are the exceptions.

Small independent retailers frequently meet strong competition from large retail chains, supermarkets, discount houses, and department stores. The small independent generally buys its inventory from wholesalers or other middlemen, rather than directly from producers, so its merchandise costs are higher than those of large, direct-buying competitors. Thus, it often has to charge higher prices (to

[2] During the 1960s the newly evolved convenience food store chains (such as 7–11) developed at a rapid pace, often at the expense of small independent grocers.

cover its costs) than its competitors. In most instances, then, small independents must use something other than the price appeal to attract trade. The more successful find some way to differentiate their stores in their customers' minds. It may consist of nothing more than personalized service and friendly relations with customers. Or the independent may stay open longer hours than larger competitors and offer such extra services as credit and delivery. A convenient location, too, may be attractive to customers. As long as substantial numbers of ultimate consumers continue to consider such things important, small independent retail stores are likely to stay in business.

LARGE INDEPENDENT RETAILERS

Large independent stores are most important in retail fields where corporate chains, department stores, and other integrated retail institutions either have no operating advantages or are at a competitive disadvantage. In retailing women's clothing, for instance, the independent store buys most of its merchandise directly from manufacturers, the same source from which the chain women's clothing store and the women's clothing departments of the department store must buy. Whereas the chain may buy larger quantities than the independent, any quantity discounts it receives are generally too small to permit it to use the lower price appeal effectively. Possibly of even greater significance is the fact that most items of women's clothing are not at all standardized, either in appearance or construction. In large towns and cities, several women's clothing outlets may handle the same manufacturer's line, but, because they normally handle very few identical garments, the consumer has little opportunity to make price comparisons. In small towns there is even less likelihood that competing retailers will represent the same manufacturers, or sell identical garments if they do, so that it is virtually impossible for the consumer to make direct price comparisons. This makes merchandise selection especially important in retailing women's clothing; the local independent can offer dresses and sportswear in tune with consumer preferences in its own locality; chain organizations, with their centralized buying, find it hard to adjust to unique preferences of local markets. Other lines that offer similar competitive advantages to the independent retailer are men's clothing and furniture.

Some large independent stores are successful because their owners have specialized knowledge that enables them to "run rings around" larger competitors. Examples abound in the retailing of such goods as Oriental rugs, musical instruments, and sports equipment. Numerous consumers hesitate to buy such items without professional advice. Chain stores and department stores sell these items, but usually they have to use less well-informed personnel than those who staff independent specialty stores.

Specialty Store

Another group of large independent retailers has succeeded in building local reputations as quality stores. Some handle large

Quality Store

assortments of related merchandise—for example, men's or ladies' apparel—and feature the latest fashions. Others deal in lines, such as jewelry, where consumers consider the store image as important as merchandise quality. Independents often find it easier to build prestige reputations than their chain-store or department store competitors. Furthermore, many independent quality stores are old and well established; it is not easy for competitors to acquire quality reputations locally in the space of a few months or years.

COMPETITIVE ADVANTAGES OF INDEPENDENT STORES

In comparison with their competitors, successful independents, both large and small, possess significant advantages. The most important is that they can more easily adapt their operations to fit the unique needs of the communities in which they do business. Furthermore, the owner-managers of many successful independent stores often are more able and more aggressive than the hired managers of department store and chain-store units. Nor should it be overlooked that many consumers are loyal to locally owned and operated stores and look askance at stores controlled from out of town.

The competitive strength of the independent retailer varies considerably from one line of retailing to another (as well as from one location to another). In retailing many convenience goods, such as food and drugs, independents account for only a small portion of total volume, and these independents obtain their competitive advantage through convenience of location or offering additional services. In other retailing lines, where chains and other mass retailers can gain little price advantage through volume buying and where the independents can adjust more nearly to market needs, independents frequently account for important shares of the market.

Large-Scale Integrated Retailers

Mass Retailers

The large-scale or *mass retailers* achieve their growth in three main ways. First, some grow by increasing the physical size of the operating unit to cater to more customers. As a store becomes larger, its power to attract customers increases because of the greater variety of merchandise offered for sale; moreover, up to a certain size, its costs per dollar of sales decrease. Beyond the optimum size, costs increase faster than sales. Optimum size of a retail establishment is also limited by the geographical extent of its market. For example, a department store that has its market limited to a single trading area does not have the growth potential of a mail-order retailer, whose market area may be as broad as the reach of the postal system or the United Parcel Service.

Second, a retailer can also expand by acquiring additional

stores in different market areas. Such multiple outlets may be operated in any of three ways: (1) a branch store operation may be established, with the parent store servicing the branches' merchandising and operating needs; (2) the outlets may be operated independently, being tied to the parent organization solely on a financial basis; or (3) a central management office may be responsible for all aspects of the retail stores' operations.

Third, retail growth may come through integration. An integrated retail institution reduces marketing costs by eliminating, simplifying, or consolidating various activities involved in the marketing process. When a retailer bypasses a wholesaler to buy directly from a producer, some part of that wholesaler's activities are taken over by the retailer. If the retailer performs these activities more efficiently than the wholesaler, its costs are reduced accordingly. Most large-scale retailing operations grew through some combination of larger outlets, additional outlets, and integration.

MAIL-ORDER HOUSES

Mail-Order Houses

History Several factors contributed to the founding and early growth of the larger *mail-order houses.* Montgomery Ward and Sears Roebuck, founded in 1872 and 1886, respectively, both owed much of their early success to the completion of the transcontinental railroads and improvements in postal service, including the advent of rural free delivery. These developments, coupled with the comparative isolation from retail centers of most of the then predominantly rural population, set the stage for an enthusiastic reception for mail-order merchandising. General stores, formerly the chief source of supply for the farm population, found themselves hard pressed to meet either the prices (achieved through integration of wholesaling and retailing) or the extensive merchandise offerings of the mail-order houses. Consumers in small towns were also attracted by the mail-order catalogs, even though most such towns had stores that collectively offered nearly as wide a merchandise selection.

Mail-Order Retailing of General Merchandise Until the 1920s, both Montgomery Ward and Sears Roebuck confined themselves solely to mail-order operations. In 1921 Montgomery Ward opened its first retail store, and in 1925 Sears Roebuck followed this move. The opening of retail stores was hastened by the spectacular growth in automobile ownership and by considerable improvements in rural roads, both of which helped transform many rural consumers into small-town shoppers and lessened the relative attractiveness of mail-order buying. Furthermore, the nation's population was rapidly shifting from predominantly rural to predominantly urban. The managements of Ward's and Sears were alert to the marketing significance of these changes; hence their decisions to open retail outlets. Today, the bulk of the sales of both concerns comes from the sales of their retail stores, although mail order still accounts for sizable proportions of their business. Indeed, the retail stores of both companies feature catalog order desks, which solicit orders for delivery by their mail-order operations. In some locations, too, both Sears and Ward's maintain catalog order stores at which consumers place mail orders either in person or by telephone.

Mail-order houses such as Ward's, Sears, Spiegel, and Penney's offer wide assortments of articles within each of a large number of merchandise lines. They buy directly from the producer, often contracting for a large share or even all of a producer's output. Many small manufacturers are completely dependent on one or the other of the large mail-order houses for distributing all they produce. Most of the over 20,000 sources of supply for Sears, for instance, are small manufacturers. Indeed, the company is on record as stating that "it prefers to work with smaller factories, which concentrate on production, and look to it for a substantial part of their distribution."[3] In the case of Sears, such small manufacturers are the main suppliers of Sears' own brands—Kenmore, Homart, Craftsman, Silvertone, J. C. Higgins, Charmode, and others.

Other Types of Mail-Order Retailing The mail-order method is also used for retailing more limited selections of merchandise. Small manufacturers often use this method to sell much or all of their output. Among the items retailed directly by such manufacturers are shirts, men's and women's apparel, toys, bird houses and feeders, and rugs. Some of these manufacturers distribute catalogs to consumers, but more often they use direct-mail promotional literature and small advertisements in magazines and newspapers. Mail-order retailing is an important distribution method, too, for many growers of trees, shrubs, plants, and seeds, who distribute their catalogs to homeowners throughout the country.

Mail-order retailing is also used by the many "of-the-month" clubs. Typically, these clubs provide the service of preselected merchandise, thus relieving their members of the need for choosing their purchases from a large number of possible alternatives. Book-of-the-Month Club, for instance, informs its members of monthly selections which must be rejected by members if they do not wish to receive them. Members not sending in rejections automatically receive monthly selections and are billed accordingly. Generally, members of "of-the-month" clubs must accept a given number of selections during their first year of membership, after which they may, on their own initiative, write the club canceling their memberships. Club members, therefore, are in the position of finding it easier to accept rather than to reject selections (this is the feature consumer activists refer to as the *negative option system*) and to continue rather than discontinue their memberships. Because of their operating scheme, the clubs are often said to provide automatic distribution for products

Negative Option System

[3] "How Sears Stays on Top," *International Management*, Vol. 23 (April 1968), p. 61.

chosen as monthly selections. Most of the clubs are true middlemen, for they make their purchases from producers and resell them to consumers. The book clubs are the longest established in the field, but similar organizations engage in mail-order retailing of such items as food, fruit, toys, gifts, and foreign imports.

DEPARTMENT STORES

Department Store

History and Growth The *department store* was a European, not an American, retailing innovation. The Bon Marché and other Paris department stores came into existence and flourished during the French Second Empire (1852–1871). Leading American retailers of the 1850s and 1860s visited Paris and other European market centers regularly on buying trips and observed the operating methods of the Bon Marché and other European department stores.[4] The result was that the idea was transplanted to the United States. Among the firms that began operating as department stores during this period were R. H. Macy (New York), Jordan Marsh (Boston), Marshall Field (Chicago), Scruggs-Vandervoort-Barney (St. Louis), Meier & Frank (Portland, Ore.), Thalhimer Brothers (Richmond, Va.), and Rich's (Atlanta). Not all of these would have qualified as department stores at the time of their founding; most started as other types of businesses and converted later to department store operations. By the close of the 1870s, department stores were well established in nearly every major U.S. city and in many smaller cities and towns.

Nature of Operations Formally defined, a department store is a large retailing business unit that handles a wide variety of shopping and specialty goods—including women's ready-to-wear and accessories, men's and boys' wear, piece goods, small wares, and home furnishings—and is organized into separate departments for purposes of promotion, service, and control. Thus, the two main features of the department store are a broad merchandise offering and departmental organization. Responsibility for buying and selling is decentralized to individual departments, each carrying different lines of goods, and each under the control of a merchandising executive called a buyer or department manager. Buyers are relatively free to operate their departments as they see fit, provided their operations produce profits considered adequate by the store's top management and their merchandise lines fit into the overall store image in terms of price and quality. In addition to exercising general supervision over merchandising activities, the store's central administrative organization operates and maintains the physical facilities, provides such services as credit and delivery for the customers, and assists the merchandising department with such activities as advertising and promotion.

[4] P. H. Nystrom, *Economics of Retailing* (New York: The Ronald Press Company, 1932), p. 127.

Originally, department stores relied on the great breadth of their merchandise offerings to attract customers. Gradually, however, the more aggressive stores, seeking to build their trade, broadened the range of services offered to customers. Today, it is a rare department store that does not provide such customer services as charge accounts, installment plans, and home delivery. Some offer such additional services as elaborate restaurants and tearooms, nurseries to care for small children, and free instruction in arts and crafts. A few of these services are self-supporting; others are not. But even though some services may show an accounting-type loss, they are generally maintained because of their proven power to pull in customers.

By its very nature, the department store is a horizontally integrated retail institution. It brings together under one roof a range of merchandise offerings comparable to the combined offerings of many stores specializing in single or fewer merchandise lines. Although this exposition-like character is the source of much of the department store's drawing power, it is not without its disadvantages, particularly in purchasing. Some departments do enough business to justify direct buying from manufacturers, but many do not. The small-volume departments, particularly in individually owned stores, are often unable to buy in large enough lots to qualify for the quantity discounts offered by manufacturers and, hence, must buy through wholesalers and agents, resulting in high merchandise costs.

Buying Groups

Department Store Buying Groups Because of the disadvantages they encounter in purchasing, some independently owned department stores join buying groups. Member stores cooperatively own, maintain, and use the services of resident buying offices located in such market centers as New York and Chicago. Through consolidation of the orders of member stores, the buying office achieves considerable savings by placing orders for lots larger than any member could buy individually. Furthermore, the combined bargaining power often results in lower price quotations by suppliers. A secondary, though important, activity of the resident buying office involves providing member stores with current information relating to prices, availability of new items, and fashion trends.

Ownership Groups

Department Store Ownership Groups Many previously independent department stores have been absorbed into ownership groups. Most department store ownership groups were put together originally by financiers rather than by merchandisers. They were intended to result, primarily, not in improved operating efficiency, but in immediate profits for the organizers who, as financial middlemen, were most interested in profiting from the flotation of new issues of common stock. But, over time, central managements of the ownership groups lost their solely financial orientations and began to emphasize the improvement and standardization of operating policies and procedures. One early development was the centralized buying offices, which enabled stores in the group to buy many standard stock items and some fashion goods at lower costs. Nevertheless, many types of merchandise are still bought by stores individually. Among these are high-fashion items, where speed of procurement and direct contact with the producer are important, and articles needed to satisfy purely local demands. Top managements of the department store ownership groups have also worked toward greater uniformity in nonmerchandising activities, such as in the standardization of personnel policies and store-operating systems and records.

Generally, each store in an ownership group plans its merchandise offerings to cater to classes of trade in its own selling area. Because the inventory is mainly shopping goods (items customers shop around for and compare before buying) and specialty goods (items customers spend considerable time searching for), and because consumer preferences for such articles vary considerably from one area to another, most department stores, whether or not they belong to ownership groups, find it difficult to standardize the merchandise offerings of stores in different locations. Furthermore, stores in the same ownership group often attract different classes of trade in different cities.

The uniqueness of the merchandise offering and of the classes of trade catered to results in each store's having a distinctive image. Thus, most department store ownership groups continue to operate stores under the names they had when they were independently owned. Allied Stores Corporation, for instance, operates, among others, Jordan Marsh in Boston, Titche-Goettinger in Dallas, the Bon Marché in Seattle, Dey Brothers in Syracuse, and Joske's in San Antonio and Houston. Federated Department Stores operates, among others, Filene's in Boston, Shillito's in Cincinnati, the Boston Store in Milwaukee, Bloomingdale's in New York, Abraham & Strauss in Brooklyn, Burdine's in Miami, and Bullock's in Los Angeles. Each of these stores has a distinct image in its own trading area.

CHAIN-STORE SYSTEMS

Chain-Store System

A *chain-store system* is a group of retail stores of essentially the same type, centrally owned and with some degree of centralized control of operation. This definition is broad enough to include not only the well-known A & P and Woolworth chains, but also Ward's and Sears' retail stores and the different department store ownership groups. Thus, basically, the distinguishing feature of a chain-store system is that it owns and controls a group of stores. The department store ownership group is one type of chain-store system, the retail stores of Montgomery Ward are another, and the F. W. Woolworth stores represent still another type. However, by long-established and customary usage, the term chain-store system refers to a multi-unit retailing operation that cannot be categorized as a department store ownership group or the retail outlets of a mail-order house.

An indication of the relative importance of chain-store systems is provided by the information in Table 11–3. Chain-store systems made up of eleven or more stores collectively account for over 30 percent of the nation's total retail sales. Notice, too, that since 1964, chain stores have been increasing their proportion of total retail sales.

Table 11–3 Total Sales of Retail Stores and Chain-Store Systems with Eleven or More Stores: 1964 to 1972*

YEAR	SALES OF ALL RETAIL STORES	TOTAL SALES OF CHAIN-STORE SYSTEMS**	PERCENT CHAIN-STORE SYSTEM SALES OF ALL STORES SALES
1972	448,379	137,650	30.7
1970	375,527	110,848	29.5
1968	339,324	94,194	27.8
1966	303,956	80,323	26.4
1964	261,870	68,306	26.1

*In millions of dollars.
**Based on sales of organizations operating 11 or more retail stores.

Source: Department of Commerce, Bureau of the Census; *Monthly Retail Trade Report*, Monthly data in Office of Business Economics; *Survey of Current Business.*

Table 11–4 indicates the relative importance of chain-store systems in various retail fields. They are of the most importance in the variety store field, where they account for over 80 percent of that field's total sales. In the nation's largest retail field—groceries—they transact more than half of the total sales. They hold relatively small shares of the market in retail fields such as furniture and appliances, restaurant operations, and men's and boys' wear.

Strengths from Horizontal Integration Certain strengths of the chain-store system trace to its horizontal integration (that is, its operation of multiple stores). With each new store, the system extends its reach to another group of prospective customers. Also, each store added means greater sales volume and, consequently, increased opportunity to effect economies through buying in larger sized lots. It also means that the costs of central administration and of providing highly specialized merchandising, buying, and promotional services can be spread over more stores. Thus, such costs are reduced for each store in the system. Furthermore, other economies

Table 11–4 Sales of Chain-Store Systems in Various Retail Fields, 1973[1]

KIND OF BUSINESS	SALES IN 1973	PERCENT OF TOTAL SALES IN FIELD, 1973[2]
Total sales	154,546	30.7
Durable goods stores[3]	9,606	5.6
Tire, battery, accessory dealers	2,210	27.9
Furniture and appliance group	2,085	8.7
Nondurable goods stores[3]	144,940	43.5
Apparel group[3]	6,569	27.3
Men's and boys' wear stores[4]	749	13.4
Women's apparel, accessory stores[5]	2,393	26.2
Shoe stores	1,908	45.1
Drug and proprietary stores	5,857	37.9
Eating and drinking places	3,193	8.4
Food group[3]	55,865	52.8
Grocery stores	55,165	56.1
Variety stores	6,627	80.7

[1]In millions of dollars. Data based on sales of organizations operating 11 or more retail stores.
[2]Multiunit sales as percent of all retail sales.
[3]Includes data not shown separately.
[4]Comprises men's and boys' clothing, furnishings stores, and custom tailors.
[5]Comprises women's ready-to-wear, other apparel, accessory, speciality shops, and furriers.

Source: Dept. of Commerce, Bureau of the Census; *Monthly Retail Trade Report*, and unpublished data.

are effected through standardization of store systems and procedures and adoption of uniform personnel policies. These strengths, all due primarily to horizontal integration, are reflected in lower costs for the merchandise handled and in generally lower operating expenses than those incurred by most independent retailers.

Merchandising and Operating Economies Relative to most of its competitors, particularly those that are independent stores, the chain realizes significant savings in merchandising and operating expenses. Some are secured through eliminating or limiting such customer services as credit and delivery. Others are obtained by limiting merchandise variety—by stocking, for example, only three different brands of canned peas in each of two sizes rather than three brands in four sizes.

Other economies are realized through application of the basic merchandising philosophy of the chain, which is to squeeze the maximum sales out of each dollar invested in inventory. The chain, in other words, gears its operation so that it has a small inventory relative to its sales volume. One aspect of this philosophy relates to decisions on composition of inventory; the chain seeks to maximize the number of items with a short shelf life (the fast sellers) and to minimize the number of those with a long shelf life (the slow movers).

The most significant aspect in applying the chain's basic merchandising philosophy is its approach to making sales. It attempts to build a large sales volume by pricing its merchandise lower than many of its competitors, which means, in effect, that it is satisfied with a comparatively low profit per item sold. Successful application of this merchandising philosophy, then, results in a large sales volume relative to size of the inventory. Thus, besides taking care about the makeup of its inventory, the typical chain "works its inventory harder" than do many competitors. The chain stresses high sales volume and low unit profits, while many competitors are satisfied with low sales volume and high unit profits.

Buying Policy Because the chain-store system is a high-volume operation, it ordinarily gets its merchandise directly from producers or through their agents. Rarely does a chain buy from merchant wholesalers, for the system is usually able to buy in larger quantities and with larger discounts than wholesalers can. Thus, by operating its own warehouses, the chain-store system effectively becomes its own wholesaler. Chain-store systems, therefore, are also vertically integrated; they take over and perform for themselves marketing activities that would otherwise be performed by separate wholesale institutions.

Weaknesses Most weaknesses of the chain-store system stem from its horizontal integration and its merchandising philosophy. Centralized decision making often means that individual chain units cannot react to changing local conditions as quickly as alert local competitors. When individual chain units lag behind the independents in making new products and brands available—and frequently they do—centralized purchasing is usually at fault. Furthermore, in keeping with the high sales volume and low-profit merchandising philosophy, the chain economizes on other costs and often dispenses with such services as charge accounts and delivery. In doing this, it, in effect, concedes to competitors the patronage of consumers desiring these services. Moreover, because of its integrated nature, the chain has many stores and requires many managers. Recruiting, training, and retaining managers in the numbers needed are formidable tasks. Individual chains, of course, have found ways to deal with, or minimize, these inherent weaknesses; nevertheless, these weaknesses, together with the impersonal and cold character of most chains, serve to offset many competitive advantages chains have over independents.

Convenience Goods Chains

Distribution of Convenience Goods Chain-store systems are important links in the distribution system for many convenience goods—those goods that consumers generally want to buy frequently, immediately, and with minimum shopping effort. Both large and small manufacturers of food products (where chains account for over 50 percent of total volume) and drug products (where chains account for roughly 38 percent of total volume), for instance, know that their brands cannot be made sufficiently available to large masses of consumers unless chain outlets stock them. Manufacturers of items sold largely through variety stores find that, if they are to achieve any sales volume at all, they need chain-store distribution.

Offering producers of convenience goods the tempting prize of widespread and high-volume retail distribution at a relatively low selling cost, skilled chain-store buying specialists drive hard bargains. They push for and usually obtain the lowest possible prices and the most advantageous promotional allowances (which are payments made by manufacturers for advertising and otherwise promoting products at the retail level). Chains handling convenience goods generally expect most suppliers to promote their own products with heavy consumer advertising to minimize the in-store selling effort needed. In the case of products that do not lend themselves to such promotion, the chain often prefers to handle its own store brands, packed for it either under contract by outside manufacturers or by captive (that is, owned by the chain) canning or processing plants.

Shopping Goods Chains

Distribution of Shopping Goods Chain-store systems are also important retailers of shopping goods—items that consumers select and buy only after doing some "shopping around." Chains are active, for instance, in the retailing of men's and women's apparel, dry goods, and shoes. In contrast to many of their independent competitors in these lines, however, shopping-goods chains tend to concentrate on low-priced and fast-selling items. In other words, chains that specialize in shopping goods seek items that resemble convenience goods as closely as possible. To obtain them, chains often have to pass up high-fashion merchandise in favor of more staple items. Because of this, as well as because of the need for large sales volumes, shopping-goods chains generally cater to middle- and lower-income consumer groups.

Commonly, shopping-goods chains have manufacturers under contract to supply them with goods according to the chain's own specifications. The supplying manufacturers need not be especially large, but they must be large enough that they can produce enough to fill the chain's requirements.

Some shopping-goods chains are the retail arms of the manufacturers who own and control them. Bond Clothes, a retailer of men's and boys' clothing, makes its own suits and coats. The Thom McAn stores are operated by Melville Shoe Corporation. Other manufacturers, such as Genesco, sell part of their output through their own retail outlets and the rest through other types of retailers. But even when chain-store systems are controlled by manufacturers, there is a need for outside sources of supply. Thus, a manufacturer-controlled shoe chain, such as Thom McAn, retails not only shoes but related items, such as hosiery and shoe polish, bought from outside sources.

Summary

Discussion in this chapter introduced the field of retailing and focused on the operating methods of major classes of retailers. Retailing occurs in all marketing channels for consumer goods, with most producers of consumer products relying heavily on separately owned retail institutions to distribute their outputs to ultimate consumers. Thus, retailers serve as marketing intermediaries for producers and wholesalers and as sources of supply for ultimate consumers. Because of the many possible ways of adjusting to the expectations of suppliers and customers, retailers are the most diverse, as well as the most numerous, of all marketing institutions.

House-to-house selling, one of the most ancient retailing methods, today is mainly important in only a few lines of trade, even though several large concerns rely heavily upon it for their retail distribution. Although house-to-house selling eliminates the expenses of retail store operations, it is generally a high-cost retailing method. Nevertheless, some manufacturers find retail distribution through house-to-house selling appropriate, especially those with products that benefit from demonstration in the home or that consumers will usually not shop for in retail stores.

Independent retailers, both small and large, take a variety of forms. The general store, perhaps the oldest type, has all but disappeared. Small independent retailers, generally concentrated in fields involving relatively small capital investments, usually do not try to compete on a price basis but find various ways to differentiate their stores in the eyes of their customers. Large independent retailers are most important in fields where integrated retailers either have no operating advantages or are at competitive disadvantages.

The large-scale integrated retailers achieved their growth in various ways. The large mail-order houses, capitalizing on several environmental changes, integrated wholesaling and retailing for a wide range of merchandise and made effective use of catalog selling and the price appeal; later, capitalizing on further environmental changes, they also became important operators of retail stores. The department stores, featuring broad merchandise offerings and departmental organizations, relied both on their exposition-like character and various customer services to attract trade. Chain-store systems, applying a basic philosophy of small inventory relative to sales volume, capitalized on their integrated nature, horizontally and vertically, and made effective use of competitive prices; today, chains are highly important distributors of convenience goods sold to mass markets and shopping goods sold to middle- and lower-income market segments.

You should now have a good "feel" for retail distribution. Specifically, at this point, you should be well acquainted with not only the nature and importance of retailing but the characteristics and operating methods of house-to-house retailers, small and large independent stores, and the large-scale integrated retailers (mail-order houses, department stores, and chain-store systems). You should also have a clear idea as to the particular circumstances under which producers should include each of these classes of retailers in their marketing channels.

QUESTIONS AND PROBLEMS

1. Discuss the various reasons which lead certain manufacturers to use house-to-house selling.
2. What do you see as the disadvantages of house-to-house selling? Explain.
3. When direct (house-to-house) selling costs run as high as 60 percent of selling price, is it really possible in your opinion to justify this method of retail distribution from a cost standpoint? Explain.
4. Explain what is meant by an "independent" store.
5. Explain the decline of the general store.
6. Would you agree that in most instances the small independent retailer is an uneconomical operation—that is, the proprietor could earn more money working the same number of hours for someone else? Why do such operations continue?
7. How would you explain the high failure rate among independent retailers?
8. In what ways can a small retailer compete effectively with large retailers? Discuss.
9. Give your assessment of the present state of retailing in terms of its efficiency and ability to effectively serve consumers. Justify your stand.
10. Explain the various ways in which large-scale or "mass" retailers have achieved their growth. If you were a retailer, which particular way would you try to expand? Discuss.
11. Identify and analyze the advantages of large-scale retailing over small-scale retailing. Which advantage do you think is most important? Why?
12. A main reason for patronizing mail-order houses in the nineteenth century was inaccessibility of other buying sources. What would you say is the main reason for patronizing such outlets today?

13. Do you feel there will always be a place for mail-order retailing in the United States? Why?
14. "The future of the department store depends on the continuing demand on the part of consumers for services, such as credit, delivery, and many more exotic ones, and their willingness to pay for these services." Do you agree?
15. Compare the department store buying group with the department store ownership group.
16. How would you assess the future of department stores in light of newer forms of retail competition?
17. What is a "chain-store system"? Discuss.
18. What is meant by "horizontal integration"? Do you think that horizontal integration is potentially dangerous in that it can lead to creation of a monopoly by a given retailer? Explain.
19. Does the fact that chain stores are horizontally integrated constitute their main competitive advantage? What other factors contribute to their success?
20. Explain the typical chain-store merchandising philosophy with respect to decisions on inventory composition. Do you feel the philosophy is realistic? Comment.
21. Analyze the weaknesses of chain-store systems.

CASE PROBLEM

Madden's Sports Center, a small independent retail sporting goods store located in a Boston suburb of 25,000 population, sold a wide line of sporting goods. For years the Sports Center was known as a quality sporting goods outlet, carrying brand names such as Wilson, Spalding, McGregor, Rawlings, and many other top brands of baseball, football, hockey, basketball, golf, tennis, bowling, and skiing equipment and supplies.

Dick Madden, proprietor, had built an excellent reputation for the store over the 20 years of its existence. In addition to serving retail customers, Madden's Sports Center supplied equipment and uniforms for all of the town's public school athletic teams and most of its youth teams in the community, such as Little League baseball, Pee Wee hockey, Bantam basketball, and Pop Warner football.

Recently, however, Dick Madden had become quite concerned over the increasing competition from discount houses and department stores, especially those in nearby shopping centers. The vigorous competition resulted primarily from the lower prices charged by the bigger stores. He was not overly concerned about his "wholesale" or school and league business, because his relationship with the administrators was solid and he had always provided them with the best products and the best service.

He was, though, concerned about the possibility of losing some of his retail patronage to the price competition of the bigger stores. Madden felt that his assortment of sporting goods was competitive with those of the discount houses and department stores, but he knew he could not compete with them on the basis of price.

How can Dick Madden's Sports Center meet the strong competitive threat of the bigger retail sporting outlets? Must he compete on a price basis in order to survive or are there other, or nonprice, ways for him to compete?

When you have mastered the contents of this chapter, you should be able to:

1. Compare retailer cooperatives and wholesaler-sponsored groups with respect to their organization and operating methods.
2. Discuss the nature of consumer cooperatives, their operating policies, and the settings conducive to their success.
3. Contrast supermarkets and discount houses with respect to basic characteristics, operating philosophy, and buying practices.
4. Analyze the conditions under which a marketer should seek to have its product sold through automatic vending machines.
5. Evaluate franchising as a method of retail distribution.
6. Discuss the implications of shopping centers for central city shopping districts and for manufacturers.
7. Explain the "wheel of retailing" hypothesis.
8. Outline the circumstances under which producers should include in their marketing channels the following classes of retailers: members of retailer-owner cooperatives, members of wholesaler-sponsored groups, consumer cooperatives, supermarkets, and discount houses.

CHAPTER 12

DISTRIBUTION: OTHER ASPECTS OF RETAILING

The highly competitive nature of retail distribution makes for tremendous variety and frequent change in types of institutions and retailing methods. From time to time, both in the United States and abroad, new or different types of retail institutions and retailing methods appear on the retail scene and those that succeed make their impact upon older types of institutions who, in order to survive, modify their ways of doing business. Discussion in this chapter focuses on the following newer retail institutions and retailing methods: (1) retailer cooperatives, (2) wholesaler-sponsored groups, (3) consumer cooperatives, (4) supermarkets, (5) discount houses, (6) automatic selling, (7) franchising, and (8) shopping centers.

Retailer Cooperatives

With the expansion of chain-store systems in the 1920s, independent stores suffered serious patronage losses. While some independents thought they could safely ignore their new competitors, others searched for ways to improve their waning competitive positions. Particularly alarming was the fact that chain outlets were selling at retail prices lower than the independents' own wholesale costs. The low chain prices were apparently clear evidence that substantial savings in merchandise costs were possible through circumventing the wholesaler. Independent retailers began to devise schemes for reducing their own wholesale costs.

COOPERATIVE BUYING CLUBS

Cooperative Buying Clubs

Some independent retailers formed *cooperative buying clubs.* They hoped that the club could obtain lower merchandise costs, and thus enable its members to meet chain-store prices. Most cooperative buying clubs were failures because, generally, they had no formal organization and their buying operations were sporadic. Many manufacturers refused to deal directly with them, often because of pressure from wholesalers. Furthermore, the independents who formed buying clubs too often failed to recognize that the low prices of the chains did not result solely from their buying advantage. They traced chiefly to practices the chains had adopted from the very first: the cash-and-carry system, the self-service store layout, and the advertising of *loss leaders.* (A loss leader is an item priced under cost that draws customers into the store.) Most independents provided credit and delivery services, operated full-service stores, and made little use of advertising; consequently, they had to charge higher retail prices to cover their costs of services and merchandise.

Loss Leaders

RETAILER-OWNED COOPERATIVES

Retailer-Owned Cooperatives

Gradually, groups of independents recognized the need for more formal organizations that would operate continuously and there evolved the *retailer-owned cooperative,* an enterprise owned and controlled by retailer-stockholders, who patronize it and share in any savings in proportion to their patronage. In contrast to the buying club, the retailer cooperative has a warehouse, carries inventory in stock, and employs a manager. Even more significantly, it renders advice and assistance on retail merchandising problems, such as store layout and location, store operation, record systems, advertising methods and layouts, and personnel policies. Often, too, the retailer cooperative persuades its members to adopt a uniform name, store front, and sign, and to engage in cooperative advertising. The net effect is an organization more in the image of a chain-store system. However, most retailer cooperatives place more emphasis on group buying than on group promotional activities. Experience indicates, nevertheless, that heavy group promotion is an important key to success. When retailer-owned cooperatives emphasize group promotion, their members generally become more effective competitors of chain-store outlets.

Wholesaler-Sponsored Groups

Wholesaler-Sponsored Groups

In other instances, wholesalers took the initiative in organizing independent retailers into voluntary groups. Each retailer affiliating with a voluntary group owns and operates his or her own store but is associated with the sponsoring wholesaler for buying and merchandising. The retailer members agree to concentrate their purchases with the sponsoring wholesaler. They also agree to operate their stores under the group name and to display uniform store signs, thus maintaining identity among their stores and in their promotional efforts. The wholesaler, in turn, agrees to supply the retailer members with merchandise at the lowest possible prices. In addition, the wholesaler prepares and places advertising in local media and provides advice and assistance on merchandising, store layout and operation, cost control, and other problems. Retention of a wholesaler's profit as a part of the total cost structure makes it a neat trick for the sponsor to offer its affiliated retailers lower prices than would be available from competing wholesalers. Therefore, the wholesaler-sponsor often makes its main contribution and justifies its role through providing promotional assistance and management advice.

Whereas the early voluntary groups admitted any independent retailer of any size, the more recent trend is to restrict membership to large retailers. In the most successful groups, the sponsoring wholesaler and the retailer members pay considerable attention to advertising and store-operating efficiency. The largest voluntaries are in the food industry where there are such nationwide organizations as *I.G.A., Red and White,* and *Clover Farm Stores.* However, voluntaries in other fields, such as in hardware and drugs, are growing in importance.

Retailer cooperatives and voluntary groups are important distributors of convenience goods. Buyers for the larger cooperatives and voluntaries drive as hard a bargain with suppliers as do their chain-store counterparts. Manufacturers regard cooperatives and voluntaries in much the same light as the chains and, consequently, deal with them in almost identical fashion.

Consumer Cooperatives

Consumer Cooperatives

A *consumer cooperative* is a retail business owned and operated by ultimate consumers to purchase and distribute goods and services primarily to its members. The earliest known consumer cooperative was started in Scotland, but the modern form traces to an English cooperative founded in 1844—the Rochdale Society of Equitable Pioneers. This organization was the first to lay down the principles which serve as the keys to successful operation of consumers' cooperatives. These principles, which are really operating policies, are: (1) open membership—any consumer is free to join; (2) democratic control—each member has but one vote regardless of the number of cooperative shares held; (3) limited interest is paid on capital invested by members; (4) all sales are made at prevailing market prices and for cash only; and (5) members receive patronage dividends proportionate to their purchases.

There are some large consumer cooperatives in the United

States, but their total impact on American retailing has been negligible. They have not been as successful in the United States as in Europe because other types of retailing institutions grew up here and provided the strongly competitive setting that kept retailing costs and profits low. In Europe the high and often exorbitant profits of retailers furnished the stimulus for consumers to band together to open their own retail stores. While the consumer cooperative movement was expanding in Europe, chain stores and their competitors in the United States were learning how to provide quality merchandise at low prices. While European retailers were still relying on high unit profits and low sales volumes, the newer American retail institutions were emphasizing low unit profits and high sales volumes. Retailers in this country early recognized that the economies of mass marketing, like those of mass production, are realized only through a combination of large sales and attractive prices.

Most U.S. consumer cooperatives are in the grocery retailing field because their organizers have been impressed with the large part that food purchases play in total consumer spending. Most consumer cooperatives in the grocery field begin as small and inadequately financed enterprises, housed in poorly situated buildings with scanty stocks and underpaid managements. These are almost insurmountable handicaps for any new firm. They are especially difficult to overcome in the grocery retailing business where the sensational successes of the chains and supermarkets have so dramatically demonstrated the importance of large size, adequate financing, well-planned inventory, and efficient management. It is small wonder, then, that consumer cooperatives have experienced rough sledding in the retail grocery field.[1]

Consumer cooperatives have more chance for success in the United States when they handle other merchandise lines than groceries. For instance, they have been highly successful in operating college and university bookstores. The consumer cooperative in this field is often more efficient than its privately owned competitors, mostly small independent stores. In marked contrast to grocery retailing, where low unit profit margins are the rule, the book and school supply trade is characterized by relatively high margins. This combination of favorable factors has enabled cooperative college stores to pay patronage dividends of as much as 12 to 13 percent of members' purchases.

However, there is little motivation for consumers to organize cooperatives in nonfood fields, chiefly because potential savings on small monthly expenditures per member seem hardly to justify the effort. Most cooperative college stores were organized to fill existing retail vacuums. In the early decades of the twentieth century, independently operated bookstores in many college communities were

[1] "Co-ops; Co-operate or Else," *Economist,* May 31, 1969, p. 60.

coping inadequately with several problems. They were unable to communicate with or obtain the cooperation of faculty members, resulting in incomplete and inadequate stocks of books, causing many students to get a late start in course work. Because these stores were not established solely to serve the students, they were often located downtown, away from campuses, and their incomplete stocks made it necessary for students to visit several stores. Existence of such retail vacuums provides a setting conducive to the establishment of successful consumer cooperatives. Leading university cooperatives, such as the Harvard Co-op, the University Book Store at the University of Washington, and the University Co-op at The University of Texas at Austin have been so successful in the textbook and supplies business that they have added many other merchandise lines, thus broadening their appeal. These multimillion dollar retailing businesses are large enough to hire competent professional managers and, consequently, operate at respectable levels of efficiency.

Supermarkets

Supermarkets

The first *supermarkets* appealed to consumers by offering lower prices than their chain-store competitors. The low prices were made possible by large sales volumes, high turnover, low markups, low rents, and minimal services. Supermarkets first appeared in the early 1930s during the depth of the Great Depression. The pioneer supermarkets opened in vacant warehouses and, through use of mass merchandise displays and heavy advertising, succeeded in transacting what were then tremendous volumes of business. They featured low prices and operated on a cash-and-carry basis. That the stores were physically unattractive was of little importance; widespread unemployment and shortages of purchasing power made the low-price appeal unusually attractive.

The first operators of supermarkets were independents, but by 1937 nearly all leading food chains were building supermarkets as fast as they could find suitable locations—and closing up three or four of their existing smaller stores to make way for each new supermarket. By this time, of course, the "cheapy" supermarkets that had located in vacant warehouses were rapidly giving way to more attractive stores on sites more convenient to customers. As this new retailing concept caught on, with more and more businessmen recognizing the great profit possibilities of supermarket operation, a revolution in food retailing gathered steam. Three decades later supermarkets were still growing, both in numbers and in dollar volume.[2]

The basic characteristics and operating philosophy of the

[2] "Supers on the March," *Statist,* Vol. 191 (March 31, 1967), p. 648.

supermarket are indicated in its definition: a large retailing business unit selling mainly food and grocery items on the basis of the low-margin appeal, high turnover, wide variety and assortments, self-service, and heavy emphasis on merchandise appeal. Originally, supermarkets were devised as food-retailing businesses, and they continue to emphasize the mass selling of food and grocery items. However, in order to widen their merchandise appeal and at the same time improve their profit potentials, increasing numbers of supermarkets add such nonfood lines as drugs, household utensils, hardware, and garden supplies. This trend toward "scramble merchandising," together with the spreading habit of many consumers to shop only once or twice per week for groceries, has enabled the supermarket to increase the dollar value of the average order sold each customer on each trip to the store.[3] To stimulate store traffic, the supermarket typically promotes its low prices through heavy advertising and mass merchandise displays; many also feature premium and trading stamp plans. Because the supermarket needs a high sales volume for profitable operation, large merchandise stocks are displayed on the selling floor to achieve maximum merchandise exposure. Readily accessible reserve stocks and adequate checkout counters, along with check-cashing facilities and a parking lot large enough to handle peak volumes of business, also make for high volume. How much is enough parking space? Early supermarket operators believed that one square foot of parking space for each square foot of selling space was adequate. Today, at least four times this amount is considered minimal. Operators of most newly opened supermarkets provide more than adequate parking space.

Scramble Merchandising

Many buying practices of supermarkets are routine. Certain staples and nationally advertised items are carried by nearly all supermarkets. The responsibility for buying varies with the company's size and organizational structure. Large supermarket chains have specialized buyers whose function is to bargain with and make purchases from suppliers, and store managers requisition most items from warehouses. In smaller companies, a single executive often negotiates and makes all purchases. Managers of produce and meat departments often have authority to buy for their own departments. Supermarkets affiliated with retailer cooperatives and voluntary groups generally make most of their routine purchases through the wholesaling units of such organizations. Ordering and shelf-stocking of perishable items, such as crackers and cookies, are often handled by manufacturers' salesmen under supervision of the owner, manager, or other individual responsible for buying. The ordering and stocking of nonfood lines are often taken care of by rack jobbers with minimum supervision by supermarket personnel.

[3] G. H. Snyder, "New Slant on Non-Foods," *Progressive Grocer*, August 1971, pp. 52–58.

Discount Houses

Discount Houses

A *discount house* is a retailing business unit that features a large selection of general merchandise (often including food), competes on a low price basis, and operates on a relatively low markup with a minimum of customer service. Most discount houses today are full-line, limited-service, promotional stores that closely resemble and actually are department stores. In fact, the term discount house is used increasingly to refer to any retail establishment whose main promotional emphasis is on selling nationally advertised merchandise at prices below those of conventional dealers.[4]

Some discount houses appeared in the late 1930s, but they were neither numerous nor widespread until after World War II. After the first rush of postwar buying subsided, discount houses began to set up in the so-called *hard-goods* lines—that is, appliances, furniture, and other consumer durables of relatively high unit price. Manufacturers of major appliances and other consumer durables, encouraged by strong immediate postwar demand, had greatly expanded their production facilities. Soon they recognized that their expanded facilities were capable of producing far more than their established outlets, using traditional retailing methods, could sell. These outlets were for the most part conventional department stores and small independent dealers. Manufacturers either had to persuade these outlets to improve their selling efficiency or had to obtain more outlets to help in retailing the expanded production. In this setting, manufacturers began to turn to discount houses that were capable of providing the needed additional sales volume.

Hard Goods

In the late 1940s and early 1950s, then, circumstances were ripe for the establishment and growth of discount houses. Traditional appliance outlets, such as department stores and small dealers, had grown accustomed to high markups—often 35 to 40 percent of the retail price—and they were also used to selling at manufacturers' full "list" prices. Furthermore, appliance manufacturers had promoted their brand names to the point where consumers no longer depended on retailers to guarantee the product. Every reputable manufacturer now stood behind its products regardless of the outlets from which consumers bought them. Discount-house operators found that they could sell appliances and other consumer durables profitably at prices as much as 30 percent below those of conventional outlets. Because the conventional retailers first maintained their own total sales and profits, for a few years they did not put up much of a competitive battle. By the time they realized that they had to meet or undercut discount-house prices, discount houses had already won strong customer loyalty.

By the 1960s, the selection of merchandise offered by discount

[4] A complete listing of discount house characteristics can be found in Delbert Duncan, Charles Phillips, and Stanley Hollander, *Modern Retailing Management* (Homewood, Ill.: Richard D. Irwin, Inc., 1972), pp. 20–21.

houses had broadened appreciably. To the original lines of hard goods, broad lines of *soft goods*—including clothing for men, women, and children, linen and bedding, and giftwares—had been added. Today, soft-goods lines occupy roughly half of the selling floor space in the typical large discount house. The early hard-goods discount houses depended strongly upon brand, attracting customers by offering well-known brands at discount prices. Since brands are far less important in soft-goods lines, today's discount houses with broadened lines of merchandise find it more difficult to prove that their prices are really lower. Instead, they must build consumer confidence in their pricing structures.

Soft Goods

In the late 1960s and early 1970s, discount houses continued to grow, both in terms of number of outlets and total sales.[5] This growth came partly from continuing expansion by the pioneer discounters and partly from invasions of the discount field by other types of retailers. Table 12–1 shows the kinds of retailers and some of the leading retail organizations currently operating discount houses. Increasingly, companies operating conventional department stores, variety stores, or food stores have invaded the field, setting up separate discounting divisions. Among companies in the variety store field, for example, S. S. Kresge Company had over 300 of its K-Marts open in 1969, a year which also saw another variety chain, F. W. Woolworth, open an additional 30 new Woolco stores.[6] Discount retailing has increasingly became an industry of giants.

Discount houses buy their merchandise stocks both from wholesale distributors and directly from manufacturers. Early in their growth, they did nearly all of their buying from distributors. Sometimes so-called legitimate retailers, not wanting to compete on a price basis, put pressure on distributors to stop supplying the discounters. When their supplies were cut off, discount houses would buy from other retailers, either legitimate or discount types, on a cost-plus basis, or work out exchange arrangements with other discount houses whose supplies had not been cut off.

As discount houses grew larger and became important outlets for many consumer durables, and as chains of discount houses such as E. J. Korvette were organized, more and more manufacturers began to make direct sales to them. The majority of large discount houses now have as many direct-buying privileges as the largest chains. In fact, discount chains count among some of the largest retail chains today. Although discount houses are hard buyers, they are also fast buyers. Manufacturers appreciate a fast buyer when they find themselves with unexpectedly large inventories that more conventional retail outlets seem incapable of moving. In fact, one of the most distinguishing characteristics of the modern large, broad-line

[5] "Discounters Coming On Stronger Than Ever," *Publishers' Weekly,* July 12, 1971, p. 63.

[6] R. Drew-Bear, *Mass Merchandising: Evolution and Revolution* (New York: Fairchild Publications, 1970), p. 477.

Table 12–1 Kinds of Retailers and Some Leading Retail Organizations Engaged in Discounting

1. The Prepioneers (who were discounting before the discounters)
   - Klein Department Stores, Inc.
   - Ohrbachs
2. The Pioneer Discounters
   - Vornado, Inc.
   - E. J. Korvette
   - Spartan Industries
   - Gibson Products Company
3. Department Store Operators
   - Allied Stores Corp.—Almart Stores
   - J. C. Penney Company—Treasure Island Stores
   - Mangel Stores Corp.—Shoppers Fair
4. Variety Store Operators
   - S. S. Kresge Co.—K-Mart
   - F. W. Woolworth Co.—Woolco Division
5. Corporate Grocery Chain Operators
   - Grand Union—Grand Way Division
   - Stop and Shop—Bradlee's Division
   - Kroger

discount house is its strong emphasis on specially priced "distress" merchandise offered on a "one-time" basis.

COMPARISON OF SUPERMARKETS AND DISCOUNT HOUSES

The supermarket and the discount house have a great deal in common. Both rely on the appeal of low prices, wide variety and assortments, self-service, and the handling of well-known brands of merchandise. Both seek to keep their prices down by combining operating expense economies with a high-volume business in fast-selling items. However, the supermarket is, by definition, a large retailing business, whereas the discount house may be any size—from very small to very large.

The larger discount house is the one most resembling the supermarket—as a matter of fact, many large discount houses feature grocery departments and offer tough competition to supermarkets. Because a discount house, like a supermarket, must transact a large total sales volume if it is to offer low prices, many operate their grocery departments at no profit or even a loss, considering them mainly as a means of getting people into the store and of obtaining the required overall level of sales. Nearby supermarkets have found it difficult to match the discount house's nonprofit grocery pricing policy—tough competition indeed!

Automatic Selling

Automatic Vending

Automatic selling or, as it is more commonly known, *automatic vending* involves the sale of goods or services to ultimate consumers through coin-operated machines. Whereas most automatic vending machines are still coin-operated, machines that will make change for one-dollar bills see expanding use. This procedure for changing currency is overcoming a long-time disadvantage of automatic vending—the inability to serve customers who do not have the proper change. Automatic selling is not really a new retailing method; the Tutti-Frutti Company installed chewing-gum machines at elevated railroad stations in the 1880s. Historically, the major portion of vending machine volume has come and still comes from soft drinks, cigarettes, and candy. Two out of every ten candy bars sold are sold through vending machines, as are 16 out of 100 packs of cigarettes and more than one out of four soft drinks.

Among the many attempts that have been made to use vending machines for products other than soft drinks, candy, and cigarettes, those with packaged milk and ice cubes have been most successful. But many have failed. Filene's, a Boston department store, once installed machines in the Boston Greyhound bus terminal selling goods ranging from men's hose and ties to ladies' panties and babies' rattles. After two years the experiment was abandoned as a failure. The Grand Union supermarket chain has conducted a round-the-clock supplementary vending operation for certain grocery staples on an experimental basis.

One area of considerable success in vending is in the sale of "fast foods." Vending machines are located in areas where large numbers of people congregate, such as office buildings, factories, sports and entertainment areas. They offer a selection of hot and cold foods and beverages that can make up a meal.

Although automatic selling still accounts for only a small percent of all retail sales—only $6.9 billion out of an estimated $448 billion total in 1972—vending machines are becoming increasingly important as outlets for many types of products. The National Automatic Merchandising Association estimates that there are 6,100 vending machine operators in the United States operating more than 6.5 million machines, selling products that literally range from soup to nuts. Vending machine volume expands with each new technological improvement in machine design and operation. The first coffee vending machine, for instance, was installed in 1946 and by 1972 such machines were selling coffee at an annual rate of $432 million. N.A.M.A. states that the average person spends about $22.50 annually on purchases from coffee machines.[7] The association pointed out that annual vending volume had more than doubled (from $2.1 billion to $4.5 billion) from 1958 to 1967 and that it had increased by more than that amount in the next five years (to $6.9

[7] "Census of the Industry, '73," *Vend*, May 1973, pp. 61–80.

billion in 1972), so it was likely to double again in the decade 1968–1977. Actually, this estimate may be too conservative because, judging from the rapid progress automation is making in other fields, technological advances in vending machines are likely to come with increasing frequency in the years ahead.

Franchising

Franchises

A *franchise* is permission given to a retailer to market the franchise company's products or services. Generally, franchise companies have a product or service that has been successful locally, but they lack sufficient capital to expand their own retail outlets. The recent and rapid growth of franchising leads some people to regard it as a new retailing concept, but franchising started very early in the twentieth century. Most of the pioneer automobile manufacturers, for instance, were too financially weak even to handle their own wholesaling (let alone their own retailing), so they turned to independent wholesale distributors who, in turn, granted retailing franchises to dealers throughout their territories. As manufacturers grew larger and improved their finances, they absorbed the distributors and granted franchises direct to auto retailers. Another early user of franchising was the petroleum industry, which has been using the method almost as long as there have been gasoline service stations. As a company using franchising gains financial strength, it often moves to reduce the number of its franchised dealers through buying out the most profitable ones and converting them to a retail chain operation; this tendency has been particularly evident throughout the petroleum industry.

Until the 1960s franchising accounted for rather a small share of total U. S. retail sales, but during that decade many new industries, particularly service industries, adopted the franchising concept and its total impact increased enormously. By 1968 more than 800 companies were granting franchises and there were approximately 400,000 franchised retail outlets whose total sales (some $700 billion) accounted for more than one-fourth of all U. S. retail sales.[8] During this period of rapid expansion, however, because of the high profits earned by a few highly successful franchisees in some of the new fields, service fields particularly, the unsophisticated investor came to think of a franchise as a sure road to riches. Investors with a little capital bought franchises in retail fields where they had no prior experience, and often located in markets already oversaturated with similar outlets. This resulted in numerous failures among franchise holders. Thus, recently, the growth of franchise retailing has slowed considerably. Nevertheless, franchise retailing is still very much an important part of the total retail scene. Table 12–2 lists some of the

[8] R. Metz, *Franchising: How to Select a Business of Your Own* (New York: Hawthorne Books, Inc., 1969), pp. 3–4.

Table 12–2 Some Franchising Companies That Achieved Rapid Growth During the 1960s

Robo-Wash—automatic car wash
Western Auto—automobile parts and accessories
Budget Rent-a-Car—car rental
Snap-on Tools—sale of auto repair tools and equipment
Puppy Palace—sells dogs
Dunkin' Donuts—doughnut shop
McDonald's Hamburgers—hamburgers and soft drinks
International House of Pancakes—pancakes
Colonel Sanders Kentucky Fried Chicken—chicken dinners
Burger King—hamburgers and drinks
Dairy Queen—soft ice cream, sandwiches, and soft drinks
Shakey's Pizza Parlor—pizzas and soft drinks
Mr. Steak—restaurants specializing in steak dinners
Arby's Restaurants—roast beef sandwiches
One Hour Martinizing—fast cash-and-carry dry cleaning
Culligan Soft-Water Service—water conditioning service
Mary Carter Paint Company—paint and painting supplies
Manpower, Inc.—provides temporary office help at low cost
General Business Services—provides bookkeeping and tax service for all small business
A to Z Rentals—rents tools and household equipment
Convenient Food Mart—convenience food stores
Aero-Mayflower—moving and trucking service
Servicemaster—carpet and furniture cleaning
Howard Johnson—restaurants and motels

better-known and more successful franchise companies. In recent years, as is evident in this table, franchising has expanded greatly in fields such as prepared foods, dry cleaning, and equipment rentals. But automobiles and gasoline are still the two most important products sold mainly through franchised dealerships.

The main attraction of franchise retailing to the franchising company is that it provides a way to secure many of the advantages of having its own outlets without actually having to finance them. If a manufacturer, for example, sells its products through completely independent dealers, generally it has little or no control over their promotion or how they are retailed. If the same manufacturer, however, sells through franchised dealers, it retains considerably more control over marketing practices and can specify retailing procedures in detail. This aspect of franchising can be an advantage for both parties, since a large manufacturer can afford to hire experienced professionals to design highly effective retail operating systems and procedures.

One disadvantage of franchising is that adjusting to unique local conditions is difficult. An additional disadvantage is that it is next to impossible to control managerial performance within the franchised dealerships. Standardized operating procedures and professional advice are not enough to compensate for sloppy or ineffective local management, as demonstrated by the high failure rate among franchised dealers nearly everywhere.[9]

Shopping Centers

Shopping Centers

The Urban Land Institute defines a *shopping center* as "a group of commercial establishments, planned, developed, owned, and managed as a unit, with off-street parking provided on the property (in direct ratio to the building area) and related in location, size (gross floor area) and type of shops to the trade area that the unit serves—generally in an outlying or suburban territory."[10] Shopping centers are classified according to their size, which is determined by the trading area served and which, in turn, determines the kinds and variety of stores included.

NEIGHBORHOOD CENTERS

The neighborhood center is the smallest and most common type of shopping center. A supermarket is usually its focal point with the smaller stores geared to supply convenience goods and services (drug and hardware stores, beauty and barber shops, laundry and dry cleaning establishments, gasoline stations) to some 7,500 to 20,000 people living within six to ten minutes' driving distance. Neighborhood centers may have only a dozen stores, but the total

[9]In addition to the above disadvantages, certain problems have arisen in the franchise system of distribution, among them (1) the fact that franchising has come under increased attack from the courts as being "anti-competitive," (2) that franchisors treat their franchisees unfairly, and (3) that franchisors engage in deceptive practices in selling franchises and in negotiating franchise agreements. For an excellent analysis of these and other aspects of franchising, including whether or not franchisees need protection from deceptive selling practices and an evaluation of some legislative proposals designed to protect franchisees, see Shelby D. Hunt, "Full Disclosure and the Franchise System of Distribution," in *Marketing Education and the Real World,* eds. Boris W. Becker and Helmut Becker, Proceedings of the American Marketing Association, 1972 Fall Conference (Chicago: American Marketing Association, 1972), pp. 301–4.

[10] "Shopping Centers Re-studied," *Technical Bulletin No. 30* (Washington, D.C.: Urban Land Institute, May 1957). The American Marketing Association defines a shopping center as "a geographical cluster of retail stores, collectively handling an assortment of goods varied enough to satisfy most of the merchandise wants of consumers within convenient travelling time, and, thereby, attracting a general shopping trade." The A.M.A. definition includes both planned and unplanned shopping areas. Unplanned shopping areas, usually called "shopping districts," are nonintegrated, i.e., they have no overall plan with respect to the merchandise stocked by each retailer. In contrast, the shopping center defined by the Urban Land Institute is an integrated, planned unit. For that reason, the definition provided by the Urban Land Institute seems more relevant for this discussion.

area occupied, including parking space, is likely to range from four to ten acres. Generally, a neighborhood center is well located if there are no strong competitors within about two miles.

COMMUNITY CENTERS

The community center is a large operation and usually features a variety store or a small department store in addition to the supermarket and small stores also found in the neighborhood center. Thus, the community center provides a merchandise offering that includes a selection of shopping goods, such as clothing and home furnishings, as well as convenience goods. The community center serves a market of from 20,000 to 100,000 persons and occupies from ten to thirty acres. According to experts, a community center should not have strong competitors within a radius of three to four miles.

REGIONAL CENTERS

The regional center is the largest of all. Two or more large department stores provide its main drawing power, further enhanced by 100 or more smaller stores. Some regional centers, though not all, include one or two supermarkets to add further to total shopping attractiveness. Shoppers, therefore, may select from a very wide range of goods. Regional centers are usually set up to serve 100,000 to 250,000 people living within a radius of five to six miles. Such centers, more closely resembling central city shopping districts than the smaller centers, are slowly but surely changing consumer shopping habits, especially because they reduce the need or urgency to go to the central city to shop.

IMPLICATIONS FOR CENTRAL CITY SHOPPING DISTRICTS

Because of their relatively generous parking facilities, easy accessibility by automobile, and nearness to the suburban middle-income market, regional centers threaten both the central city's downtown shopping district and the older "main street" suburban business district. It is estimated that there were roughly 300 regional shopping centers in 1975. One Cleveland retailer estimated that, in the late 1950s, of every \$20 million spent in shopping centers, \$10 million comes out of "downtown's hide."[11] Today, even more comes out of "downtown's hide," as evidenced by the recent closing of numerous, long-established central city stores. Central city merchants press for measures to alleviate traffic congestion and for improved parking facilities, but they are not likely ever to match the convenience of the outlying shopping centers.

Figure 12–1 shows the evolutionary development of shopping

[11] *Business Week*, December 5, 1959, p. 82.

centers in a rapidly growing American city of moderate size—Austin, Texas. The shopping centers are numbered in order of their dates of completion. Center number one, a moderate-sized community center, was built in 1958 as a small community center and enlarged in 1963. Centers 2 and 3, moderate-sized regional centers, were built in 1959 and 1963, to serve northern areas of the city experiencing rapid population growth. Center 4, a large community center, was built in 1970 to serve southern areas of the city experiencing moderate population growth. Center 5, a large regional center with three large department stores, was completed in 1971 and has considerably more square feet of retail floor space than the downtown central business

Figure 12–1 Austin, Texas: city and major retail shopping centers

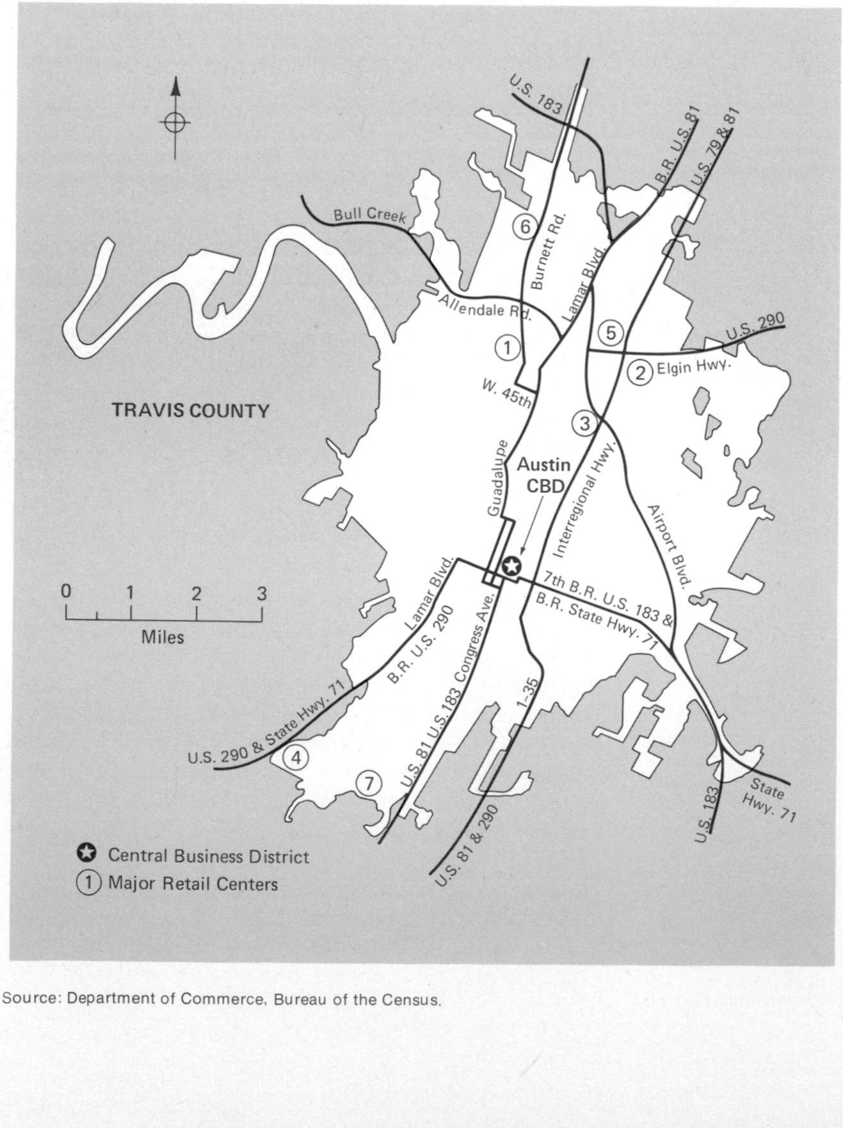

Source: Department of Commerce, Bureau of the Census.

district. Center 6, a regional center with two large department stores, and Center 7, a smaller regional center, were opened in 1975. During the seventeen years from construction of the first community center to construction of the newest regional center, Austin's population grew from 170,000 to 300,000 and the main direction of growth was toward the north, so that four of the five regional centers are nearer the city's population center than is the central business district. This pattern of retail growth is typical of most small- to medium-sized cities that have experienced recent rapid growth—usually, the central business district regresses to the position of an unplanned shopping center for nearby residents and downtown employees, while outlying and suburban shoppers increasingly patronize the regional centers.

In addition to competing with central city shopping areas and smaller centers, expanding regional centers have increasingly become competitive with each other. Research has indicated that driving time to the center is highly influential in determining consumer shopping preference.[12]

IMPLICATIONS FOR THE MANUFACTURER

For the manufacturer, the main marketing significance of the planned shopping center is that it is an integrated retail unit. Consumers view the center as a single large shopping convenience and not as a conglomeration of individual stores, each going its separate way. Recognizing this, shopping center developers sometimes restrict the classes of merchandise individual stores are permitted to handle. But, in large centers, controlled competition among stores handling similar merchandise lines is allowed. A manufacturer of lighting fixtures, accustomed to selling its line through both hardware stores and department stores, encounters three different distribution situations in shopping centers: (1) in some, the line is restricted to the hardware store, (2) in others, it is restricted to the department store, and (3) in still others, both the hardware store and the department store are free to handle the line. This same manufacturer even finds instances where shopping center branches of department stores are not permitted to handle its line even though the parent stores have stocked it for years. The great need for information about such situations explains why manufacturers should maintain close contact with their dealers operating, or planning to operate, stores in shopping centers. In addition, the extensive use of self-service in shopping centers has caused many manufacturers to redesign product packages and add more information to the labels. And, with the growing importance of the regional centers, manufacturers have been led to reexamine their advertising practices, espe-

[12] J. A. Bonner and J. L. Mason, "The Influence of Driving Time on Shopping Center Preference," *Journal of Marketing*, April 1968, pp. 57–61.

cially with respect to advertising in media that are aimed specifically at the trading areas of shopping centers.

The Wheel of Retailing Hypothesis and Trends of Future Growth

Wheel of Retailing

Changes in retailing evolve rather gradually over the years. According to the *wheel of retailing* hypothesis, advanced by Professor M. P. McNair, new forms of retailing institutions generally obtain a foothold on the retail scene through emphasizing a price appeal made possible by low operating costs inherent in the new form of institution. Over time the new institutions upgrade their facilities and services, necessitating added investments and higher operating costs. At some point they emerge as high-cost, high-price retailers, vulnerable to newer forms of retailers who, in turn, go through a similar metamorphosis. Mail-order houses and department stores, for example, were originally low-cost retailers soliciting business mainly through use of the price appeal, but eventually the wheel turned and they became vulnerable to chain-store systems, discount houses, and other newer institutions.[13] As another example, conventional supermarkets in the late 1960s encountered new competition from the new food discount stores, which, in line with the wheel notion, were featuring lower prices made possible by lower operating costs due to stripped-down services.[14]

There is a marked trend toward giantism in retailing in the United States today. Only in the case of the highly specialized, single line stores can the small entrepreneur still start on a shoestring and, as mentioned earlier, even here much of the new growth has been in franchised outlets. Electronic data processing has now made possible the central management of multiple-unit retail organizations, such as chains, with greater efficiency than previously was thought possible. In the sector of retail merchandising, however—that is, in the selec-

[13] See M. P. McNair, "Significant Trends and Developments in the Postwar Period," *Competitive Distribution in a Free, High-Level Economy and Its Implications for the University*, ed. A. B. Smith (Pittsburgh: University of Pittsburgh Press, 1958), pp. 17–18. See also S. C. Hollander, "The Wheel of Retailing," *Journal of Marketing*, July 1960, pp. 37–42. Dr. Hollander concludes "the wheel of retailing hypothesis is not valid for all retailing . . . (it) does, however, seem to describe a fairly common pattern in industrialized, expanding economies."

[14] For a most provocative analysis that bears directly on the wheel of retailing hypothesis, see Arieh Goldman, "The Role of Trading Up in the Development of the Retailing System," *Journal of Marketing*, January 1975, pp. 54–62. Prof. Goldman cites evidence that indicates that, while many new retailing institutions have penetrated the retail system using a price appeal, some (e.g., department stores, discount stores, and supermarkets) have entered combining low prices with a regular level of services and appearance (rather than the "no-service, low-status" profile suggested by the wheel of retailing hypothesis). Goldman's conclusion is that the wheel of retailing hypothesis correctly identifies the low price factor as the major aspect of the appearance of new retailing institutions, but does not provide an adequate explanation of "why."

tion of what is to be sold—many a small retailer still enjoys a clear-cut advantage over its larger competitors.

Summary

You should now have a good understanding of retail distribution. In addition to what you learned from the last chapter about the operating methods and characteristics of various major classes of retailers, you should now know the operating methods and characteristics of retailer cooperatives, wholesaler-sponsored groups, consumer cooperatives, supermarkets, discount houses, automatic vending, franchise distribution, and the different kinds of shopping centers. All of these institutions and retail distribution methods—in their present forms, at least—represent relatively recent innovations in retailing. All developed as responses to changes either in the competitive environment or in consumer markets or in producers' marketing requirements. With the background knowledge that you now have of both wholesale distribution and retail distribution, you are ready to move on to an analysis of marketing channels—the subject of the next chapter.

QUESTIONS AND PROBLEMS

1. What is the fundamental reason behind the establishment of cooperatives? Explain.
2. Distinguish between cooperative buying clubs and retailer-owned cooperatives.
3. If you were an independent grocery retailer and were offered the opportunity to join either a retailer cooperative or a voluntary group, which would you join and why?
4. If you were a wholesaler, in the process of organizing independent retailers into voluntary groups and were talking with a small independent retailer who was having a difficult time meeting the competition of large retailers, what reasons would you cite to get the small retailer to consider joining your wholesaler-sponsored group? Discuss.
5. From the wholesaler's point of view, what are the advantages of sponsoring a voluntary group of independent retailers? Explain.
6. What are the "Rochdale principles"? Discuss.
7. Why have consumer cooperatives had such little impact on retailing in the United States? Explain.
8. "Although most United States consumer cooperatives are in the grocery retailing field, the retail grocery chains have provided such formidable competition as to render such consumer cooperatives

ineffective and less popular than they otherwise might be." Agree or disagree? Why?

9. Explain why producer cooperatives have been so much more successful than consumer cooperatives in the United States.
10. Supermarkets are described as integrated marketing institutions. What kind of integration is represented by this kind of store? Why should independent supermarkets find it desirable to be members of voluntary chains?
11. What problems would a salesman attempting to sell a new product likely have in selling to a supermarket chain that uses a buying committee to make decisions on adding new items?
12. What are the reasons underlying the trend toward "scramble merchandising" by supermarkets? Explain.
13. Some of the new discount houses have been described as soft-goods supermarkets. Is this description accurate? How similar are the operating methods of the two types of institutions (discount houses and supermarkets)?
14. "Twenty years ago it was easy to distinguish between a discount house and a department store. Today, however, the lines of distinction are much less clear and, in some cases, it is impossible to tell the difference between these two types of retail institutions." Agree or disagree? Why?
15. Can you foresee the possibility that all convenience goods may eventually be sold in vending machines? Comment.
16. What do you think are the major reasons for the high rate of failure among franchised dealers?
17. Distinguish between the three types of shopping centers—neighborhood, community, and regional.
18. Does the evolution of large, planned shopping centers spell the ultimate elimination of downtown shopping centers? In what ways do downtown merchants have an advantage over merchants in the shopping centers.
19. If you were in the process of developing a community shopping center in your local area, specifically, what two retailers would you try to contract as your first "tenants"? Explain your choices.
20. Critically evaluate the "wheel of retailing" hypothesis. What lessons might a retailer learn from this hypothesis?
21. Over the years, retail institutions have changed their character and operating methods in response to changing needs and expectations on the market. Do you feel that the adjustment has been satisfactory and that retailing is fulfilling the demands placed upon it by the consuming public? What further changes do you feel are required? Discuss in detail.

CASE PROBLEM

Mr. Bruce Blyth, owner and operator of Blyth's, Inc., a long established family-owned jewelry firm, was approached by a real estate developer to consider moving his store to a large regional suburban shopping center. Blyth's, Inc., was located in the heart of the downtown district of a major metropolitan city and had achieved an outstanding, prestigious reputation as the area's finest jewelry store, specializing in custom-designed jewelry. Much of Blyth's jewelry sold for over $10,000.

The real estate developer had already lined up most of the stores to be included in the regional center. In addition to the usual benefits of shopping centers—better parking, easier accessibility, one-stop shopping, and the like—the developer appealed to Mr. Blyth on the basis that the jewelry store would fit nicely with the image that was being sought by this particular shopping center. The real estate developer also felt that Blyth's name would be a drawing card as it was very well known in the area.

Mr. Blyth had seen several stores in the downtown district forced to close their doors because of the competition from similar stores located in shopping centers. At the same time, however, Blyth's, Inc., had withstood all competitive challenges and, in fact, was enjoying its best year ever. Nevertheless, Mr. Blyth wondered whether his business might in the near future be one of those affected adversely by suburban shopping centers. He consented to give the matter his careful consideration.

Should Blyth's, Inc., relocate to the new regional shopping center? What factors should be taken into account in the decision to move or not to move?

When you have mastered the contents of this chapter, you should be able to:

1. Outline the conditions under which producers find it appropriate to use each main type of marketing channel.
2. Explain the various factors influencing channel usage.
3. Illustrate the two types of "dual distribution."
4. Identify the key problems producers face in the initial determination of marketing channels.
5. Demonstrate the use of *tradeoff analysis* in the determination of marketing channels.
6. Discuss the three general degrees of distribution intensity and the factors influencing the distribution intensity decision.
7. Analyze the problems producers face in obtaining channel usage initially and in building and maintaining middlemen's cooperation.

CHAPTER 13

MARKETING CHANNELS

Analysis in the three preceding chapters focused on the middlemen who operate on the wholesale and retail levels of distribution. These middlemen constitute the building blocks that producers seek to link together into marketing channels to bridge the gap between themselves and the target markets. Marketing channels are the distribution networks through which producers' products flow to market. More formally defined, a marketing channel, or channel of distribution, is a path traced in the direct or indirect transfer of ownership to a product, as it moves from a producer to ultimate consumers or industrial users. As emphasized throughout Part Four, to understand distribution, you must understand both marketing institutions and marketing channels. Discussion in this chapter focuses on (1) the different types of marketing channels, (2) various factors influencing their usage, and (3) producers' problems in determining and using them.

Types of Marketing Channels

Marketing Channels

Marketing channels can vary widely, from the simple one employed by a spark plug manufacturer selling its entire output to one automobile manufacturer to the long and complex channels employed in moving nonperishable farm products to market. Marketing channels are made up of different kinds of building blocks including producers, consumers or industrial users, wholesale institutions (both agent and merchant wholesalers), and retail institutions. Thus, the possible number of different channels is large. Figure 13–1 illustrates the more commonly used marketing channels and shows that the various channel building blocks bear a hierarchical relationship to each other. For example, if agent middlemen are present in a marketing channel, they are generally situated farther back in the channel than wholesalers and/or retailers.

MANUFACTURER TO CONSUMER OR USER

There are two levels in the shortest marketing channel. They are the producer and either the ultimate consumer or industrial user. The direct producer-to-industrial-user channel is used in marketing many types of industrial goods. There are several reasons for this: many industrial products have markets composed of relatively few potential users; the users of particular industrial products are clustered together in only a few market areas; some industrial products have special servicing and installation requirements which the manufacturer can best provide; others are so technical that manufacturers must deal directly with prospective users; and, in many cases, industrial users insist on buying directly and can buy in quantities large enough to make direct sales by producers economically feasible.

The direct producer-to-ultimate-consumer channel is not nearly so important. But farmers sometimes deal directly with consumers at roadside stands or from stalls in public markets. And small businesses, such as bakeries and dairies, and larger businesses, such as tire manufacturers, quite often sell directly to consumers, either through their own retail outlets or on a house-to-house basis. There are even a few manufacturers, in such lines as shoes and shirts, who sell directly to consumers through mail-order departments. However, very few manufacturers of consumer products rely wholly or even principally on the producer-to-ultimate-consumer channel,

Figure 13–1 Marketing channels commonly used in the distribution of industrial and consumer goods

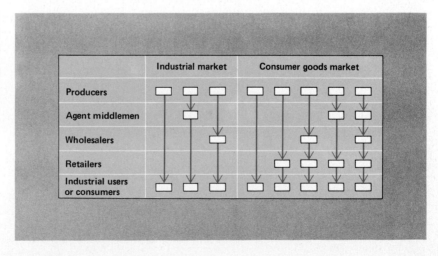

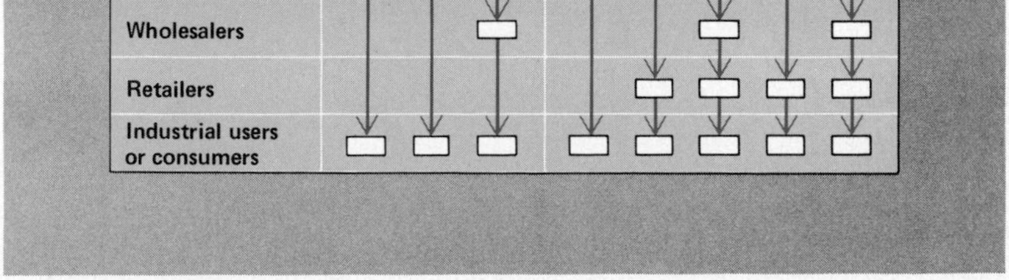

because ultimate consumers are numerous, widely scattered, and accustomed to buying in very small quantities.

MANUFACTURER THROUGH AGENT MIDDLEMAN TO CONSUMER OR USER

Some producers use agent middlemen as intermediaries between themselves and the next level of distribution. Agent middlemen, who generally operate at the wholesale level, are much used in marketing agricultural produce, partly because most farmers are too small to handle their own distribution efficiently and partly because the main growing areas are separated geographically from the larger markets.

In marketing both industrial and consumer goods, agent middlemen are used usually, although not exclusively, by manufacturers who want to rid themselves of much of the marketing task. A manufacturer's entire output may be turned over to one or a small number of agent middlemen for marketing, in which case the manufacturer, in effect, delegates the formulation of overall marketing strategy to one or a few outside organizations, the manufacturer's participation being limited to the selection of the agent(s). In other instances, the manufacturer uses agents to market its product in some areas—generally ones with limited sales potentials—and either uses its own sales force or merchant middlemen in other market areas.

When agent middlemen are used, they negotiate the transfer of legal title to the producer's merchandise with institutions active on the next distribution level. In marketing consumer goods, they negotiate with either merchant wholesalers or retailers or both, or the agent makes arrangements for further negotiations to be handled by other agent middlemen situated farther along the marketing channel and nearer the ultimate consumer. For products sold through a limited number of retail outlets, such as furniture, the agent ordinarily negotiates directly with retailers. For products sold through numerous retail outlets, such as most grocery items, the agent usually negotiates with merchant wholesalers, who, in turn, sell to retailers. However, in marketing grocery products, agents may also deal directly with such large-volume retailers as grocery chains and retail cooperatives. In marketing industrial goods, agents usually negotiate directly with industrial users; but in some lines, such as small hand tools, it is common for them to negotiate with merchant wholesalers, such as industrial distributors or mill supply houses, which, in turn, sell to industrial users.

MANUFACTURER-RETAILER—ULTIMATE CONSUMER

This is one of the most common marketing channels for consumer products. Manufacturers using it generally have some compelling reason for avoiding wholesale middlemen: their products may be perishable, either physically or fashion-wise—hence, speed in distribution is essential; the retailers involved may be predominantly large (such as chains, department stores, and mail-order houses) and, as a policy matter, refuse to buy through wholesalers; the retailers handling the product may be located near each other, thus making it convenient for the manufacturer to sell them directly; the available wholesalers may be unable or unwilling to provide the promotional support that the manufacturer feels its product requires; or the manufacturer may desire closer contact with ultimate consumers than that afforded through channels containing more distribution levels.

Manufacturers who distribute their products directly to retailers must be able to finance the inventories that would otherwise be carried by merchant wholesalers. Furthermore, they should have either a product line wide enough to permit their salesmen to write large orders or a narrower line generally ordered by retailers in large quantities. If individual retailers do not ordinarily buy in large quantities, a manufacturer should have some other compelling reason for selling them directly.

One important reason for distribution direct to retailers is the manufacturer's desire to use franchising. A franchise is a continuing relationship between a manufacturer (or an expert in the performance of some service) and a retailer in which, for a consideration, the manufacturer supplies the retailer with manufacturing and marketing techniques, a brand image, and other knowhow. This method of operation, which has existed for many years in such fields as petroleum marketing, has increased enormously in importance during the past decade. The franchisor-franchisee relationship requires continuing close contact so that the franchisor can provide advice, supervision, and help when needed. The manufacturer-to-retailer-to-ultimate-consumer marketing channel meets this requirement.

MANUFACTURER-MERCHANT WHOLESALER-RETAILER—ULTIMATE CONSUMER

This consumer goods channel is often called the traditional or orthodox channel. A manufacturer finds it suitable under some or all of the following conditions: it has a narrow product line; it is unable to finance distribution direct to retailers or can put the funds to more productive use elsewhere; retail outlets are numerous and widely dispersed; wholesalers are able and willing to provide strong promotional support or the product does not require such support; the products are staples, not subject to physical or fashion deterioration; the manufacturer's advertising to ultimate consumers exerts a strong pull in causing retailers to stock the product. Manufacturers using this channel but desiring closer contact with retailers often employ "missionary" salesmen who, while calling on retailers, refer any orders they obtain to local wholesalers for filling and delivery.

MANUFACTURER-MERCHANT WHOLESALER – INDUSTRIAL USER

This marketing channel is used by many producers of industrial items such as small tools and other standard pieces of equipment. These are products of comparatively small unit value used by numerous and diverse industrial establishments. Merchant wholesalers serving the industrial market, though their operations in many ways resemble those of consumer goods wholesalers, sell directly to industrial users and are known as industrial supply houses, mill supply houses, industrial hardware distributors, or equipment distributors.

Factors Influencing Channel Usage

THE PRODUCT

The product's nature, its technical characteristics, its degree of differentiation from competitive products, whether it is perishable, whether it is a staple or a nonstaple – these and other product characteristics may limit the possible channel alternatives. Individually or in combination, they may restrict the alternatives to those in a given line of trade, to those containing a certain number of distribution levels, to those where middlemen are equipped to provide technical service and repair, or to those where middlemen have specialized storage facilities (for example, for frozen foods) or are specialists in some phase of marketing (for example, fashion merchandising).

The crucial marketing needs of a given product, of course, may be quite unique. For example, the marketing needs for a line of power garden tools are quite different from those for a line of imported children's clothing. Often, formal marketing research is required to uncover crucial marketing needs, particularly for radically new products.

The product's characteristics also generally determine the length of the channel (i.e., number of distribution levels) through which it can be marketed. The product's unit value sets the limit as to how short the channel can be – a unit value in the thousands of dollars indicates a short direct-sale type of channel; a unit value of only a few cents (unless a large number of units make up the average sale) indicates a longer channel. Perishability of the product influences channel length – perishable items must move through relatively short channels to get them to final buyers quickly. The product's complexity is a determinant – highly technical products requiring specialized selling and/or servicing talent normally move through the shortest channel available. The degree of product standardization is a factor – highly standardized items should often be marketed through long and complex channels; custom-made items are generally best distributed direct to the user.

THE MARKET

Market factors exert powerful influences on channel usage. Customer buying habits are perhaps the most important; when customers are used to buying a particular product from a particular source, for instance, it is difficult to switch them to a different source. Market size and location are also important: If the number of final buyers is very large, then the channel is likely to contain at least one layer of middlemen; if the final buyers are widely dispersed geographically, generally the product moves through a channel containing one or more layers of middlemen.

Dual Distribution Certain market factors cause products to move through multiple marketing channels. In some instances, the factor is average order size—a manufacturer sells direct to a large chain organization because of its large purchases but uses wholesalers to reach smaller retailers. In other instances, the factor is that the product has both an industrial and a consumer market—a manufacturer of carburetors sells original equipment direct to automobile manufacturers but replacements through retailers to ultimate consumers.

Dual Distribution

Dual distribution involves selling through two or more marketing channels either a single brand or two brands of essentially the same product. An example of the first type of dual distribution is the practice in petroleum marketing of selling a single brand of gasoline and related products both through franchised independent outlets and through company-owned stations. An example of the second type of dual distribution is the practice of some appliance manufacturers who sell a nationally advertised brand through a network of wholesalers and retailers and an almost identical product under a private brand through a large chain or mail-order retail organization. Dual distribution may make it possible for a manufacturer to achieve deeper penetration of a market than it could obtain through a single marketing channel. However, there is a risk of alienation of channel members in either or both of the channels if they encounter strong competition from the other.

Many large manufacturers use multiple channels because of both market factors—average order size and a product with both a consumer and industrial market. For instance, Figure 13–2 shows the multiple channel system a typewriter manufacturer uses in selling direct to large users and mass retailers and through wholesalers and retailers to other industrial and consumer market segments.

THE PRODUCER

Factors within the producer's own organization strongly influence channel usage. Management's experience and ability are important—unless management is capable of setting up and controlling a direct sales force, channels including middlemen or agents are needed. Financial strength is important—short channels require a much larger outlay for fixed selling expenses than do long channels. The producer's desire for control over the product's sale to end buyers also influences channel length; if, for example, management wants to ensure the product's aggressive promotion, it chooses the shortest available channel.

The reputation of the producer and/or its products also influences channel usage. Middlemen willingly accept a well-known product line but hesitate to take on unknown items made by unknown companies. In other words, the better and more favorably known a manufacturer and its products are, the more freedom its management enjoys in putting together the combination of middlemen it wants.

The width of the manufacturer's product line also influences channel length. If a wide line of related products is to be sold to the same general class of buyers, a short channel is feasible. The manufacturer with a wide product line can sell directly to the retailer, or sometimes even to the consumer, and still secure orders large enough to be profitable. When the product line is rather narrow, by contrast, or consists of items sold to different markets, the distribution network is likely to include one or more levels of middlemen.

THE MIDDLEMEN

Marketing channels are sometimes dictated by the middlemen available, their willingness to represent particular manufacturers, and the relative costs of using them. A manufacturer may be re-

Figure 13–2 Multiple marketing channel system of a typewriter manufacturer

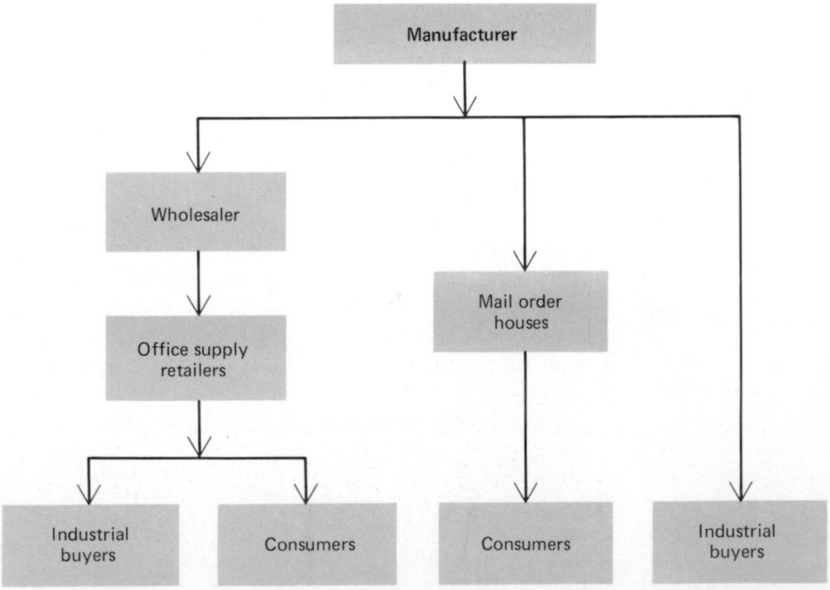

stricted in its choice of channel by the availability of particular middlemen; thus, if middlemen of the type it wants are not available or those it wants are unwilling to take on its product line, it may have to take second choices. Some middlemen may be willing to take on the manufacturer's product line but unwilling to accept its distribution policies, with respect to price, required promotional effort, and the like. Furthermore, the cost of using different middlemen relative to its own sales and profit goals influences the manufacturer's channel choice.

Producers' Problems in Channel Determination and Usage

Producers face several key problems both in the initial determination of marketing channels and later in using them. Those faced in making the channel decision include: (1) adjusting to buyers' needs and expectations, (2) determining the best channel alternative(s), and (3) determining distribution intensity (i.e., deciding on how many middlemen should handle the product on each distribution level). Problems faced by producers later on include: (1) obtaining initial channel usage, and (2) building and maintaining middlemen's cooperation.

ADJUSTING TO BUYERS' WANTS AND EXPECTATIONS

A producer's main role in the determination of marketing channels is that of adjusting to buyers' wants and expectations on each distribution level. In consumer goods marketing, for instance, the final buyers are ultimate consumers, and they buy from those retailers who best serve their needs. This tendency is vividly illustrated by what happened in the early history of discount houses, when certain manufacturers of nationally advertised products refused to permit them to handle their lines. Nevertheless, discount houses managed to obtain these products (through "bootleg" channels) and to obtain competitive lines from producers less particular about their retail outlets. Ultimate consumers, in ever-increasing numbers, demonstrated that they preferred to buy such items from discount houses rather than from conventional retailers. Manufacturers, realizing the hopelessness of trying to keep their products out of discount houses—and the potential loss in sales volume if they succeeded—relented, many actively seeking retail representation through discount houses.

At other distribution levels, also, buyers' wants and preferences are important. Once the producer determines which kinds of retailers are most acceptable to ultimate consumers, it must find out the type of supplier from which retailers prefer to buy the product. Retailers may customarily buy directly from manufacturers, or they may buy from merchant wholesalers, or they may buy through agents of some sort. Whatever the normal buying pattern of retailers, a producer is well advised to make its product available through the same sources. Similarly, the producer must analyze the wants and expectations of buyers at other distribution levels.

DETERMINING THE BEST CHANNEL ALTERNATIVE(S)

From the producer's standpoint, determining the best channel alternative(s) involves: (1) recognizing what "best" means, and (2) comparing the various alternatives in terms of this meaning. If, as in most cases, best means most profitable, the producer must estimate for each channel alternative both the sales volume potential and the costs of channel usage, and then compare the alternatives in terms of their relative contributions to long-run profit. Certain market statistics are required for making such comparisons. The most basic relate to the potential market. The producer must have long-run estimates of market potential and from these, perhaps by applying some "target share-of-the-market percentage," its management must derive long-run estimates of the firm's sales potentials. After considering these sales potentials, together with data on the "reach" of outlets at each distribution level, management determines whether a single channel or a number of channels are needed.

Marketing cost analysis is used to determine probable costs of performing required marketing activities under each arrangement. In each channel there is implied some scheme for dividing up performance of marketing activities, apportioning some to the producer and others to different channel members. The costs of performing each activity at each distribution level and the total costs of accomplishing the entire marketing task must be estimated for each channel.

Tradeoff Analysis

Then the two sets of estimates—sales and costs—are combined, generally in the form of a *tradeoff analysis*. Figure 13–3 shows a hypothetical tradeoff analysis comparing the projected results of selling direct to retailers and using a selling agent. As indicated, channel usage costs rise with sales volume for both alternatives but at different rates. The costs of using a selling agent are mostly variable, while those incurred in selling direct (through the company's own salesmen) to retailers are mostly fixed (assuming that the salesmen are paid mainly on a straight salary basis). Under this set of conditions, channel usage costs rise more rapidly with additional sales through the selling agent than they do through company salesmen.

Notice that at sales volume *T* (the tradeoff point) channel usage costs are identical for both channels. This indicates that the selling agent is the best alternative at any sales volume lower than *T*, while the direct-to-retailer channel is the best at any sales volume higher than *T*. If the manufacturer believes that in all likelihood sales will be

Figure 13–3
Tradeoff analysis—selling agent vs. direct sales to retailers

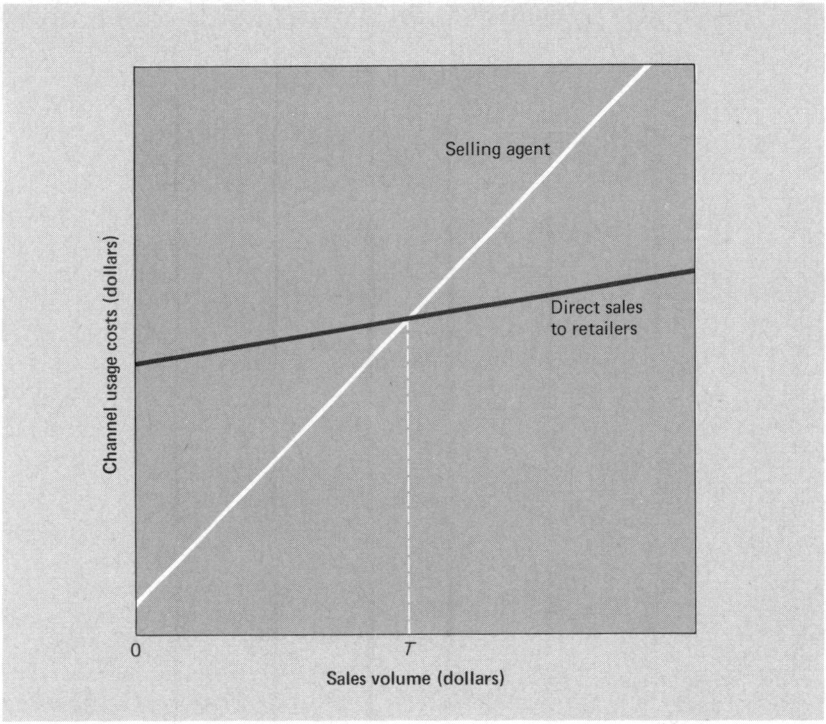

less than T (and assuming no other important considerations), then it should use the selling agent; otherwise, it should sell direct to the retailers.

DETERMINING DISTRIBUTION INTENSITY

Not only must the manufacturer decide the kind of middlemen it should use on each distribution level, it must decide how many middlemen there should be on each level. If it decides to sell directly to retailers, it must choose from among many different kinds of retailers; if it decides to use wholesalers, it must choose from among the different kinds of wholesale institutions. Then it determines how many retailers of the chosen types are needed to reach the consumers it wants to reach; and, assuming that it decides to use wholesalers also, how many wholesalers of the chosen types are required to reach all the retailers it desires to use. The manufacturer must decide not only the kinds of building blocks to include in its marketing channel(s) but the number of each kind.

Distribution Intensity

Decisions on the number of middlemen relate to distribution intensity. There are three general degrees of *distribution intensity:* mass, selective, and exclusive. These are arbitrary classifications since there are many intermediate gradations. Distribution intensity should be regarded as a broad band with mass distribution at one end and exclusive distribution at the other. Within this broad band, a large number of points represents different degrees of selective distribution.

Mass Distribution

Exclusive Distribution

Extremes of Distribution Intensity The two extremes are mass and exclusive distribution. *Mass distribution* provides maximum sales exposure for a product, whereas *exclusive distribution* involves using a single middleman—a retailer, for example—in each market area. Generally, a manufacturer must use multiple channels, and frequently some rather long channels, to achieve mass distribution intensity. By contrast, a manufacturer using exclusive distribution tends not only to use a single channel but also to sell directly to the chosen outlets.

Selective Distribution

Selective Distribution Most manufacturers have neither complete mass distribution nor complete exclusive distribution but, rather, some form of *selective distribution.* Voluntarily or involuntarily, in pursuing a policy of selective distribution, manufacturers restrict the number of outlets at each distribution level. Voluntary restriction occurs when a manufacturer decides—in a given market area, for instance—to use not every conceivable outlet for its product but only a few desired outlets. Involuntary restriction occurs either when certain desired outlets refuse to handle a manufacturer's product or when the available outlets in a given market are fewer than the number that the manufacturer would like to have. Sometimes the number of middlemen is limited to those that can best serve the manufacturer (that is, that can be the most profitable), but the more modern view is that the number of outlets should be limited to those that can best serve sufficiently large numbers of ultimate buyers (that is, not necessarily including only those outlets most profitable to the manufacturer but also other outlets, such as those situated in locations more convenient to ultimate buyers).

If skillfully implemented, selective distribution commonly results in greater profits for each channel member. The manufacturer gains because it sells to a smaller number of accounts (thus reducing selling expenses), and at the same time it should be able to sell more to each account. The middlemen gain because fewer of their competitors handle the manufacturer's product, permitting them to attract trade that might otherwise go elsewhere. Better merchandising practices are also likely to augment the profits of manufacturer and middleman alike; there are fewer "out-of-stocks" because more adequate inventories are handled; more valuable retail display space tends to be used; at all levels there is more desire to cooperate in coordinating promotional efforts. Even the manufacturer's small order problem may disappear almost entirely.

Deciding Distribution Intensity Particularly important in deciding distribution intensity are a product's marketing characteristics. The more frequently final buyers purchase a product, the stronger the argument for mass distribution or for an extensive form of selective distribution. The greater the gross margin is for the middlemen, the more persuasive the argument for something closer to exclusive distribution. The amount of product service expected by final buyers may vary from none at all (a point in favor of mass distribution) to a large amount (an argument for exclusive distribution). If the useful life of a product is very long, distribution should be quite selective or even exclusive. Similarly, the more searching time final buyers are willing to devote to finding a product outlet, the fewer outlets a manufacturer can afford to have.

The anticipated or actual market position of a brand also influences the decision on distribution intensity. If a brand has consumer preference, the manufacturer can afford to use some selective distribution. If a brand is so fortunate that final buyers insist on it and refuse substitutes, highly selective distribution is feasible and exclusive distribution may be possible.

Many other factors influence the decision on distribution intensity. A manufacturer must take into account the strength of its desire to control price at each distribution level and its relation to the size of the policing problem. Management must appraise the market risk involved in each alternative—for example, exclusive distribution is like putting all the marketing eggs in a limited number of baskets, and in a specific market area, it is like putting all the eggs in one basket. Management must know the attitudes of distributive outlets: some actively seek and enthusiastically support exclusives, others want no part whatever of exclusives, and still others accept exclusives chiefly to deprive competitors of them. The manufacturer must also compare the alternatives in relation to its advertising program—both as to probable waste circulation (that is, appearance of its advertisements in geographic areas other than those where it contemplates having distributors) and as to problems in coordinating middlemen's promotional efforts with its own. Management's attitudes toward competition must also be considered. Someone has to decide whether it is more desirable to have competition inside or outside retail outlets and the amount of protection that should be sought from in-store competition and in-market competition.

OBTAINING CHANNEL USAGE

Obtaining channel usage requires that approaches be made to individual members of the prospective channel team. The producer's proposal must be sold to the managements of channel members and, once this is done, there is usually also need to follow through and sell the team members' sales staffs. In other words, for each channel member's organization, someone must convince both the executives and those who do the actual selling of the marketing worth of the product.

The decision each prospective channel member must make—either to accept or to reject the manufacturer's proposal—is a product selection decision and such decisions have to be made at each distribution level. To put it another way, while the manufacturer thinks of the situation as that of putting together a marketing channel, each middleman (i.e., prospective channel member) thinks of it in terms of "Should I add or not add this product to my stock?" If a consumer product, for instance, is to be marketed through wholesalers and retailers, such decisions are made at three levels—wholesale, retail, and consumer. Before the consumer can decide to accept or reject the product, the retailer must have already decided to accept it; and, before the retailer can make this decision, the wholesaler must have decided to accept it.

BUILDING AND MAINTAINING MIDDLEMEN'S COOPERATION

Building and maintaining middlemen's cooperation is a highly critical matter. When a manufacturer determines its marketing channels and obtains middlemen to assist in the distribution process, it is in effect casting its lot with them. If they succeed in selling the product, the manufacturer also succeeds; if they fail, it fails. Middlemen are charged with making the payoff sales—unless the supply of product finally flows through to final buyers, the marketing channel becomes clogged, and all previous marketing efforts are wasted. It is important, then, for the manufacturer to recognize that middlemen are customers for the product, even though they are not final buyers. At least as much attention, therefore, should go toward securing and maintaining a harmonious working relationship with the middlemen as to building a good reputation among final buyers.

Whether middlemen actively promote, simply recommend, or just handle the manufacturer's products depends largely upon their attitudes toward the manufacturer and its salesmen. If they value these associations, the manufacturer's chances of obtaining satisfactory cooperation are very good. If they stock the product line merely for their customers' convenience, the manufacturer finds it considerably more difficult to capitalize on market opportunities. Sometimes, despite the adverse attitudes of middlemen, it is possible, through heavy advertising and promotion to final buyers, to pull a product through the marketing channel. But forcing middlemen to handle a product generally involves unnecessarily high marketing costs—it is both less costly and more effective to win and hold middlemen's loyalty and cooperation.

Situations in which middlemen are not merely apathetic but outwardly hostile to the manufacturer and its products are the most serious. Many manufacturers who experience this type of difficulty have little personal contact, such as through salesmen, with their middlemen, relying instead on the pull type of advertising to final buyers. Middlemen who stock products only because the number of calls generated through advertising forces them to do so may put the product under the counter, keep it in the backroom, or provide it with the least desirable shelf or counter positions. If they handle competing brands, they may attempt to sell substitutions when their customers ask for the manufacturer's brand—this, of course, is all the more serious when the brand possesses few features differentiating it from competitors.

Appraisal of Marketing Policies The manufacturer seeking to build and maintain mutually beneficial relations with its middlemen should make critical appraisals of the product, the services rendered in connection with it, and other policies followed in its marketing. The manufacturer should ascertain how well or how poorly the product matches middlemen's merchandising requirements and the extent to which it conforms to their evaluations of their customers' wants. Manufacturer-performed services, such as installation and repair, should be offered in response to recognized needs of middlemen and their customers. All of the manufacturer's distribution and promotion policies and practices must be intelligently conceived, uniformly and fairly applied, and fully understood by middlemen; otherwise the manufacturer's marketing efforts cannot begin to approach full effectiveness.

Similarly, the manufacturer should closely examine its pricing practices. When a manufacturer uses unwise pricing, such as granting excessive discounts for large orders, its product may become a "price football" for large middlemen competing on the basis of price. This frequently happens after the product becomes well known and is in strong demand because of continued heavy advertising to final buyers. In these circumstances, smaller dealers may not even try to meet their larger competitors' resale prices, instead devoting their efforts to promoting substitutes for the manufacturer's brand. The underlying difficulty here, as in most cases of unwise pricing, is that some middlemen believe they receive inadequate compensation for handling the product. Oftentimes, the solution to problems traceable to unwise pricing is found through revising decisions on marketing channels and distribution intensity.

Analysis of Communications with Middlemen Lack of or insufficient personal contact of middlemen with the manufacturer often contributes to their failure to give the manufacturer their wholehearted cooperation. Particularly when the marketing channel includes several layers of middlemen, when personal selling plays little or no part in the promotional program, or both, there are likely to be defects in the manufacturer's communications system with its distributive network. Although its product, distribution, promotion, and pricing policies may all appear fundamentally sound, a manufacturer's remoteness, institutionally if not geographically, from certain middlemen and their problems may cause certain of its policies to be inappropriate for them. When competitors have closer personal relationships, such as through salesmen, with these same middlemen, they may regard the manufacturer as too distant to deserve their attention or cooperation. They may continue to handle the manufacturer's product, but mainly because of its already established demand among their own customers. To improve such a situation, the manufacturer must improve its communications with its middlemen.

There are many ways to improve communications with middlemen. Sometimes drastic changes in channel policy may be required—for example, a manufacturer may switch from the use of wholesalers to direct-to-retailer selling, thereby obtaining closer personal contact with retailers. Or it may be sufficient to supplement wholesalers' efforts with a force of "missionary" salesmen. A program involving occasional visits to middlemen by sales and other executives may do wonders in improving communications and in cementing relationships; similar benefits may come from company sponsorship of national or regional conventions for middlemen. Such relatively inexpensive methods as personal letters or telephone calls from marketing executives, the circulation of specially edited dealer magazines, or advertising to the trade sometimes prove effective not only in improving communications, but in building and retaining dealer cooperation.

Summary

Marketing channels are the distribution networks through which direct and indirect ownership transfers are effected as products move from producers to final buyers. Except where producers deal directly with those making up target markets, all channels represent cooperative arrangements of producers and middlemen toward the end of making products available for purchase by final buyers. In all cases, the particular channel used is influenced by factors related to the product, the market, the producer's own organization, and the middlemen—the relative influence of each factor varying with the situation.

In the determination of marketing channels, the producer's main role is that of adjusting to the wants and expectations of buyers on each distribution level. Generally, the producer regards the best channel alternative(s) as the most profitable and, consequently, must estimate and compare for all alternatives both sales potentials and channel usage costs. As management decides on the type of channel and the kinds of middlemen to use on each distribution level, it must also decide on distribution intensity, that is, determine how many middlemen should represent the manufacturer on each level.

In implementing the channel aspects of its distribution strategy, the producer faces problems both at the outset and later on. In obtaining initial channel usage, it must recruit the individual members of the prospective distribution team, convincing them of the merits of its proposal. After the producer succeeds in linking its chosen middlemen together into a marketing channel, it faces problems in building and maintaining cooperative relationships with them; in resolving these problems, the producer must appraise all aspects of its overall marketing strategy and its system for communicating with the distributive network. Any producer using a marketing channel that includes middlemen needs their wholehearted cooperation in order to achieve marketing efficiency.

You should now understand how decisions on marketing channels and their implementation fit into distribution strategy. You should know not only the main types of marketing channels but, more important, the reasons for using each type. You should know both the factors influencing channel usage and the problems producers face in determining and using channels. If you know these things, you understand the channel aspects of distribution strategy.

QUESTIONS AND PROBLEMS

1. Explain the meaning and significance to marketing of each of the following statements:
   a. The producer does not always enjoy complete freedom in selecting marketing channels.
   b. Manufacturers make channel selection decisions whereas middlemen make product selection decisions.
   c. A manufacturer should consider the middlemen on its channel team as simply extensions of its own marketing organization.
   d. Effective usage of marketing channels requires a continuous review and evaluation of the marketing uncontrollables.
2. Illustrate how product and market factors might affect the initial screening of channel alternatives for each of the following products:
   a. cigarette lighters intended to retail at $15
   b. portable, small-screen, transistorized television sets
   c. prefabricated swimming pools for homeowners
   d. office furniture
   e. college textbooks
   f. electric shavers for women
   g. neckties
3. Analyze the relationship of sales forecasting and marketing cost analysis to the determination of marketing channels.

4. What are the factors which cause many manufacturers to use dual marketing channels?
5. To what extent does a manufacturer's use of certain marketing channels place constraints on its decisions with respect to the addition of new products? On its decisions to drop certain products?
6. Under what conditions would you advise a manufacturer to merge with a middleman handling its products? Under what conditions would such a merger be illegal?
7. Outline the steps an importer of foreign automobiles might go through in securing an exclusive dealer in a particular city.
8. A producer of machine tools has been selling industrial users directly through its own force of 20 salaried salesmen. What arguments might be put forth to persuade this manufacturer to discontinue direct selling and to use industrial distributors instead? (NOTE: Industrial distributors in this field normally receive a 20 percent discount off the manufacturer's list price.)
9. Manufacturers of consumer products who use wholesalers to reach retail outlets often also employ salesmen to call on wholesalers' customers. Why? Since, in such cases, the manufacturer's salesmen already call on retailers, why shouldn't the wholesalers be eliminated entirely?
10. Why is it that manufacturers who desire to make use of franchising generally sell direct to retailers?
11. What influence do each of the following factors have on the choice of marketing channels? The product. The market. The manufacturer's organization. The middlemen.
12. What is the producer's main role in the determination of marketing channels? Discuss.
13. How can tradeoff analysis be used in determining the best channel alternatives? Explain.
14. "Normally, a manufacturer must use multiple channels, and frequently some very long channels among them, to achieve mass distribution intensity." Why?
15. Under what conditions might a manufacturer involuntarily use a policy of selective distribution in a given market area?
16. Why would a manufacturer using exclusive distribution normally tend to sell directly to its chosen outlets?
17. Generally speaking, a manufacturer's brand must enjoy some degree of consumer preference before it is wise for the manufacturer to adhere to a policy involving selective distribution. Why?
18. How should a manufacturer go about building and maintaining middlemen's cooperation? Discuss.

CASE PROBLEM

Mr. Bob Tarwater, marketing manager of Russell Ellen Company, a manufacturer of dinnerware, was considering a new system for the distribution of the dinnerware. Up to that time, Russell Ellen products were sold through nearly 2,000 retail department, jewelry, and specialty stores. A number of factors, however, had led Mr. Tarwater to consider setting up a distribution system whereby the company's own salesmen would call directly on ultimate consumers and sell them "in their homes." If this system of direct distribution were to become a reality, Mr. Tarwater would discontinue selling the Russell Ellen line through the existing marketing channels and outlets.

What factors should be taken into account by Mr. Tarwater in making this decision?

When you have mastered the contents of this chapter, you should be able to:

1. Explain the various factors influencing decisions on size of inventory.
2. Contrast the relative strengths and weaknesses of each of the three decision alternatives on geographic deployment of inventory.
3. Outline the conditions under which a marketer should (a) operate its own branch warehouses, or (b) use public warehouses.
4. Explain how the marketer should make decisions on modes of transportation.
5. Discuss the marketing significance of decisions on materials handling, order size, and order processing.
6. Explain the total cost approach to the management of physical distribution.
7. Describe the various applications of operations research to physical distribution problems.
8. Summarize the inputs and decisions that comprise distribution strategy.

CHAPTER 14

PHYSICAL DISTRIBUTION

Physical Distribution

Physical distribution—a critical element in distribution strategy—involves the actual movement and storage of products after their production and before their consumption. All producers and final buyers and most middlemen (i.e., all except for one type of merchant wholesaler—the drop shipment wholesaler—and several types of agents) in varying degrees perform physical distribution activities. Total costs of physical distribution bulk large in the overall cost of goods, generally ranking third in size and exceeded only by the costs of raw materials and labor. Efficiency in physical distribution, therefore, significantly influences a company's chances for marketing success. In this chapter discussion focuses on (1) the various interrelated facets involved in managing physical distribution including inventory control, storage, transportation, materials handling, order size control, and order processing; and (2) the total distribution system.

Decisions on Size of Inventory

Inventories

Inventories are, in effect, reservoirs of goods held in anticipation of sales—that is, of filling demands from farther along the marketing channel. Incoming quantities of the product ready for sale arrive, usually at irregular intervals, and are added to the inventory reservoir. The outgoing product flow is more continuous but still fluctuates considerably. The volume in the inventory reservoir pulsates but not always with a regular rhythm; for, day to day, changes occur in the rates and quantities of input and output. Therefore, in deciding on inventory size, management must determine both maximum and minimum allowable limits. Setting these upper and lower limits involves both sales and cost considerations.

SALES CONSIDERATIONS

The main objective in maintaining any inventory is to meet market demands; that is, to make sales and to fill customers' orders. Since inventories are kept in anticipation of market demand, the upper and lower control limits should be attuned to forecasted sales. Thus, the more accurate the sales forecast, the greater the opportunity is for gain from economical inventory operations. The less accurate the forecast, the greater the need is for substantial buffer stocks over and above normal inventory levels. Both a sales forecast and some notion of its probable accuracy are needed for setting the control limits.

Two additional factors, however, need considering. One is management's concept of an acceptable level of customer service. Experience indicates that, in a typical business, about 80 percent more inventory is needed to fill 95 percent of customers' orders from stock on hand than to fill just 80 percent of such orders.[1] Each firm, then, must strike a balance between what it considers reasonable customer service and costs, in line with overall marketing objectives. It should recognize that many customers regard consistency of delivery as at least as important as speed of delivery, particularly if they buy for resale.[2] Settling on some objective as to the proportion of all customers' orders which the stock on hand could satisfy without delay has a definite bearing on the upper inventory limit.

Distribution System Responsiveness

The other factor is *distribution system responsiveness*—the ability of a system to communicate needs back to the supplying plant and get needed inventory into the field. The amount of responsiveness determines how quickly management can adjust inventory to demand changes. Thus, distribution system responsiveness directly influences the lower inventory limit.

COST CONSIDERATIONS

Three main types of costs are associated with the inventory.

Holding Costs

Holding costs include warehousing and storage charges, costs of capital tied up in inventory, costs of adverse price movements, obsolescense, spoilage, pilferage, and taxes and insurance on inventory.

Costs of Shortages

Costs of shortages (that is, of having negative inventories) include special clerical, administrative, and handling costs and, most impor-

[1] J. F. Magee, "The Logistics of Distribution," *Harvard Business Review,* July–August 1960, p. 62.

[2] D. J. Bowersox, "Physical Distribution Development, Current Status, and Potential," *Journal of Marketing,* January 1969, p. 66.

Costs of Replenishing

tant, losses of specific sales, of goodwill, and even of some customers. *Costs of replenishing* inventory differ in composition depending upon whether a business does its own manufacturing. Inventory-replenishing costs in a make and sell business are mainly manufacturing costs: labor and machine setup costs, costs of material used during setup testing, cost of production time lost during setups, clerical and administrative costs, and so on. Inventory-replenishing costs in the buy and sell type of business include those for clerical and administrative work, transportation and unloading, placement in warehouses or stores, and performing necessary related activities.

Inventory decisions should seek to balance the three types of costs. Whereas holding costs rise as inventory increases, the costs of both shortages and inventory replenishment decrease as inventory increases. Holding, shortage, and replenishment costs are all related, then, to inventory size; total costs are a function of the amount stored. Determining how much to store in order to minimize total costs involves balancing inventory-holding costs against either costs of shortage or costs of replenishment or both.[3]

Decisions on Storage and Inventory Location

Decisions on storage and inventory location are closely linked to decisions on inventory size. For instance, a decision to restrict inventory size drastically, so as to operate almost from hand to mouth, reduces total need for storage space. It is often necessary to increase some physical distribution costs to reduce others by a greater total amount. Marketers make three important storage decisions: geographic deployment of inventory, ownership of warehouse facilities, and number and location of warehouses.

GEOGRAPHIC DEVELOPMENT OF INVENTORY

Geographical Deployment of Inventory

There are three decision alternatives on *geographical deployment of inventory:* (1) concentration at or near the plant or at some other central location, (2) dispersion at several distribution points located in or closer to the main markets, and (3) concentration of substantial inventories at a few distribution centers and redistribution to a larger number of distribution points dispersed throughout the market. The first two alternatives are opposite extremes; the third is a compromise between them.

[3] For an excellent analysis of the importance of costs and cost reduction opportunities in overall distribution operations, see Wendell M. Stewart, "Physical Distribution," in *Handbook of Modern Marketing,* ed. Victor P. Buell (New York: McGraw-Hill Book Co., 1970), pp. 4-61–4-65.

Inventory Concentration

Inventory Dispersion

Comparison of inventory concentration and dispersion reveals opposite sets of strengths and weaknesses. The company that concentrates its inventory can minimize the number of customers' orders unfilled because of stock-outs; but in so doing it may increase total transportation costs and delay customer service. The firm that disperses its inventory needs a larger total inventory investment and, in effect, commits each subinventory to sale only in a particular market area; but it reduces total transportation charges and speeds up customer service. The concentration decision permits more rapid adjustment to changes in the makeup of incoming orders because unexpected demands originating from only a few markets usually can be met at once; the dispersion decision requires either that a large enough reserve stock be maintained at each branch to meet most emergencies or that there be some provision for moving stocks among branches. Thus, the dispersion decision requires the greater inventory investment because the sum of many small reserve stocks scattered over the whole market is greater than one large reserve stock held at a single location. Similarly, operating one large central warehouse should mean greater warehousing efficiency at lower costs per unit of product handled than can be achieved through decentralized operation of smaller storage facilities. But if the product line consists mostly of bulky and low-unit-value items—the kind that must usually be shipped by truck or rail—total transportation costs may be lower when decentralized warehouses are used. This is because railroads and truckers normally charge less for full carloads or truckloads than for shipments in less-than-carload lots. Both alternatives, then, have general strengths and weaknesses, and whether a marketer chooses one or the other—or adopts the third as a compromise—depends upon its evaluations of the relative importance of each factor. These evaluations, in turn, are influenced by the product line, target markets, marketing channels, promotional strategies, pricing policies, and competitors' practices.

INVENTORY DISPERSION AND WAREHOUSE OWNERSHIP

Manufacturers deciding to disperse their inventories may choose between operating their own branch warehouses or using public warehouses. This choice depends upon the amount of sales volume originating in particular markets, the preference for fixed or variable warehousing costs, the degree of flexibility desired in making changes in the pattern of inventory deployment, relative warehousing efficiency, and marketing channel(s) used. There is relationship and interaction among these factors. If the volume of goods moved is substantial and shows little seasonal fluctuation, a good case can be made for branch warehouses owned and operated by the manufacturer. The costs of branch warehousing are mainly fixed and, with a large and steady flowthrough of goods, the costs per unit of product moved are likely to be low. Because public warehouses base their charges on the space and labor actually used, the scales generally tip in their favor only when a small volume is to be handled or when a large volume with great seasonal fluctuations is to be stored. The variable costs associated with the use of public warehouses also provide greater flexibility in changing the geographical deployment of inventory. Because most cities have many public warehouses, the manufacturer can easily close out stocks in some locations and place them in others.

Public Warehouses

The chief economic justification for the public warehouse is that it dovetails local small storage needs of many manufacturers which, in turn, results in a large enough storage facility to make efficient use of storage space, warehousing labor, and mechanized handling equipment. However, with a large and steady sales volume of its own, a manufacturer may realize comparable efficiencies in its own branch warehouses. Furthermore, if its product requires either specialized handling and technical service or special storage facilities, it may be forced to own and operate branch warehouses. Although some cities have public warehouses that provide individualized handling and technical services (for example, those specializing in appliance warehousing) and warehouses that offer specialized storage facilities (for example, those with refrigerated storage space), they cannot be found in all cities. Thus, the manufacturer who needs them may have to operate its own facilities in certain market areas.

Spot Stocks

Accredited Lists

Some manufacturers use public warehouses as substitutes for wholesalers, for local sales representatives, or for both. These manufacturers place "spot stocks" in public warehouses and furnish the operators with "accredited lists" of customers (including "credit limits") authorized to receive deliveries. The public warehouseman not only fills orders but often attends to billing and collections. Generally, public warehouses are not aggressive sales representatives so the manufacturer using them for that purpose may have to rely on exclusive retail outlets or heavy consumer advertising to move the goods out of the warehouse. Still another reason for using public warehouses is that they issue warehouse receipts, which may be used as collateral for bank loans; however, this is only a source of short-term credit during the time the goods remain unsold.

NUMBER AND LOCATION OF WAREHOUSES

One problem confronting a manufacturer who decides on a policy of inventory dispersion is determining the number of locations of warehouses. The nature of this problem is influenced by several important variables including customers' buying patterns and delivery expectations, freight rate structures, service characteristics of alternative transportation media, warehouse operating costs, location of factories, production capacities and product mix of individual factories, and costs of building or renting suitable warehouses in different cities. It is possible to gather statistics and related information on each of these variables, but the number of possible combinations of the many sets of complex, and to some extent interrelated, variables is staggering. Thus, in the past, largely because of the mountain of work involved in calculating the probable results of each combination of variables, most decisions on number and location of warehouses were made intuitively. With the advent of the high-speed digital computer, such computations became more routine.

Operations researchers have devised simulation techniques that permit mathematical representations of a company's distribution system, present and proposed, to be programmed on a computer. In a comparatively short time, a computer can provide the probable operating results under many different combinations of numbers and locations of warehouses. Such simulations often furnish marketing executives with much additional information needed for decisions on related problems.

Decisions on Modes of Transportation

Decisions on modes of transportation are related to those on size of inventory and on storage location, both of which are themselves interrelated. No one of these decisions should be made without considering the possible effects on the others. For example, decisions that seek only to optimize transportation costs may drastically increase inventory and storage costs. The overall total costs of physical distribution are more important than the costs of any one aspect of a physical distribution system.

Significant improvements are being made in transportation services. Truck transportation is improving with the construction of more superhighways, the increase in truck speeds, and the use of larger trailers. Rail freight transportation is improving as more roads provide *piggyback* service (rail movement of loaded tractor trailers), "unitized" trains, and other service innovations. Air freight transportation is improving with the larger jet air carriers and the use of "containerized" (giant containers holding many smaller shipments) loading and unloading systems. These are only a few of the many improvements being made in transportation services, but they indicate the strong general trend toward providing shippers with more rapid and efficient transportation services.

Too often, decisions on modes of transportation are made solely in terms of comparative shipping costs. In these cases, management ignores the fact that transportation is only one part of what should be a totally integrated physical distribution system. When transportation decisions are made in isolation, shipping costs may be minimized but total physical distribution costs are usually not. Shipping decisions that aim only to reduce transportation cost may be more than offset by increases in warehousing costs, costlier packing, and the costs of carrying larger-than-necessary inventories.

Decisions on modes of transportation should be made with the objective of optimizing the efficiency of the total physical distribution system. Relative costs, although important, provide only one basis for comparing the contribution of different modes of transportation to total system efficiency. There is a general trend, as mentioned earlier, toward providing shippers with more rapid transportation services (for example, increased truck speeds and rail freight "piggyback" service). *Transport time*—the time required for moving goods from warehouses, for example, to customers—is a major determinant of efficiency in the distribution system. Reductions in transport time, though commonly accompanied by increased shipping costs, often result in significant savings in warehousing costs, packing costs, and inventory investments. For instance, switching from a distribution system composed of surface transportation and branch warehouses to one involving air transportation direct to the customer normally results in higher transportation costs but much lower storage costs. Net savings often result from such changes, largely due to reductions in storage and inventory costs.

Transport Time

However, physical distribution costs can sometimes be cut through using slower and lower cost modes of transportation. For instance, Westinghouse Electric Corporation switched from air to surface transportation for deliveries of rush orders. By making improvements in all the distribution steps before shipment, Westinghouse saved so much time that it could use the slower surface transportation and benefit from the lower cost. Generally, transportation decisions should be based both on cost and transport time, and the relative significance of each depends on their combined relationship to the overall efficiency of the total physical distribution system.

Materials Handling Decisions

Materials handling is the area of physical distribution that has experienced the greatest change and improvement in recent decades. The first major improvement was the elimination of "manhandling" of goods. Thirty years ago it was common to use manpower to transfer goods from storage to transportation and back to storage. Today, most goods are not handled by human labor at all until they reach the retail or final buyer level. Improved conveyor systems and fork lift equipment make possible almost total mechanization.

Containerization

The second improvement in materials handling was *containerization*—the development of methods by which a large number of units of a product are combined into a single compact unit for storage and transportation. Containerization has evolved from the simple pallet to complex and special-purpose containers. Containerization reduces both materials handling costs and time, because it allows goods to be moved greater distances in bulk form, increasing mechanized handling and reducing manhandling.

Materials handling decisions and costs are interrelated with other decisions and costs. Improved materials handling not only reduces the cost of handling goods, it also improves the relative effectiveness of transportation and storage. For example, containerization so drastically reduces the "loading turnaround time" for ships that it has greatly lessened their "comparative speed" disadvantage. At the same time, improved materials handling makes possible more effective utilization of storage space and, hence, a reduction of investment in facilities. Improved materials handling may increase the utilization of warehouse storage space by 50 or more percent, since it makes possible "ceiling-high" stacking of goods. Similarly improved materials handling, by speeding up the processing of orders and movement of shipments, should also contribute to improved customer service.

Order Size Decisions

Order size decisions are also complicated because of the interrelationships of order sizes to other facets of physical distribution. For example, when orders are for quantities less than the contents of a normal pallet or container, the goods must be handled entirely by hand instead of by machine. Such manhandling raises costs appreciably. Less-than-pallet-size orders also increase the costs of storage and inventory control and add to their complexity. The size of an order may also affect the level of shipping costs, since bulk or carload shipping rates are generally a good deal lower than rates for smaller quantities. It is important, therefore, for management to make decisions concerning minimum order sizes, units of increment in order sizes, and preferred order sizes so that customers' orders will be of sizes consistent with the objective of optimizing total physical distribution costs.[4]

Order Processing Decisions

The methods a marketing organization uses for processing customers' orders affects its service to them in two ways. First, reorder time is affected; second, the consistency of delivery time is affected. Variations in these two time variables exert influences upon the buyers' profits by changing their minimum investments in inventory, altering their ordering costs, and changing the probability that they will

[4] A good discussion of order size decisions, complete with examples, may be seen in Arthur J. Schomer, "An Approach to Inventory Management," *Journal of Accountancy*, August 1965, pp. 75–77.

be out-of-stock. Because of these considerations, buyers tend to shift their orders to suppliers providing superior order processing service. In a study of 700 retailers, it was found that store buyers could discriminate among even small differences in order service time and that their rating of this factor influenced their overall rating of a supplier.[5] Even small improvements in order processing service can provide a supplier with a competitive advantage; thus, it is worthwhile exploring possible avenues leading to greater efficiency in order processing.

The Total Distribution System

Physical distribution is intimately related to other aspects of marketing. Consider what takes place as products move through marketing channels, over time and through space, from production to consumption. Inventories are normally held by manufacturers, by middlemen at each distribution level, and by ultimate buyers at the end of the channel. In the distribution of consumer goods, for example, consumers add to their stocks by buying from retailers. This reduces retailers' inventories and eventually the retailers place replenishing orders with wholesalers, who, in turn, replenish their stocks by placing orders with manufacturers. Thus, while products are flowing forward to final buyers, there is a reverse flow of orders causing alternating subtractions from and additions to inventories at each level. Each time a manufacturer ships an order, it initiates this chain reaction in the performance of transportation, inventory control, storage, and other physical distribution activities.

The details and manner of performing physical distribution activities at each level in the marketing channel may vary considerably. Often, the size of inventory varies between distribution levels and among individual middlemen on the same level. When a channel includes drop-shipment wholesalers or agent middlemen, there may be no inventories at all on their levels. Other middlemen differ markedly with respect to order quantities and frequency of order placement. Both the forward flow of products and the reverse flow of orders encounter interruptions of varying and often unpredictable durations. Either flow, and sometimes both, may fall to "just a trickle" or rise to "flood-stage proportions." A manufacturer may centralize warehousing and shipping activities at one or a few locations, or it may decentralize them through branch warehouses or by using public warehouses. Middlemen—especially chains or other multiple establishments—have similar options. Furthermore, in moving products from one distribution point to the next, different transportation methods may be selected. These factors, present in all distribution systems, make managing physical distribution a challenging task.

[5] R. P. Willet and P. R. Stephenson, "Determinants of Buyer Response to Physical Distribution Service, *Journal of Marketing Research,* August 1969, pp. 280–283.

Even though the way total distribution costs are divided among the various physical distribution activities varies widely in different firms, it is possible to generalize about the relative role of each activity in terms of costs. Table 14–1 shows the average division of physical distribution costs found in a sample made up of twenty-six large companies. Carrier or transportation charges were the largest cost element (44 percent of the total), while warehousing and handling costs, including storage charges and materials handling costs, were the second largest cost element (20 percent of total physical distribution costs).

From the manufacturer's standpoint, physical distribution management requires integrated planning of all transportation, storage, and supply requirements, plus the implementation of inventory policy. This requires decisions on the deployment and size of inventory at specific times and places, ensuring that the right products are in the right quantities at the right places at the right times. The solution should strike an optimal balance between physical distribution costs and the expectations of end buyers and users of the product.

Because manufacturers generally reach final buyers through intermediate distribution levels, they cannot completely control (that is, direct and regulate) physical distribution. They are bound to find distribution levels and points where they have little, if any, control over the inventory size and disposition. A manufacturer does direct and regulate inventories at the factory and at its own warehouses; and here, at least, physical distribution decisions can be optimal, but only in the sense that they are the best under the circumstances—considering such factors as costs, demand characteristics, and in-

Table 14–1 Physical Distribution: Major Elements of Cost in Twenty-Six Large Companies

COST ELEMENT	PERCENT OF TOTAL DISTRIBUTION COST
Carrier Charges	44
Warehousing & Handling	20
Inventory Carrying Cost	18
Shipping Room & Administrative (Includes order processing costs)	18
Total	100

Note: Averages for survey sample as a whole, based on available company data and/or author's estimates. Percentages assigned to various items vary as much as ±20% among the twenty-six individual companies.

Source: R. P. Neuschel, "Physical Distribution—Forgotten Frontier," *Harvard Business Review*, March-April 1967, p. 132.

ventory eccentricities of distribution points farther down the channel.

Normally, a manufacturer must work toward optimum performance of the total distribution system by coordinating its inventory policies and practices with those of other channel members. How middlemen manage their inventories definitely affects the manufacturer's costs and profits. Their actions also determine the quality of service and product availability at the times and places desired by final buyers. If middlemen are overstocked, they may cut prices to make sales, thus jeopardizing future sales at normal prices, possibly damaging the manufacturer's reputation for product quality, and perhaps making themselves less enthusiastic about future relationships with the manufacturer. If middlemen follow unintelligent inventory practices, such as "hand-to-mouth" buying, the manufacturer is forced to enlarge inventories and, consequently, to increase costs. Furthermore, the manufacturer and the middlemen suffer hidden costs from being out of stock and unable to fill orders when buyers want them. Unfortunately, out-of-stock costs are rarely identified because they are not recorded by conventional accounting systems, but profits and sales are both reduced when customers are sent away empty-handed.

Estimates of physical distribution costs indicate that they account for as much as one-third of the manufacturer's selling price and from one-fifth to one-fourth of the price paid by the final buyer. Any area accounting for so much of total costs should be a prime target for management's efforts to increase efficiency. Gains in physical distribution efficiency should be accompanied by improvements in net profits. Such improvement, however, can be achieved only by periodic, complete reviews of the entire distribution process.

Applications of Operations Research to Physical Distribution Problems

Physical distribution decisions generally involve an attempt to optimize several variables. The conventional manual "pencil and paper" approach to such decisions is not only tedious but rarely very effective, since restrictions of time and manpower require drastic simplifications of problems. Consequently, business executives have searched for new approaches involving computer use. Among these new approaches are those involving mathematical simulation, linear programming, heuristic programming, and integer programming.

MATHEMATICAL SIMULATION

The essential parts of a company's physical distribution system can be reduced to a mathematical representation and, through use of a computer, can then be used to test various schemes management may be considering for improving distribution methods and/or lowering distribution costs. Management, by comparing the results simulated for each of the various alternatives, can then better select those distribution alternatives that come closest to meeting its objectives.

Mathematical Simulation

Such a *mathematical simulation* can easily be set up to analyze, for instance, which of a hundred possible warehouse configurations should be used or which of a dozen different combinations of shipping arrangements should be used. Mathematical simulations are particularly useful in dealing with the scheduling of shipments, an area in which many puzzling problems confront those concerned with physical distribution. However, since an answer reached through a mathematical simulation may involve assumptions and simplification, it is not necessarily an optimum solution to the problem under investigation.

LINEAR PROGRAMMING

Linear Programming

The transportation technique of *linear programming* is used in planning shipments from different origins to different destinations in ways that minimize total shipping costs. For example, the origins may be factories or other sources of supply, distribution centers, or warehouses; the destinations may be distribution centers, warehouses, customers, or stores. Thus, knowing customer demand for the product at various locations and the amount of supplies at a number of warehouses, it is possible through linear programming to determine which warehouse should ship how much product to which customer in order to minimize total shipping costs. Until the development of the transportation technique, no simple procedure more scientific than the "cut and try" method was available for solving problems of this sort.[6]

A more general method of linear programming, the simplex method, is used to find solutions to multidimensional distribution problems. The transportation technique is used only with two-dimensional problems, such as those involving shipments between several origins and several destinations. Dimensions above and beyond this may include various time periods, different products, and one or more intermediate storage points in the distribution system.[7] For example, one large oil company uses such a model to plan optimal means of transportation to serve a number of widely dispersed terminals by relating probable costs to projected changes in product mix and volume at each terminal.

[6] H. C. Bunke, *Linear Programming: A Primer* (Iowa City: Bureau of Business and Economic Research, College of Business Administration, State University of Iowa, 1960), p. 5.

[7] For an explanation of the application of linear programming techniques to multidimensional distribution problems, see J. W. Metzger, *Elementary Mathematical Programming* (New York: John Wiley & Sons, 1958), pp. 54–58.

HEURISTIC PROGRAMMING

Heuristic Programming

A *heuristic* is any device or procedure used to reduce problem-solving effort—that is, it is a rule of thumb used to solve a particular problem. A *heuristic program* is a collection or combination of heuristics used for solving a particular problem. Such programs are basically sets of instructions making possible computerized solutions to problems. Heuristic programming is not so much concerned with finding the one best answer after a lengthy search as with rapidly finding a good answer.[8] Thus, heuristic programming provides a way of finding a good enough answer rather than the very best answer to a complex problem, such as those in physical distribution, with considerably less computational effort than that involved in using, say, linear programming to solve the same problem.

INTEGER PROGRAMMING

Integer Programming

Integer programming is a variant of linear programming in which the optimal solution is constrained to consist only of answers which are whole numbers. The principal advantage of this technique is its ability to determine the optimum solution from among a considerably larger number of alternatives than with linear programming, and without excessive time and effort. Recent application of integer programming to physical distribution decisions has been made by several companies.

Summary

Physical distribution activities are involved in moving the product through time and space from the producer to the final buyer. Products often do not reach final buyers until months after their production, and this time element makes inventory control and storage necessary, sometimes at several different distribution levels. Marketing also requires moving products from points of production to points of consumption, sometimes many thousands of miles, and this "space element" makes transportation, materials handling, and order processing necessary.

Recognition that all facets of physical distribution should be treated as a unified managerial responsibility reduces the possibility that certain facets will be emphasized at the expense of others. Awareness of the opportunities for cost savings in the area of physical distribution has become greater with more widespread understanding of the sound logic inherent in the total cost approach to the management of physical distribution. Physical distribution decisions are major decisions, as difficult to make on rational bases as

[8] See J. D. Weist, "Heuristic Programs for Decision Making," *Harvard Business Review,* September—October 1966, pp. 130–131.

they are to reverse or change. They require considerable market information, both qualitative and quantitative and, in using this information, decision makers are helped considerably if they clearly conceptualize the nature of the total physical distribution system, each of its facets, and the relationships each facet bears to others and to the total system.

You should now, therefore, be familiar with the various interrelated facets of physical distribution, know the problems involved in managing each facet, and have an appreciation of the total cost approach to physical distribution management. You should also have concluded that in order to optimize the "mix" of physical distribution decisions, a single executive should be responsible for the entire area. And you should recognize that since the various facets of physical distribution are complex individually, it is frequently necessary to use operations research techniques as aids to making decisions in this area of marketing.

Summary on Distribution

Part Four (Chapters 10 through 14) has covered the inputs and decisions that comprise distribution strategy. Figure 14–1 shows the four main elements of overall marketing strategy (product-market, promotion, distribution, and price strategies). This figure also shows a graphic representation of the various aspects of distribution strategy.

Marketing institutions—wholesalers and retailers—not only constitute the building blocks producers seek to link together into marketing channels, but also play important roles in implementing distribution strategy, including making critical decisions on physical distribution. In the three chapters on marketing institutions (Chapters 10 through 12) we placed particular stress on their dynamic nature. In the past 200 years the rate of institutional change has greatly accelerated. New institutions have appeared, scored great successes, and settled back as significant but not dominating features of the scene; others have gradually faded away. Traditional institutions have had to modernize their operating methods to stay in business. Many of these changes in marketing institutions and their operating characteristics represent a continuation of long-range trends; a few represent a reversal of previous trends. They have come about, in almost all cases, as the result of attempts to adjust operating methods more closely to the needs and expectations, often changing, of the market.

Chapter 13 dealt with marketing channels—the distribution networks through which direct and indirect ownership transfers are effected as products move from producers to final buyers. Major emphasis in this chapter was on the relationships of various channel members to one another and to final buyers. Channel usage, as well as producers' choices of channels, is determined by diverse factors,

Figure 14–1 Distribution strategy and overall marketing strategy

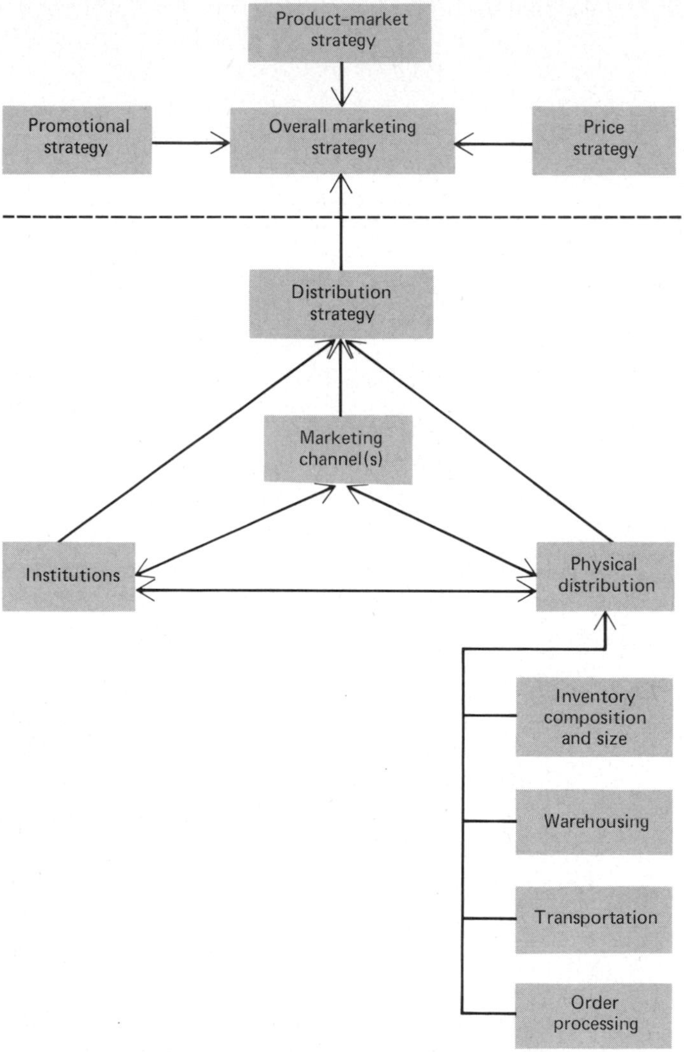

including the products' nature, the target market(s), the producer itself (its financial strength and knowhow), and the middlemen available.

Physical distribution deals only incidentally with ownership transfers, focusing mainly on the physical movement of goods both through space and through time.

The three elements of distribution strategy illustrated in Figure 14–1 are interrelated and interdependent. Marketing channel decisions and physical distribution decisions are made by marketing institutions—producers, wholesalers, and retailers. In a similar manner, marketing channels assume the movement of goods, and the movement of goods assumes eventual transfers of ownership. Various combinations of these elements constitute the distribution strategy input to overall marketing strategy.

QUESTIONS AND PROBLEMS

1. Explain the meaning and significance to marketing of each of the following statements:
   a. Managing physical distribution involves balancing distribution costs against an acceptable level of customer satisfaction.
   b. When the price level in an industry is rising, the relative competitive position of the most distant producer in the industry tends to improve.
   c. Viewed from the channel position of the manufacturer, physical distribution management requires logistical planning.
2. Explain the meaning of the following:
   a. distribution system responsiveness
   b. spot stocks and accredited lists
   c. "simulation" technique
   d. containerization
   e. heuristic
3. What is meant by the "total cost" approach to physical distribution? Contrast this approach with the management of physical distribution activities before its development.
4. Why is it that manufacturers cannot completely "control" (i.e., direct and regulate) physical distribution?
5. Explain and illustrate the relationship of accuracy in sales forecasting to decisions on inventory size.
6. What factors determine the upper and lower inventory control limits?
7. What kinds of costs are associated with the inventory? Explain how inventory costs are "balanced" in making inventory decisions? How does middlemen's management of inventories affect the manufacturers' costs and profits?
8. Contrast and compare inventory concentration and inventory dispersion from the standpoint of their respective strengths and weaknesses.
9. Under what circumstances should a manufacturer use public warehouses? Own its own warehouses?
10. Would you advise a fertilizer manufacturer to use public warehouses as a substitute for wholesalers? Why or why not?
11. Explain the significance of "transport time" to physical distribution efficiency.

12. What improvements have been made recently in materials handling? Of what significance are they to marketing?
13. Explain how order size decisions are related to decisions on materials handling.
14. What is meant by "reorder" time? How does it relate to efficiency in order processing?
15. Should a manufacturer attempt to minimize the costs of inventory size, inventory location, materials handling, order processing, and shipping separately or collectively? Why?
16. What applications of operations research techniques have been made to physical distribution problems? Appraise the likely future uses of these and other operations research techniques.

CASE PROBLEM

Onondaga Distributors, Inc., manufactured and sold a very wide line of industrial parts. In going over the sales records for the past two years, Mr. Bob Borgman, sales manager, noted a substantial increase in the number of small orders sold by Onondaga. As a result, he requested Mr. John Fleming, chief sales analyst for the firm, to conduct a detailed investigation of the order size of sales.

Mr. Fleming's research revealed that nearly 30 percent of the orders filled by Onondaga were clearly unprofitable, falling well below the $22.50 per order needed to break even. The average order size of the 30 percent unprofitable orders was $10.35.

Mr. Borgman could easily see that Onondaga Distributors was losing money on some orders and he was aware that distribution costs directly affected the profitability of the company. However, he was uncertain as to what course of action he should take to correct the small order problem.

What alternatives are available to Mr. Borgman?

PART FIVE

PROMOTION

When you have mastered the contents of this chapter, you should be able to:

1. Explain the relationship of overall marketing strategy to marketing communications.
2. Describe the five stages in the communications process.
3. Define the following terms: noise, feedback, source effect, promotional mix.
4. Contrast the nature and distinctive characteristics of the following forms of promotion: personal selling, advertising, point-of-purchase display, packaging, direct mail, trading stamps, premiums, sampling, and couponing.
5. Analyze the various factors influencing the "inputs" that should be incorporated in particular promotional mixes and strategies.
6. Explain the relationship of promotional objectives to the total appropriation for promotion.
7. Discuss the relationship of promotion to demand stimulation in terms of each of the three general promotional objectives.

CHAPTER 15

PROMOTIONAL STRATEGY

Product-Market Strategy

Distribution Strategy

Promotional Strategy

Promotional strategy is the third key element in overall marketing strategy. *Product-market strategy,* the first key element, focuses on the marketer's efforts to fit the product and its features to the target market's needs and wants. *Distribution strategy,* the second key element, concerns the marketer's activities in joining with middlemen to provide marketing channels for the product and to handle its physical distribution. *Promotional strategy*—the topic of the three chapters in Part Five—relates to the marketer's efforts to make the product actually flow through the marketing channels and to the target market. Thus, promotion involves the marketer's activities in communicating both with members of the product's target market and the middlemen to increase the chances that the planned sequence of sales (i.e., ownership transfers) takes place smoothly and efficiently. Discussion in this chapter covers (1) the role of communications in overall marketing strategy, (2) the nature and distinctive characteristics of the different forms of promotion, (3) the factors involved in blending different forms of promotion into promotional mixes and strategies, and (4) the total promotional appropriation.

Overall Marketing Strategy and Marketing Communications

Figure 15–1 shows the relationship between overall marketing strategy and marketing communications. Management combines the four controllables—product-market, distribution, promotion, and price strategies—into an overall marketing strategy. Establishing and maintaining communications with target market segments are the main missions assigned to promotion. Thus, promotion involves

Figure 15–1
Relationship of overall marketing strategy to marketing communications

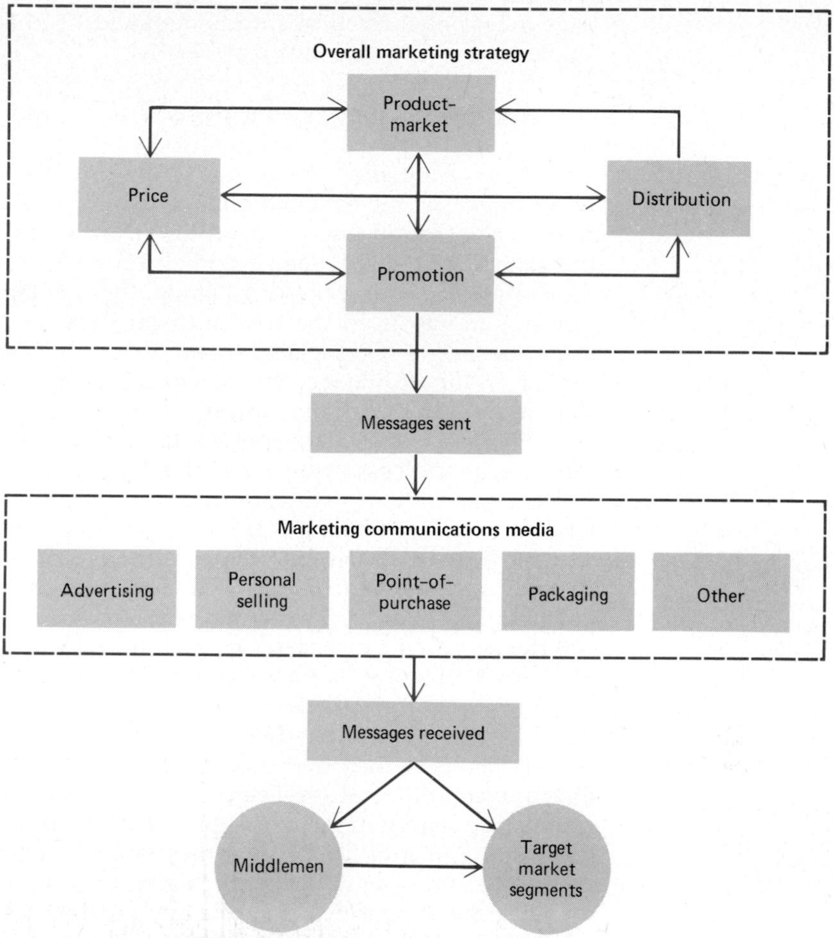

sending messages to target markets and intervening middlemen through various marketing communications media—advertising, personal selling, point-of-purchase materials, packaging, and other media such as samples and coupons. The "messages sent" relate to various aspects of the overall marketing strategy that management feels might contribute to favorable buying responses on the parts of middlemen and members of target market segments. However, as implied in this figure, the "messages received" are not necessarily identical to the "messages sent," thus emphasizing the very important point that successful promotion comes about only through effective communications!

Communications and Promotion

Communications requires a sender (or source), a message, and a receiver. Unless a sender's message is received by someone, no communication takes place. And, clearly, a marketer's promotional message must be received by middlemen and/or those making up target markets, if it is to achieve its objective.

THE COMMUNICATION PROCESS

Communication Process

The *communication process,* as Figure 15–2 shows, consists of five stages.[1] At the first stage the source originates the communication. In the second stage – encoding – the idea to be communicated is translated into a language or medium of expression suitable for transmission. During the third stage, the message carrying the idea flows or moves from the source toward the receiver. In the fourth stage, decoding takes place; in other words, the message is interpreted. In the fifth stage, the decoded message reaches the receiver, the target of the communication.

Noise

Figure 15–2 also shows two other elements affecting the communication process – noise and feedback. *Noise* consists of extraneous interferences with communication, thus making it less effective. It can be actual noise, such as the sound of an airplane interfering with a salesman's presentation, or other kinds of interference, such as "snow" or a double image disturbing a television commercial. Even a distracting remark or action by another that interferes with the message's reception is considered noise. Any sort of distraction vying for the receiver's attention or interfering with the reception of the message is noise. In all communication processes, noise is present to some degree or another.

Feedback

Feedback is the other element and, normally, it is essential for effective communication. Feedback is important to the information source (the sender of the message) – to determine the effectiveness of the communication, the source needs feedback to tell whether the "message sent" was actually the "message received." Feedback takes many forms: it might consist of a nod, an expression of interest, or a smile from the listener or reader; it might consist of a marketing research report or a returned coupon from the receiver of an advertising message. Marketing management needs effective feedback in order to identify and rectify the causes of communication breakdown.

[1] E. Crane in *Marketing Communications* (New York: John Wiley & Sons, 1965), p. 11, builds communication around only three stages – source, message, and receiver.

Figure 15–2 The communication process

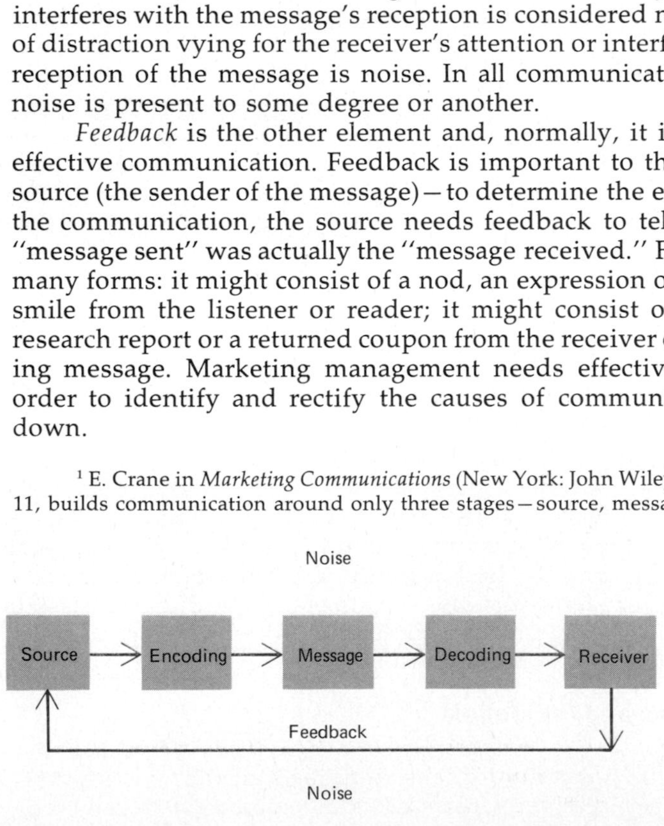

Several factors may interfere with effective communication. A breakdown at the message stage may mean that no communication whatever takes place. An error in encoding or decoding may mean that the message received differs from the message sent. The source might say "What a place!" intending to mean "How nice it is!" The receiver may hear it as "How dreadful it is!" A receiver's different background and way of thinking may cause him or her to interpret the message's meaning in a way not intended by the source. Therefore, for example, in oral communications, such as in salesmen's presentations or those conveyed through radio or television, semantics are important. An expression or word may convey different meanings in different parts of the country, and such differences may be even wider between nations. Words such as "closet" and "napkin" have considerably different meanings in the United States and Great Britain, differences that could prove embarrassing to the message source. Often, differences are even more marked when a message is translated into a foreign language.[2]

SOURCE EFFECT

In marketing communication, it is important to recognize the effect of the message source's reputation upon the way a message is received. The audience's feeling about the message source (for example, concerning its credibility) helps determine the message's effectiveness in persuading receivers to take some action or change an attitude. If the source is highly prestigious or credible, the message is much more likely to influence the audience. For example, for most people an article in *Fortune Magazine* about the future role of business is much more credible and, hence, much more influential than the same article published in a daily newspaper. This phenomenon is known as *source effect*. The source may exert as strong an influence on the receiver as the message itself. The more familiar and prestigious a source is, the more it is likely to be able to influence the receiver with its promotional message.

Source Effect

Forms of Promotion

Personal selling and advertising are the two best-known forms of promotion. They are also the most important forms in terms of cost and market impact. Personal selling is almost always an important part of promotional programs, and it is commonly supported by advertising. Other forms of promotion, such as point-of-purchase display, are less well known but often make important contributions to successful promotional programs.

[2] For a detailed discussion of communications theory, see C. I. Hovland and L. Janis, eds., *Personality and Persuasibility* (New Haven: Yale University Press, 1959), pp. 229–240.

PERSONAL SELLING

Personal Selling

The main mission of *personal selling* is to match up specific products with specific customers to secure ownership transfers. In other words, personal selling seeks to pair the right products with the right customers. Basically, it consists of communicating product and service features in terms of benefits and advantages to the buyer and of persuading him or her to buy the right kind and quantity of the product. Since most people do not like to admit that they have been "sold" anything, most ultimate consumers underestimate the influence of personal selling on their patterns of buying behavior. This is in marked contrast to the sale of industrial products where buyers generally admit that they rely heavily on salesmen as sources of product information and advice. Personal selling, however, plays an important role in marketing even the most heavily advertised and promoted consumer products, such as detergents. The consumer buys detergents on a self-service basis and generally without the help of a sales clerk: however, what is often forgotten is that a considerable personal selling effort is usually required to persuade retailers to stock the particular brand of detergent and to ensure that it is given adequate display and shelf space. Ultimate consumers are not exposed directly to the detergent producer's personal selling effort but, nevertheless, it plays a critical role in promotional strategy.

Personal selling is potentially both the most effective and the most costly form of promotion. Its effectiveness traces to its personal one-to-one approach. The salesman directs his or her message to a single prospect so it can be tailored specifically to fit that prospect's needs. The flexibility inherent in personal selling is a great advantage favoring its use. In addition, in interpersonal communication, there is maximum opportunity for feedback. When the prospect has a question about the salesman's message, he or she can ask for clarification, and the salesman then has a chance to adapt the message accordingly. Clearly, however, this personal one-to-one relationship results in a high cost per message received.

ADVERTISING

Advertising

Advertising is an impersonal form of promotion and involves transmitting standard messages to large numbers of intended receivers. The advertiser has a wide choice of message media including: purely visual media, such as newspapers and magazines; purely aural media, such as radio; and combined aural and visual media, such as television. Although the same message is used, it can be directed only to selected prospects through appropriate media choices. For example, an advertising message can be directed primarily to housewives by placing it on daytime television or in a homemakers' magazine, such as *Good Housekeeping*. One noteworthy weakness of advertising is the great difficulty in obtaining accurate feedback to evaluate message effectiveness. There is no automatic feedback mechanism, as with personal selling, and the mechanisms most advertisers use for obtaining feedback are not very sophisticated or effective. In addition, advertising is relatively inflexible compared with personal selling, since the same message must be directed to large numbers of prospects (some of whom may not even be bona fide prospects, thereby falling under the category of "wasted audience").

Advertising's importance in marketing is frequently overrated by the average citizen. Since it is mainly directed toward consumers, and since the typical consumer is exposed to a large number of advertising messages each day, many are more aware of it. Also, there is a tendency to be impressed with the importance of advertising and with its apparent costs, which might be $50,000 for a single magazine advertisement, or $100,000 for the advertising on a television program. However, while an advertising budget of $1 million a year may appear very large, companies with that kind of advertising effort often have sales forces of 500 or more each costing $20,000 per year to keep in the field, representing a total personal selling cost of $10 million.

Advertising costs are relatively low per promotional message received. A television commercial may be seen by hundreds of thousands, or even millions, of viewers, so even though the total cost seems high, the cost per message received may be only a few cents. However, largely because of its impersonal nature, advertising can seldom move the prospect to buying action as well as can personal selling. Generally, the role most effectively served by advertising is to acquaint prospects with the product and its strengths so that they will be more favorably disposed toward it in later buying situations. Because of advertising's low cost per message, it is highly appropriate for developing initial product awareness or acceptance, which makes the final selling job easier. Also important to remember is that advertising is an out-of-pocket cost; a commitment to spend $100,000 on an advertising campaign is made without any guarantee of return on the investment.

POINT-OF-PURCHASE DISPLAY

Point-of-Purchase Display

The *point-of-purchase display* (for instance, in a retail store) is the silent salesman that calls the prospective buyer's attention to the product and, hopefully, makes the prospect decide to buy. Some research indicates that promotion at the point of purchase is more effective than any other.[3] Retailers rely heavily on instore displays to familiarize customers with products and their features and to allow them the opportunity to examine them. Some displays even make it possible for the customer to try out the product.

Displays vary widely, ranging from a showing of new automobiles with promotional literature and pricing information in a dealer's showroom to a display rack for candy and chewing gum beside the cash register in a supermarket. The automobile showroom

[3] R. T. Peterson, "Experimental Analysis of Theory of Promotion at Point of Consumption," *Journal of Marketing Research*, August 1966, pp. 347–350.

display makes it easy for prospective buyers to become familiar with the different features of the cars on display and to set their own pace while doing so. Display plays a similar role in the promotion of many other large, complex, and "big ticket" (i.e., expensive) items, such as home appliances, furniture, and musical instruments, and for numerous soft goods, such as clothing, piece goods, and linens and bedding. The candy display by a cash register has a different objective—that of reminding customers to buy.

Display, as a form of promotion, is not restricted to retail stores or, for that matter, to consumer products. Merchandise marts provide display booths for manufacturers or distributors to show their product lines to retailers who visit the mart to buy. Display is also an important form of promotion at trade shows and expositions, where industrial buyers are provided with opportunities to examine and test products, too bulky for a salesman to demonstrate on the prospect's own premises, before making their buying decisions.

Marketers rarely use display as their only form of promotion. Even with products sold in self-service stores, the product's ability to sell itself with the help of a point-of-purchase display depends importantly upon brand recognition, which is generally built up rather slowly through frequent exposures of prospective buyers to advertising messages over long periods. And, as mentioned previously, the manufacturer's salesmen must convince the retailer to handle the product before it can be put on display in the store. In fact, it is usually also necessary for the manufacturer's salesman to sell the retailer on erecting the display! The situation is similar for most big ticket items, such as automobiles: not many people buy a car without examining it in the showroom (and in most cases even test-driving it), but few buy *solely* because of what they see and do in the showroom. Advertising is generally necessary to get the prospective car buyer sufficiently interested to visit the showroom. And, most important, it generally takes a live salesman to clinch the sale. Display serves both as a reminder of the product's existence and as a trigger for buying decisions. However, for maximum effectiveness, display must generally be used in combination with personal selling and/or advertising.

PACKAGING

Packaging

Packaging, besides serving to differentiate or protect a product, is also an important form of promotion. The package plays two critical promotional roles: First, it calls shoppers' attention to the product in retail stores, an especially critical role in self-service stores where the package and the display (if any) are the only ways the manufacturer has for communicating with shoppers. Second, it carries selling messages and other items of information that many shoppers need to make buying decisions. As mentioned earlier (in Chapter 9), the package essentially must provide product protection, ease of handling, selling ability (in the absence of a salesman), convenience, and information.

Good package design, from a promotional standpoint, must be capable of attracting the shopper's attention away from an enormous selection of other products and brands also competing for attention. If three competing brands are located side by side on the same retail shelf, the attention of most shoppers is drawn to the best-designed package. Good package design involves a proper blend of color, design, and type style, but the proper blend varies in different situations. For example, research has demonstrated that certain combinations of color are most effective in attracting the attention of shoppers; but, if the packages of the leading competitive brands already carry these color combinations, a particular marketer will find it advantageous to use a different combination to set its brand apart and divert attention away from the competitive packages.

DIRECT MAIL

Direct Mail Promotion

While *direct mail promotion* serves much the same purpose as other printed advertising, it usually allows greater precision in selecting target receivers. For the same cost, a single newspaper advertisement might reach 10,000 readers and direct mail only 100 prospects. But if the mailing list is compiled carefully, the 100 direct mail messages may reach more real prospects than the newspaper advertisement.[4] For example, an art gallery with a $1 million Van Gogh painting to sell might be better off if it sent a direct mail piece to 100 carefully screened individuals than if it advertised in *The New York Times* with its large readership. Direct mail also contrasts with most advertising in that it can be made more personalized. Even a form letter, when individually typed on an automatic typewriter, can convey the impression of person-to-person communication. When the number of prospects is small, each can be sent an individually designed message, thus increasing the potential impact.

Direct mail, like other forms of promotion, is rarely used alone. Its main use is as a supplement to other forms of promotion. It provides an excellent way to maintain contact with customers of industrial products between salesmen's calls. Also, like advertising, it can help develop the product awareness or acceptance that increases purchase probabilities when buyers are contacted by salesmen or see displays.

OTHER FORMS OF PROMOTION

There are many other forms of promotion which, although used less frequently than those already mentioned, are effective in certain situations. Special forms of promotion are often designed to get consumers to try a new product. *Sampling* is one widely used form of special promotion. Sampling of new food products is often carried on in retail stores. Other samples of consumer products, such as deter-

Sampling

[4] For an excellent example of the variety of mailing lists that may be purchased by marketers, see *Catalog of Mailing Lists*, published by Fritz S. Hofheimer, Inc., New York, 1974.

gents or personal care and grooming products, are mailed or delivered to residences. Pharmaceutical manufacturers rely heavily on sampling to make doctors aware of new products. *Couponing* plays a similar role in stimulating purchases of new or improved products. Coupons offering a price reduction on purchases of various brands of numerous products are made widely available to prospective buyers, being inserted as "tear-outs" in magazines or newspapers or through the mail or by distribution in stores and other public places. Trading stamps can provide powerful promotion in situations where it is difficult to develop strong customer store or brand preferences. Special premiums can be used periodically for similar reasons. For example, breakfast cereal manufacturers use premiums, usually choosing varieties that are attractive to children, their largest market segment.

Couponing

The variety of forms of promotion is nearly as broad as man's ingenuity. When a special promotional need arises, it seems a new form of promotion (or a new twist on an old form) is developed to serve it. While these special forms of promotion are relatively unimportant in terms of the total promotional dollars spent by business, they frequently play key roles in the overall marketing strategies of individual companies.

Promotional Mixes and Strategies

Promotional Mix

Most promotional strategies involve the use of various combinations, types, and amounts of different forms of promotion—marketing professionals use the term *promotional mix* to refer to the combination, types, and amounts of different forms of promotion used by a marketer. Generally, a combination is needed, because most forms of promotion used alone are seldom effective and/or efficient. Advertising by itself, for instance, is not usually effective in actually making sales; generally, its effectiveness is increased when it is used with personal selling or display. Even personal selling, which can sometimes produce sales without the support of any other form of promotion, often proves an expensive way to make sales when it is used alone—a small expenditure for advertising to pave the way for the salesman may enormously increase sales productivity and thus reduce the selling cost per sales dollar.

Figure 15–3 shows the relationship of the promotional mix, promotional strategy, and overall marketing strategy. Various combinations, types, and amounts of personal selling, advertising, and other forms of promotion are brought together into a promotional mix which becomes the promotional strategy. For each component of the promotional mix—personal selling, advertising, and so forth—management sets objectives, determines policies, and formulates strategies. These individual strategies are blended together into the promotional strategy which, in turn, needs blending with product-

Figure 15–3
The promotional mix, promotional strategy, and overall marketing strategy

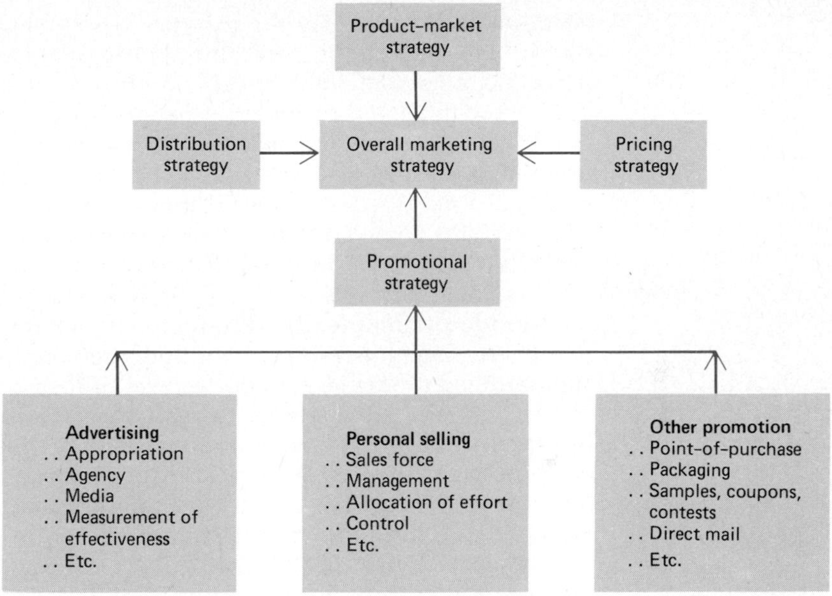

market, distribution, and pricing strategies into an overall marketing strategy.

Thus, in blending the various forms of promotion into a promotional mix and strategy, management's task is to determine the forms most effective for achieving the promotional objectives and optimize the expenditure on each.[5] There is no ideal promotional mix that fits all marketing situations. Various factors influence the promotional inputs that should be incorporated in a particular promotional mix and strategy, but the most critical are the other components of overall marketing strategy (product-market, distribution, and pricing strategies) and the relative costs of different forms of promotion.

PRODUCT-MARKET FACTORS

Nature of the Product Different products require markedly different promotional mixes. Staple branded convenience items, such as many grocery and drug products, are best promoted primarily through mass consumer advertising, combined with good display at the retail level. The needed display space is obtained by using personal selling to persuade dealers and providing them with display materials of proven effectiveness. By way of contrast, impulse convenience items, such as gift boxes of candy, are usually most effectively promoted through heavy emphasis on personal selling aimed to per-

[5] For a good discussion of the various stages in promotional planning and strategy, see J. F. Engel, H. G. Wales, and M. R. Warshaw, *Promotional Strategy* (Homewood, Ill.: Richard D. Irwin, Inc., 1971), pp. 33–37.

suade dealers to display the product where shoppers will see and buy it. Specialty goods generally require major emphasis on advertising (to persuade final buyers to shop or look for the product) blended with personal selling (to persuade dealers to stock and push the product). Many industrial products—particularly those of high unit value, such as machine tools—require an entirely different promotional mix, often composed almost entirely of personal selling with perhaps some advertising or direct mail or space at industrial expositions to locate customers or pave the way for the salesman.[6]

Product Complexity Products of a complex and technical nature are much more dependent upon personal selling than simple, standardized products. A manufacturer of road graders sends highly trained salesmen to confer with road contractors and governmental buyers, explaining the machine's unique advantages and how the machine pays for itself in increased productivity. They must prove the machine's capabilities to each buyer's satisfaction. For many such products, an actual demonstration is an integral part of the sales presentation. By contrast, a razor blade manufacturer relies far less on personal selling, concentrating instead on advertising to consumers to develop brand recognition and/or preference. The razor blade manufacturer supports this advertising effort with point-of-purchase displays to remind the consumer to buy, but relies upon personal selling to persuade dealers to stock the product.

Brand Differentiation The degree to which a marketer's brand is differentiated from competitors' brands also affects the promotional mix. Individual brands of bread and sugar generally have little to differentiate them, and their promotion emphasizes personal selling to get the product stocked in as many retail outlets as possible and to secure maximum effective shelf space display. With clearly differentiable products, such as cosmetics and sporting goods, advertising aimed at preselling consumers is a major element in the promotional mix.

Purchase Frequency How often final buyers buy the product is another factor influencing the promotional mix. When final buyers buy a product frequently, as consumers buy soap or as industrial buyers purchase typing paper, the marketer is usually justified in investing a considerable sum in advertising to develop brand recognition or preference and a generally favorable predisposition toward the product. But, when final buyers buy a product only infrequently, as consumers do in buying garden tools, it is generally very difficult to justify the expense of preselling through advertising or direct mail to final buyers. Instead, the emphasis in the promotional strategy for

[6] Theodore Levitt argues persuasively that it pays an industrial products marketer to be favorably well known (through advertising and direct mail) when the salesman attempts to make the sale. See his "Communications and Industrial Selling," *Journal of Marketing*, April 1967, p. 21.

such products is on using personal selling to persuade the proper outlets to stock the product and to push it over competitive brands when final buyers come in to make a purchase decision.

Nature of Market Different markets require different promotional mixes and strategies. Most marked, of course, is the contrast between industrial and consumer markets. Advertising plays more of an informative and less of a persuasive role for industrial buyers than for consumer buyers while, by contrast, personal selling reverses the emphasis on these two roles in cultivating the two types of markets. Thus, advertising's and personal selling's places in the promotional mix depend on the market to which each is directed. Other differences among final buyers in consumer markets—such as those of sex, income, age, education, religion, and place of residence—also influence the promotional mix most appropriate for selling a particular product. Similarly, other differences among final buyers in industrial markets—such as relative size, bargaining power, and buying responsibility—influence the type of promotional mix that is most appropriate for selling given industrial products.

Stage in the Product Life Cycle The promotional mix varies with the stage in the product's life cycle.[7] Promotional mixes vary during the product's different life cycle stages, because different kinds of people buy the product during each phase of the diffusion process.[8] During a new product's market pioneering stage, the first buyers (i.e., the innovators) differ considerably in their needs for information from those who first buy the product during its market maturity stage. Generally, innovators want to learn considerably more about the product and its features because they must make fairly independent judgments. Thus, they usually require more personal selling than members of the early and late majorities (who buy at various times during the product's market growth and market maturity life cycle stages), who are for the most part merely following the crowd. Early adopters, who buy a new product later than the innovators, are more skeptical and also rather more demanding in their requirements for product information than even the innovators; generally, they seek this information both from the marketer's advertising and the dealer's personal selling. The promotion for a mature product generally is directed toward reminding existing customers of its nature and value, while the promotion for a radically different new product usually aims to provide the early buyers with the information they need to make buying decisions. Different promotional mixes vary in their effectiveness in attaining these two quite different promotional objectives.

[7] The product life cycle is discussed in detail in Chapter 8.

[8] The diffusion process, involving the spread of acceptance of a new product, is discussed in detail in Chapter 3.

Market Penetration

Sustaining Promotion

Market Penetration The relative degree of the product's market penetration also influences the promotional mix and strategy.[9] When a brand has significant *market penetration*—that is, when it is already well known to final buyers and middlemen and has a substantial market share—*a sustaining promotional strategy* is appropriate (i.e., one aimed at sustaining this market position). Such a brand already benefits from the special treatment of retailers and other middlemen who are anxious to stock and push easily marketed best sellers. Consequently, the promotional mix for a brand with significant market penetration usually contains a rather large proportion of advertising.

Developmental Promotion

When a brand has insignificant market penetration—that is, when it is still struggling for recognition from final buyers and middlemen and has a very small market share—a *developmental promotional strategy* is appropriate (i.e., one aimed at improving the brand's market position). Many middlemen are reluctant to stock or push the less popular or new brand because they assume that the risk of not reselling it at a profit is high. Similarly, final buyers, having never heard of or knowing little about the brand, hesitate to buy it even when they find an outlet stocking it. Thus, the promotional mix for a brand with insignificant market penetration generally requires large dosages of both personal selling (to get dealers to stock and push the brand) and advertising (to get final buyers to ask their dealers to handle the brand or to convince them to go out and buy).

However, even the marketer of a product that has significant market penetration often must use a developmental promotional strategy in cultivating certain markets. Many, perhaps even most, established, successful products have uneven patterns of market penetration in different areas. In those where the brand has deep penetration, sustaining promotion is appropriate; in those where there is shallow penetration, developmental promotion is required.

Market Size and Location Variations in the size of the product's market influence the promotional mix and strategy. For example, a narrow market (in terms of numbers of potential buyers), such as that for shoe manufacturing machinery, is reached effectively through direct mail, whereas a broad market, such as that for cigarettes, is reached more effectively through mass advertising. Location of the market is also important—different promotional mixes and strategies, for instance, are required for markets concentrated in urban areas and for those widely dispersed in rural areas.

Characteristics of Prospective Buyers Also strongly influencing the promotional mix and strategy are the characteristics of prospective buyers. Experienced professional buyers, such as industrial purchasing agents, are usually most receptive to promotional

[9] This section leans heavily on R. M. Fulmer, "How Should Advertising and Sales Promotion Funds be Allocated?" *Journal of Marketing*, October 1967, pp. 8–11.

messages individually tailored to their specific needs, such as those delivered through salesmen. By contrast, many an inexperienced young housewife is most receptive to impersonal appeals delivered through advertising media which cause her to feel she is following the leads of older, more experienced women. Other characteristics of prospective buyers—such as the relative importance the buyer attaches to the purchase, the amount of time the buyer has available for shopping or searching for the product, and the influence of friends, relatives, and associates—all similarly affect the promotional mix and strategy.

DISTRIBUTION STRATEGY

The product's relative degree of market penetration, as noted earlier, has important implications for the promotional mix and strategy. Companies fighting to gain market position for their brands generally need to invest heavily in both personal selling and advertising to get middlemen to stock and push the product and in many situations to get final buyers to pull the product through the marketing channel. Those companies with already established market positions for their brands generally have little need to invest in promotion to keep their current distribution intensity, as dealers are quite willing to keep on selling brands that sell themselves. But, still, such dealers must be frequently reminded to buy by the marketer's salesmen—otherwise, they carry insufficient stocks and may be out-of-stock when consumers come in to buy the product.

The product's marketing channels also influence its promotional mix and strategy. If the product is sold direct to the user or consumer, major reliance is generally placed on personal selling and advertising is cast in a supporting role. For products sold through longer channels (i.e., those including one or more levels of middlemen), generally the marketer places less reliance on personal selling by its own salesmen and more reliance on its advertising to final buyers and on distributors' and/or dealers' selling efforts. For consumer products sold through channels containing self-service retail outlets, advertising to final buyers is generally important, effective promotional packaging essential, and effective display often critical.

PRICING STRATEGY

Pricing strategy influences the promotional mix and strategy, both with respect to the brand's price compared to those of competitive brands and the markups allowed middlemen. If the brand is priced higher than the competition, considerable personal selling is then needed to get middlemen to stock and push the brand; likewise, heavy advertising to final buyers is required to help the middlemen sell the brand and to get final buyers to buy it. If the brand is mainly sold on the basis of low price, then little promotion is used, except perhaps for some personal selling (to keep dealers handling the brand) and for a little advertising (to publicize the brand's low price and remind final buyers to keep on buying it). Similarly, if the marketer allows middlemen markups on the brand higher than those they obtain on competitive brands, it often can get them to push the brand enthusiastically and may need little consumer or trade advertising. By contrast, if markups on the brand are lower than on competitive brands, the marketer must often use heavy advertising to final buyers in order "to force" the middlemen to handle its brand and must use considerable personal selling to retain its present dealers and secure new ones.

RELATIVE COSTS OF DIFFERENT FORMS OF PROMOTION

Different forms of promotion vary considerably in the cost per message delivered. When a company's funds available for promotion are limited, management must put together a promotional mix of relatively low-cost forms of promotion. For example, a marketer with limited promotional funds might make heavy use of direct mail because it is possible to aim each message directly at a known prospective buyer of the brand. If the marketer transmits the same message through advertising media such as television or magazines, the cost per message received by bona fide prospects is much higher—even though the marketer reaches a much larger total audience. In other words, differences in economies of scale may allow a marketer to use direct mail when its total promotional funds are not sufficiently large to allow it to use other advertising effectively.

When promotional funds are sufficiently adequate so as not to dictate the choice of forms of promotion, the marketer should attempt to optimize the combination of cost per message received and the productivity of the form of promotion. For example, it may cost $50 to $75 for each call salesmen make on prospects, while it may cost only a few cents per message for an advertisement to reach the same prospects. However, the ad alone may result in few if any sales, while the salesmen's calls will result in some sales. An appropriate combination of the two forms of promotion (advertising and personal selling) should increase the chances that salesmen's calls will result in sales, while also reducing the total cost of making each sale.

The Promotional Appropriation

The amount of the total appropriation for promotion depends directly upon the marketer's promotional objectives. The costs of reaching promotional objectives, in turn, depend upon the marketer's choice of particular forms of promotion and the costs of using each form in the required intensities. The marketer should work out the appropriations for personal selling, advertising, and other forms of promotion more or less simultaneously and in conjunction with each other. If the marketer has arrived at an optimum promotional mix and strategy, it should be fairly easy to determine the amounts of the appropriations for the different forms of promotion in the mix. To clarify this, consider the steps the marketer has to go through—first, in arriving at an optimum promotional mix, management sets the objectives it expects each form of promotion to achieve; the next step is to determine what activities have to be performed (and in what volume) in order to attain the objectives set for each form of promotion; then management estimates how much it will cost to perform the required volume of activities; thus determining the amount of the appropriation for each form of promotion. Note the really important point here—the marketer can determine the optimum promotional appropriation only if it has found the optimum promotional mix which, of course, requires considerable planning.

Promotion and Demand Stimulation

Often, one hears the criticism that because promotion creates or stimulates demand, it makes people do what they might not otherwise do or what they do not really want to do. The implication is that promotion has some coercive control over people. While some marketers may wish they had such control, none of them actually do. When people buy items that are needlessly extravagant or frivolous, it is convenient to find a scapegoat—the marketer—to explain away such behavior, since it does not fit into stereotypes of "economic man."

Promotional Objectives

Promotion cannot and does not make people do what they do not want to do, but it does stimulate demand by relating products to prospective buyers' latent needs and wants. Demand is stimulated through promotion aimed at achieving any or all of three rather general promotional objectives: (1) to *inform* prospective buyers about the existence of a product and its need- and want-satisfying capabilities; (2) to *remind* present and former users of the product's continuing existence and its various roles in consumption; and (3) to *persuade* prospective buyers that the product's need- and want-satisfying capabilities make it worth buying. Clearly, the objective of persuading prospects to buy is the most ambitious of the three, and generally the most difficult and expensive to achieve.

Summary

If you thoroughly understand the material in this chapter, you have gained numerous important insights on promotion as a key element in overall marketing strategy. You should know how promotion, as a communications process, plays various roles in overall marketing strategy. You should know and understand the nature and distinctive characteristics of the various forms of promotion—personal selling, advertising, point-of-purchase display, packaging, direct mail, and other forms—that comprise the communications media through which the marketer seeks to achieve promotional objectives. (The two generally most important forms of promotion—personal selling and advertising—only briefly discussed in this chapter are covered in detail in the next two chapters.) You should know the significance of the several factors that influence the marketer in choosing and blending the different forms of promotion into promotional mixes and strategies, including those factors involved in other components of overall marketing strategy (product-market, distribution, and pricing strategies) and the relative costs of different forms of promotion. You should also know why the marketer should develop appropriations for each of the forms of promotion more or less simultaneously and in conjunction with one another, and why executives can determine the optimum promotional appropriation only if they have found the optimum promotional mix. If you have gained these insights and understand the reasoning that lies behind them, you have a good understanding of the various roles that promotion can play in overall marketing strategy. And you are ready to proceed to Chapters 16 (Personal Selling) and 17 (Advertising) to gain additional insights on planning and managing these two important forms of promotion.

QUESTIONS AND PROBLEMS

1. Promotion is described as a process of communication between seller and buyer. In what ways significant to marketing does this communication process differ for personal selling and advertising?
2. Is there a contradiction between the following two statements? (1) Communication is built around three essentials. (2) There are five stages in the communication process. Explain.
3. Evaluate the more important promotion methods with respect to the importance of feedback and the ease or difficulty of achieving it.
4. Does the concept of "noise" have particular relevance in the application of communications theory to promotional strategy?
5. How might recognition of "source effect" influence the promotional mix for a manufacturer of heavy industrial products?
6. If a marketer were restricted to the use of only one promotion method, which method would most likely be chosen? Why? Can you think of any exceptions?
7. Would a large consumer products marketer, such as General Mills or Lever Brothers, likely allocate a larger portion of its promotional budget to personal selling or to advertising? What possible roles might point-of-purchase display play when used with these two main promotion methods?
8. Differentiate between a "push" strategy and a "pull" strategy.
9. What is the difference between a sustaining promotional strategy

and a developmental promotional strategy? When is each appropriate?

10. What is the most important difference between advertising and direct mail in terms of their respective uses?
11. List five specific products that are heavily dependent upon packaging for marketing success. Explain why you think each of these packages is or is not as successful as it could be.
12. Name and describe three important objectives of promotion, with respect to demand stimulation.
13. Describe the type of promotional campaign that would probably be most appropriate and effective for salt, shampoo, men's suits. Explain why the mix should be different for each of these products.
14. Explain how a television set manufacturer might adjust its promotion mix to the stages in the product life cycle: introduction, growth, maturity, and decline. Would similar adjustments be appropriate for appliances? Furniture?
15. What is wrong with using the cost per message delivered as a basis for evaluating alternative promotion methods?
16. Evaluate the following statement. "The larger the promotional budget is, the greater the economic waste is to society."

CASE PROBLEM

Needham Machinery, Inc., manufactured a line of packaging machinery and distributed its products to a wide variety of consumer goods packagers throughout the country. The company was relatively small by most industry standards, yet it enjoyed a fine reputation as a producer of quality packaging machinery. The Needham sales force was considered one of the company's major assets.

The company was in the process of a full-scale evaluation of its promotional program. In reality, it was an evaluation of the personal selling program since, except for occasional displays at packaging exhibitions, the firm's entire promotional program consisted of personal selling. No advertising was done currently, although several years back the company had done a limited amount of advertising in "trade" publications. However, this was soon discontinued because management was unable to measure the advertising's effect and was doubtful as to its value.

Mr. Bill Coughlin, vice-president for marketing, had ordered a complete appraisal of Needham's promotional program to determine its effectiveness and, especially, to reconsider the feasibility of its "no advertising" approach. He had noticed that most of Needham's competitors, although they too relied heavily on personal selling, did considerable advertising. He wondered whether or not he was mistaken as to the value of advertising, that perhaps a mix of personal selling and advertising would result in a more effective promotional program.

Should Needham Machinery, Inc., engage in advertising? What factors influence the inputs that should be incorporated in a promotional program?

When you have mastered the contents of this chapter, you should be able to:

1. Give examples of the various types of qualitative and quantitative personal selling objectives.
2. Explain the nature and purpose of sales policies and their relationship to personal selling objectives and personal selling strategies.
3. Identify and compare the four basic styles of selling.
4. Describe how management should decide the size of the sales force.
5. Discuss the several problems involved in determining and allocating the personal selling appropriation.
6. Explain how the sales manager implements personal selling strategy through the various tasks performed in managing the sales force.
7. Contrast the three basic methods for compensating salesmen.
8. Discuss the use of job descriptions and quotas in appraising salesmen's performances.

CHAPTER 16

PERSONAL SELLING

Salesmen are in many respects the "unsung heroes" of marketing. Success in marketing for many, perhaps most, companies depends importantly upon salesmen's skills in matching company products with customers' needs and, of course, in effecting ownership transfers (i.e., making sales). Thus, formulating personal selling strategy and managing the salesmen who implement it are not only critical but challenging tasks. Discussion in this chapter relates to (1) planning the personal selling operation, including the setting of objectives, determination of policies, and formulation of strategies; and (2) management of the sales force.

Personal selling is a highly distinctive form of promotion. Like other forms, it is basically communication; but, unlike others, it is two-way rather than one-way communication. Thus, personal selling involves social behavior, both the salesman and the prospect (by what they say and do) influencing each other. The outcome of each sales situation depends importantly upon the success both parties have in communicating with each other and in reaching a common understanding of needs and goals.

The social character of personal selling makes it an activity particularly difficult to manage. Generally, management must leave each salesman free to interact with individual customers in the manner the salesman feels is the most effective. Yet, at the same time, management must direct and control the sales force in order to achieve marketing and personal selling objectives.

Planning the Personal Selling Operation

Figure 16–1 shows how personal selling fits into the promotional program. Management's first task, of course, is to decide just what role, if any, personal selling should play in the promotional mix. Some companies shift the entire personal selling activity to middle-

Figure 16–1
Personal selling as part of the promotional program

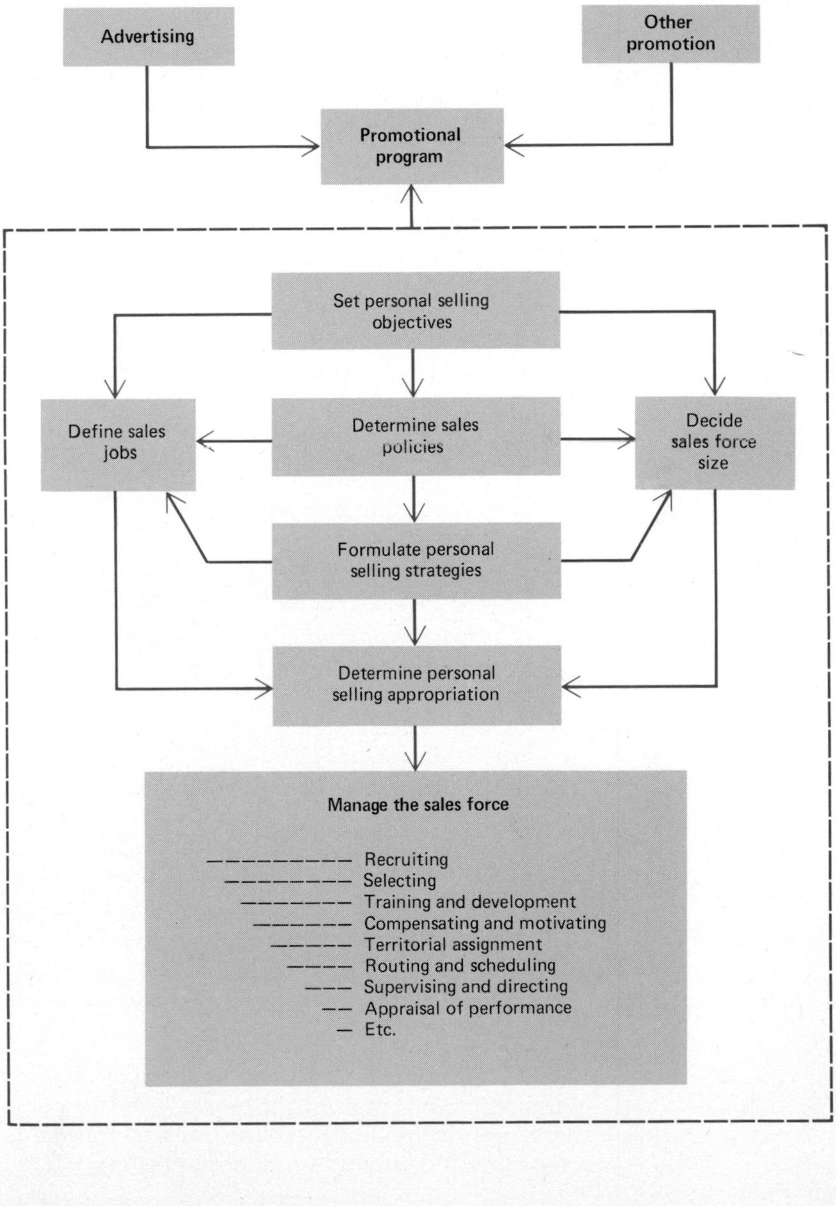

men (such as to a selling agent), but this is by no means common. Most producers, especially those who are manufacturers, must set personal selling objectives, determine sales policies, formulate sales strategies, determine the personal selling appropriation, and manage the sales force. As Figure 16–1 indicates, these interrelated tasks collectively make up the personal selling portion of the promotional program. As you read the rest of this chapter, you will find it helpful to refer frequently to this figure.

PERSONAL SELLING OBJECTIVES

Personal selling has both long-term and short-term objectives. The long-term objectives are broad and general, changing very little over time, and concern mainly the contributions management expects personal selling to make to the achievement of overall company objectives. The short-term objectives are more specific and relate chiefly to the role(s) management assigns to personal selling as a part of both the promotional program and the overall marketing strategy. In certain instances, personal selling's role is minimal, perhaps that of simply having salesmen take orders from the customers. But in most instances personal selling plays considerably more important roles. Depending upon the overall marketing strategy and the nature of the promotional mix, the objective(s) of personal selling may be:

Personal Selling Objectives

1. to do the entire selling job (as when there are no other elements in the promotional mix)
2. to "service" existing accounts (i.e., to maintain communications with present customers, take orders, etc.)
3. to search out and obtain new customers
4. to secure and maintain customers' cooperation in stocking and promoting the product line
5. to keep customers informed on changes in the product line and other aspects of marketing strategy
6. to assist customers in selling the product line (as through "missionary selling")
7. to provide technical advice and assistance to customers (as with complicated products and custom-designed products)
8. to assist with (or handle) the training of middlemen's sales personnel
9. to provide advice and assistance to middlemen on various management problems
10. to collect and report market information of interest and use to company management

This list, as you should recognize, is only illustrative of the many objectives that might be assigned to personal selling. Besides these mainly qualitative objectives, certain quantitative objectives are generally assigned to personal selling, such as:

1. to obtain a specified sales volume
2. to obtain sales volume in ways that contribute to profit objectives (e.g., by selling the proper mix of products)
3. to keep personal selling expenses within specified limits
4. to secure and retain a specified share of the market

SALES POLICIES

Sales Policies

Sales policies are the general rules management sets up to guide itself in making decisions on the nature and direction of the personal selling effort. Specifically, sales policies guide management in formulating sales strategies, defining the sales job, and deciding sales force size. Sales policies should derive directly from, and be wholly consistent with, the personal selling objectives. If, for example, one of the personal selling objectives states that "this company expects its salesmen to provide first-class engineering assistance to both new and old customers," then a sales policy (or policies) is needed to describe how, in general, this objective is to be attained.

FORMULATING PERSONAL SELLING STRATEGY

Personal Selling Strategy

A company seeks to achieve its personal selling objectives through both its sales policies and its *personal selling strategy*. Whereas sales policies provide the general guidelines for making decisions on the personal selling effort, personal selling strategies are adaptations of sales policies—personal selling decisions individually tailored to fit particular marketing situations. Formulating personal selling strategy requires management to (1) define the nature of the sales job, and (2) decide the size of the sales force—the two main determinants of the personal selling appropriation.

Sales Job Definition

Defining the Sales Job Both personal selling objectives and sales policies influence the nature of the sales job and the kind of salesmen who should make up the sales force. The nature of sales positions varies from company to company because, although salesmen in different companies may have similar duties and responsibilities, differences in personal selling objectives and sales policies cause them to vary their emphasis on specific tasks. Personal selling objectives and sales policies differ, of course, because no two companies use exactly the same overall marketing strategies.

In some situations salesmen must aggressively seek orders, and in others they need only take orders that come to them. But, the degree of emphasis on order-taking and order-getting varies with different selling jobs. The driver salesman for a soft drink bottling

Order-Taking

company is primarily an *order-taker,* since the product is strongly presold to consumers, and retailers reorder automatically for stock.

Order-Getting

The salesperson calling on householders to sell encyclopedias is much more of an *order-getter,* since he or she has the primary responsibility for creating demand.

The complexity of the product or product line is another important factor influencing personal selling objectives, sales policies, and the nature of the sales job. When the product is highly technical, the selling job is considerably different than when the product is simple. The computer salesman and the office stationery salesman have very different jobs.

Similarly, the type of customer affects not only personal selling objectives and sales policies but also the nature of the sales job. The industrial user buying for its own operations needs to be dealt with differently than the middleman buying for resale. Differences in salesmen's roles and tasks call for differences in sales job descriptions. Nevertheless, it is possible to group sales jobs into a limited number of categories, at least to draw certain generalizations. Specifically, it is possible to identify four basic styles of selling that cut, to a large degree, across industry boundaries: trade selling, missionary selling, technical selling, and new-business selling.[1]

Trade Salesman

The *trade salesman* develops long-term relations with a relatively stable group of customers. For the most part, this style of selling is low key with little or no pressure, and the job tends to be on the dull and routine side. This style of selling, which predominates in marketing food and apparel and in wholesaling, applies primarily to products that have well-established markets. In such cases, advertising and other forms of promotion are often more important than personal selling. One of the trade salesman's important responsibilities is to help the customers build up their volume by providing promotional help. For example, the salesman for a line of breakfast cereals devotes much time to promotional work with retailers and wholesalers—taking stock, refilling shelves, suggesting reorders, setting up displays, and the like.

Missionary Salesman

The *missionary salesman* is responsible for increasing the company's sales volume by assisting customers with their selling efforts. The missionary is only incidentally concerned with order-taking and order-getting, since any orders obtained are by-products of the missionary's public relations and promotional efforts with customers of customers (the company's indirect customers). The missionary's job is to persuade indirect customers to buy from the company's direct customers. For example, the salesman for a pharmaceutical manufacturer calls on retail druggists to acquaint them with a new product and to urge them to stock it, hopefully persuading them to order from drug wholesalers (the company's direct customers). Some missionary salesmen also call on individuals and institutions who do not buy the product themselves, but who influence its purchase by others—for example, the "medical detail man" calling on doctors and hospitals to

[1] D. A. Newton, "Get the Most Out of Your Sales Force," *Harvard Business Review,* September-October 1969, pp. 131–141.

acquaint them with new drugs. Missionary selling, like trade selling, is low key and generally does not require high-level technical training or ability.

Technical Salesman

The *technical salesman* deals primarily with the company's established accounts and aims to increase their purchases through providing technical advice and assistance. Frequently, though not always, the technical salesman needs a technical background and formal education in engineering or science. The technical salesman performs advisory functions similar to those of the missionary salesman but, in addition, makes sales direct to industrial users and other buyers. Technical salesmen devote most of their time to acquainting industrial users with technical characteristics of products and with new product applications, and to helping them design installations or processes that incorporate their company's products. In this style of selling the ability to identify, analyze, and solve customers' problems is important. Technical salesmen often specialize, either by products or by markets: in selling heavy made-to-order installations, such as steam turbines and electric generators, different technical salesmen working with different items in the product line. Other technical salesmen specialize in servicing either industrial accounts or governmental procurement agencies.

New-Business Salesman

The *new-business salesman* is mainly responsible for securing new customers—converting prospects into customers. Some experts argue that many companies that now have a single sales force should divide and specialize their salesmen into two separate groups—one to concentrate on retaining existing customers and one to specialize in converting prospects into customers.[2] The argument is that different sets of talents are required—retaining existing customers mainly involves performance of rather routine duties, while converting prospects into customers requires much creativity, ingenuity, and resourcefulness (all rather scarce talents). Salesmen specializing in new business are a difficult group to manage; turnover among them tends to be high because only a few can continue indefinitely without becoming discouraged by failures to convert prospects into customers.

Deciding Sales Force Size One important consideration in deciding sales force size is the rate of sales force turnover. If a company has 100 salesmen, needs all 100 for the coming year's operations, and has a 10 percent annual turnover, ten new men must be recruited during the year. The *sales force turnover rate* is defined as the number of salesmen separated, resigned, fired, and so on per 100 on the sales force. Every sales force should have some turnover. When there is no turnover, the sales force may be growing stale, inefficient salesmen staying on because management has failed to replace them. Management should try to optimize turnover so as to

Sales Force Turnover Rate

[2] G. N. Kahn and A. Shuchman, "Specialize Your Salesmen!" *Harvard Business Review*, January-February 1961, pp. 94–95.

eliminate "dead wood" and at the same time keep costs of turnover as low as possible.

Management's decision on the size of the sales force boils down to estimating the total number of salesmen needed to achieve the company's personal selling objectives. Consider, for example, the objective with respect to sales volume: if the sales job has been defined accurately and completely, it should be possible to estimate the number of sales dollars that each salesman should produce; dividing this amount into forecasted sales and making an allowance for the rate of sales force turnover should indicate the number of salesmen needed. Management should make similar estimates for each of the personal selling objectives, the purpose in each case being that of determining the total number of people required to achieve the objective. Difficulties in making these estimates vary both with the objective and the nature of the salesman's activities related to its achievement. It is considerably less difficult, for instance, to estimate the number of people required to reach a quantitative objective (such as total sales volume for the company) than to estimate those required to attain a qualitative objective (such as "securing and maintaining customers' cooperation" or "building goodwill among the customers of customers"). But, out of the composite of such estimates, management determines the size of the sales force it needs to implement the personal selling strategy.

DETERMINING THE PERSONAL SELLING APPROPRIATION

The logical starting points for determining the amount of the personal selling appropriation are the specific personal selling objectives set by top management for the period just ahead. The personal selling strategy, formulated with a view toward achieving these objectives, must ultimately be translated into the types and amounts of personal selling effort required (as in the definition of the sales job and the decision on sales force size). Sooner or later, management must also deal with the problem of converting these types and amounts of personal selling effort into dollar estimates of the costs involved. Thus, an increase in the sales volume objective may call for the hiring of a certain number of new salesmen, their training, providing them with expense allowances, securing and assigning additional supervisors, and the like. Therefore, in building the personal selling appropriation, management must (1) estimate the volume of performance for each required activity, and (2) convert these performance volumes into dollar cost estimates.

Although the kind and size of sales force are the main determinants of the total size of the personal selling appropriation, management must make further decisions concerning how it is to be spent. In deciding among various uses, management must answer such questions as: Should we hire five additional salesmen at a total cost of $150,000 or should we invest the same amount in refresher training for present salesmen? Should we add sales supervisors or use the same number of dollars for conducting sales contests? If such questions were resolved rationally, there would be an equating of the marginal productivities of alternative ways of spending the personal selling appropriation. But, in practice, such allocations are largely made intuitively. Management experiments constantly and is always striving for an improved allocation pattern. Since there is no known way for measuring or predicting the relative effectiveness of expenditures on the different activities, such allocations continue to be made on the basis of management's best judgment.

Managing the Sales Force

The sales manager's job is to ensure that the sales force plays its assigned roles in implementing the personal selling strategy. This executive's major responsibilities for sales force management include recruiting and selecting, training and development, compensating and motivating, making territorial assignments, routing and scheduling, supervising and directing, and appraising salesmen's performance.

Sales Job Descriptions

In every company *the job description,* outlining the duties and responsibilities of the salesman, lies at the heart of sales force management. Effectiveness in sales force management, to put it another way, depends importantly on the completeness and accuracy of the sales job description. Through analysis of the duties and responsibilities making up the job, management derives the set of *qualifications* that salesmen should possess. This furnishes guidance in searching out the best source of recruits and in selecting those with the best qualifications. Comparison of the desired set of qualifications with the qualifications of newly hired sales personnel indicates the needed breadth and depth of initial sales training. Similarly, comparing the job description with the qualifications possessed by the veteran salesman is a basic technique of salesman evaluation and assists in determining the content of refresher sales training. Furthermore, the job description provides guidance for management in designing the sales compensation plan, planning programs for motivating salesmen, and arriving at the best methods for supervising salesmen.

Sales Job Qualifications

RECRUITING AND SELECTING SALES PERSONNEL

Recruiting Sales Personnel

Recruiting involves identifying the sources of recruits and choosing recruiting methods. Each previously used source should be analyzed according to the number of recruits obtained and their success or failure as company salesmen. Although internal sources, such as other departments and nonselling sections of the sales department, occasionally provide promising recruits, most companies must look to external sources for an adequate supply of recruits. Among the external sources are educational institutions—universities, colleges, and, of greatly increasing importance, junior colleges. Other external sources include the experienced salesmen of competitors and other companies, job seekers registered with employment agencies, and "walk-in volunteers." Recruiting methods vary with the source: personal recruiting by executives is used mainly for tapping internal sources and recent graduates, while indirect recruiting methods (e.g., placing classified advertisements in newspapers or trade journals) are used for attracting experienced salesmen.

Selecting Sales Personnel

Systems used for selecting salesmen range from simple one-step procedures, consisting merely of an informal personal interview, to complex multistep systems utilizing numerous and varied devices and techniques for gathering information on prospective salesmen. A selection system should be a set of successive "screens," at any one of which job candidates may be dropped from further consideration. The number and relative sophistication of the screens, of course, depend upon the resources management is willing to invest in its selection of salesmen. Considering its own needs, each company should devise its own selection system. Among the commonly used selection screens or steps are the interview application, the interview(s), the formal application form, references and recommendations, physical examination, credit reports, and psychological tests (aptitude, intelligence, personality, and others).

TRAINING AND DEVELOPMENT OF SALESMEN

The modern sales executive, while considering on-the-job experience as the best sales training, believes strongly that formal sales training contributes significantly to selling effectiveness. Most companies conduct training programs both for newly hired personnel and for their veteran salesmen. Building an effective training program of any kind requires clear definition of objectives, decisions on program content, selection of training methods, and execution of the actual training—professional sales trainers call these steps the A-C-M-E procedure—*a*im, *c*ontent, *m*ethod, and *e*xecution.

For new salesmen the content of the sales training program generally includes product data, sales techniques, markets, and company information, while for more experienced salesmen the content is more specialized to meet particular needs. Training methods include both individualized techniques, such as on-the-job training, and group techniques including lectures, group discussion, role playing, and simulations. Executing the training program requires decisions on training duration, the training site, training the trainers, and training materials and aids.

COMPENSATING AND MOTIVATING SALESMEN

The duties and responsibilities inherent in each sales job determine the amount of compensation that must be paid to attract and hold people of the desired caliber. Because salesmen enjoy high job mobility, ordinarily they must be paid approximately what competitors' salesmen are paid. Generally, too, because of the strong pull exerted by other firms employing salesmen of similar quality, salesmen are paid more than either production or office workers.

Compensation Methods Each method for compensating salesmen is a combination of all or some of four elements: (1) a fixed portion (salary), (2) a variable portion (commission, bonus, or a share in profits), (3) either reimbursement of expenses or an expense allowance, and (4) such "fringe benefits" as paid vacations, pensions, and insurance. Because "expense" provisions and fringe benefits are never used alone, the three basic compensation methods are (1) straight salary, (2) straight commission, and (3) a combination of salary and one or more variable features.

Each basic method presents a different balance of two underlying purposes of compensation: providing management with power to direct salesmen's activities and furnishing salesmen with the incentive to work productively. At the two extremes are the straight salary and straight commission. The straight-salary method, in theory, provides management with the maximum power to direct salesmen's efforts along the potentially most productive lines. The company guarantees a total fixed income to the salesmen and has the right to ask them to engage in activities not directly productive of sales. Under the straight-commission method, where the salesmen's earnings are closely related to their selling efforts, they generally resent demands on their time not directly productive of sales. The justification for the straight-commission method is that it provides salesmen with the maximum of direct financial incentive to strive toward high selling efficiency. Neither straight salary nor the straight commission, however, is as widely used as the combination method. By including both a fixed element and one or more variable elements in their plans for paying salesmen, companies using combination methods seek both to secure needed control and to furnish salesmen with necessary motivation.

Other Incentives While the basic compensation plan is the most important motivator of salesmen, most companies also use other forms of incentives to good advantage. Sales meetings provide opportunities for motivating individual salesmen, and for strengthening feelings of group identification. Sales contests offer a mechanism through which salesmen are motivated not only to increase profitable sales volume but to achieve other specific objectives. The judicious use of both sales meetings and sales contests builds both individual and sales force morale and assists in the accomplishment of personal selling objectives.

ASSIGNING SALESMEN TO TERRITORIES

Assigning a salesman to a territory focuses his or her efforts on a given geographical area containing a grouping of customers and prospects. Each territory represents some potential volume of sales to the company. Whenever a salesman is assigned to a territory, management has, in effect, matched a specific level of selling skill with the amount of sales opportunity that it believes to be present in that territory.

Therefore, both the relative abilities of salesmen and the relative sales potentials of territories should be considered in assigning salesmen to territories. Too often, however, management treats problems of appraising salesmen's efficiency and evaluating territorial sales potentials independently. Because salesmen differ in efficiency, and because territories differ in sales potential, a rational assignment would put the best salesman in the most fertile territory, the second-best salesman in the second-most fertile territory, and so on. Only if the assignment is made in this way is it possible to maximize total sales in the entire market.

ROUTING AND SCHEDULING SALESMEN'S CALLS

Companies fielding trade or missionary salesmen often route and schedule salesmen's calls for them. Besides increasing the chances that salesmen will be on the job when they are supposed to be, formal route and call schedules make it easier to contact them to provide needed and helpful information or last-minute instructions. Planning a salesman's route, if done intelligently and efficiently, eliminates much backtracking, travel time, and waiting time. Providing a salesman with a call schedule makes it possible to adjust more precisely the frequency of call to fit customers' needs, thus securing improved territorial coverage.

Companies fielding technical or new-business salesmen do not generally use formal route and call schedules. Evidently, most believe that each salesman is the best judge of how time should be spent. In addition, in numerous situations, management finds it difficult to predict the amount of time each call will require—as, for example, when salesmen sell products designed to the customer's specifications or when they sell such products as encyclopedias on a house-to-house basis.

SUPERVISING AND DIRECTING SALESMEN

Most salesmen—even star performers—need supervision and direction to channel their efforts along lines consistent with achievement of the company's personal selling objectives. Supervision and direction involves: observing, evaluating, and reporting on salesmen's field performances; correcting their deficiencies in job performance; clarifying their job responsibilities and duties; providing them with on-the-spot motivation; keeping them informed on changes in company policy; helping them solve business and personal problems; and continuing their sales training in the field. Thus, the overall purpose of sales supervision and direction is to improve the salesmen's job performances.

APPRAISING SALESMEN'S PERFORMANCES

Successful implementation of the personal selling strategy depends directly on the performance of the salesmen, individually and as a group; consequently, management needs ways of appraising performance. Management uses appraisal data in making and predicting the likely outcomes of decisions on such matters as which salesmen to train further, which to reward, and which to discharge. In order to distinguish good from poor performance, in other words, management needs standards or norms to use for purposes of comparison.

The Job Description Comparison of what the salesman does against what the job description says the salesman should be doing provides insight into the individual's total performance. However, one problem in using the job description for this purpose is that many of the salesman's job responsibilities do not lend themselves to quantitative measurement. How, for example, can one gauge how much goodwill a salesman builds? Or what quantitative measures are there for determining the salesman's mental alertness in dealing with customers? The most the job description can do is to define, as clearly as possible, the performance expected in connection with each duty and responsibility. Such performance definitions may include some quantitative standards (e.g., the call frequencies for different classes of accounts), but most (because of their elusive nature) have to be phrased as qualitative statements of what management expects.

Quotas

Quotas The most common yardsticks used for measuring salesmen's performances are called *quotas,* defined as "quantitatively expressed goals assigned to specific marketing units, such as to individual salesmen or territories." For instance, on the basis of past performance, a salesman might be expected to produce a predetermined volume of sales; or, on the basis of measured market and sales potentials, a territory might be expected to yield a predetermined volume of sales. Quotas may be in terms of dollar or unit sales volume, gross margin, net profit, expenses, calls, number of new accounts, amount of dealer display space obtained, or other measurable quantities.

The dollar sales volume quota presents a major difficulty. Salesmen's efforts do not always produce sales in the period for which their performance is being evaluated, and the results of a salesman's current efforts may materialize only over many future periods. In addition, each salesman has different working conditions, many influencing the relative ease of making sales. Territory by territory, variations exist in competition, required travel time, and sales potential. Thus, it is rare to find a company that is justified in assigning identical sales volume quotas to all salesmen. Because of competitive, physical, and sales fertility differences among territories, the sales volume quota for each salesman should be set individually. Another important reason for individually set quotas is that salesmen vary in selling efficiency because of differences in training, experience, and native abilities.

Distinguishing sales results produced by the salesman from those due to other causes is another major difficulty. Advertising, for instance, is often an influence in making many sales, but it is usually the salesman who writes the actual order. At other times, the salesman's supervisor or branch manager may actually have been the major influence in the customer's buying decision. In such cases, it is next to impossible to determine the salesman's contribution precisely.

The sales forecast should be the main basis for setting sales volume quotas since carefully prepared forecasts, when intelligently broken down, result in reasonable and attainable quotas. By breaking the forecast down into manageable parts—that is, into sales volume quotas for individual salesmen—management defines the results it expects from the efforts of each. However, it should be recognized that a sales volume quota can be no better than the sales forecast on which it is based. If the forecast is little more than a wild guess, the quota derived from it will be no better. Improvements in sales forecasts and sales volume quotas go hand in hand.

Summary

If you have mastered the material in this chapter, you have gained important insights on planning the personal selling operation and managing the sales force. You should have learned: how, in setting personal selling objectives, management defines the general and specific roles it expects personal selling to play; how, in determining sales policies, it provides itself with guidelines for making decisions in this area; how, in formulating personal selling strategies, management tailors sales policies to fit particular marketing situations and in the process defines sales jobs and decides the size of the sales force; how the kind and size of sales force largely determine the amount of the personal selling appropriation; and how the sales manager implements personal selling strategy through the various tasks this executive performs in managing the sales force. If you understand all of these things thoroughly, you understand the part personal selling plays both in the promotional program and in overall marketing strategy.

QUESTIONS AND PROBLEMS

1. How do you explain the fact that manufacturers are more inclined to shift the advertising activity to agencies than they are to shift the personal selling activity to middlemen?
2. In which of the following situations should the major promotional emphasis be placed on personal selling rather than on advertising? Give your reasons in each case.
   a. selling extension telephones to homeowners
   b. persuading retailers to stock a new soft drink
   c. selling a landscaping and grounds maintenance program for industrial plants
   d. selling life insurance to individuals
3. In what ways do the objectives of personal selling depend upon overall marketing strategy and the nature of the promotional mix?
4. Clearly distinguish between sales policies and personal selling strategy.
5. Why is it necessary to clearly define sales jobs?
6. Compare the following types of salesmen:
   a. order-taker and order-getter
   b. missionary salesman and technical salesman
   c. missionary salesman and trade salesman
   d. trade salesman and new-business salesman
7. In each of the following situations, what would you regard as the salesperson's main task? His or her other tasks?
   a. A salesman selling aluminum drains and gutters to homeowners on a house-to-house basis
   b. An automobile dealer's salesman charged with making fleet sales to business and local government agencies
   c. A salesman of automatic packaging machinery used by brewers, soft-drink bottlers, and food processors
   d. A salesman for a hardware wholesaler calling on retail hardware and variety stores
   e. A manufacturer's salesman selling furniture to department stores and discount houses

8. Do you favor or oppose the proposal that salesmen should specialize either in sales maintenance activities (retaining existing customers) or in sales development (converting prospects into customers)? Why? If you worked for a company that specialized its sales force in this way, would you rather be assigned to sales maintenance or sales development? Why?
9. The formula for calculating the rate of sales force turnover is:

$$\text{Rate of Sales Force Turnover (Expressed as \%)} = \frac{\text{Number of Separations}}{\text{Average Size of Sales Force}} \times 100$$

   Now consider the following problem: The sales force of a certain manufacturer numbers 50 people at the start of the year and 80 people at the end of the year. Twenty salesmen either resigned, were fired, were promoted, or otherwise left the sales force during the year.
   a. Compute the rate of sales force turnover.
   b. Assuming continuation of the present rate of sales force turnover, how long will it take to replace the entire sales force?
   c. Supposing this manufacturer says: "What good does it do me to know my rate of sales force turnover? How do I use this statistic?" What advice would you give?
   d. Later on, this manufacturer hears of a small company which had five salesmen at the start of the year, eight at the end, and lost two during the year. He concluded that since this company and his own both had the same rate of sales force turnover, both must have been equally well managed. Would you agree? Why or why not?
10. The formula for determining the number of salesmen needed is expressed as:

$$N = \frac{S}{P} + T(S/P)$$

which reduces to:

$$N = \frac{S}{P}(1 + T)$$

where:

N is the number of salesmen
S is the forecasted sales volume
P is the sales productivity of an individual salesman
T is the allowance for rate of sales force turnover, and
$\frac{S}{P}$ is the average size of sales force desired over the year.

Now, consider the following problem:
Suppose a certain manufacturer has a forecasted sales volume of $8 million, the sales productivity of an individual salesman is $160,000, and the expected rate of sales force turnover is 20 percent. Assume further that there are presently 40 persons on the sales force.
a. What is the "needed" size of the sales force in this case?
b. What is the anticipated average size of sales force?
c. Suppose that it costs $10,000 to bring a new salesman up to the $160,000 sales productivity level. How much money can this manufacturer save if it succeeds in holding the rate of sales force turnover to 10 percent?

11. What are the factors influencing the determination of the personal selling appropriation?
12. What is a sales job description? Suggest some ways a company might go about obtaining job descriptions for its salesmen. Discuss the relationship of the sales job description to recruiting, selecting, training, supervising, and controlling salesmen.
13. What sources should be used in recruiting new salesmen for the following companies? Why?
    a. A company selling fine china and kitchenware house-to-house
    b. An importer of fancy Italian foods selling in the New York and Philadelphia market areas
    c. A manufacturer of high-quality men's clothing sold through exclusive men's stores
14. What are the A-C-M-E decisions? How should they be made?
15. Answer the following questions pertaining to salesmen's compensation:
    a. What factors should be taken into account in setting the compensation level?
    b. What are the main factors influencing the decision as to compensation method?
    c. Compare the three basic compensation methods from the viewpoints of (1) management, (2) the salesmen, and (3) the customers called on by salesmen.
    d. Explain how control and incentive are balanced under each of the three basic compensation methods.
    e. Why do managements generally prefer to use the commission or bonus element in compensation as the main instrument for recognizing performance differences among salesmen?
16. What information does management need to make rational assignments of salesmen to territories? What methods might be used in obtaining this information?
17. Under what conditions should companies use formal routing and scheduling of salesmen's calls? Under what conditions should salesmen route and schedule themselves?
18. Why must management have measures of the performance of

salesmen? How useful is the job description in making performance appraisals? What problems are encountered in using quotas as yardsticks of sales performance?

19. Discuss the relationship of sales forecasting to the setting of sales volume quotas.
20. Some cities have enacted laws, known as "Green River Ordinances," which regulate or sometimes even prohibit house-to-house selling. Why are such ordinances passed? Why not pass similar ordinances to prohibit or regulate the activities of salesmen calling on business establishments? Why not pass laws requiring salesmen to be licensed and to meet certain minimum requirements, such as successful completion of a formal educational program or passage of a state-conducted examination?
21. "With almost complete literacy in this country, with the progress of automation, with the tremendous coverage afforded by radio and TV, and with the increasing effectiveness of advertising, the age of the salesman is fast disappearing. By the time we reach the year 2000, salesmen will be as rare as dinosaur's eggs." What is your reaction to this statement by a critic of personal selling? Are salesmen in general in any great danger of being supplanted? What about retail salespeople? Wholesalers' salesmen? Manufacturers' salesmen?
22. Professor Dale Houghton of New York University reported that 64 percent of the consumer goods companies he studied spent more for the sales force than for advertising. Professor Houghton also found that among industrial goods companies the cost of the sales force almost invariably exceeded by many times the cost of advertising. What conclusions might be drawn from these findings?

CASE PROBLEM

The Deluxe Office Machine Company manufactured and sold office machines. Its product lines consisted of portable, manual, and electric typewriters, as well as adding machines, printing calculators, and accounting machines. Distribution was effected through more than 300 branch sales offices and a network of sales agencies. Sales quotas for the branch offices were established by the general sales office in New York City. The number of salesmen assigned to each branch office was under the control of the general sales manager, whose philosophy was that the number of salesmen working out of each sales branch should be closely tied in with the sales quota assigned that branch. When Mr. Walter Carpenter, branch sales manager in Detroit, received his annual typewriter sales quota, he saw that the figure had been increased to such an extent that another salesman would have to be hired. The typewriter quota for the Detroit branch was set at \$9,500 per month, or \$114,000 for the year.

The number of typewriter salesmen needed to reach the quota was arrived at by dividing the total monthly quota by \$2,500. This \$2,500 was equivalent to one unit of manpower since all salesmen carried this figure as their monthly quota. When Mr. Carpenter received the quota information for the year, he also received a letter from the general sales manager commenting on the necessity for securing an additional salesman.

The area covered by typewriter salesmen working out of the Detroit branch office consisted of five counties in eastern Michigan. These five counties were divided into three sales territories covered by as many salesmen. The question of manpower was at issue because, if each of the three present typewriter salesmen attained 100 percent of their individual quotas, their combined volume would amount to only $7,500. Exhibits 1, 2, and 3 contain information that was available to Mr. Carpenter and provided the basis upon which he was to decide what action should be taken.

What action should be taken by Mr. Carpenter, branch sales manager of Deluxe Office Machine Company?

Exhibit 1 Personal Data on Present Typewriter Salesmen

SALESMAN	AGE	LENGTH OF SERVICE	ANNUAL EARNINGS	COMMISSION RATE
Joe Alexander	58	25 years	$15,000–$18,000	20%–30%
Wally Mors	45	10 years	$10,000–$12,000	15%–20%
Ed McGee	27	5 years	$10,000–$12,000	15%–20%

Exhibit 2 Typewriter Sales Territories, Detroit Branch Office

TERRITORY	SALESMAN	NUMBER OF COUNTIES	POPULATION
1	Joe Alexander	4	180,900
2	Wally Mors	½	243,500
3	Ed McGee	½	243,500

Exhibit 3 Quota Record of Typewriter Salesmen, Detroit Branch Office (in percent)

SALESMAN	1972	1971	1970	1969	1968
Joe Alexander	165	160	161	160	150
Wally Mors	108	103	105	103	101
Ed McGee	103	98	103	102	95

When you have mastered the contents of this chapter, you should be able to:

1. Give examples of several types of advertising objectives.
2. Explain the nature and purpose of advertising policies and their relationship to advertising objectives and advertising strategies.
3. Discuss the two key policy decisions relating to advertising organization.
4. Analyze the factors management should consider in deciding whether to use an advertising agency.
5. Explain how management should go about formulating advertising strategy.
6. Differentiate demand expansibility and price elasticity of demand.
7. Contrast the several approaches to determining the advertising appropriation.
8. Describe the chief problems involved in managing the advertising effort.
9. Discuss the problems involved in measuring advertising effectiveness.

CHAPTER 17

ADVERTISING

Advertising's contribution to marketing success is more indirect than personal selling's, but generally advertising effectiveness and marketing effectiveness go hand in hand. Achieving advertising effectiveness through skilled planning and management of the advertising effort is a key responsibility of marketing management. Discussion in this chapter focuses on (1) planning the advertising effort, including the setting of objectives, determining policies, and formulating strategies, and (2) managing the advertising effort.

Advertising

Advertising, in sharp contrast with personal selling, generally seeks to convey the marketer's messages to masses (i.e., large groups) of potential buyers. It takes, in other words, a "shotgun" approach, while personal selling "zeroes in" on individuals with a "rifle-like" approach. While the emphasis in this chapter is on planning and managing advertising from the marketer's standpoint, you should also keep in mind advertising's role as a source of information for members of the target audience. Under the marketing concept a communications medium can serve the marketer's purposes only if it also serves the target audience's needs for information.[1]

Planning the Advertising Effort

Figure 17–1 shows how advertising fits into the promotional mix. Management must first decide what role advertising should play in

[1] B. Stidsen, "Some Thoughts on the Advertising Process," *Journal of Marketing,* January 1970, p. 47.

Figure 17–1
Advertising as part of the promotional mix

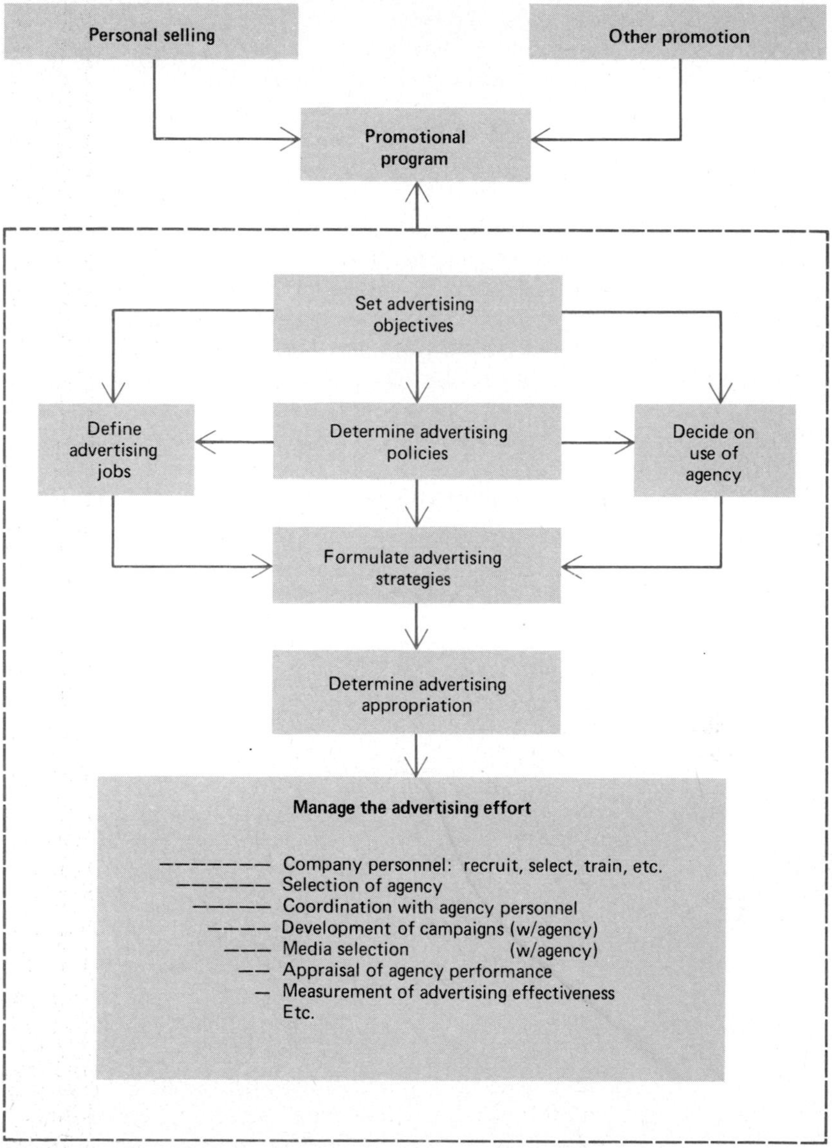

the promotional mix. In some situations, particularly in industrial marketing, management decides that advertising's role should be minimal or even nonexistent. But in most situations—both in consumer and industrial marketing—producers, especially manufacturers, must set advertising objectives, decide on advertising organization, determine advertising policies, formulate advertising strategies, determine the advertising appropriation, and manage the advertising effort. As this figure indicates, these interrelated activities collectively make up the advertising portion of the promotional mix. As you study the rest of this chapter, you will find it helpful to refer frequently to this figure.

Advertising Objectives

The long-term objectives of advertising, like those of personal selling, are broad and general, and concern the contributions advertising is expected to make to the achievement of overall company objectives. Most companies regard advertising's main objective as that of providing support for personal selling and other elements of promotion. But advertising is a highly versatile communications tool and, depending upon the marketing situation, companies use it to achieve such other long- and short-term objectives as the following:

1. to do the entire selling job (as in mail-order marketing)
2. to introduce a new product (by building brand awareness among potential buyers)
3. to force middlemen to handle the product (pull strategy)
4. to build brand preference (by making it more difficult for middlemen to sell substitutes)
5. to remind users to buy the product (retentive strategy)
6. to publicize some change in marketing strategy (e.g., a price change, a new model, or an improvement in the product)
7. to provide rationalizations for buying (i.e., "socially acceptable" excuses)
8. to combat or neutralize competitors' advertising (competitive advertising, perhaps comparative advertising)
9. to improve the morale of dealers and/or salesmen (by showing that the company is doing its share of promotion)
10. to acquaint buyers and prospects with new uses of the product (to extend the product's life cycle)

This list is not all-inclusive but only illustrative of the wide range of objectives that may be assigned to the advertising effort.

Advertising Policies

Advertising policies are the general guidelines management establishes to provide needed direction in making advertising decisions. Such policies should derive directly from the advertising objectives and assist management in formulating advertising strategies. The most basic advertising policy decision, of course, relates to whether the company should advertise at all; if management decides on a "no advertising" policy, as the Hershey Company had for many years, then there is no need for other advertising policies. Most companies, however, have policies spelling out, in general, the conditions under which they will or will not advertise. Among the most common advertising policy areas are those treated in the following discussion.

GENERAL SCOPE OF ADVERTISING EFFORT

Top management generally sets relatively specific limits for its advertising effort. Sometimes the policy is to permit only product-related advertising, but more frequently management also permits a limited amount of institutional (i.e., company image-building) advertising. Less frequently, a few companies, such as the Warner and Swasey Company (a diversified marketer of machine tools and other industrial goods), permit some advertising aimed to mold general public opinion. Oil companies and public utilities, in response to negative public attitudes concerning their role in the energy shortage (not to mention the large profits in times of rising prices), have been known to change the scope of their advertising effort to include advertising aimed at changing the general public's opinion toward their products, services, and policies.

ADVERTISING AND THE COMPETITION

Comparative Advertising

Horizontal Cooperative Advertising

Commonly, management spells out the general relationship that company advertising should bear to the competitors and/or their advertising. Many companies have policies prohibiting any advertising mention of competitors whatsoever, although, in recent years, more advertisers than ever before have engaged in *comparative advertising,* in which the advertiser's product is compared directly with those of competition, which are clearly identified by brand name. Some, as a policy matter, insist on matching or exceeding the advertising efforts of their competitors. In a number of industries, it is common policy for individual companies to participate, under certain conditions, in industry-wide advertising efforts (so-called *horizontal cooperative advertising*). Whether or not a given company should participate in industry advertising depends on such factors as the significance of competition from products of other industries, comparative effectiveness of its own advertising, and its normal share of the market.

ADVERTISING AND THE MIDDLEMEN

Vertical Cooperative Advertising

Another common policy relates to the use or nonuse of *vertical cooperative advertising;* that is, advertising whose costs the company shares with its middlemen according to some prearranged plan. Quite often, manufacturers use such cooperative advertising to stimulate middlemen to put more push behind the product. Others use it: to expand the amount of advertising a dollar buys (by getting dealers to pay part of the costs); to get dealers to stock the product by using the offer of cooperative advertising as bait; to secure local advertising media rates (which are usually lower than those charged national advertisers); to encourage retailers to advertise in order to identify themselves as local outlets where consumers can find the product; and to provide local advertising support for national advertising campaigns.

ADVERTISING AND THE AUDIENCE

A growing number of advertisers have policies concerning the general approach advertising should take relative to the target audience. Some, for instance, frown upon the use of humor in advertisements or testimonials. Others insist upon the use of positive appeals, strictly forbidding the use of negative or scare appeals.

Advertising Organization

Two key policy decisions relate to advertising organization: (1) the nature of advertising jobs inside the company, and (2) the use or nonuse of an advertising agency. The availability of professional outside help from advertising agencies provides an organizational alternative whereby the advertiser may shift all or part of the planning, producing, and placement of advertising to an agency. If the company decides to use advertising at all, management must then decide who will do what part of the actual work. Who should participate in formulating advertising strategy? (Sometimes agencies have major voices in strategy formulation.) Who should plan the advertising program and prepare the different campaigns? Who should write the copy, develop the appeals and themes, do the illustrations, and select the type styles? Who should determine the size and position of advertising space, arrange for the use of various media, write and produce the radio and TV commercials, choose the programs to sponsor, and draft the master advertising schedule? These are some of the many tasks involved in the actual work of advertising. Management must decide either to have company personnel do this work, or to secure the services of an advertising agency, or to use a combination.

DEFINING ADVERTISING JOBS INSIDE THE COMPANY

In a company organized under the marketing concept, the top advertising executive serves in a staff capacity and reports directly either to the chief marketing executive or to a director of marketing communications or promotion. How large the advertising executive's staff is, and the nature of their duties and responsibilities, depend upon how much, if any, of the advertising work is "farmed out" to an agency. Determination of advertising policy and formulation of advertising strategy, because of their close relationships to overall marketing strategy, are generally not, and should not be, delegated to an agency. Furthermore, when an advertising agency is used, the advertising executive, at the very minimum, should actively be involved in the agency's planning of advertising campaigns, thus ensuring that they fit in with overall marketing strategy. Top management holds the advertising manager responsible for the success or failure of the advertising, and this holds true whether the firm's own advertising department discharges the entire task of advertising or whether all or parts of it are handled by an agency.

DECIDING ON USE OF AN ADVERTISING AGENCY

Whether a company should have its own pool of talent or tap the skills of an agency depends on who can do the job best and most effectively. Important factors to consider in making this decision are the functions and cost of an agency, advertiser-agency relationships, and required advertising skills.

Advertising Agency

Nature of an Advertising Agency An *advertising agency* is a group of experts on various phases of advertising and related marketing areas.[2] In its operations, it resembles other organizations that provide expert assistance on specialized business problems—the management consulting firm, the marketing research firm, and the firm specializing in design and administration of incentive campaigns for salesmen and dealers. But in the way it normally receives its compensation, the advertising agency is distinct from other consulting organizations.

Commission System

Card Rate

Compensation of Agencies The *commission system* is the traditional and still most widely used method of compensating advertising agencies. Agencies pay for space and time used on behalf of advertisers at the *card rate* less a certain discount, usually 15 percent, and bill clients at the card rate. Thus, agencies receive their basic compensation from advertising media rather than from advertisers, and this has been the source of considerable controversy.

Advertisers, especially large ones, maintain that agencies may overspend for media because so much of their compensation comes from media commissions. Advertising agencies, as might be expected, have been the main defenders of the commission system, but some have been losing their liking for it. Part of the growing disenchantment traces to the consent decree (resulting from an antitrust suit brought by the U.S. Department of Justice) which, in effect, made it possible for media to grant commissions to other than recog-

[2] For a good discussion of the advertising agency as a force in the advertising business, see "The Advertising Agency—What It Is and What It Does for Advertising," *Advertising Age*, November 21, 1973, pp. 34 ff.

nized agencies and in general made the commission system more difficult to enforce and more open to attack.

Even more of the agencies' disaffection for the commission system results from the increasing cost of providing a wide range of services to advertisers: services that include, among others, advertising pretesting, test marketing, research on advertising effectiveness, and marketing counsel and aid in marketing research. At one time agencies performed these services free, but now many bill advertisers for these extras on a *cost plus* or *fee* basis. Fees or charges amount to roughly one-third of the gross incomes of advertising agencies. Some agencies have replaced the commission system entirely with a fee arrangement under which media commissions received are credited toward payment of the agreed fee.

Cost Plus (Fee) Basis

Advertiser-Agency Relationships Through long-standing practice, certain relationships between advertisers and their agencies have become standardized. The five most important are (1) the agency refrains from having two accounts whose products are in direct competition; (2) the advertiser refrains from using two agencies to handle the advertising for the same product; (3) the agency obtains advance approval before it commits the advertiser to expenditures; (4) the advertiser pays the agency for media and other invoices promptly and within the cash discount period; and (5) the agency passes on to the advertiser the exact dollar amounts of all cash discounts granted by media.

Required Advertising Skills The decision to use an agency often hinges upon the skills required to carry out the advertising effort. In contrast with advertising agencies, few manufacturers can afford to have in their employ all the different talents needed to develop and produce large-scale advertising programs. Characteristically, too, agencies allow much greater latitude for creative activity than is normally found in a manufacturer-controlled advertising operation. Creative people in agencies may give freer rein to their imagination because they do not work directly for the advertiser. It is usually the agency team which sees the need and the way to break with the advertiser's traditional approach and produce advertisements and campaigns that are fresh and original. When the nature of the advertising effort requires considerable and varied skills, an outside agency is more likely to have them than a manufacturer-controlled advertising operation. Table 17–1 shows the ten leading advertising agencies in U.S. billings for 1973 and 1974.

Advertising Strategy

Advertising Strategy

Advertising strategies are individualized tailorings of the advertising effort to fit particular marketing situations. An *advertising strategy* is aimed to achieve advertising objectives and should be

Table 17–1 Top Ten Advertising Agencies in U. S. Billings, 1973 and 1974 (millions of dollars)

RANK	AGENCY	1974	1973	PERCENT CHANGE 1973 TO 1974
1	Young & Rubicam International	$468.9	$390.0	+ 20.2
2	J. Walter Thompson Company	401.5	386.4	+ 3.9
3	Batten, Barton, Durstine & Osborn	373.9	339.1	+ 10.3
4	Leo Burnett Company	366.1	330.9	+ 10.6
5	Grey Advertising	290.0	277.0	+ 4.7
6	Doyle Dane Bernbach	265.1	248.3	+ 6.8
7	Ted Bates & Company	255.1	241.3	+ 5.7
8	Foote, Cone & Belding	238.8	234.5	+ 1.8
9	Ogilvy & Mather International	223.3	203.7	+ 9.6
10	D'Arcy-MacManus & Masius	222.0	200.0	+ 11.0

Source: Reprinted with permission from the February 24, 1975, issue of *Advertising Age*. Copyright 1975 by Crain Communications, Inc.

consistent with existing advertising policies (if it is not, management should then either reshape the strategy or alter the policies). Formulating advertising strategy, then, involves making advertising decisions within an appropriate policy framework so as to determine advertising's role in overall marketing strategy. Advertising strategy formulation requires management to "size up" the extent of the advertising opportunity through analysis of different aspects of the particular marketing situation (product-market, distribution, promotion, and pricing).

PRODUCT-MARKET ASPECTS

Demand Expansibility

Demand Expansibility If demand can be stimulated through advertising alone, it is said to be "expansible." A product has an expansible demand if (with no change in price) advertising results in greater sales. To stimulate *primary demand* (i.e., demand for a *type* of product, such as cassette recorders in general) on a profitable basis, then, demand must be expansible.

Primary Demand

Selective Demand

An expansible demand is not a necessary condition for the profitable stimulation of *selective demand* (i.e., demand for a specific brand, such as for Wollensak cassette recorders), inasmuch as selective demand advertising may succeed in winning away customers from competing brands. Nevertheless, existence of an expansible demand adds to the chances of success for selective, as well as primary, demand advertising. Moreover, advertising aimed at stimulating selective demand may win nonusers of the product type to the manufacturer's brand, may win some users of competing brands, and may even increase the brand's consumption among present users.

Brand Differentiation A particularly critical factor in appraising advertising opportunity is the extent to which the brand differs from competing brands. Brand differences and similarities should be identified, and appraisals made of their relative importance to specific market segments. Differences that numerous consumers consider important furnish the source of selective advertising appeals. If a brand is not very different from competing brands—and consumers know it—the most the manufacturer can hope to accomplish through advertising is brand acceptance. There must be brand differences of substantial importance to consumers if advertising is to succeed in developing brand preference or brand insistence.

For some products buyers can detect some hidden brand differences through use. If, as with many food products, the consumer must use the product in a certain way to detect hidden differences, the marketer must provide directions for use (on the package and possibly in the advertising). Thus, a cake mix manufacturer provides careful directions both on the package and in its advertising to ensure that the end result is an acceptable cake. If, as with certain drugs and cosmetics, the hidden difference is not detectable through use (e.g., it may take several weeks of using a facial cream to determine its effect on the complexion), the advertiser may attempt to convince buyers of the integrity of the firm itself or may use endorsements of the brand by public figures or experts. Whenever a brand possesses important hidden differences, there is considerable opportunity for advertising to exploit them profitably.

Stage in the Product Life Cycle The potential effectiveness of advertising depends importantly upon management's recognition of the stage in the product life cycle that the product is in and upon its skill in adjusting the thrust of the advertising effort accordingly. Relative to the product life cycle, stimulation of primary demand precedes stimulation of selective demand—consumers must want the generic product (as marketing people generally describe a type of product) before they can want some brand of it.

Thus, after introducing a new generic product, the innovating company normally should concentrate on advertising to stimulate primary demand. As the product type gains acceptance (during the market growth and market maturity stages), the innovating company gradually changes over to advertising to stimulate selective demand. For example, when R.C.A. introduced color television, the major thrust of its advertising was directed toward persuading consumers to buy color rather than black-and-white television. After General Electric, Zenith, and others entered the color television field, R.C.A. shifted its advertising emphasis to the special advantages of R.C.A. color television over competitors' color sets. An innovating company (for a new type of product), therefore, must be willing to expend considerable money on primary demand advertising, whereas followers usually must concern themselves only with selective demand advertising.

However, some products in the market maturity stage continue to benefit from advertising aimed at stimulating primary demand, because they compete directly or indirectly with some different product type. For example, tea, certainly not a new product, must continually and directly compete with coffee for primary acceptance. As another example, home organs and color television sets compete indirectly, especially since many prospective buyers cannot afford to buy both. It is not unusual, then, for mature products to be promoted through primary demand advertising.

Retentive Advertising

For most products in the market maturity stage and for some in the market decline stage, much advertising effort is directed toward retaining present customers. Usually, *retentive advertising* takes the form of reminding past buyers to buy the brand. Quite often, retentive advertising features special deals, such as two-for-one offers or reduced prices.

The Product and Consumer Needs and Wants Marketing professionals have long recognized that if a product will not sell without advertising, it will not sell with advertising. For a product to sell at all, with or without advertising, it must appeal to and satisfy some needs and wants of some consumers at least as well as competing items. Advertising, in other words, possesses no magic capable of causing people to buy things they do not need or want; however, it may help them to rationalize purchases of products they want but do not need in a strict economic sense. Who needs custom-made shirts at double the price of factory-made shirts? Only a small percentage of men who require unusual sizes actually need custom-made shirts, but many men want them for prestigious reasons. Appeals to these other wants help consumers to rationalize uneconomic but satisfying wants.

In appraising a product with regard to advertising opportunity, the really important questions to ask are: "Do potential buyers have needs or wants that this product or brand is capable of satisfying?" and "How important, or how strong, are these needs or wants?" If there are strong needs or wants for the product, the chances are that considerable advertising opportunity exists. If the product is capable of satisfying only comparatively weak and less basic needs or wants, there is not nearly so much advertising opportunity. The extent of the advertising opportunity varies with the strength of the basic underlying needs or wants that are satisfied by the product or brand.

DISTRIBUTION ASPECTS

Distribution Intensity For advertising to attain maximum effectiveness, people influenced by it must be able to find stores that carry the brand. This is a matter of achieving the proper distribution intensity, considering the time consumers are willing to spend looking for the product. If consumers will spend only a little time looking for the product, its distribution should be widespread. If consumers are willing to spend considerable searching time on the product, its distribution can be more selective. Company strategy on distribution intensity should be closely correlated with the coverage of the proposed advertising.

Middlemen's Cooperation Even with proper distribution intensity, sales and goodwill may be lost if dealers do not carry sufficient stocks to meet increased demand resulting from the advertising. In order to prevent out-of-stocks from developing, the manufacturer should make certain that dealers know of the anticipated sales increase before the advertising appears. The manufacturer should also see to it that dealers obtain reorders promptly. Securing and maintaining the needed cooperation of the middlemen is, of course, the responsibility of the sales force; therefore, it is highly important to coordinate the advertising and personal selling efforts effectively.

THE PROMOTIONAL MIX

In sizing up the extent of the advertising opportunity, management at the same time must consider the other elements in the promotional mix. Management's task is to select the appropriate elements in the proper amounts in order to achieve as near an optimum a mix as possible. Thus, in determining advertising's role in the mix, management must simultaneously consider advertising's interactions and interrelations not only with personal selling but with such other possible promotional elements as point-of-purchase display and packaging. If, for example, management concludes that a certain amount of advertising will make point-of-purchase displays twice as effective in terms of making sales, then it would probably decide to include that amount of advertising for this purpose.

PRICING ASPECTS

Advertising, Price, and the Final Buyer The final buyer should consider the advertised item worth the price at which it is offered for sale. This does not necessarily mean that the advertised item should be priced identically with its unadvertised or even its advertised competitors. Its price should represent reasonable value in the final buyer's mind. If the final buyer considers it superior to competing brands, its price may be higher; if the final buyer considers it inferior, its price must be lower. Advertising cannot persuade final buyers to pay what they consider an unreasonable price. Yet many ultimate consumers feel that advertised brands are worth higher prices than unadvertised brands because they are more confident that they are buying what they want.

Manufacturers of nationally advertised brands aiming to secure and retain consumer confidence must be careful to maintain consistent product quality and service. Generally, consumers will pay a small price premium because of their confidence in consistent benefits from their favorite advertised brands. Beyond that small premium, the favorite brand's price can exceed an unadvertised brand's price only by the amount at which its buyers value its additional advantages. Consumers determine this added value by personal observation and product use or by accepting the advertiser's claims when they are unable to observe and evaluate the differences for themselves. If the advertised brand has no important differences, hidden or otherwise, its price can be no higher than those of its competitors.

Price Elasticity of Demand In sizing up the advertising opportunity, management should also determine whether the product's demand is *price elastic*. Demand is price elastic if a price reduction increases total revenue (price × quantity sold), and if a price rise reduces total revenue. Demand is *price inelastic* if a price reduction decreases total revenue and a price rise increases total revenue. Normally, however, and contrary to the economist's usual assumption, the adjustment of revenue to a price change is not immediate. So a practical businessman may find advertising useful in "spreading the word" of a price reduction on a product with an elastic demand, thus speeding up the receipt of increased total revenue.

Price Elasticity

Price Inelasticity

The Advertising Appropriation

After management has formulated the advertising strategy, it must determine the amount of the advertising appropriation. It should do this, as emphasized in Chapter 15 (Promotional Strategy), in conjunction with its determination of the total promotional appropriation. In determining the advertising appropriation, management must secure estimates for such cost factors as media usage and advertising research studies. At some point management must decide whether the company can afford the estimated expense of the proposed advertising effort—if the answer is "no," it must then rework the advertising strategy to bring the costs into line with what the company can afford. That advertising is a big business is illustrated by the more than $23 billion spent in 1973. Table 17–2 shows the ten leading advertisers in 1973 by advertising expenditures, as well as their spending as a percentage of sales. Note the sometimes wide variation in advertising as a percent of sales, not only from industry to industry, but also from one company to another in the same general industry.

Whether the company can afford the costs involved in implementing a proposed advertising strategy depends partly on the potential ability of the advertising to return enough additional gross margin dollars to pay for itself. But it also depends on the funds the company has available. If there is not enough money to support an adequate advertising effort (i.e., to implement an effective advertis-

Table 17–2 Top Ten U. S. Advertisers, 1973

RANK	ADVERTISER	1973 EXPENDITURE (Millions of Dollars)	Percent of Sales
1	Procter & Gamble	$310.0	6.3
2	Sears, Roebuck	215.0	1.7
3	General Foods	180.0	8.1
4	General Motors	158.4	0.4
5	Warner-Lambert	141.7	14.6
6	American Home Products	133.0	9.9
7	Bristol-Myers	132.0	12.7
8	Ford Motor Company	127.2	0.6
9	Colgate-Palmolive	120.0	12.2
10	U. S. Government	99.2	–

Source: Reprinted with permission from the August 26, 1974, issue of *Advertising Age*. Copyright 1974 by Crain Communications, Inc.

ing strategy), it is generally best not to advertise at all and to concentrate instead on other promotional methods.

Whether the sales resulting from the advertising are immediate or deferred is also significant. If advertising results in quick sales, the advertising costs may be met largely as they are incurred from the greater number of gross margin dollars available. If the advertising investment pays off only over or after a considerable time period, financing the advertising requires a much larger outlay. Companies short of working capital are often able to advertise under the first condition but not under the second; this, in turn, causes them to use advertising strategies aimed to result in quick rather than deferred sales. Better-financed companies may choose advertising strategies aimed to produce either quick or deferred sales or both, depending on the relative attractiveness of the different payoffs.

There is a difference between the way advertisers should determine their appropriations, and the way most of them actually do. The majority, mainly because of difficulties encountered in isolating the effectiveness of advertising, rely on such traditional methods as the percentage-of-sales approach. The method advertisers should use is called the incremental approach, but it can only be applied when the advertising strategy is directed solely to the achievement of profit-related objectives.

INCREMENTAL APPROACH

Marginal Analysis

The incremental approach is derived from the analytical tool economists call *marginal analysis*. It puts the problem of determining the appropriation (when the advertising strategy is totally profit-related) into an appropriate conceptual framework since, logically, the advertiser should set the appropriation at the amount that maximizes advertising's net profit contribution. It is necessary, in other words, to analyze the relationship of advertising as a cause and sales as the effect.

Figure 17–2 depicts the relationship of advertising to unit sales volume as marketing theoreticians suggest it exists. Some sales would be made even without any advertising expenditure, and this is indicated at point X_1. As advertising expenditures are begun and as increments of expenditure are added, unit sales volume first expands rather slowly, then more rapidly, and, finally, additional expenditure has less and less effect. This indicates that there must be a minimum size appropriation beneath which expenditures for advertising are unduly costly in terms of the resulting sales. It also indicates that beyond a certain point, increases in the advertising appropriation are accompanied by diminishing returns in terms of unit sales volume.

Figure 17–3 shows how to obtain the optimum appropriation if the marketer knows the nature of the advertising-to-sales relationship and makes two assumptions. One assumption is that price remains constant, which means that total sales revenue (*TR*) varies at a constant rate with changes in sales volume. The second assumption is that total variable nonadvertising costs (*TVC*) vary at a constant rate. In order to determine the advertising appropriation that maximizes net profit, one must find the point on the advertising-sales curve (*DR*) where a tangent can be drawn parallel to the total sales revenue curve (*TR*). One such line is QQ_1, but the point of tangency on this line obviously is one where total costs exceed total revenues.

Figure 17–2
Relationship of advertising to unit sales volume

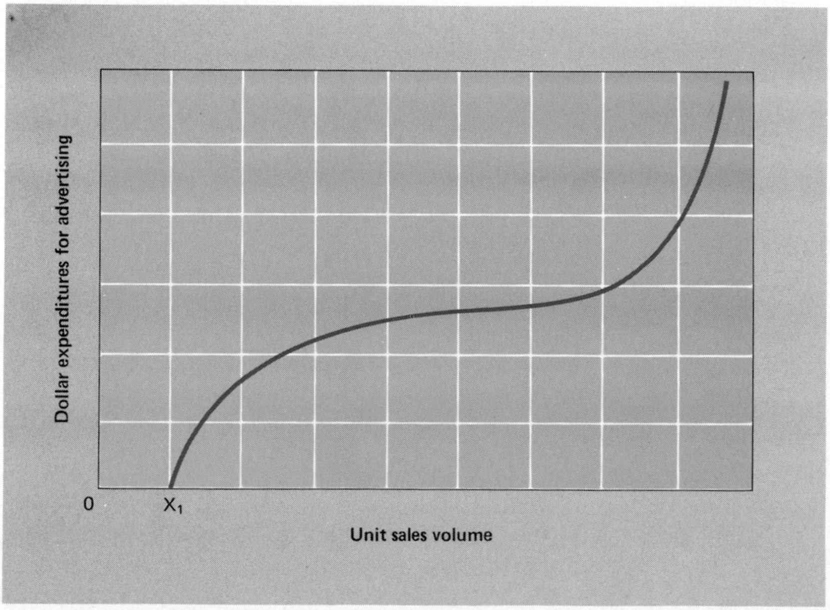

Figure 17–3
Determining the optimum advertising appropriation

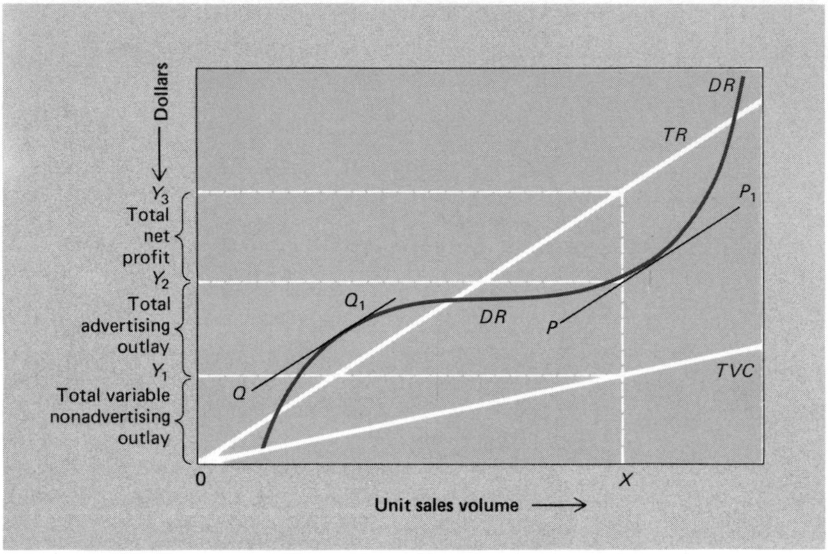

Source: Adapted from J. Howard, *Marketing Management: Analysis and Planning*, rev. ed. (Homewood, Ill.: Richard D. Irwin, Inc., 1963), p. 407.

The tangent line the decision maker should seek is PP_1, for here the point of tangency is also the profit-maximizing point. On the vertical axis, the optimum advertising appropriation is represented by the distance Y_1Y_2, total variable nonadvertising outlay by OY_1, and total net profit by Y_2Y_3.

PERCENTAGE-OF-SALES APPROACH

This is a widely used traditional method of determining the advertising appropriation. In this method management applies some arbitrary percentage to past sales figures, forecasted sales, or some combination of the two and, supposedly, up comes the amount of the appropriation. This simplicity, in fact, is about the only good thing about this approach because it is difficult to defend on logical grounds, especially if advertising objectives are all profit-related. It assumes, for one thing, that the advertising cost per unit of product remains constant regardless of the sales volume; this is not a valid assumption because, as shown in Figures 17–2 and 17–3, sales do not have a straight-line relationship with advertising. More important, it implicitly assumes that advertising follows sales and not the other way around. Further, the percentage figure in most cases can come only from past sales records and past advertising expenditures—there is little assurance that past percentage relationships will hold in the future.

OBJECTIVE-AND-TASK APPROACH

There are three steps in this method: (1) define objectives in terms of desired sales volumes, net profits, and the like; (2) estimate the amount of advertising space and time needed to achieve these objectives; and (3) express this amount of advertising in dollars to arrive at the amount of the appropriation. This method is logical in that it treats advertising as a cause of sales rather than as an effect. If used to maximize the net profit contribution of advertising, this method is equivalent to the incremental approach; however, unfortunately, most users appear to concentrate more on the effect of advertising on sales than on net profit. Without a profit maximization emphasis, this method may produce an appropriation that increases costs rather than profits.

OTHER APPROACHES

Three other common approaches to determining the advertising appropriation should be mentioned. The first is the *arbitrary method,* in which the appropriation is decided either "by pure guess" or "by allotting all the advertiser can afford." The second is called *matching competitors' expenditures;* the advertiser, in effect, permits its competitors to set its appropriation. The third is the *tax per unit of product,* in which a fixed sum is put into the "advertising pot" for each unit of the product sold or expected to be sold. As should be clear, none of these approaches is defensible on logical grounds.

Managing the Advertising Effort

COMPANY ADVERTISING PERSONNEL

Implementing the advertising strategy is one of the advertising manager's most important responsibilities. The people who do the actual advertising work may be company employees (those in the advertising department), agency personnel, or some combination. As advertising department head, the advertising manager recruits, selects, trains, motivates, supervises, directs, and appraises that department's staff. Managing an advertising department can be a challenging assignment, especially when (as is often true) people having the needed talents prefer the more free-wheeling environment of, and greater glamor associated with, advertising agencies. Difficulties in recruiting and retaining people with scarce creative talents largely explain why so many advertising departments are small, often consisting only of an advertising manager, perhaps one or two assistants, and a few clerical workers and secretaries.

SELECTION OF THE ADVERTISING AGENCY

There are no standardized procedures for selecting advertising agencies. Advertisers decide to use agencies mainly because they require unique or additional talent to help them carry out their advertising efforts. The problem of agency selection, then, importantly involves evaluating the qualifications of competing agencies and requires comparisons of their pools of talent. Therefore, an advertiser should, for each agency, investigate the backgrounds and professional qualifications of the key personnel who may be assigned to the account. Keeping in mind the objectives of the company's advertising strategy, management should appraise each agency according to whether it appears to possess the required talents. It is advisable, too, to analyze each agency's record in serving other accounts, especially those having similar marketing and advertising problems. In most companies, several executives including the advertising manager participate in evaluating the agencies competing for the account, but the final selection is usually made by an individual—most often the president, and next most often the advertising manager.

COORDINATION WITH AGENCY PERSONNEL

When an advertising agency is used, the advertising manager working along with the agency account executive or account supervisor is responsible for coordinating its activities with related company activities. At the very minimum, the advertising manager should be actively involved in the agency's planning and conduct of advertising campaigns, thus ensuring that they are consistent with company advertising and overall marketing strategy. Beyond that, the advertising manager must be concerned with such matters as checking out the agency's proposed campaigns with company legal personnel, making certain that advance approval is given before the agency commits the company to various expenditures, and coordinating research studies conducted by the agency and company.

DEVELOPING ADVERTISING CAMPAIGNS

Campaign Objectives

Defining Campaign Objectives The first step in developing an advertising campaign is the clear definition of its objectives.[3] *Campaign objectives* should be consistent with the objectives the company sets for its overall advertising effort, and they should be specific. Some campaign objectives can be expressed quantitatively—for example, "to introduce a new product in a particular market area and

[3] An excellent discussion of the various stages and elements of a complete advertising campaign may be seen in Otto Kleppner, *Advertising Procedure*, 6th ed. (Englewood Cliffs, N.J.: Prentice-Hall, Inc., 1973), pp. 532–545.

obtain a 10 percent market share within the first year." Whenever possible, campaign objectives should be stated quantitatively, as that greatly simplifies later appraisals of the extent of their achievement. Sometimes, however, certain campaign objectives are qualitative, such as "building dealer loyalty" or "improving salesmen's morale." Such objectives are important and appropriate; however, it is difficult to measure the extent of their achievement.

Campaign Budget

Determining the Campaign Budget Determining the *campaign budget* involves estimating how much it will cost to achieve the campaign's objectives. If the campaign objectives are profit-related and stated quantitatively, then the amount of the campaign budget is determined by estimating the proposed campaign's effectiveness in attaining them. If campaign objectives are not directly related to profit (e.g., if the objective is to build a particular type of company image), then generally there is little basis for predicting either the campaign's effectiveness or accurately determining the budget required.

Creation of the Advertisements The actual preparation of the advertisements for a campaign involves creativity of a high order. It is difficult and probably impossible to evaluate such creativity quantitatively. The actual advertisements are produced by the advertising field's creative people—the copy writers and artists—but the overall qualitative evaluation and approval of their outputs are the responsibilities of agency executives and the advertiser's marketing and advertising executives.

An important early step in producing an advertising campaign is to develop a campaign theme—a keynote idea or concept that will provide continuity over time and result in significant impact upon the target market segments. Some advertisers change themes annually or even seasonally. Others continue with a single theme almost indefinitely, until it loses most of its appeal. Maidenform's "I dreamt I . . ." theme was continued for more than a dozen years because it lost little of its power to draw readers', viewers', and listeners' attention to the product.

The next step is to create language or visual messages projecting the central theme. Most advertisements use both language and visual messages. An effective message generally meets three criteria: (1) it attracts the audience's attention, (2) it is clearly understandable, and (3) it is believable. In a society where most people are exposed daily to hundreds of advertising messages, creating an ad capable of attracting attention is difficult and requires rather unusual talent—it is not only possible to come up with an ad that fails to attract much attention but also possible to succeed too well so that other elements in the ad divert attention away from the product (which is a potential pitfall for ads featuring humor). Likewise, constructing a message that conveys the desired impression clearly without confusion or misunderstanding is not easy. Clarity in communications is an art, and it is often difficult to tell in advance whether or not an audience will understand a particular message in the way intended. Similarly, special care is needed to ensure that the audience will believe the message conveyed. If, for example, an ad states that the advertiser's product is more effective than any competitive product, generally the audience must be provided with sufficient proof. Otherwise, much of the audience may reject the entire message as a wild and unsubstantiated claim that should not be believed.

Media Selection Most of the campaign budget is used for purchasing space and time in different media. Advertising media include (among others) newspapers, magazines, television, radio, outdoor posters, and transportation cards. Even though the agency usually handles the actual media selection, the advertiser should evaluate its selections.

Media Selection Factors

What main factors influence media selection? The most fundamental, of course, are the nature of the target market segment and the type of product. The distinctive characteristics of various media are important—for instance, because newspapers are issued daily, some advertisers use them and others avoid them. The campaign budget is important—small budgets usually require a concentration of expenditures in a few media for best results, whereas large budgets ordinarily must be spread over many media to avoid a premature onset of diminishing returns. Ideally, but rarely attainable, media circulation (general exposure) should cover only those geographical areas where the advertiser has distribution (otherwise there is "waste circulation").

Conceptually, media selection is a problem in determining optimum allocation of the campaign budget. It involves dividing the budget among different media—newspapers, magazines, television, outdoor posters, and so on—so as to equate the marginal returns from each. Practically speaking, this is difficult to accomplish; consequently, most companies, relying largely on data on past media expenditures and past results, use a "try, try again" approach—starting with some feasible allocation, testing it to find possible improvements, and making those changes that seemingly would raise total effectiveness. Computer models for media selection have been developed in an attempt to simplify the task; but their one great limitation lies in the difficulties in quantifying certain factors used in comparing media—for example, the value of a particular medium's prestige with its audience.

Media Cost Comparisons

Relative cost is often used as a selection factor when making choices among media in the same classification—for example, between two magazines. Because each medium has a different size of circulation and a different advertising rate, the comparison technique is to convert circulation and rate figures to a common basis. Magazines, for instance, are compared according to the cost of reaching 1,000 readers with a given amount of advertising space; thus, the cost of using a full page of magazine space is calculated as follows:

$$\text{Cost per 1,000} = \frac{\text{Page Rate} \times 1{,}000}{\text{Circulation of Magazine}}$$

Cost comparisons of other media follow similar patterns. For radio and television, the rate for a given amount of time is multiplied by 1,000 and divided by the size of the audience. For outdoor posters and transportation (car) cards, the rate for a given showing of posters or cards is multiplied by 1,000 and divided by the circulation.

Agate Line

Milline Rate

For newspapers, the technique varies slightly—newspapers quote their rates by the *agate line,* of which there are fourteen in a space one column wide and one inch deep; thus, the cost comparison yardstick for newspapers is called the *milline rate*—the cost of reaching one million readers with one agate line of advertising—which is calculated as follows:

$$\text{Milline Rate} = \frac{\text{Agate Line Rate} \times 1{,}000{,}000}{\text{Circulation of Newspaper}}$$

APPRAISAL OF AGENCY PERFORMANCE

Because the agency plays a critical role in the advertising effort and is a part of the promotional mix and overall marketing strategy, the advertiser should continually appraise the agency's services and effectiveness. The key criteria for evaluating agency performance are (1) its effectiveness in meeting specific campaign objectives, and (2) its contribution to the reaching of the advertiser's advertising and overall marketing objectives. Formal reviews of the agency's performance should occur at least once a year. News of an advertiser's dissatisfaction with its present agency's performance travels fast, and other agencies are generally sensitive to signs of such dissatisfaction. Consequently, there is considerable agency switching by advertisers, and this serves as a partial brake on the inclination of some agencies to perform sloppily or to overspend their clients' funds.

MEASURING ADVERTISING EFFECTIVENESS

Advertising effectiveness should be measured in terms of criteria derived from campaign objectives and the advertiser's overall advertising and marketing objectives. Unfortunately, however, most measures of advertising effectiveness in current use are rather superficial; they include such measures as size of audience, program ratings, readership scores, and numbers of inquiries received (all of which pertain almost exclusively to campaign objectives alone).

If advertising objectives are directly sales-related (i.e., if they are aimed to increase sales, to improve market share, etc.), then it is possible, of course, to determine (usually through special research studies) whether or not the advertising has been effective in reaching them. However, as should now be clear, advertising is only one of the causes of sales, market share, and the like. Other aspects of the overall marketing strategy (product-market, distribution, other forms of promotion including personal selling, and pricing) all contribute to the making of sales, and it is difficult to isolate the sales effect of any one of these aspects.

Some advertisers seek to pretest advertising effectiveness before the advertising is run, rather than relying only on predictions of effectiveness by advertising professionals. Pretesting may take such forms as "consumer opinion panels," actual sales in "test markets," or "attitude studies" made among consumers to determine the likely impact of prototype advertising appeals and approaches. Motivation research studies, too, are used by some advertisers in attempts to determine in advance the relative effectiveness of different advertising appeals and media.

Summary

If you have mastered the material in this chapter, you have gained important insights on planning and managing the advertising effort. You should have learned: how, in setting advertising objectives, management carefully defines both the broad and specific roles it expects advertising to play in the promotional mix and in the overall marketing strategy; how, in determining advertising policies, it sets up the general rules to guide itself in making advertising decisions; how, in approaching the question of advertising organization, it defines advertising jobs within the company and decides on the use of an advertising agency; how, in formulating advertising strategies, management fits the advertising effort to particular product-market, distribution, promotion, and pricing aspects making up the total marketing situation; how, in determining the advertising appropriation, management simultaneously determines the total promotional appropriation and balances the proposed advertising strategy with what the company can afford; how, in managing the advertising effort, management concerns itself with administering company advertising personnel, selecting an advertising agency, developing advertising campaigns, appraising agency performance, and measuring advertising effectiveness. If you thoroughly understand all of these things, you understand the part advertising plays both in the promotional mix and in overall marketing strategy.

1. Explain the meaning of the following terms:
   a. generic product
   b. brand differentiation
   c. advertising agency
   d. advertising media
   e. milline rate
   f. cost per thousand
   g. advertising campaign
   h. advertising strategy
2. Explain and contrast the terms in each of the following pairs:
   a. primary demand and selective demand
   b. demand elasticity and demand expansibility
3. Analyze the relationships that the different short-term advertising objectives should bear to marketing management's long-term goals.
4. What is an "advertising opportunity"? How can advertising opportunities be detected?
5. Under what conditions are consumers likely to be willing to pay more for an advertised product than for an unadvertised product? Using your own shopping experience as a guide, provide some examples of instances where you paid more for an advertised product when competing unadvertised products were available?
6. Currently, a certain manufacturer sells 5,000 units of its product in a given marketing area each year. The product is distributed through retailers and the manufacturer has not used local advertising in this particular area for several years. Retailers pay the manufacturer $20.00 per unit of the product and price it at $25.00. The manufacturer estimates its total costs per unit at $17.50. This manufacturer now wants to launch a local advertising campaign in the marketing area and estimates that the cost of an adequate campaign would amount to $20,000. How much additional sales volume should this advertising campaign produce in order for the manufacturer to break even on the cost?
7. How does a company's financial condition affect management's decision to use advertising for the purpose of producing immediate sales? For the purpose of producing deferred sales? What arguments might a management use in an attempt to secure a bank loan for purposes of carrying on an advertising campaign?
8. What is the relationship between effective advertising strategy and the product life cycle?
9. How are advertising decisions affected by each of the following:
   a. company policy on distribution intensity
   b. marketing channels for the product

c. competitors' advertising practices
d. price of the product

10. Is it absolutely essential to use an advertising agency?
11. If you were the marketing manager of a large manufacturing company which had an advertising budget of millions of dollars, would you favor or oppose the commission system of compensating advertising agencies? Why? Would you take the same position if you were the president of a large advertising agency? Why? If you were the owner of a large city newspaper, what would be your position on this question? Why?
12. Under what circumstances would you advise a manufacturer to switch advertising agencies? Under what circumstances might an advertising agency voluntarily "resign" a manufacturer's account?
13. "The size of the advertising appropriation should be based on advertising effectiveness." Bearing this "should be" statement in mind, how might you, as the manager of a marketing research department, contribute to the decision on size of the advertising appropriation?
14. Compare and contrast the following approaches to determining the size of the advertising appropriation:
    a. incremental
    b. percentage-of-sales
    c. objective-and-task
    d. arbitrary
    e. matching competitors' expenditures
    f. tax per unit of product
15. To what extent should the sales forecast be considered in determining the size of the advertising appropriation? In selecting media?
16. "Everyone connected with advertising—the advertiser, the agency, and the media—has a sincere interest in finding out whether advertising is successful." Agree or disagree? Why?
17. What are the social responsibilities of advertising? Do you feel advertising successfully carries out these responsibilities?
18. Comment on the following two statements:
    a. "Advertising's job, purely and simply, is to communicate, to a defined audience, information and a frame-of-mind that stimulates action. Advertising succeeds or fails depending on how well it communicates the desired information and attitudes to the right people at the right time at the right cost."
    b. "The average consumer is subjected to roughly 1,600 advertising impressions per day. As a result, he is developing an imperviousness to advertising in general and an increasing ability to shut off advertisers' messages."

19. From time to time, certain politicians suggest that a tax should be placed on advertising, not only to raise revenue but to protect consumers from "further commercial invasions of their homes." As a marketing executive, what position would you take with regard to this proposal? As the "target" of advertisers' messages, what is your attitude? Justify the positions you take.
20. In a certain city there are two large newspapers—a morning and an evening paper—both of which reach similar audiences and have the same circulation areas. Advertising rates per column inch are: $7.00 in the morning paper and $10.50 in the evening paper. The morning paper has a circulation of 200,000 and the evening paper has a circulation of 250,000. Calculate and compare the milline rates of these two papers. Under what conditions might an advertiser use the paper with the higher milline rate?
21. A book publisher wants to insert a page of advertising in one of two monthly magazines, both of which are directed primarily to male audiences. The first magazine has a page rate of $6,500 and a circulation of 875,000, while the second has a page rate of $7,100 and a circulation of 1,140,000. Assuming that the audiences of both magazines are roughly comparable (i.e., from the standpoints of age, income, geographical location, etc.), which is the better buy? Under what conditions might the publisher decide to use the other magazine?
22. Western Pretzel Works, Inc., has retained an advertising agency to handle its advertising for the forthcoming year. Media expenditures are anticipated as follows:

		MEDIA COMMISSION
Consumer Magazines	$100,000	15%
Dealer Magazines	24,000	10
Newspapers	46,000	15
Outdoor Posters	6,000	16 2/3
Television	43,000	15
Total	$219,000	

Costs of art work, typography, and so on are estimated at $2,250, and the agency will bill the company for these items at cost plus 15 percent. Western Pretzel has a long-standing policy of taking all cash discounts and plans on paying invoices received from the agency within the cash discount period. The discount will amount to 2 percent of the net costs of space and time.

Assuming that the agency is to be compensated on the commission basis, what is:

a. the total amount Western Pretzel will pay the agency?
b. the total amount the agency will pay to all media and services?
c. the total amount the agency will receive as compensation?

CASE PROBLEM

Newton Packing Company is a medium-sized packer located in eastern Washington. For several years, annual sales have been approximately $5 million. Newton handles its own wholesaling of the fresh and smoked meat and meat products it processes. In addition, the company wholesales the products of other manufacturers not engaged in direct distribution in the territories covered by Newton. The company sells its products to independent retail meat markets and meat departments, to large chain grocery organizations, and to certain high-class restaurants and hotels. Newton salesmen cover territories in Washington, Oregon, Idaho, Montana, and northern California.

In the past, this company did not use an advertising agency, but recently arrangements have been made for a small Seattle agency to handle the company's account. The Newton advertising manager, working in cooperation with the account executive, has proposed the following advertising budget for the coming year:

Costs of artwork, typography, etc., and all overhead expenses		$ 16,000
Media Costs:		
Magazines	$42,000	
TV spot announcements	7,000	
Dealer cooperative advertising	14,000	
Dealer display materials	20,000	83,000
Reserve for Contingencies		1,000
		$100,000

a. As president of Newton Packing Company, what questions might you ask the advertising manager about this proposed budget? What further information might you ask for?
b. What further refinements in the method of presenting this budget should be made?
c. What method was used to determine the size of this advertising appropriation? What should be the relationship between past sales history, anticipated future sales, and the advertising budget?

PART SIX

PRICING

When you have mastered the contents of this chapter, you should be able to:

1. Discuss the various internal and environmental factors influencing pricing decisions.
2. Calculate break-even points, given the necessary data.
3. Analyze the relationship of costs and competition to pricing decisions.
4. Identify the main types of long-run pricing objectives.
5. Explain the three policy alternatives concerning pricing relative to the competition.
6. Differentiate between full-cost pricing and contribution pricing.
7. Define the following terms: one-price policy, variable-price policy, quantity discount, trade discount, F.O.B. pricing, delivered pricing, freight absorption.
8. Describe the policy decisions involved in pricing a product line.
9. Outline the reasons why certain marketers use or do not use: (a) resale price maintenance, (b) a guaranty against price decline.

CHAPTER 18

PRICING DECISIONS, OBJECTIVES, AND POLICIES

Prices

Without prices there can be no marketing. Products may be matched with markets, but only when buyers and sellers agree on *prices* do ownership transfers actually occur. Either a buyer or a seller may propose a price, but it does not become one until accepted by the other.

Generally, the seller, regarding pricing as a controllable, makes the offer and the buyer decides whether to accept it. Modern marketers, except in rare instances, enjoy a great deal of freedom in making pricing decisions of all kinds. This freedom comes from their success in manipulating other controllables (products, distribution, and promotion) so as to improve their ability to compete on a nonprice, rather than on a price, basis.[1] In other words, only when pricing is a controllable (made so by successful manipulation of other controllables) can a marketer compete on a nonprice basis. Nevertheless, in most marketing situations, pricing decisions, both individually and collectively, do influence the relative ease with which "ownership transfers" are effected. While pricing is not usually the most critical element in marketing, it is an essential element.

Discussion in this and the following chapter (all of Part Six) focuses on pricing's role as a controllable and its place in overall marketing strategy. This chapter covers (1) factors influencing pricing decisions, (2) long-run pricing objectives, and (3) price policies.

[1] See J. C. Udell, "How Important Is Pricing in Competitive Strategy?" *Journal of Marketing*, January 1964, pp. 44–48.

Factors Influencing Pricing Decisions

Many factors, both internal to the company and environmental, as Figure 18–1 indicates, influence pricing decisions. Among the internal factors are the company's objectives and desired public image, the other strategic components of overall marketing strategy (product-market, distribution, and promotional strategies), and costs. The

Figure 18–1 Factors influencing pricing decisions and relationship of pricing strategy to overall marketing strategy

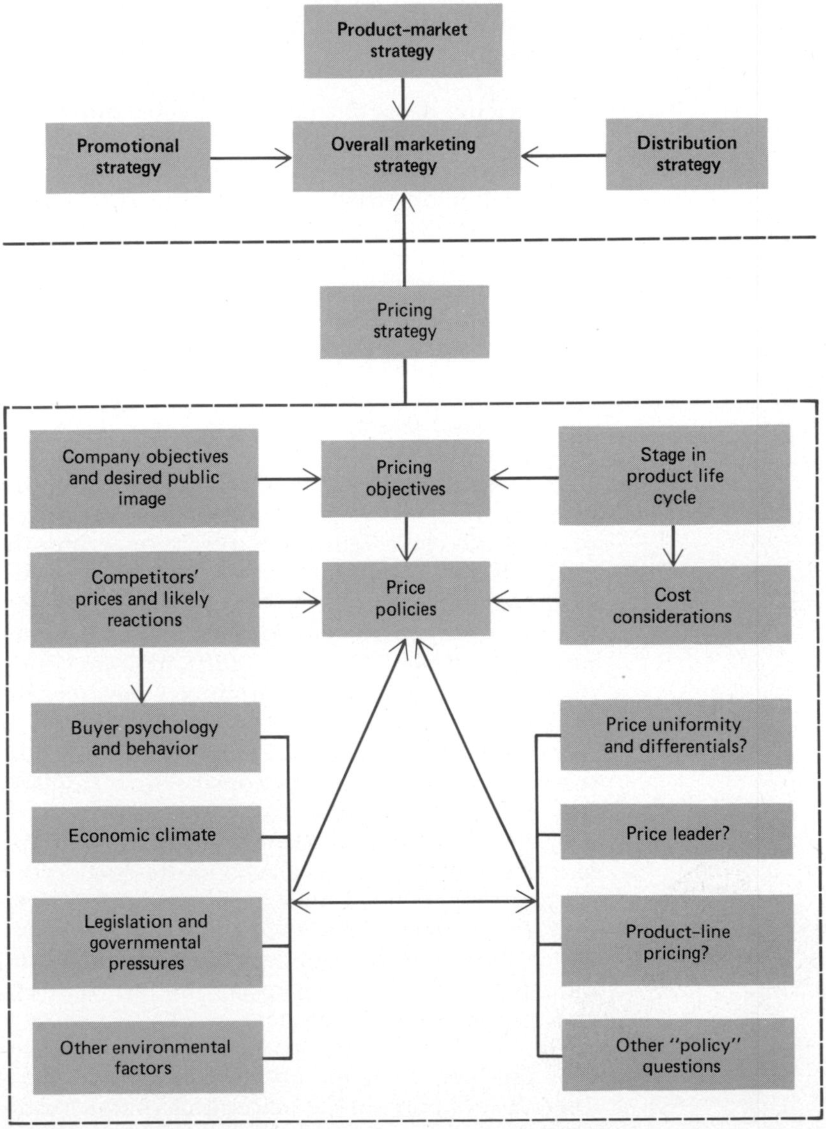

environmental factors, most of them "uncontrollables," include the competition, buyer psychology and behavior, economic climate, and legislation and governmental pressures. Interacting in complex ways, both the internal and environmental factors influence the setting of pricing objectives, the determination of price policies, and the formulation of pricing strategies. As you study this and the next chapter, you should find it helpful to refer frequently to this figure.

COMPANY OBJECTIVES AND DESIRED PUBLIC IMAGE

Pricing decisions must be consistent with company objectives and the desired public image. Unwise pricing can damage, or needlessly alter, a favorable image that has taken years to build. Therefore, pricing objectives should derive directly from company objectives (which, as a composite, reflect top management's vision of the kind of company it is trying to build). Similarly, price policies should be consistent with pricing objectives. And pricing strategies (i.e., the ways in which policies are implemented) should be in line with both price policies and pricing objectives.

PRODUCT-MARKET FACTORS

Stage in Product Life Cycle The amount of freedom management has in making pricing decisions varies with the stage in the product life cycle. During market pioneering, the innovator enjoys wide discretion ranging from setting the initial price very high to skim the market to setting it very low to achieve market penetration quickly. Competitors enter during the market growth stage, but nonprice competition prevails and, at first, individual companies (because of differentiated products) have considerable freedom in pricing. During later phases of market growth and early phases of market maturity, different competitors see opportunities to widen the market, and price reductions become key factors in securing further market expansions. Sometime during market maturity, however, the market approaches saturation and price reductions no longer expand sales, emphasis shifts from selling to new users to making replacement sales to present users, usually through introducing new models or using other forms of product differentiation, and prices stabilize. Finally, during market decline, sporadic price reductions occur as different companies clear out stocks and discontinue the product.

Product Differentiation Competing on a nonprice basis depends not only on the amount of product differentiation but also on its relative importance to prospective buyers. Customers who consider product differentiation important do not ignore price completely, but they are not likely to buy competing brands solely because of small price differences. A prospective new-car buyer with a strong preference for Chevrolet, for example, will not buy a Ford or a Plymouth because of a price difference unless it is substantial. Price is not unimportant to such buyers, and they may shop around among several Chevrolet dealers to get the best terms; but, in selecting the brand, they regard product differences as more important than price. The particular characteristics differentiating a brand may range from fashion and styling to quality and durability or product service. To the extent that members of target market segments regard such features and services as important, the marketing significance of price in attracting buyers is lessened and price becomes more of a controllable.

Price Elasticity

The Product's Price Elasticity of Demand *Price elasticity*—the relative sensitivity of a product's sales volume to changes in its price—varies widely among different products. Demand for fresh strawberries is price elastic, since a relatively small price change increases (or decreases) their sale considerably. Demand for coal is price inelastic, since a relatively small price change has little effect on the amount sold. These generalizations, of course, hold only within certain limits. A substantial increase in the price of coal, for instance, may cause buyers to switch to less expensive fuels or to conserve fuel.

When a product has a price inelastic demand, its marketer has little incentive to cut the price, since sales revenue per unit of product decreases more rapidly than unit sales increase. The marketer is much more tempted to raise it, as sales revenue per unit of product increases faster than unit sales decline. However, the availability and prices of substitute products limit the profitability of any sizable price increase.

When a product's demand is price elastic, pricing decisions are generally no less difficult. Unless a company has no strong competitors at all (a very rare situation except during market pioneering), it cannot hope to take business permanently away from competitors through a price reduction, since they can and probably will quickly match or better it. Price reductions in such cases are profitable to individual companies only if they expand the industry's total sales so that the increase in the quantity the industry sells more than offsets the loss of sales revenue per unit. And, if close substitutes exist, declines in their prices may cancel out or reduce anticipated sales increases. Price increases are no more attractive unless competitors follow; but even if they do go along, availability and prices of substitute products limit the profitability of any sizable price increase.

Other Product-Market Characteristics Other characteristics of a product's market may affect pricing decisions. The size of the potential market makes a considerable difference: if a marketer can anticipate a large sales volume, it can realize substantial economies in physical distribution and promotion, thus reducing total marketing costs, and it may use an accordingly low price to improve the chances of attaining that sales volume. The relative density of the potential market (i.e., the degree of concentration of possible buyers) also affects marketing costs and, consequently, offering prices. Any factor that may change marketing costs affects pricing, since it shifts the level at which the price can be set and still be profitable.

DISTRIBUTION STRATEGY

Distribution strategy influences pricing decisions. Specifically, the producer's pricing decisions must take into account the size of the gross margins middlemen expect. Such expectations reflect individual middlemen's costs and their profit objectives as well as the scope and importance of the activities each is to perform for the manufacturer. In fact, each middleman's costs and the services it performs are related; that is, services involve costs. A wholesaler carrying an inventory and handling repairs, for instance, has higher costs and expects more gross margin than one who neither carries an inventory nor handles repairs. If the channel includes more than one level of middleman, the gross margin requirements and services performed by each level need considering.

Similarly, if the marketer follows an exclusive or highly selective distribution policy, there are implications for pricing. Companies having such policies generally expect dealers to provide additional services, such as local advertising and product service. Dealers, in turn, expect larger margins. The manufacturer using mass distribution bears such costs himself; consequently, its dealers obtain lower gross margins on the product.

PROMOTIONAL STRATEGY

Promotional strategy affects pricing decisions. If a manufacturer, for example, uses massive advertising to "pull the product through the channel," it will probably allow middlemen somewhat less than normal gross margins. If it expects them to assume some of the advertising burden, they will expect greater than normal gross margins. If the manufacturer minimizes its use of advertising and other promotion, it may then offer middlemen lower prices (and higher gross margins) to get them to provide needed promotional support.

COSTS

The extent to which costs can or should enter into pricing decisions varies. Over the long run, sales revenues (i.e., prices × unit volumes) must be sufficient to recover all costs. But short-run prices do not necessarily have to cover all short-run costs.

Nature of Cost Data Cost figures are often not as accurate as they appear on the surface. Although costs are expressed in exact dollar amounts, their computation requires many subjective judgments. Production cost accounting involves numerous arbitrary allocations of overhead costs to arrive at unit cost. Marketing cost accounting requires even more arbitrary allocations.

Furthermore, cost data adequate for accounting purposes are often not suited for pricing decisions. Accountants work mostly with historical costs and are mainly concerned with controlling current operating costs. Pricing decisions are more closely related to future costs than to either present or past costs. Thus, pricing decision makers are more interested in estimated than in known costs.

Estimating production costs accurately is particularly difficult for joint-cost products. A manufacturer making several products in the same plant, often on the same machinery, may find it impossible to allocate total costs among them except on a wholly arbitrary basis. The unreliability of the resulting cost data often leads to pricing individual products according to "what the traffic will bear," using cost data only as a general guide to ensure that total sales revenue on all products is enough to cover total costs.

Cost Concepts The two cost concepts most relevant to pricing decisions are *fixed costs* and *variable costs*. Fixed costs, often called "overhead costs," do not vary with the amount of sales and include salaries, rent, heat, light, depreciation, property taxes, bond interest, and the like. By contrast, variable costs vary somewhat automatically with the amount of sales and include such costs as raw materials, labor paid on a piece rate or hourly basis, salesmen's commissions, and packaging, packing, warehousing usage, and shipping.

Fixed Costs

Variable Costs

Break-Even Computations Because the interrelationship of costs and sales volume determines the amount of profit (or loss), break-even analysis helps in estimating the effects of different prices on profits.[2] Figure 18–2 is a typical break-even chart. Notice that the break-even point occurs where total costs equal total sales revenue, indicating that this is the number of units of product which must be sold at a particular price for the seller to barely cover its total costs. If sales volume goes beyond this point, each additional unit sold brings in some profit; each sale before reaching this point is at a loss.

[2] Break-even analysis also helps in evaluating the likely effects on profits of various alternative solutions to many other marketing problems. It can be used, for example, to show the effects on profits of altering the amounts invested in advertising, of changing the sales compensation method, of adding a new product, or of changing a marketing channel. Break-even analysis helps in analyzing any marketing problem in which alternative solutions differ as to their impact on costs and/or sales volume.

Figure 18–2
Typical break-even chart

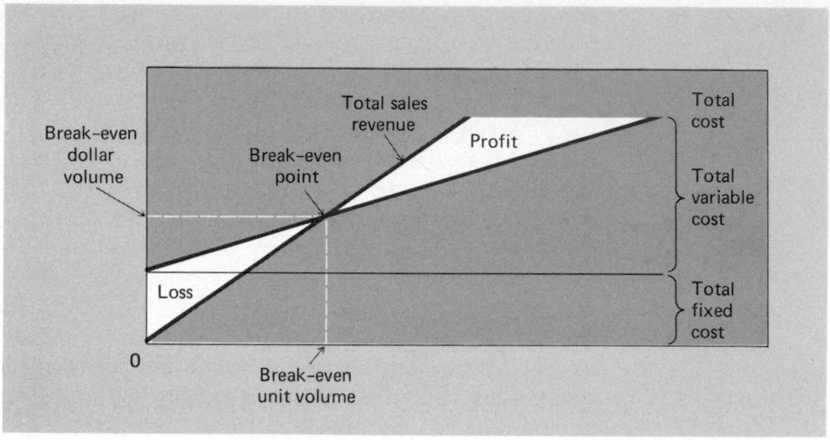

If we want to determine the break-even point mathematically, rather than graphically, there are three steps: First, compute total *fixed costs for the operating period* (at a predetermined volume of output) and *variable costs per unit* (calculated by dividing total variable cost by the number of units made or sold. Second, compute the *unit contribution to fixed costs* as follows:

Unit Contribution

$$\text{Unit Contribution to Fixed Costs} = \text{Selling Price per unit} \text{ minus } \text{Variable Costs per unit}$$

Break-Even Point

SKIP

Third, compute the *break-even point* itself—that is, the total number of units which must be sold to cover total fixed costs—as follows:

$$\text{Break-Even Point (in units)} = \frac{\text{Total Fixed Costs}}{\text{Unit Contribution to Fixed Costs}}$$

Then if we multiply *break-even unit volume* by the *selling price per unit*, we determine the dollar sales volume needed to reach the break-even point.

To illustrate, suppose a marketer has total annual fixed costs of \$40,000, variable costs per unit of \$1.50, and is thinking of pricing its product (assume it has only one product) at \$3.50 each. Unit contribution to fixed costs is \$3.50 minus \$1.50, or \$2.00 per unit, and break-even unit volume is:

$$\frac{\text{Total Fixed Costs}}{\text{Unit Contribution}} = \frac{\$40{,}000}{\$2} = 20{,}000 \text{ units}$$

To obtain the break-even volume in dollars, multiply break-even unit volume (20,000 units) by selling price (\$3.50), which yields \$70,000. To check this, add total fixed costs (\$40,000) to variable costs per unit multiplied by break-even unit volume ($1.5 × 20,000 or $30,000), which means that total dollar costs are also $70,000. At the break-even point, total costs equal total sales dollars.

Suppose, now, that the marketer wants to determine the different effects on the break-even point of pricing its product at $3.00 and $4.00. At the lower $3.00 price, break-even unit volume rises to 26,666+ units; at the higher $4.00 price, break-even unit volume falls to 16,000 units. The marketer, in deciding which of the three prices to use, would then go on to determine the chances of exceeding each break-even unit volume and by how much, compute the total sales revenues expected under each price, deduct the total costs involved, and compare the resulting estimated profits.

Thus, in using break-even analysis in pricing decisions, it is not enough to compute only the different break-even points. The effect of each alternative price on demand must also be considered. Furthermore, in many cases changes occur in fixed costs and unit variable costs at different output levels, requiring adjustments in break-even computations. The seller, in other words, is more interested in the amount of profit it can expect at different sales levels than it is in break-even points as such. Prices, sales volume, and costs all have effects on profits.

COMPETITORS' PRICES AND LIKELY REACTIONS

While most modern marketers seek to compete on a nonprice basis to the utmost extent, they cannot entirely ignore competitors' prices. Nonprice competition may enable a marketer to gain partial control over a market segment as, for example, through product differentiation or selective distribution. This may enable the marketer to obtain higher prices than competitors, but when their prices change, it must keep its own prices generally in line; otherwise, its control over the particular market segment gradually slips away.

Furthermore, in making price changes, a marketer must consider competitors' likely reactions. Will they follow a price rise? A price cut? How soon? A price change is the easiest switch in marketing strategy to copy, and copying can be almost instantaneous. That, perhaps, is why most marketers prefer nonprice competition—product, distribution, and promotion changes are neither easy to copy nor can they be followed quickly. The first competitor making a profitable nonprice move gains more than a temporary advantage.

BUYER PSYCHOLOGY AND BEHAVIOR

The effectiveness of relative price as a factor in making sales varies with buyer psychology and behavior. Buyers shopping for high fashion items often regard their prices as of secondary importance and frequently are more interested in buying quality or prestige. In shopping for a dress to wear on a special occasion, for example, a woman may regard price—within limits, of course—as much less important than cut or styling. Similarly, in industrial marketing, buyers of machine tools give first consideration to such product attributes as quality and durability, price usually being important only in choosing from among two or more comparable makes of tools. Moreover, the relative prestige of certain products in the consumer goods field varies directly with their prices; for instance, many buyers of prestige automobiles, such as the Continental, buy mainly because others will know they paid a high price. However, low price is a very important aid in selling products which are difficult to differentiate (e.g., sugar, gasoline, and certain industrial raw materials), and a price even slightly below competitors' may result in large increases in sales volume.

The frequency with which the typical buyer purchases a product also influences pricing decisions. Products which ultimate consumers buy very frequently, for instance, are sold profitably by middlemen at low markups because of fast inventory turnover. When sales are high relative to inventory investment, a small profit per sale returns a large annual profit. High turnover products, such as most grocery items, are profitably retailed at 15 to 20 percent markups, whereas slow turnover products require higher retail markups—hardware, for instance, carries a 35 to 40 percent retail markup.

The quantity of a product usually bought at one time by a typical buyer may affect offering prices. The larger the quantity bought at a time, generally the lower the marketing cost is per unit. Thus, for instance, it usually costs a retailer very little more to sell six of an item than to sell one, so cost savings make possible profitable price reductions for quantity purchases. Purchases in larger quantities tend to increase the buyer's total consumption because the item's increased availability often causes him or her to use more.

The relative bargaining power of potential buyers influences pricing decisions. A marketer of a consumer product, for instance, may be "bargained into" giving special low prices to large buyers, such as corporate chains, in order to get them to handle its product at all. Similarly, marketers of industrial products often must make price concessions to large customers in order to gain, or retain, their patronage. However, the giving in to buyers' demands for special prices is limited in the United States by legislation outlawing price discrimination among like buyers (see Chapter 20).

ECONOMIC CLIMATE

Administered Prices

Because of the stickiness of *administered prices* (i.e., ones set by management and held stable for a time), the company emphasizing nonprice competition tends to adjust slowly to changing economic conditions. Slowness in changing administered prices causes delays in price reductions at the beginning of a recession, causes inventories to build up to abnormally high levels, and necessitates even larger price cuts later on. Similarly, during periods of rapidly rising costs, which are often characteristic of business upturns, increases in administered prices lag behind the need, resulting in cost-price squeezes. Therefore, the company emphasizing nonprice competition should be alert to impending economic changes and make needed and timely price adjustments.

LEGISLATION AND GOVERNMENTAL PRESSURES

Practically every country has legislation that influences pricing alternatives. In the United States, for instance, at the federal level, the Clayton Act, as amended by the Robinson-Patman Act, prohibits several pricing practices that discriminate among like buyers: cumulative quantity discounts, noncumulative quantity discounts in excess of actual cost savings, "dummy" brokerage payments, and discriminatory promotional allowances. At the state level, some states have Unfair Trade Practices Acts prohibiting sales at prices below costs (or cost plus some designated markup). However, most states have also broadened pricing alternatives through passage of Fair Trade Laws that modify specific legal prohibitions against price fixing to allow a manufacturer to set the minimum price at which dealers may resell its product.

The possibility that governmental pressures will be brought to bear is a factor that decision makers, particularly in basic industries where price increases might be regarded as inflationary, should consider. In industries whose members produce less basic and more differentiated products, the likelihood of governmental intervention is more remote but still possible. In fact, governmental intervention in pricing decisions is likely to become increasingly frequent and more influential in the future, especially during inflationary periods.

Pricing Objectives

Long-run pricing objectives should derive directly from company objectives. They also should provide guidance to decision makers in determining price policies, formulating pricing strategies, and setting actual prices. Probably, most companies have profit as a main pricing objective.

It is not at all clear, however, that profit maximization is the main objective. Occasionally, a company "charges what the traffic will bear"—this may be short-run profit maximization but it is not usually the way to maximize long-run profit. Most experts suggest, in fact, that companies should deliberately refrain from maximizing short-run profits in order to maximize them in the long run. But it is impossible to prove that a short-run pricing strategy actually leads to maximum long-run profits. We agree with a writer who concludes, "Long-run profit maximizing is elusive and perhaps unmeasurable."[3]

Profit maximization, then, is more an ideal than a usable pricing objective. Recognizing the elusiveness of profit maximization, realistic decision makers focus on other long-run pricing objectives related, in one way or another, to securing, if not the maximum, at least a satisfactory long-run profit. One study of twenty large corporations found that the most typical long-run pricing objectives were (1) to achieve a target return on investment, (2) to stabilize prices, (3) to hold or obtain a target market share, and (4) to meet or keep out competition.[4]

TARGET RETURN PRICING OBJECTIVES

Return on Investment (ROI)

Many companies have pricing objectives aimed to achieve either a certain target return on investment (*ROI*), or a certain return on net sales, or simply some targeted dollar profit.

Target ROI In working toward a target ROI objective, pricing decisions are made so that total sales revenues will exceed total costs by enough to provide the desired rate of return on the total investment. Since the objective is to secure the targeted return on the total investment, pricing decisions for specific products, groups of products, or company divisions need not be individually designed to produce precisely the specified ROI; rather, the objective is for the company's entire operations to earn, on the average, the specified ROI. Additionally, "on the average" means *standard sales volume*—that is, the average sales level experienced over several years' operations. ROI pricing objectives are more common among manufacturers than middlemen and among large companies than small ones.

Standard Sales Volume

Target Return on Sales Many middlemen set their pricing objectives as a targeted return on sales, stated as some percentage of dollar sales. Then they price their inventories with sufficiently high markups so that sales revenues will cover total costs and yield a desired profit on the year's operations. Various items in the inventory will carry different markups—some will be priced to return more than the targeted return, some less.

Targeted Dollar Profit In many small businesses, particularly small manufacturers, the pricing objective is a targeted amount of

[3] R. A. Lynn, *Price Policies and Marketing Management* (Homewood, Ill.: Richard D. Irwin, Inc., 1967), p. 99.

[4] See R. F. Lanzillotti, "Pricing Objectives in Large Companies," *American Economic Review*, December 1958, pp. 921–940.

dollar profit. Typically, such companies are managed by their owners, who simply want to earn a good living. Consequently, they set prices to return that dollar profit which represents in their minds "a good living."

PRICE STABILIZATION AS AN OBJECTIVE

Some companies seek to keep their prices relatively stable over long periods, hoping to even out, possibly even to eliminate, cyclical price fluctuations. During periods of depressed business, they work to keep prices from falling too far; during periods of good business, partially perhaps out of a sense of social responsibility, they try to keep prices from rising to "what the traffic will bear." A price stabilization objective is often paired with a target ROI objective, both are typically long-run pricing objectives.

Price stabilization is also an important pricing objective in other situations. Marketers of products vulnerable to price wars, such as tires and gasoline, regard price stabilization as highly desirable. Companies promoting their products through national advertising in which prices are featured also attach considerable importance to price stabilization. Fairly often, such companies resort to Resale Price

Fair Trade Laws

Maintenance (*fair trade*) laws in efforts to stabilize prices. More frequently, they simply suggest resale prices to their middlemen.

TARGET MARKET SHARE AS A PRICING OBJECTIVE

Pricing products to obtain a target market share is nearly as common as target ROI pricing. A dominant company in an industry may set a target market share pricing objective defensively—that is, to emphasize the importance of holding the market share it already has, or to restrain itself from becoming too dominant in the industry (which might increase its vulnerability to antitrust prosecution). Smaller and younger companies set target market share pricing objectives offensively—that is, to establish benchmarks for their growth in the industry. Some giant retailers, such as Sear, Roebuck and A & P, also have aggressive target market share objectives, generally trying to increase their market share both geographically and for individual product lines.

MEETING OR KEEPING OUT COMPETITION AS A PRICING OBJECTIVE

In certain industries, meeting or keeping out competition is an important pricing objective. If a company is its industry's price leader, for instance, it may set prices designed to discourage new competitors from entering the market. Similarly, companies that are price followers set their prices in order to meet competitors' prices, including those of the price leader. The meeting-competition pricing objective often is used with the target market share objective—thus, a company working to retain a given target market share might have to meet competitors' price cuts in order to hold that share.

Price Policies

Price Policies

Price policies constitute the general framework within which management makes pricing decisions. Thus, they provide the guidelines within which management formulates and carries out pricing strategy. Although price policies should be reviewed continually, they form an important part of the company's image and should be changed only infrequently. Each company needs a "bundle" of price policies appropriate not only to company and pricing objectives but to its overall marketing situation.

PRICING RELATIVE TO COMPETITION

Every company adheres to some policy, either explicitly or implicitly, regarding the prices of its products relative to those of competitors. If competition is mainly on a price basis, then each company generally prices its products at the same level as its competitors. If there is nonprice competition, each marketer chooses from among the three alternatives discussed below.

Meeting Competition This is the alternative usually chosen. Marketers competing on a nonprice basis simply meet competitors' prices, hoping thereby to minimize the use of price as a competitive weapon. A "meeting competition" price policy does not mean meeting every competitor's prices, but only the prices of important competitors—important in the sense that what such competitors do in their pricing may lure customers away.

Pricing Above the Competition This is a less common policy but appropriate in certain circumstances. Sometimes higher-than-average prices convey an impression of above-average product quality or prestige. Many buyers relate a product's price to its quality, especially when it is difficult to judge quality before actually buying. In these instances, buyers may pay a little more for an item whose higher price implies higher quality.[5]

[5] For some excellent analyses of the price-quality relationship, see Benson P. Shapiro, "Price Reliance: Existence and Sources," *Journal of Marketing Research*, August 1973, pp. 286–294; Kent B. Monroe, "Buyers' Subjective Perceptions of Price," *Journal of Marketing Research*, February 1973, pp. 70–80; David M. Gardner, "An Experimental Investigation of the Price/Quality Relationship," *Journal of Retailing*, Fall 1970, pp. 25–41; and Zarrel V. Lambert, "Product Perception: An Important Variable in Pricing Strategy," *Journal of Marketing*, October 1970, pp. 68–71.

Sometimes, too, a manufacturer suggests higher-then-average resale prices in the hope of improving middlemen's cooperation. If the manufacturer wants middlemen to exert especially aggressive selling and promotional efforts, it may set relatively high "list" prices at which it suggests they resell the product to secure above-average markups. The higher markups are passed on to final buyers in the form of higher prices, but the increased cooperation of the middlemen may more than offset the sales-depressing tendency of the higher prices and may even increase total sales. Generally, for a product to compete successfully at a price above the market, it must either be so strongly differentiated that buyers believe it superior to competitive brands or middlemen must enthusiastically and heavily promote it.

Pricing Under the Competition Many firms price under the market. Some have lower costs because their products are of lower quality. Others substitute lower prices for the promotional efforts (which also cost money) of their competitors. In all cases, marketers following this policy must either have very low costs or be willing to accept a very low profit per unit of product sold.

PRICING RELATIVE TO COSTS

Every company also has a policy regarding the relationships it should seek to maintain between its products' prices and the underlying costs. Long-run sales revenues must cover all long-run costs but short-run prices do not necessarily have to cover all short-run costs. Thus, management needs some policy to guide short-run pricing decisions toward attainment of long-run pricing objectives. There are two main alternatives.

Full-Cost Pricing

Full-Cost Pricing Under this policy, no sale is made at a price lower than that covering total costs including both variable costs and an allocated share of fixed costs. The reasoning is that if prices cover short-run costs, they will also cover long-run costs. Nevertheless, rigid adherence to this policy is not only difficult but often downright stupid: the price buyers are willing to pay may bear little or no relationship to the seller's costs, and there are complex problems involved in determining real costs. Furthermore, prices on items already on hand oftentimes must be cut below full cost in order to sell at all. While most businesses should try to keep prices above short-run costs in most situations, they should also permit below-cost prices when necessary. A full-cost pricing policy should be regarded only as a flexible guide to decision making.

Contribution Pricing

Contribution Pricing A company with a contribution pricing policy uses full-cost pricing whenever possible but will price, under

Incremental Costs

certain conditions, at any level above the relevant *incremental costs.*[6] Suppose, for example, a seller is offered a special contract to supply a large buyer, who will not pay the going price. The buyer may argue that the price differential is justified because of savings to the seller in selling time, credit costs, handling expenses, and the like. Still, the demanded price concession may exceed the likely savings, so that total income from the proposed transaction is not enough to cover total costs. Emphasizing the short-run aspects, most economists would advise the marketer to accept the order if the resulting revenues were large enough not only to cover all incremental costs but to make some contribution to fixed costs and/or profits. After all, current sales at established prices may already be large enough to cover the fixed costs, and the proposed sale at a special price will not raise fixed costs (assuming the incremental costs are all variable costs) so this sale need not bear an allocated share of fixed costs to yield net revenue. In other words, the argument is that so long as the proposed price more than covers the out-of-pocket costs of the transaction, then the excess over these costs represents profit.

Economists, however, often do not clarify all the conditions under which they make this recommendation. The major purpose of a contribution pricing policy, then, is to specify the conditions under which offers at prices under full cost will be considered. Two important conditions should both be present for such offers to be accepted: (1) the company has the capacity and can put it to no more profitable use, and (2) the portion of the output sold below full cost is destined for a different market segment. Both conditions are important but the second is critical to the continuance of prices at full cost or above for the bulk of the output.

UNIFORMITY OF PRICES TO DIFFERENT BUYERS

Every marketer should have a policy outlining the conditions under which it will charge different buyers identical prices and those under which it will allow price differentials. A contribution pricing policy, as just explained, details one set of conditions under which it might charge differential prices. But the question of uniformity of offering prices also arises in other circumstances.

One-Price Policy

One-Price vs. Variable-Price Policy Generally, marketers prefer to sell on a one-price basis—that is, by offering all like buyers exactly the same price. In the United States, the one-price policy is used in selling most consumer products and many industrial prod-

[6] Incremental costs are those incurred in changing the level or nature of an activity—for example, making and/or selling a larger quantity of a product, entering a new market, or switching or adding marketing channels. Incremental costs may be either variable or some combination of variable and fixed costs. You should recognize, however, that both variable and incremental costs are added costs.

ucts. Elsewhere, especially in the developing countries, sellers commonly use variable pricing even for most consumer items.

Sellers regard the one-price policy as attractive for three reasons: (1) it provides a uniform return from each sale, simplifying the forecasting of profits; (2) selling costs are lower, since prices are not negotiated with individual customers; and (3) there is less risk of alienating customers because of preferential prices given others.

Variable-Price Policy

Variable pricing, however, is common where individual sales are large. It is hardly worth a consumer's or retailer's time to bargain over the price of a pound of coffee, and the loss of an individual sale is not important enough to a retailer to cause it to reconsider its price. But, in buying an auto, many consumers will exert considerable effort to obtain a lower price, and the sale is important enough to the dealer for it to hesitate to lose a sale because of a few dollars.

The bargaining power of individual buyers varies with the transaction size. In the industrial market, a large buyer generally represents a greater potential for future business than a small buyer so a seller may make concessions to gain or retain the large buyer's patronage. In addition, some buyers have greater bargaining power because of their ability to pay cash. For these reasons, negotiated pricing (under variable price policies) exists in many industrial markets and even in some consumer markets. Reluctant as many sellers of consumer durables are to admit that their prices are not fixed, very often they hold to one price and negotiate on the value of "trade-ins" instead.

PRICE DIFFERENTIALS

Most marketers vary their prices under certain conditions even though they generally adhere to one-price policies. Price differentials may be based on size of purchase, type of customer, or buyers' geographical locations. Normally, the marketer using these kinds of price differentials extends them to all buyers meeting the specified requirements.

Quantity Discounts

Quantity Discounts Granting price reductions on large purchases is common. Through such reductions, called quantity discounts, sellers try to increase sales by passing on to buyers part of the savings resulting from large purchases. These can be substantial savings for it may take little, if any, more of a salesman's time to sell a very large order than a small one. And the same holds for order-processing, order-filling, billing, and transportation costs (because quantity rates are offered by carriers).

Firms using quantity discounts in the United States must keep two legal restrictions in mind (both included in the Clayton Act): (1) the price reduction can be no greater than the actual savings resulting from the larger quantity order, and (2) discounts must be made available on proportionately equal terms to all like purchasers.

Within these restrictions, quantity discounts provide a possible way to reduce marketing costs and increase sales volume.

Trade Discounts

Trade Discounts A marketer often sells the same product to different classes of buyers. A paper manufacturer, for instance, sells typing paper to wholesalers, to retail chains, and to businesses buying for their own use. Some buyers in each class buy approximately equal quantities on each order, and one might expect the manufacturer to sell at the same price. But other conditions may cause the manufacturer to offer different "trade discounts" from the list price to each class of buyer. Assume it makes 70 percent of its sales through wholesalers: this marketing channel is essential to its success, and it hesitates to do anything that might antagonize or threaten the existence of its wholesalers and the retailers they serve. If the manufacturer gives a corporate chain the same price it gives wholesalers, its outlets may underprice their independent retailer competitors served by the wholesalers. For this reason, some manufacturers extend lower prices to wholesalers than to even very large retail chains regardless of the amounts purchased.

Cash Discounts
Special Promotional Discounts
Seasonal Discounts

Other Types of Discounts Many marketers grant other types of discounts. Some give *cash discounts* for prompt payments by buyers. Others allow *special promotional discounts* to middlemen providing local advertising or other promotional support, though generally such discounts are not offered continuously but periodically, as for a few weeks during the spring and fall. Still others use *seasonal discounts* to persuade buyers to place their orders in advance of the normal buying season.

GEOGRAPHICAL PRICE DIFFERENTIALS

The policy a marketer adopts with respect to who should pay the freight has a direct bearing upon its price quotations to buyers in different geographical locations. In general, the farther away the customer is from the factory, the higher the freight charge is for a given size of shipment. There are three major policy alternatives: (1) "F.O.B." or "free on board" pricing, (2) delivered pricing, and (3) "freight absorption."

F.O.B. Pricing

F.O.B. Pricing The marketer using this policy quotes its selling prices at the factory (or other point from which it makes sales), and buyers pay all the freight charges. Thus, buyers in different places have different "landed costs"—each pays the price at the selling point, plus the freight from there to its location, thus determining its total costs for the delivered shipment. Variations result not only in buyers' costs but in resale prices of the product in different parts of the country. This prevents the marketer from advertising the resale price nationally except in a general way, such as "Priced at $19.95—prices at your local dealer may vary slightly." The main attraction of F.O.B. pricing for the manufacturer is that it simplifies price quotations to those with whom it deals directly.

Delivered Pricing

Delivered Pricing The marketer using this policy pays all freight charges but, of course, builds them into its price quotations. In effect, it averages total freight charges for all customers and incorporates some amount, which may or may not be the exact average, into the price quoted. Prices quoted buyers are really F.O.B. destination prices—and the marketer's net return varies with the buyer's location. Delivered pricing is most appropriate when freight charges account for only a small part of the product's selling price or when a marketer attempts to maintain resale prices or to advertise them nationally. Standardized resale prices are most likely to be obtained when the marketer assures middlemen of uniform markups regardless of their locations.

Freight Absorption

Freight Absorption Some marketers use a freight absorption policy to counter stiff price competition from sellers located closer to prospective buyers. Generally, this policy takes the form of quoting a price to the buyer that is the usual F.O.B. factory price plus an amount equal to that which the competitive marketer located nearest to the customer would charge. Thus, freight absorption pricing is often adopted to lessen the competitive disadvantages of F.O.B. pricing, especially where strong locally based competition is met in certain markets.

POLICY ON PRICE LEADERSHIP

Price Leadership

All marketers should decide whether, as a matter of policy, they will initiate or follow price changes. In some industries there are well-established patterns of price leadership and following. In selling basic industrial materials, such as steel and cement, one company is the price leader and is usually the first to raise or cut prices; other industry members simply follow—or, sometimes, fail to follow, as fairly often happens with price increases, thus causing the leader to reconsider and perhaps to cancel the announced increase. Similar patterns exist in marketing such consumer products as gasoline and bakery goods where, usually in each market area, one company serves as the price leader while others follow. Generally, price leaders have rather large market shares and price followers small market shares.

Even when final buyers are not particularly price conscious, most producers know that the middlemen handling their products are extremely sensitive to price changes. In response to even very small price changes, up or down, they will consider switching suppliers. Thus, even the marketer of a consumer product competing on a nonprice basis must be alert to impending price changes—the important policy question is whether to initiate or simply to follow price changes. The answer depends largely upon the marketer's relative market position and the image of leadership it desires to build.

PRODUCT LINE PRICING POLICY

Price Space

Pricing the individual members of a product line calls for certain policy decisions. The different items in a product line tend to compete with each other—that is, a buyer who wants one member of the line usually does so to the exclusion of others. One policy decision concerns the amount of *price space* that should exist between the prices of individual members of the line. Having the proper amount of price space is critical—too little may confuse buyers and too much may leave gaps into which competitors can move and make sales. Determining the proper amount of price space requires thorough knowledge of the market, of buyers' motivations, and of competitors' offerings and prices.

Other important policy decisions concern the pricing of the top (highest-priced item) and the bottom (lowest-priced item) of the line. Generally, companies try to price the in-between members of the line so that they account for the greatest sales volume, using the bottom of the line as a traffic-builder and the top of the line as a prestige-builder. As the traffic-builder, the lowest-priced item ordinarily affects the line's total sales far more than the price of any other item in the line—thus, price changes on it often have a magnifying effect on sales of other line members. As the prestige-builder, a change in the price of the top of the line also tends to strongly influence sales of other line members.

OTHER POLICY QUESTIONS

Resale Price Maintenance

Resale Price Maintenance Some manufacturers wish to control the resale prices at which middlemen sell their products. *Resale price maintenance* may be either informal or formal. The informal type involves suggesting prices to middlemen—perhaps by printing the price on the package or through suggestions by the manufacturer's salesmen. The formal type is effected by taking advantage of the various states' so-called "fair trade" laws.[7]

Manufacturers adopt resale price maintenance policies for various reasons. One wants to establish a customary resale price for its product, a price that consumers can become familiar with, one that

[7]It is possible that by the time this book goes to press Congress will have repealed the McGuire Act (the enabling legislation that makes the state fair trade laws legal). There seems to be little organized opposition to a strongly supported move for repeal. In any case, two more such laws were repealed at the state level during 1974.

they can normally expect to pay; without some control, resale prices among different retailers may vary considerably. Another wants to prevent its products from being used as price leaders, so it controls resale prices to protect its dealers from the competition of price cutters. Still another maintains its products' resale prices because it believes that they bear on consumers' evaluations of the products' quality.

Most manufacturers, however, do not have resale price maintenance policies. One large group is not bothered by resale price differentials on their products and actually welcomes any pricing action by resellers that increases sales. Another large group recognizes that a price maintenance policy is difficult to administer and enforce, particularly when marketing channels are long and/or the product is mass distributed. In addition, in states without fair trade laws, manufacturers can only suggest, not enforce, resale prices.

Guarantees Against Price Decline

Guaranty Against Price Decline Some marketers, whose products are subject to frequent price fluctuations, have policies guaranteeing the stability of the price for a specified period after the sale. Sugar refiners and coffee roasters, for instance, often grant *guarantees against price declines* to their middlemen because their selling prices tend to parallel price fluctuations in the sugar and coffee commodity markets. Buyers' fears, therefore, that they are buying at the wrong time are alleviated by the manufacturer's promise to refund an amount equal to the price change on all unsold stock left in buyers' hands.

Policy on Using Pricing as a Promotional Device Some companies have formal policies concerning the extent to which they will use pricing as a promotional device. Many follow a policy of temporarily reducing prices for promotional purposes under certain conditions, such as in introducing a new product, or to counter the effects of competitors' increases in promotional activity. Others, as a policy matter, refrain from such temporary price reductions, relying instead upon increased advertising and other promotion.

Summary

You should now know and understand the many factors influencing pricing decisions, the various pricing objectives, and the different kinds of price policies. Most marketers enjoy considerable freedom in pricing, yet in making nearly all pricing decisions management must consider numerous and varied internal and environmental factors. Management must make certain that its pricing decisions are consistent with the company's objectives and image and, in addition, it must take into account such factors as the other strategic components of the marketing program (product-market, distribution, and promotion), costs, the competition, buyer psychology and behavior, the economic climate, and legislation and governmental pressures.

Pricing objectives should derive directly from company objectives. But the general elusiveness of the profit maximization objective forces management to set other pricing objectives related to securing, if not the maximum, at least satisfactory long-run profits. These include such objectives as achieving a target return on investment or sales, stabilizing prices, holding or obtaining a target market share, and meeting or keeping out competition.

Price policies, collectively making up the framework within which management makes pricing decisions, should be consistent with, and contribute to the achievement of, pricing and company objectives. Accordingly, marketers need price policies for such matters as company prices relative to the competition, the relationships of prices to costs, uniformity of prices to different buyers, use of price differentials, price leadership (or followership), product line pricing, resale price maintenance, guaranteeing buyers against price declines, and the use of pricing as a promotional device.

You should once again—before leaving this chapter—review Figure 18–1, making certain that you understand the significance of all the elements in the various "boxes" and the "arrows" connecting them. When you are certain that you have this understanding, you are prepared to move on to the next chapter, Pricing Strategies and Procedures.

QUESTIONS AND PROBLEMS

1. Which of the following would generally regard pricing as an uncontrollable rather than a controllable? State your reasoning in each instance.
   a. a bicycle manufacturer
   b. a cattle farmer
   c. an electrical utility
   d. a commercial photographer
   e. a taxi operator
   f. a newspaper publisher
   g. a strawberry grower
   h. a lumber mill
2. Explain how an administered price differs from a market price.
3. Illustrate how a marketer might go about manipulating other marketing controllables in ways that would improve its ability to compete on a nonprice basis.
4. If pricing is usually a marketing controllable, why is it that the marketing manager so rarely has full authority over pricing?

5. During which stage of the product life cycle does management have the most discretion in making pricing decisions? The least discretion?
6. Suppose a seller of fireplace wood can sell 50 cords at $20 and 75 cords at $15. Is the demand for fireplace wood price elastic or inelastic?
7. "Since price elasticity of demand applies to industries rather than to the products of individual firms, price elasticity should not be a factor in the pricing decisions of individual firms." Agree or disagree?
8. What "tradeoffs" exist between:
   a. the nature of a product and its price?
   b. marketing channels and price?
   c. promotional strategy and price?
9. Why are marketers generally much more reluctant to use price than promotion as a competitive weapon?
10. How are variable costs and incremental costs different? How are they similar?
11. The problem of finding the optimum combination of product, marketing channels, promotion, and price is extremely complex. Explain how, for purposes of planning short-run operations, it is possible to simplify this problem.
12. "The existence of administered prices tends to increase the economic impact of fluctuations in price levels." Do you agree? Why?
13. "The larger a company is, the more vulnerable it is to governmental pressures being brought to bear on its pricing decisions." Do you agree? Why?
14. Suppose a company produces a single product, which it forecasts will reach a sales volume of 50,000 units in an "average" year. The total capital employed in the business amounts to $7.5 million. At the 50,000 unit sales level, total unit costs (i.e., fixed costs per unit + unit variable costs) amount to $300. If the targeted ROI is set at 25 percent before taxes, what should be the selling price per unit?
15. A retailer estimates that next year its total costs (including both operating and merchandise costs) will be $1,250,000. The retailer desires an 8 percent targeted return on net sales. What is the targeted dollar profit?
16. Why do industry leaders often have price stabilization as an important pricing objective?
17. Which of the following might set target-market-share pricing objectives defensively? Offensively?
   a. a large chain of discount department stores
   b. a leading tire manufacturer
   c. a transcontinental airline

   d. the largest manufacturer of electrical apparatus
   e. a regional gasoline marketing company

18. Pricing above the competition is less likely to be successful with products sold in self-service than in full-service stores. Why?
19. Why do you suppose so many marketers rely primarily on cost rather than market factors as the basis for setting prices on their products?
20. A certain company has a contribution pricing policy. Under what circumstances should it accept private-brand orders?
21. Do you agree or disagree with each of the following statements? State your reasoning in each instance.
   a. A company using contribution pricing also is using a variable pricing policy.
   b. Automobile dealers find it hard to adhere to a one-price policy because prospective buyers have trade-ins and play one dealer off against another.
   c. In implementing a "meeting competition" pricing policy, a company must meet the prices of all its competitors.
   d. No product should ever be sold at a price below full cost.
22. Distinguish among the following:
   a. quantity discounts LARGE P
   b. trade discounts –
   c. cash discounts – prompt payment
   d. promotional discounts –
   e. seasonal discounts – to persuade buyers
23. "It is clearly unethical, if not illegal, for a manufacturer to sell its products at lower prices to wholesalers than to retailers who buy similar quantities." Do you agree? Explain.
24. Would you agree that the competitively strongest companies are more likely to prefer a one-price policy, and the weakest prefer to negotiate prices? Explain.
25. "An F.O.B. pricing policy is a great deal more fair to buyers than any delivered-pricing policy can possibly be." Discuss.
26. Prepare a list of several products that might be sold under:
   a. F.O.B. pricing
   b. delivered pricing
27. Under what conditions might a marketer use a freight absorption policy?
28. What reasons do marketers have for using guaranty-against-price-decline policies?
29. Give some examples of items in a product line that "compete" with each other. What pricing problems do such items present?
30. Would you agree that resale price maintenance is clearly to the disadvantage of the consumer? Explain.

CASE PROBLEM

Par-Maker, Inc., a small manufacturer and marketer of golf balls (its only product), had total fixed costs amounting to $100,000 annually; variable costs were 57 cents per unit. Par-Maker sold its golf balls to wholesalers at a price of $9.00 per dozen.

Based upon the above data, answer the following questions: (a) what is the break-even point in dollars? (b) what is the break-even point in units of product? and (c) what is the value of break-even analysis?

When you have mastered the contents of this chapter, you should be able to:

1. Illustrate the pricing strategy of a marketer whose product has lasting distinctiveness.
2. Outline the conditions under which a marketer whose product is in the market pioneering stage should use (a) price skimming, or (b) penetration pricing.
3. Contrast the pricing strategies during market growth of (a) the innovating marketer, and (b) its competitors.
4. Compare pricing strategy during the market maturity stage under conditions of (a) oligopolistic competition, and (b) monopolistic competition.
5. Explain the meaning of "run-out" strategy.
6. Discuss how price-setting procedures vary under different competitive conditions.
7. Explain cost-plus pricing, and markup pricing.
8. Demonstrate the *practical* use of break-even analysis for price setting.
9. Discuss the two main approaches to estimating demand.

CHAPTER 19

PRICING STRATEGIES AND PROCEDURES

Marketers seek to attain their long-run pricing objectives through both price policies and pricing strategies. Management uses price policies as general guidelines in making pricing decisions over long periods. The pricing decisions management makes to fit the changing competitive situations encountered by specific products are its *pricing strategies.* Thus, price policies are general and long-run, while pricing strategies are specific and in effect for shorter periods. Setting the price itself is a key element in the formulation of pricing strategy and, as the competitive situation changes with different stages in the product's life cycle, the relative amount of freedom management has in setting prices also changes. Discussion in this chapter focuses first on pricing strategies under different competitive situations and then on price-setting procedures.

Pricing Strategy and the Competitive Situation—an Introduction

Pricing strategy varies considerably with the competitive situation. At one extreme, pricing is an uncontrollable, and forces outside management's control determine prices. For example, many farm prices are determined by the relationship between available supply and market demand, as described in classical economic theory. Thus, lettuce growers have no need for a pricing strategy—their only pricing decision is to accept or reject the current market price. At the other extreme, in those rare cases where the marketer has a long-term monopoly, pricing is almost 100 percent a controllable. Generally, the monopolist, so economic theory indicates, sets its price to maximize profits by "charging what the traffic will bear," but, in the "real world," various external pressures prevent it from obtaining a pure monopoly-type price. Nevertheless, a *monopolist's price* is the purest example of an administered price—one set by management and held stable over a long period.

Monopolist's Price

In the vast majority of the in-between cases, pricing is a controllable but hardly ever to the extent that it is with the monopolist in economic theory. Pricing becomes a controllable through a combination of marketing skill and luck. Most modern marketers differentiate their products, hoping to reduce the incentive prospective buyers have for choosing competitors' offerings solely on a price basis. Most use promotion in an effort to differentiate their products further in prospective buyers' minds. Similarly, they differentiate other aspects of their "total offerings" through their individualized choices of marketing channels and middlemen, physical distribution systems, and the like. Most modern marketers, in other words, manipulate the other controllables to enhance their ability to use pricing as a controllable—only when pricing is a controllable does management need to formulate pricing strategy and set specific prices.

Joel Dean identifies three kinds of competitive situations met by particular products as those where the product has (1) lasting distinctiveness, (2) perishable distinctiveness, or (3) little distinctiveness.[1] A product has "distinctiveness" to the extent that it can be sold at a price above or below those of competitors without causing changes in their prices or sales.

Clearly, the relative distinctiveness of most products varies with the stage of the product life cycle. Very few products have lasting distinctiveness—except perhaps for such things as diamonds and ermine furs in certain market segments—if lasting means more than ten years, and distinctiveness means that no acceptable substitutes exist.[2] Most products in the market pioneering stage have perishable distinctiveness, which gradually diminishes in the market growth and market maturity stages. This happens as competitors introduce their own versions, which become progressively closer approximations of the innovator's product, and as their overall marketing strategies come more and more to resemble that of the innovator. Products of perishable distinctiveness ultimately become products of little distinctiveness sometime during the market maturity stage and continue as such during their market decline. Since both the prod-

[1] J. Dean, *Managerial Economics* (Englewood Cliffs, N.J.: Prentice-Hall, Inc., 1951), p. 402.

[2] *Ibid.*, p. 403.

uct's relative distinctiveness and overall marketing strategy vary with the stage of the product life cycle, so does pricing strategy.

Pricing Strategy for Products of Lasting Distinctiveness

As mentioned earlier, very few products, have lasting distinctiveness, so this type of competitive situation is exceedingly rare. But when it occurs, the marketer essentially enjoys the monopolist's pricing freedom. Figure 19–1 shows the "pricing model" that economists say the monopolist should use. According to this model, the marketer of a product of lasting distinctiveness (with a demand curve *D*), should price it at *P* and sell it in a quantity *Q*, thus equating marginal costs (*MC*) and marginal revenue (*MR*) and maximizing profits. The shaded area in Figure 19–1, the lower-right-hand corner of which is cut by the average total costs curve (*ATC*), represents the total profit at price *P* and volume *Q*.

But in the real world the marketer of a product of lasting distinctiveness is not likely to use price *P* in an attempt to maximize its profits. Other factors cause it to choose some price lower than *P*: possible adverse public reactions to monopoly pricing, the threat of governmental intervention, and the possibility of weakening its bar-

Figure 19–1
Pricing a product of lasting distinctiveness to maximize profit (monopoly pricing)

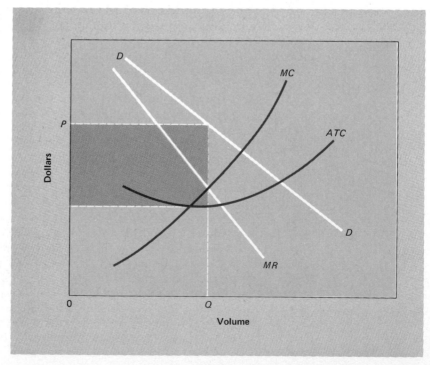

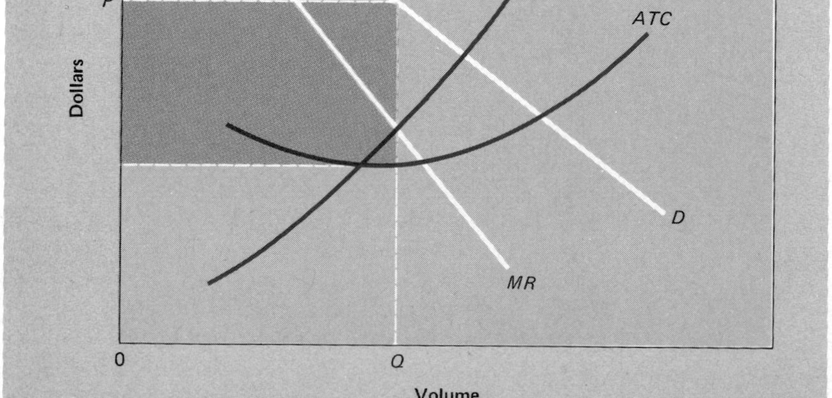

gaining position with organized labor. Even when a monopolist starts out with a profit-maximizing price (P), sooner or later it is almost certain to encounter outside pressures that force it to lower this price.

Pricing Strategy During Market Pioneering

During market pioneering, the marketer's appropriate pricing strategy depends both upon how distinctive its new product is and how long it expects this distinctiveness to last. The more distinctive the new product is, the more freedom the marketer has in pricing it. If it is highly distinctive—that is, a revolutionary new product with no close substitutes—the marketer can choose from a wide range of possible profitable prices. If it is only slightly distinctive—that is, if it represents only comparatively minor changes from existing and substitute products—the marketer's range of possible profitable prices is restricted, the most likely price being very slightly above those of the competitive substitutes. Similarly, the longer the period during which a marketer expects its new product's distinctiveness to last, the wider the range of possible profitable prices.

Most new products, however distinctive they are initially, have only a limited period free from competition. The length of this period is determined by factors such as the relative uniqueness of the product innovation, its patentability, the rate at which it gains market acceptance, and potential competitors' product development capabilities. During the market pioneering stage, the innovating marketer generally enjoys considerable pricing discretion, but rarely can it count on more than three years of freedom from competition. For most products, then, the marketer must formulate pricing strategy during the market pioneering stage on the assumption that product distinctiveness will deteriorate in a relatively short time as competitors enter the market.

PRICE-SKIMMING AND PENETRATION-PRICING STRATEGIES

Price-Skimming

Penetration-Pricing

During the market pioneering stage, the marketer has a choice between two pricing strategies—*price-skimming* or *penetration-pricing*. A price-skimming strategy uses a high introductory price to skim the "cream" of demand, while a penetration-pricing strategy uses a low introductory price to speed up the product's widespread market acceptance. Neither of these strategies is intended to maximize profits—both aim toward achieving other short-range pricing objectives, price-skimming perhaps to recoup product development costs quickly and penetration-pricing usually to capture a certain market share before competitors enter the market.

Whether to use price-skimming or penetration-pricing during the product's market pioneering stage depends importantly on its price elasticity of demand (i.e., on the relative sensitivity of the product's sales to its price). Figure 19–2 shows two contrasting demand curves—*DD* for a new product with an inelastic demand and *D'D'* for one with an elastic demand. For the product with an inelastic demand, the marketer's best pricing strategy is to choose a skimming price (such as P_1) and plan on selling a volume of Q_1. For the product with an elastic demand, the best pricing strategy is to use a penetration price (such as P_3) and plan on selling a volume of Q_3. An intermediate price, such as P_2, is probably too low a price for the product with an inelastic demand and too high for that with the elastic demand. At price P_2, in both cases a volume of Q_2 would be sold, and sales revenues would be lower than if price-skimming had been used for the product with the inelastic demand and penetration-pricing had been used for that with the elastic demand.

ATTRACTIONS OF PRICE-SKIMMING

Five factors make price-skimming an attractive strategy for many marketers. First, if the product is highly distinctive, it tends to have a more price inelastic demand at first than it will have later on, because advertising and personal selling generally have more influence on sales than price does during a product's market pioneer-

Figure 19–2
Pricing products of perishable distinctiveness: skimming versus penetration strategies

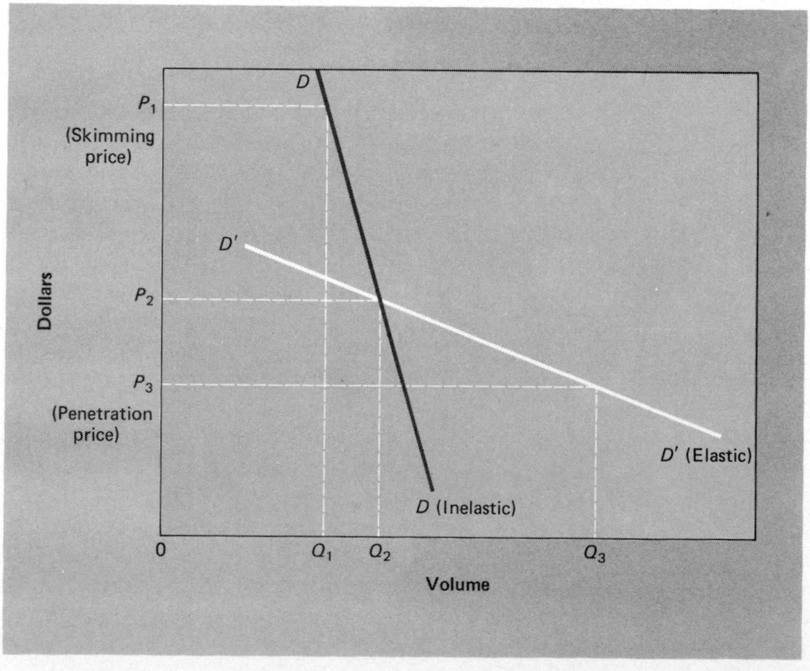

ing stage. Second, a high introductory price divides the market into segments according to their responsiveness to price—the skimming price taps the market segment that is relatively insensitive to price, later price reductions can reach more price-conscious market segments. Third, if an introductory price is too high it is easy to reduce it, but if it is too low it is difficult and awkward to raise it. Fourth, a high introductory price often generates greater dollar sales and profits than a low introductory price—thus, price-skimming provides funds the marketer can use later in expanding sales to other market segments. Fifth, price-skimming gives the innovating marketer a chance to recoup its product development expenses before competitors, whose product development expenses should be lower, enter the market.

CONDITIONS MAKING PENETRATION-PRICING APPROPRIATE

Management should seriously consider using penetration-pricing under any or all of four different conditions: (1) when the new product's demand is highly price elastic, even early in the market pioneering stage; (2) when the marketer can realize substantial manufacturing and marketing economies if it obtains a large sales volume (such economies, of course, bring down average total costs); (3) when the marketer expects strong competition very soon after introducing the product—that is, when it expects the product's market pioneering stage not to last long; and (4) when there is little or no elite market for the product—that is, a market segment made up of buyers who will probably buy regardless of price.

COMPETITORS' LIKELY REACTIONS

Probably the innovating marketer's single most important consideration in choosing between price-skimming and penetration-pricing is the relative ease and speed with which competitors can launch their own versions of the new product. For revolutionary new products which have large potential markets, penetration-pricing is usually the most appropriate strategy. This is because the existence of a large potential market is almost certain to attract many large competitors soon after introduction of the innovation. Penetration-pricing helps to discourage prospective competitors by making the market appear less attractive (i.e., less profitable) than if the innovating marketer uses a price-skimming strategy. If the marketer expects that competitors will need considerable time and will encounter great difficulties in coming up with their own versions of the product type, then, of course, price-skimming is an appropriate strategy. Clearly, too, if the marketer's new product is only slightly distinctive, then, as implied earlier, the best choice is penetration-pricing—at a price either at or very slightly above those of the competitive substitutes.

Pricing Strategy During Market Growth

INNOVATING MARKETER'S PRICING STRATEGY

During the market growth stage for a product of perishable distinctiveness, the innovating marketer's pricing strategy must increasingly take direct account of the pricing strategies of its competitors as, one by one, they enter the market. If the innovator used price-skimming during the market pioneering stage, it may either switch to penetration-pricing when significant competition first appears or, alternatively, reduce its price in several successive steps as more competitors enter the broadening market. If the innovating marketer used penetration-pricing during market pioneering, it is likely to continue with that strategy during the market growth stage. In either case, during market growth, the innovator's main pricing objective is generally that of retaining a particular market share.

PRICING STRATEGIES OF COMPETITORS ENTERING DURING MARKET GROWTH STAGE

Competitors new to the market always take note of the innovator's pricing strategy, and tend to price with the objective of gaining and holding some target market share. If the innovator has been using price-skimming, the first few competitors to enter the market may seek to underprice the innovator slightly and, as it steps down its price, some try to time their price cuts (also in steps) so as to precede the innovator's price cuts. Competitors entering the market later during market growth are much more likely to use penetration-pricing from the outset. If the innovator has been using penetration-pricing all along, generally all new competitors have no choice but to do the same though, as will be explained later, it is not necessary that all use identical penetration prices.

NONPRICE COMPETITION DURING MARKET GROWTH

During the market growth stage, while each marketer's pricing strategy becomes increasingly dependent upon those of its competitors, nonprice competition also increases. Different competitors seek to gain advantages through promotional efforts, changing or improving the product, extending its distribution, and the like. Those that succeed in becoming leading brands often also succeed in pricing their entries at a "price above the market"—that is, they find it possible to use a premium-pricing strategy. Those that do not succeed in becoming leading brands must generally price either at competitive levels or under the market. Consequently, each competitor in formulating its own pricing strategy considers not only the nonprice components of its own overall marketing strategy but also those of its competitors. As market growth proceeds, all competitors find that both their pricing and overall marketing strategies are increasingly interlocked.

Pricing Strategy During Market Maturity

During market maturity a product of perishable distinctiveness loses its distinctiveness at an increasing rate. Brands become more and more alike, and there is increasing substitution among brands. Market shares among brands tend to stabilize and, in the contest to maintain market shares, leading brands cannot command as high a price as before. As production methods stabilize and as individual manufacturers develop excess production capacity, private-label competitors enter and secure important market shares, usually by offering private labels at under-the-market prices.

The net effect of these developments on pricing strategy depends mainly on the ease of entry into the market and on the number of competitors. If market entry is difficult and the number of competitors small, an oligopolistic pricing situation may develop (if it has not done so during market growth). If market entry is easy and the number of competitors large, then monopolistic competition prevails and governs individual marketers' pricing strategies.

OLIGOPOLISTIC PRICING

Oligopolistic Pricing

For products of perishable distinctiveness, an *oligopolistic pricing* situation may develop either during a late phase of market growth or an early phase of market maturity. An oligopoly, by definition, is a market that has such a small number of sellers that each has a significant effect on the market price. Each, therefore, in making price changes must consider the likely effect on competitors.

Figure 19–3 illustrates the pricing situation confronting each oligopolist. The demand curve *BAC* is "kinky," with segment *BA* relatively elastic and segment *AC* relatively inelastic. If the industry's prices are stable, the individual marketer may expect to sell a volume Q_1 at price P_1. If it decides to raise its price to P_2, it will sell less – Q_2 if its competitors do not follow its price rise and Q'_2 if they do (in the latter case, the kink shifts to A'). In other words, if the competitors do not raise their prices at all, or raise them to something less than P_2, the marketer's sales will be off more sharply than if all had matched the price increase.

What will happen if the marketer cuts its price? If it cuts the price to P_3, it cannot expect to sell more than a volume of Q_3. Competitors, it must assume, will match any price cut since if they do not

Figure 19–3
Oligopolistic pricing and the kinky demand curve

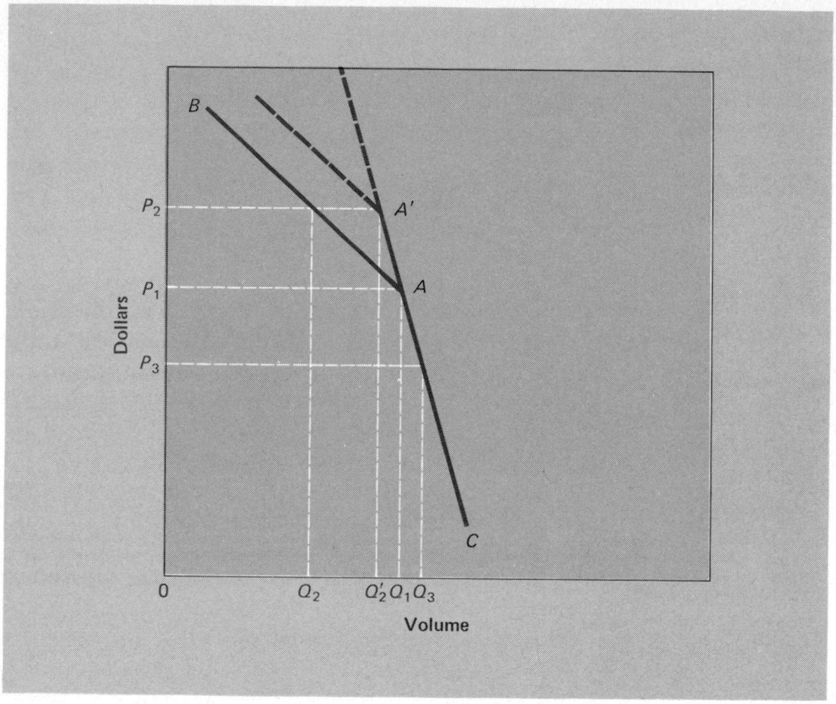

they will lose market share. Usually, it can also assume that they will refrain from further undercutting the price, because of fears of starting a price war. The demand segment *AC* is quite inelastic, and all competitors should anticipate lower total dollar revenues if the price drops below P_1. Consequently, under oligopolistic competitive conditions, any price change, up or down, is likely to result in lower total dollar sales. Since all industry members are aware of this, all tend to refrain from making price changes and the price stabilizes.

PRICING UNDER MONOPOLISTIC COMPETITION

Figure 19–4 illustrates the pricing situation under monopolistic competition (i.e., when market entry is easy and the number of competitors large). The demand curve *DD* indicates the various quantities each firm can sell at different prices. Each competitor—according to the economic theorist—attempts to maximize profits by setting its price at the point where marginal revenue (*MR*) and marginal costs (*MC*) are equated. At this price (*P*), it sells a volume of *Q* and secures the profit represented by the shaded area. (*ATC* denotes average total costs.)

Notice that the demand curve (*DD*) in Figure 19–4 is highly price elastic. This is typical of products in the market maturity stage

Figure 19–4
Pricing under conditions of monopolistic competition

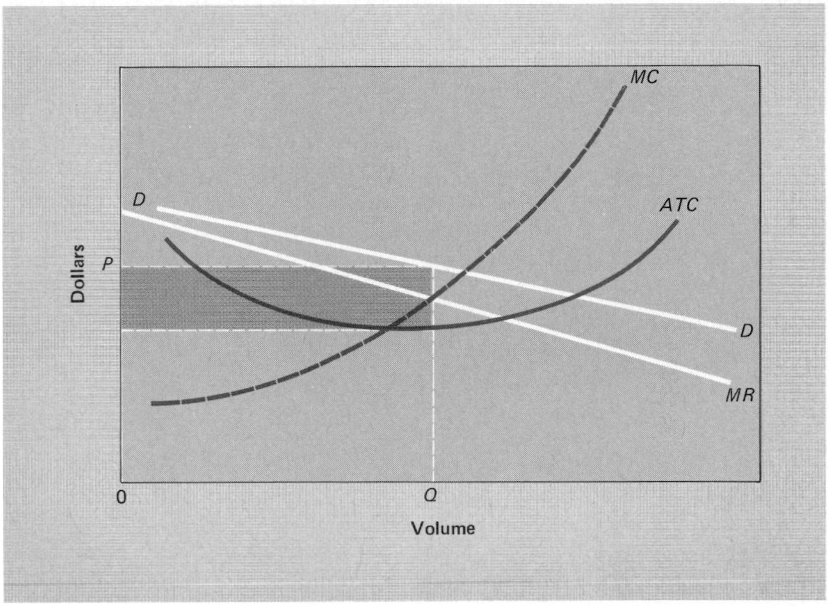

where there are numerous competitors, since many close substitutes exist for each marketer's brand. Furthermore, under conditions of monopolistic competition, the ease of entry into the market forces each marketer to struggle continuously to hold its market share.

Under monopolistic competition, then, the range of different marketers' prices narrows. Some manage to obtain premium prices, providing their brands retain some distinctiveness (and/or if they succeed in keeping various nonprice advantages gained during the market growth stage). But the amount of a marketer's price premium cannot exceed the average price by much or the marketer loses market share, as its fringe buyers switch to lower priced substitutes. If a marketer's brand loses its distinctiveness to the extent that it becomes indistinguishable from many competing brands, the marketer may be forced to lower its price below the market's average.

However, greater flexibility in pricing strategy is possible under monopolistic competition than under oligopolistic competition. The number of competitors is large, and a price change by any one tends to affect each of the others only slightly. If one competitor, for example, cuts the price, it may increase its sales, while each of its competitors loses only a small amount of business. Therefore, unlike under oligopolistic competition, the chances are against a price cut's inviting instant retaliation by competitors. Nevertheless, a marketer contemplating a price cut must consider the ever present possibility that too drastic a reduction may set off a *price war*, with the impact spreading from one company to another throughout the entire industry.

Price War

Pricing Strategy During Market Decline

A product in the market decline stage is of little or no distinctiveness. Generally, by the time this life cycle stage is reached the number of competitors has dwindled considerably, with only a few remaining. Why do some competitors remain? A marketer may keep such a product in its line offering for any of several reasons: the marketer may need it to round out its line, it may have a hard core market that continues to insist on buying it, it may still be profitable, and so on. Marketers of products in the market decline stage generally price them competitively hoping to secure a sales volume large enough to return a profit. But if the product has a sizable hard core market, the marketer may even raise its price a bit, thus obtaining a slight premium price; at this point the marketer also cuts promotional costs to the bone, and thus may realize considerable profit through this "run-out" strategy.[3]

Price-Setting Procedures

Procedures for setting prices also vary with competitive conditions. At one extreme, as brought out earlier, pricing is an uncontrollable, market prices being determined by the forces of supply and demand.

Commodities

For some *commodities,* organized commodity exchanges exist and provide the mechanism which determines market prices—for example, cotton, coffee beans, raw sugar, wool, potatoes, corn, wheat, oats, soybeans, eggs, copper, and silver. For other commodities, such as tobacco and most livestock, prices result from auctions, where prospective buyers make bids and prospective sellers decide whether to accept them. For other farm commodities, such as many fruits and vegetables, no formal price-making mechanism exists and buyers and sellers arrive at prices through individual negotiations. Sellers of most commodities, in other words, have very little power in setting the prices on their outputs: market prices are determined by interactions of supply and demand and vary from day to day, even from one sale to another. At the other extreme, where monopolies exist, pricing is largely a controllable, purely administered prices being set and held stable by management.

Products of Perishable Distinctiveness

However, for *products of perishable distinctiveness*—that is, for those that go through more-or-less normal life cycles, marketers enjoy varying amounts of freedom in setting specific prices. Management has considerable price-setting freedom in the first two stages of product life cycles. This freedom diminishes considerably if oligopo-

[3] A run-out strategy involves a marketer cutting back all support costs, such as promotional costs, to the minimum level that will optimize the product's profitability over its limited foreseeable life. See W. J. Talley, Jr., *The Profitable Product* (Englewood Cliffs, N.J.: Prentice-Hall, Inc., 1965), p. 8, fn 2.

listic competition develops and an industry price leader emerges (as often happens), in which case other industry members set their prices at or very near the leader's price. If monopolistic competition develops instead, an industry price leader is less likely, although most competitors set their prices fairly close to the industry average. Sometime, then, either late in a product's market growth or during its market maturity stage, management's freedom in setting specific prices lessens—with most competitors keeping an eye on each other's pricing moves. During the market decline stage, the few remaining marketers continue to price competitively but an occasional one lucky enough to retain a sizable hard core market regains some pricing freedom.

Competitive Bidding

One type of situation in which a marketer may or may not have much pricing freedom is that involving the price-setting procedure known as *competitive bidding*. If the product subject to competitive bidding is of little or no distinctiveness, then, of course, the marketer must submit a price that is not only close to but also under those of competitors if it wants to secure the business. However, if the product is highly unique or somehow involves an input of scarce talents (e.g., the scientific knowhow that goes into the design of space exploration equipment), a particular marketer may have considerable leeway in setting its "asking price."

COST-PLUS PRICING

Cost-Plus Pricing

Surveys of business practice show that *cost-plus pricing* is the most common price determination procedure. Cost-plus pricing involves making a cost estimate and adding a margin to cover marketing expenses and profit. Thus, a manufacturer, for example, might set the price for a new product by estimating the product's per unit total costs (at some predicted level of production and sales) and, then, adding a certain percentage to provide a gross margin (i.e., expenses + net profit). With per unit total costs of $5.00 and a 40 percent add-on markup, for instance, the manufacturer would set the new product's price at $7.00 (i.e., $5.00 + $2.00).

In using cost-plus pricing, however, manufacturers generally apply different markups to each cost component, as illustrated in Table 19–1. As this table indicates, cost-plus pricing applies various rules of thumb to set a price. The particular costs management considers and the percentages (or multipliers) it uses vary with its knowledge and understanding of the behavior of different kinds of costs. Each company using cost-plus pricing, through experience and trial and error, derives its own rules of thumb.

Companies using cost-plus pricing generally regard the formula-determined price as only a starting point since, in most cases, it needs adjusting for the competitive situation. One exception to this is that 100 percent cost-plus determined prices are sometimes appropriate during the market pioneering stage, especially when the product is radically new and different; this life cycle stage, as you will

Table 19–1 Illustrations of Cost-Plus Pricing

	PRODUCT A	PRODUCT B
Labor Cost/Unit	$ 5.00	$ 2.00
Materials Cost/Unit	1.00	8.50
Factory Overhead (@ 150% of Labor)	7.50	3.00
Total Cost/Unit	$13.50	$13.50
Markups:		
On Labor (100% of Cost)	$ 5.00	$ 2.00
On Materials (20% of Cost)	.20	1.70
On Factory Overhead (10% of Cost)	.75	.30
Total Markup/Unit	$ 5.95	$ 4.00
Price = (Cost + Markup)	$19.45	$17.50
	PRODUCT C	**PRODUCT D**
Labor Cost/Unit	$ 5.00	$ 2.00
Materials Cost/Unit	1.00	8.50
Total Labor and Materials/Unit	$ 6.00	$10.50
Markups:		
Labor Cost/Unit times 5	$25.00	$10.00
Materials Cost/Unit times 2	2.00	17.00
Total Markup/Unit	$27.00	$27.00
Price = (Labor & Materials/Unit + Markup	$33.00	$37.50

recall, is the only one where the innovator is entirely free of direct competition—but even here the innovator must consider the probable entry of competition in setting the introductory price. During the three subsequent life cycle stages, competitors' prices and their possible reactions are important considerations in setting prices; hence, the need for adjusting cost-plus determined prices.

MARKUP PRICING BY MIDDLEMEN

Markup Pricing

Markup pricing is the middleman's counterpart to the manufacturer's cost-plus pricing. In pricing an item, the middleman typically thinks of cost as the base and adds its markup (an amount management believes sufficient to cover both estimated expenses and desired profit). Management applies different percentage markups to different items depending upon, among other factors, the rate of stockturn, competition, trade custom, and the manufacturer's suggested resale prices. Each middleman, however, attempts to secure the overall average markup which it believes is needed to cover both its anticipated expenses and desired profit; consequently, it marks up some items above average, others average, and still others below average. Furthermore, the middleman often adjusts markup-determined prices for various reasons; for example, a book dealer who buys some books at a cost of $7.50 each may first apply a 25 percent markup on the selling price to arrive at a tentative price of $10.00 each but, considering this as a psychologically bad price, the dealer adjusts the price downward to either $9.95 or $9.98 each. (Markup pricing is discussed in greater detail in Chapter 6.)

Implications for the Manufacturer's Pricing The fact that middlemen generally use markup pricing often affects the way the manufacturer sets its prices. A manufacturer whose products are distributed through middlemen, *if* it wants to influence their resale prices on its products, must take their customary markups into account in its own price setting. Thus, if a manufacturer believes its product should retail at $5.00 and if the customary retail markup on this type of product is 30 percent on the retail price, it may then set the price to retailers at $3.50. If the manufacturer uses wholesalers to reach retailers and their customary markup is 10 percent, it may set its price to wholesalers at $3.15. Therefore, this manufacturer's price setting goes beyond merely setting its own prices and has strong influences on both its wholesalers' and retailers' resale prices.

USING BREAK-EVEN ANALYSIS IN PRICING

Break-Even Analysis

In making practical use of *break-even analysis* for price setting, management must go beyond break-even computations and estimate the probable sales at various alternative selling prices. To illustrate, assume the data shown in Table 19–2, where a marketer has variable costs per unit of $50, total fixed costs of $20,000, and is considering four different possible selling prices: $75, $100, $130, and $150. At each price, the contribution per unit is shown in column (3), and the break-even point in column (5). Figure 19–5 shows the same data graphically.

Table 19–2 Computation of Break-Even Points at Four Different Prices

(1) PRICE/ UNIT	(2) VARIABLE COSTS/UNIT	(3) CONTRIBUTION/ UNIT (1)–(2)	(4) TOTAL FIXED COSTS	(5) BREAK-EVEN POINT (4)÷(3)
$75	$50	$25	$20,000	800 Units
100	50	50	20,000	400 Units
130	50	80	20,000	250 Units
150	50	100	20,000	200 Units

To complete the analysis, the marketer needs the additional data shown in Table 19–3. Specifically, it needs estimates of the sales that can be made at each price (column 2). Then it can go ahead

Figure 19–5
Break-even points at four different prices

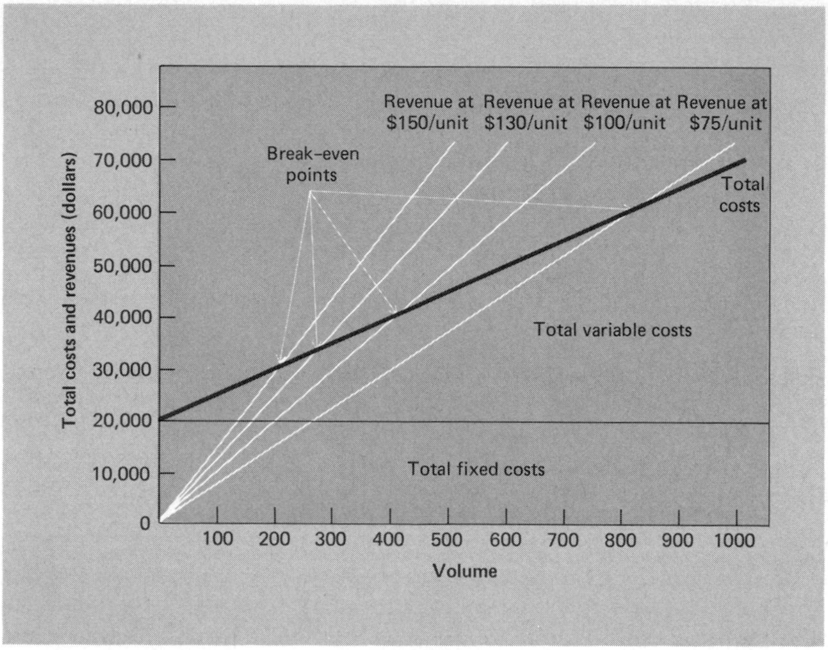

and calculate the total revenues (column 3) and total costs (column 4) at those sales volumes which, in turn, makes it possible to estimate the total profits at each price (column 5).

Table 19–3 Estimated Sales, Total Revenues, Total Costs, and Total Profits at Four Different Prices

(1) PRICE/ UNIT	(2) ESTIMATED SALES IN UNITS	(3) TOTAL REVENUE (1) × (2)	(4) TOTAL COSTS*	(5) TOTAL PROFITS (3) − (4)
$75	750	$56,250	$57,500	−$1,250
100	600	60,000	50,000	10,000
130	440	57,200	42,000	15,200
150	375	56,250	38,750	17,500

* Computed from data in Table 19–2. Total Costs = Total Fixed Costs + (Var. Cost/Unit × Estimated Sales in Units).

Figure 19–6 graphically illustrates this procedure. The total cost curves and the four revenue curves are identical to those shown on the break-even chart in Figure 19–5. Management's estimates of the quantities that the company can sell at each proposed price are indicated by points *a*, *b*, *c*, and *d*. When these points are connected,

Figure 19–6
Relationships among total revenues, total costs, and break-even points

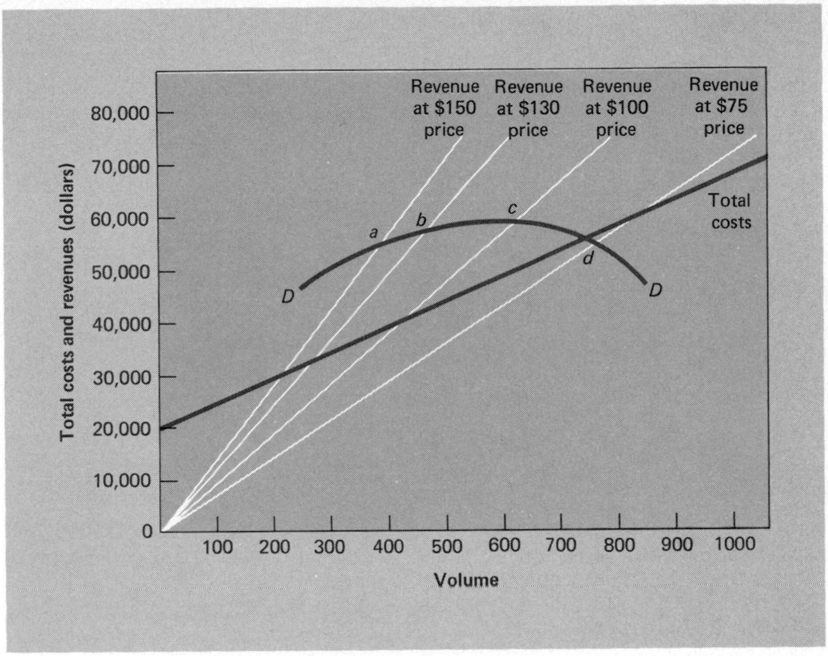

the resulting curve (*DD*) represents total demand. (Note particularly that this demand curve indicates total revenues rather than average revenues as in the conventional demand curve.) If management's pricing objective is to maximize profits, it will now choose the price at which the vertical distance between the total revenue curve (*DD*) and the total costs curve is greatest.[4] In this example, this is at the $150 selling price, where total revenues are $56,250 and total costs are $38,750, yielding total profits (i.e., vertical distance) of $17,500.

Estimating Demand Clearly, using break-even analysis together with estimates of sales at alternative prices is the ideal price-setting procedure. However, the "catch" is in "estimating how much buyers will buy at different prices," that is, in ascertaining the shape and nature of the "demand curve." Nevertheless, despite numerous difficulties, there are ways to approximate demand schedules.

There are two main approaches to estimating demand. One is to offer the product at various prices until the shape and nature of its demand curve is approximated; although these trial-and-error data may not actually represent the real demand curve, the marketer can use this experience in the market to arrive at a specific price, hopefully near the optimum. The other approach is to use formalized market tests to gauge demand at different prices—the marketer system-

[4] See E. R. Hawkins, "Price Policies and Theory," *Journal of Marketing*, January 1954, p. 234.

atically offers the product at different prices in different markets (or at different prices at different times in the same markets) under controlled conditions. Analysis of the results of the market tests should lead to a usable demand schedule. Demand schedules arrived at through properly designed market tests should provide closer approximations of the real demand curve than those derived from trial-and-error market experiences.

Summary

You should now, after completing Part Six, thoroughly understand pricing's role as a controllable and its place in overall marketing strategy. From the previous chapter (Chapter 18), you gained needed knowledge of the many factors influencing pricing decisions, the various long-run pricing objectives, and the different kinds of pricing policies. Building on this foundation, from this chapter you should have gained important perspectives on different pricing strategies, learned the conditions under which each is appropriate or necessary, and developed understanding of price-setting procedures.

Only when pricing is a controllable does management need to concern itself with formulating pricing strategy and setting specific prices. Pricing is a controllable when management succeeds in manipulating various combinations of the other controllables (product, distribution, and promotion) in ways that make it so. Of the other controllables, management's manipulation of the product has the most influence in converting price from an uncontrollable to a controllable. Most modern marketers market products of perishable distinctiveness (ones that go through more-or-less normal life cycles), so formulating appropriate pricing strategy (i.e., manipulating price as a controllable) is of considerable importance. During the product's market pioneering stage, the innovating marketer may skim the market at a high price or penetrate it at a low price. During the product's market growth stage, competitors invade the market, and both they and the innovator must take direct note of each other's pricing behavior in formulating pricing strategy; thus, price-skimming generally becomes inappropriate and each competitor tends to set prices aimed to gain or retain some target market share. During the product's market maturity stage, it loses its distinctiveness at a faster rate, both price and nonprice competition intensify, and the range of competitors' prices narrows and moves toward stability. During the product's market decline stage, most companies price competitively, but a few obtain a slight premium through successful pursuit of "run-out" strategies.

Price-setting procedures also vary with competitive conditions. The more that pricing is a controllable, the greater is the marketer's freedom in setting prices. However, sole reliance on cost-plus pricing is generally appropriate only during the market pioneering stage of a radically new and different product (i.e., for one that has no close competitive substitutes). At other stages in the product life cycle, cost-plus pricing is used appropriately only as a starting point, because of the increasing need to consider competitors' behavior in setting prices. Markup pricing—the middleman's counterpart to the manufacturer's cost-plus pricing—affects the manufacturer's price setting if management desires to influence their resale prices on the manufacturer's products. Price-setting procedures that combine break-even analysis with demand estimation are ideal, assuming that maximizing profits is the main pricing objective.

You now have the needed understanding of the fourth controllable—pricing. Coupling this understanding with what you previously learned about the other three controllables—products, distribution, and promotion—you are ready to move on to Part Seven: Overall Marketing Strategy.

QUESTIONS AND PROBLEMS

1. How does a pricing strategy differ from a pricing policy?
2. Discuss the effect of the kind of "distinctiveness" possessed by a product on its pricing.
3. How does pricing a product of lasting distinctiveness differ from pricing one of perishable distinctiveness?
4. For each of the following products, should the marketer use a skimming price or a penetration price. State your reasoning in each case.
   a. A new "cola" drink with an alcoholic content comparable to that of beer
   b. An "original" model of women's dress made by a "prestige" manufacturer
   c. A new insecticide developed to kill "selectively" only harmful insects and not to affect such harmless insects as ladybugs and bees
   d. A milk substitute for people allergic to milk
   e. A light bulb that lasts twice as long as ordinary bulbs
   f. A new deodorant for industrial use that effectively curbs noxious fumes that pollute the air
   g. An electric tractor for use in home gardening, snow removal, etc.
5. Would you agree or disagree with the following statements? Why?
   a. A price-skimming strategy is usually directed toward maximizing profits.

PART SEVEN

OVERALL MARKETING STRATEGY

When you have mastered the contents of this chapter, you should be able to:

1. Explain why answering the question, "Does marketing cost too much?" requires consideration of values added by marketing activities.
2. Contrast the conditions under which increases in marketing costs result in: (a) lower total costs, and (b) higher total costs.
3. Identify the possible offsetting benefits of nonprice competition that increases prices consumers pay.
4. Give examples of the ways in which marketing costs have been reduced in the past.
5. Evaluate the criticism that marketing induces "frivolous" and excessive buying.
6. Evaluate the criticism that marketing contributes to environmental pollution.
7. Explain how society influences marketing through public opinion and political pressure.
8. Analyze the implications for marketing strategy formulation of legal restraints on decisions involving: competitive action, products, price, marketing channels, and promotion.

CHAPTER 20

INTERACTIONS OF MARKETING AND SOCIETY

Modern marketers must recognize the significance of interactions between marketing and society. Whereas businessmen and society once viewed marketing's role as simply that of providing the mechanism through which production and purchasing power are converted into consumption, both have now broadened that view considerably. Both now recognize that marketers through their manipulation of the controllables—products, distribution, promotion, and price—exert influences on, and help to mold, not only consumption patterns but public attitudes and general economic and social well-being. Both also now recognize that society not only through its buying behavior but through public opinion, political pressure, and legislative action exerts influences on how marketers can and should manipulate the controllables. Modern marketers, in other words, in formulating and implementing overall marketing strategies, must be keenly aware that they are both influencing and being influenced by society.

How Marketing Influences Society—the Economic Aspects

Marketing, in performing its traditional economic role—that is, in serving as the mechanism through which production and purchasing power are converted into consumption—incurs substantial costs that society ultimately must pay. Since marketing costs can account for more than half of the total price paid by the final buyer, certain questions arise: Does marketing cost too much? What is the effect of marketing costs on total costs? Are there any offsetting benefits? What, if anything, can be done to reduce marketing costs?

DOES MARKETING COST TOO MUCH?

The costs of marketing bulk large in the prices that buyers pay—most experts say that out of each dollar the ultimate consumer spends, roughly 50 cents goes for the costs of performing marketing activities.[1] For some products, of course, marketing costs are a much lower proportion of the price the consumer pays—automobiles and appliances, for example, cost considerably more to make than to market. For other products, marketing costs are a much higher proportion of the price the consumer pays—perfume and cosmetics, for example, cost little to produce but a great deal to market. But, out of all the dollars the consumer spends for goods and services, about half go to pay the costs of marketing.

Table 20–1 is a breakdown of the costs involved in growing wheat, converting it into flour, and marketing the finished flour to the consumer. In this table, the various costs are listed generally in the order that they are incurred (all except for railroad and truck charges, which are incurred at several stages). Notice that all but two of the costs—farmer's growing cost and the miller's grinding costs—are marketing costs, accounting for 52 percent of the $1.00 the consumer pays for the flour.

Does marketing cost too much? To answer this question we must compare the costs and the benefits. Consider the wheat and flour example again and ask yourself, "Are the marketing activities performed here worth what they cost the consumer?" Generally, wheat is grown in different areas than those in which flour is consumed; therefore, it is certainly necessary to move the product (both as wheat and as flour) from production areas to consumption areas; the farmer's wheat marketing expenses (2 percent of the total) are mainly those of getting it to the country elevator, and other enterprises (country elevator, terminal elevator, the miller, wholesaler, and retailer) pay out another 13 percent of the total for railroad and truck charges—thus, a total of about 15 percent of the consumer's dollar goes for adding *place utility* to the product (i.e., moving it from production areas to consumption areas). Is 15 cents out of the $1.00 price too much for the consumer to pay for this added place utility?

Place Utility

Then, too, wheat is grown at one time and flour is consumed at a later time. The country elevator's marketing charges (3 percent of

[1] For a concise discussion of several studies on marketing costs, see P. D. Converse, H. W. Huegy, and R. V. Mitchell, *Elements of Marketing*, 7th ed. (Englewood Cliffs, N.J.: Prentice-Hall, Inc., 1965), pp. 622–625.

Table 20–1 A Breakdown of the Costs Represented in the Amount of Flour Sold at Retail for $1.00*

	CENTS
Farmer for growing the wheat	36.0
Farmer for marketing the wheat (mostly for transportation)	2.0
Country elevator (mostly for storage)	3.0
Terminal elevator (mostly for storage)	2.5
Flour miller for buying wheat	5.0
Flour miller for grinding wheat	12.0
Flour miller for marketing flour (including storage)	7.0
Wholesaler's costs (including storage)	3.5
Retailer's costs (including storage)	16.0
Railroad and truck charges (for transportation)	13.0
Consumer pays	$1.00

* Figures adapted from P. D. Converse, H. W. Huegy, and R. V. Mitchell, *Elements of Marketing*, 6th ed. (Englewood Cliffs, N.J., Prentice-Hall, Inc., 1958), p. 8, to reflect current conditions.

the total) are mostly for storing wheat until it accumulates enough to ship to the terminal elevator (with charges of 2.5 percent of the total) which, in turn, stores the wheat until the flour miller buys it. After the miller finishes grinding the wheat into flour, he performs storage activities until it is bought by wholesalers, who store the flour until it is bought by retailers, who in turn store the flour until the consumer finally buys. Considering all these storage operations, perhaps as much as 20 percent of the consumer's dollar goes for adding *time utility* to the product. Is 20 cents out of the $1.00 price too much for the consumer to pay for this added time utility?

Time Utility

Well, 15 cents for place utility and 20 cents for time utility adds up to only 35 cents—what does the consumer get for the other 17 cents of the 52 cents in total marketing costs? In the movement of wheat to the miller, its ownership is transferred three times—farmer to country elevator, country elevator to terminal elevator, and terminal elevator to miller. In movement of the flour to the consumer, ownership is again transferred three times—miller to wholesaler, wholesaler to retailer, retailer to consumer. Thus, a total of six ownership transfers occur from the time the farmer sells the wheat until the consumer finally buys the flour. Clearly, most of the remaining 17 cents goes for the costs of effecting ownership transfers (i.e., for adding *possession utility* to the product). These costs go for performing marketing activities such as grading (all wheat is not the same quality), buying and assembling, selling (including personal selling, advertising, display, and packaging), extending credit to buyers (i.e., marketing financing), and risk-bearing (e.g., the risks of the wheat or flour spoiling, being destroyed, stolen, etc.). Of course, each seller

Possession Utility

also expects its operation to return a profit over and above the costs it involves. Is 17 cents out of the $1.00 price too much for the consumer to pay for the added possession utility?

Generally speaking, then, marketing activities add value to a product by changing its ownership and its time and place of consumption. Kansas wheat at harvest time is of less value to the farmer than (after being converted into flour) it is six months later (change of time) after it has been shipped and received in Boston (change of place) and when it is finally bought by a housewife (change of ownership). Converting the wheat into flour, of course, also adds value to the product (through adding *form utility*), but value in this case is added by manufacturing, not marketing, operations.

Form Utility

EFFECT OF MARKETING COSTS ON TOTAL COSTS

Sometimes a company can reduce its total costs by increasing its marketing costs (thus benefiting consumers by making it possible for them to pay a lower price). For example, a company through increasing its advertising and personal selling expenditures may so increase a product's sales that the unit costs of manufacturing the product decrease more than the marketing costs have increased. Thus, the total costs are reduced. From the standpoint of society, so long as production costs fall faster than marketing costs rise, consumers benefit through lower prices—and this is the typical pattern of development for products going through the market growth stage of their life cycles.

However, increased marketing costs sometimes result in greater, not lower, total costs. As a product moves into the market maturity stage of its life cycle, for instance, competitors must fight harder to retain their shares of a total market that is first growing at a declining rate then shrinking at an increasing rate. While there is some tendency for price competition to develop, most marketers try to avoid it (largely because of fears of setting off a price war) and rely on increased marketing expenditures (e.g., for additional advertising, or for improved packaging) to help them hold their market shares. This increases total costs throughout the industry (unit production costs are generally already as low as they will get), and the tendency is for marketers to pass on the increased costs in the form of higher prices to consumers. Is paying the cost of this type of marketing activity worth it to consumers? Or does nonprice competition in this sort of competitive setting simply represent an economic loss to society? Your answers to these questions depend upon your economic philosophy and the value, if any, you attach to the possible offsetting benefits.

POSSIBLE OFFSETTING BENEFITS OF NONPRICE COMPETITION THAT INCREASES PRICES CONSUMERS PAY

Most Americans agree that strong competition is a necessary feature of capitalism. So they accept, though not enthusiastically, as one of the "costs of capitalism," additions to marketing costs that make for higher prices. They hope, of course, that the higher costs will be more than offset by other benefits of capitalism—a wider variety of competing brands from which to choose, having more ready and convenient access to sources of supply, and the like. Most Americans also realize that intense price (rather than nonprice) competition often drives many competitors out of the market, reducing the total number to a handful of large companies (i.e., an oligopoly), a situation that discourages newcomers from entering the market. You will also recall (from Chapter 19) that oligopolistic competition generally evolves to the point where prices among competitors stabilize, not necessarily at the lowest possible level, so oligopolistic competition may not reduce the price consumers pay.

REDUCING MARKETING COSTS

Not until rather recently has marketing been the target of formal cost-cutting efforts. With the development of large-scale business organizations, the early "scientific management experts" devoted most of their efforts to improving manufacturing efficiency and cutting production costs. However, certain marketing costs have been reduced through the years as enterprising businessmen detected profitable opportunities to engage in lower cost marketing operations—the mail-order house, department store, chain-store system, supermarket, and discount house all are institutions which at the time they appeared made possible lower marketing costs than those of the institutions previously existing. At the producers' and wholesalers' distribution levels, other cost-reducing developments have been taking place—for example, new and better designed warehousing facilities making possible economical usage of materials-handling equipment and mechanized order-processing systems. A few manufacturers have even set up automatic reordering systems whereby middlemen's inventory requirements are handled almost entirely by computer—thus reducing the middlemen's buying costs and the manufacturer's personal selling costs. Furthermore, more and more marketers are using marketing research: for reducing the number of product failures (incurring costs to society as well as to the marketer); for studying final buyers' needs and wants in order to provide more efficient (and lower cost) distribution; and for improving the efficiency of other aspects of marketing activities. However, many opportunities still exist for increasing marketing efficiency (and reducing marketing costs) and for passing some portion of the savings along to consumers in the form of lower prices.

How Marketing Influences Society—Buyer Behavior

Marketers manipulate the controllables—products, distribution, promotion, and price—in order to influence buyer behavior. Many marketing activities aim to provide information to prospective buyers in the hope of persuading them to buy. Critics of marketing, especially those who object to certain advertising and personal selling activities, express strong doubts about the social value of marketing's role in persuasion. Their argument is that many people are hoodwinked into wasting their money on frivolous items that contribute little or nothing either to the buyer or to society. Since many more consumers have discretionary income (to spend as they please) today than a generation ago, this criticism takes on added force. However, criticisms of this type are often related to questionable value judgments, such as those based on the belief that society would be better off if more people went to symphony concerts rather than to sports events or movies. But even the critic with this belief must admit that marketers have been instrumental in making it possible for more Americans, as well as a higher proportion of the total population, to regularly enjoy symphonic music today than was true fifty years ago—for example, marketers of records, tapes, and cassettes have brought symphony music to millions while other marketers, by paying the costs of radio and television time as part of their advertising efforts, have made it possible for millions more to enjoy symphony concerts in their homes.

The criticism that marketing induces frivolous and excessive buying, however, does have validity, particularly when it relates to buying by low-income and ghetto consumers. Studies of marketing in ghetto areas have shown that numerous low-income people are easily persuaded to buy more than they can afford.[2] Ghetto residents appear to be particularly gullible in accepting false and misleading claims about products at face value, and they are often lured into making purchases—through "easy credit terms," for example—that are beyond their means.

Language difficulties which characterize many low-income people make them less sophisticated in their buying than they otherwise would be. For the segment of the U.S. population made up of people whose native language is Spanish, English is for many only a

[2] For more information on this topic, see D. Caplovitz, *The Poor Pay More* (New York: The Free Press, 1963); and F. D. Sturdivant, *The Ghetto Marketplace* (New York: The Free Press, 1969).

partially understood second language. For much of the black population, word usage is sufficiently different to create communication problems, presenting marketers with the danger of unintentionally misrepresenting their products.

Whether the net influence of marketing on buyer and social behavior is favorable or unfavorable, critics and noncritics both agree that such influence occurs. Because of the strong marketing emphasis placed upon such items, most Americans are buyers of deodorants, detergents, automobiles, sporting equipment, and work-saving appliances, to name only a few. Marketing professionals, defending the system, argue that increased consumption makes for more business profits and jobs and, hence, rising incomes and higher standards of living. Marketing critics, attacking the system, argue that higher incomes are of no value if they are wasted on unnecessary purchases and that material things are of no value if the buyer has little time or energy left over after working hours to enjoy them.[3]

How Marketing Influences Society— the Environment

Society is increasingly concerned with ecology and the need for preserving the environment from further human pollution. Business and industry are leading contributors to environmental pollution, but there are others—for example, inadequate municipal sewage disposal facilities, lack of controls over population growth, and unwisely located airports. Marketers, in particular, must accept responsibility for certain aspects of environmental pollution.

Packaging Revolution

Packaging, a prominent feature of modern marketing, is a serious pollutant. Until the early 1900's, numerous products—among them butter, rice, crackers, coffee, and soap—were sold from bulk stock in unpackaged form. In attempting to differentiate their brands and develop buyer preferences, marketers of these products joined the "packaging revolution." Other marketers, who previously sold their products in reusable containers (such as milk, soft drinks, and beer), in increasing numbers have switched to disposable or "throwaway" packages. It is estimated that in 1975 the packaging industry turned out more than 650 pounds of packaging material per person in the United States. This means that a city of the size of Dallas, Texas, must dispose of 430,000 tons of waste packaging, and the New York

[3] For an excellent discussion of marketing as a social system, as well as the various interactions that occur between marketing and society, see Sidney J. Levy and Gerald Zaltman, *Marketing, Society, and Conflict* (Englewood Cliffs, N.J.: Prentice-Hall, inc., 1975).

City metropolitan area more than 4,100,000 tons. Complicating the problem are the disposal methods—one, incineration, is itself an atmospheric pollutant; some types of packaging—plastic, for instance—appear almost impossible to recycle or disintegrate.

Marketing also adds to environmental pollution through its development and promotion of disposable products. For example, as paper napkins replace cloth napkins, the volume of trash requiring disposal increases. The same thing happens with disposable diapers, drinking cups, bottles, and so forth. Society on the whole seems to prefer the added convenience of disposability but, increasingly, voices objections to the added pollution involved. Unfortunately, too, disposability often makes it possible to reduce the prices consumers pay—the soft drink industry, for example, estimates that it costs 30 cents to collect six nonreturnable bottles, considerably more than the cost of six tin cans or throwaway bottles.

Many critics contend that marketing contributes to environmental pollution in still other ways. Some say that marketers adversely affect the appearance of the landscape through roadside advertising and obscure natural beauty with outdoor billboards. Others object to "pollution of the airwaves" through excessive numbers of commercials on radio and television programs.

How Society Influences Marketing—Public Opinion and Political Pressure

The modern marketer recognizes the need for an efficient system of information feedback to measure success in evaluating and servicing the target market's needs and wants. Unfortunately, most marketers' marketing information systems tend to have rather a narrow scope, focusing mainly on the short-term and on that portion of society the marketer considers as a target market. The manufacturer of snowmobiles, for example, can rely upon its marketing information system to provide insights about prospective buyers' reactions to its product's performance characteristics, the dealers who sell it, and its price. But this marketing information system is not likely to be of much help in providing feedback from nonusers of snowmobiles. Thus, unless the snowmobile manufacturer makes special investigations, it may not learn that nonusers find its product's noise level highly offensive, or that ecologists are worried about damage to wilderness areas from indiscriminate snowmobile usage, until it meets strong pressures from society to control—perhaps even to outlaw—its product.

Since marketers have not often bothered to investigate society's reactions to various aspects of their marketing practices, society has often taken the initiative in communicating its displeasure through various forms of social pressure against offenders. The mildest form of social pressure is public opinion aimed at causing the offending marketers to change their ways. When public opinion does not accomplish the desired result, stronger action may take the form of political pressure with an implied threat of ultimate legal action to force the offender to abide by society's wishes. And the strongest form of social pressure is restrictive legislation outlawing the unpopular product or marketing activities.

PUBLIC OPINION

Consumerism Movement

Consumers' and the general public's dissatisfaction with marketing (and the business system in general) finds expression through the *consumerism movement*. One writer defines consumerism as "the actions of individuals and organizations (consumer, government, and business) in response to consumers' dissatisfactions arising in exchange relationships.[4] In other words, consumerism may be viewed as a protest against business injustices and the efforts to correct those injustices.

Actually, consumerism is not new. The consumer movement started in the early 1900s, fueled by rising prices and Upton Sinclair's writing. Sinclair's *The Jungle*, focusing on the meat packing industry, made the public aware of the need for consumer protection and contributed strongly to the passage of the Meat Inspection Act (1906), the Pure Food and Drug Act (1906), and the Federal Trade Commission Act (1914). A second wave of consumerism was launched in the late 1920s. Two books, *100,000,000 Guinea Pigs* and *Your Money's Worth*, both published in the 1930s, were widely read and quoted, and through their impact on public opinion forced several manufacturers to modify or abandon worthless or dangerous products.[5] Consumer organizations, such as Consumers Union (a nonprofit organization set up in 1936) have developed to test and rate products and provide their members with more complete and accurate buying information. Consumers Union publishes a monthly magazine, *Consumer Reports*, and an annual *Buying Guide*, both providing comparisons and ratings of competing brands of different products which are of considerable interest to consumers.

However, the consumer-oriented publications have their greatest impact on members of upper-middle- and upper-income groups. The vast majority of middle- and low-income consumers, who would have much to gain from more complete and accurate product information, are not effectively reached by these media. Consequently,

[4] W. J. Stanton, *Fundamentals of Marketing*, 4th ed. (New York: McGraw-Hill Book Company, 1975), p. 671.

[5] See A. Kallet and F. J. Schlink, *100,000,000 Guinea Pigs* (New York: Vanguard Press, Inc., 1933); and S. Chase and F. J. Schlink, *Your Money's Worth* (New York: The Macmillan Company, 1934).

the leaders of the consumerism and ecology movements have turned increasingly to the news media. If these leaders identify a particular product defect or uncover some other marketing abuse, they are quick to prove its newsworthiness and the resulting publicity rapidly spreads through newspapers, television, and radio. During the late 1960s and early 1970s, for instance, Ralph Nader, a leading crusader for consumer protection, achieved nationwide news coverage in publicizing a number of product deficiencies and abuses. Leading groups of environmentalists and ecologists have also been increasingly successful in securing news coverage in their efforts to publicize "companies responsible for polluting and destroying the environment."

Not a great deal of research has been reported on how successful these efforts to influence business activities through the power of public opinion have actually been. But there is no doubt that some businessmen, in many instances, have yielded to the force of public opinion before it was necessary to apply political and legal pressures. The results of one research study (conducted during 1970 in Austin, Texas) illustrates the power of public opinion.[6] Local press media had carried strong criticisms of the effects of phosphate-based detergents on pollution, and the researchers arranged with several "experimental" stores for the display of information about phosphate content of each detergent brand on sale. During a three-month period, large numbers of shoppers in the experimental stores switched to brands of lower phosphate content, and the "leading brand" (which had a high phosphate content) lost 30 percent of its market share. Yet during the same period in the "control" stores (where phosphate content information was not displayed), practically no shift in the buying of different brands occurred. Thus, this study provided some evidence of the potential power that public opinion has in shifting patronage from one brand to another. The results also have a strong implication for marketers—it is not only a wise idea but also profitable to keep track of public opinion!

POLITICAL PRESSURE

When the weight of public opinion fails to bring about results desired by society, the next step often involves applying political pressure on the offending marketer. When local business executives, for instance, ignore numerous complaints, some of which have been publicized, that their companies are using misleading advertising or polluting the environment, then a demand to "cease the offense" made by the mayor or other local official may bring about the desired correction. Various officials at all levels of government—local, state,

[6] Karl E. Henion, "The Effect of Ecologically Relevant Information on Detergent Sales," *Journal of Marketing Research*, February 1972, pp. 10–14.

and federal—are in position to apply political pressure to bring about results desired by society.

Two striking examples of the application of political pressure are provided by the actions taken by recent presidents concerning price changes in basic industries. Early in the administration of President John F. Kennedy, the United States Steel Corpcration announced a price increase only a few days after Kennedy administration officials had persuaded the United Steel Workers Union to accept minimal pay increases in order to keep inflation from getting worse. President Kennedy effectively used the prestige of his office in bringing pressure to bear on U.S. Steel and other industry members to "roll back" steel prices. During his administration, President Lyndon B. Johnson succeeded in bringing about similar rollbacks of copper and aluminum prices—President Johnson used the term *jawboning* to describe the use of political pressure and leverage to bring about a desired action.

Jawboning

How Society Influences Marketing—Legislative Action

When the force of public opinion or political pressure or both proves ineffective in bringing about the actions it desires, society often resorts to legislative action. From the standpoint of the marketing decision maker, the law limits the power of decision; but the relationship of the law to marketing decision making is often vague, since law is a complex of limitations coming from different sources. There are not only both federal and state law-making bodies but courts at both levels which, in handing down judicial interpretations, set precedents for decisions in later cases. Furthermore, some governmental agencies (e.g., the Federal Trade Commission and the Food and Drug Administration) are charged with administering various pieces of legislation, while others (e.g., the Antitrust Division of the U.S. Department of Justice) carry out the enforcement provisions of other pieces of legislation. Small wonder, then, that lawyers are reluctant or unable to state what the law is in every possible situation.

Thus, by and large, the law provides no clear-cut guides for marketing decision making. But it is convenient to think of the body of law as "the rules of the game," even though the rules are subject to differences in judicial and administrative interpretation and are almost constantly changing. It is not surprising, then, that the legal implications of specific marketing decisions are often difficult to predict.

The following discussion is organized around the five main decision areas in marketing which are most affected by legal restraints: competitive action, product, price, marketing channels, and promotion. The intent of this discussion is to convey an appreciation of the legal boundaries, however vague and even ill defined they may sometimes be, within which the marketer must make certain decisions.

COMPETITIVE ACTION

Many marketing decisions have, purposely or not, considerable impact on competitors. In fact, nearly every marketing decision has at least some effect on competition. This is certainly inherent in most decisions on those marketing areas discussed later in this section—decisions on products, prices, marketing channels, and promotion. Our concern at this point is with those decisions which may directly affect competition and possibly expose the marketer to antitrust prosecution.

Decisions Involving Expansion Decisions involving expansion, particularly if the company is already large, should be made only after considering the possibilities of antitrust prosecution—the legal danger is that the company may be charged with unlawfully monopolizing or attempting to monopolize a market. There are only two avenues of corporate growth—one through gradual natural expansion, the other through merger with or acquisition of other firms. Eventually, either may lead to antitrust prosecution.

Legal restraints on growth have gradually become more restrictive. The first piece of federal antitrust legislation, the Sherman Antitrust Act of 1890, declared monopolization or attempts to monopolize illegal. The Clayton Antitrust Act, enacted in 1914, prohibits a corporation from acquiring stock in a competing corporation in the same industry or line of commerce, and prohibits a holding company from acquiring the stock of two or more competing corporations when acquisition would substantially lessen competition, or restrain commerce, or tend to create a monopoly. Generally, the courts have defined *monopoly power* as the power to control prices or the power to exclude competition—with strong emphasis on the word "power." Frequently, the extent of power has been measured in terms of relative market share—one way to describe the comparative sizes of different industry members.

Monopoly Power

The merger or acquisition route to expansion is fraught with legal complications, but companies that choose to take the natural growth route also have their problems. Once a company grows rather large, and as it gains an increasing share of the market, management begins to fear adverse action by the government. In such a company management is often inclined to suppress its competitive skills.

Decisions Requiring Cooperative Relations with Competitors Marketing decisions requiring any sort of cooperative relationship with competitors should be made only after considering possible violations of antitrust laws. Particularly vulnerable to antitrust prosecution are price agreements with competitors, for they are illegal *per se*. This means, in effect, that the courts will declare them illegal without considering any mitigating circumstances. The courts have held that it is illegal for competitors even to exchange information about prices.

It is illegal not only for competitors to fix prices among themselves, but also for them to agree upon uniform terms of sale. Use by competitors of the same basing point for pricing and collusion among bidders are also illegal.[7] Marketers "skate on thin legal ice" when they permit themselves to be drawn into any sort of pricing arrangement with their competitors.

Decisions on Competitive Tactics The law limits the tactics a marketer can use in fighting a competitor. It is illegal, for example, for a marketer to misrepresent or disparage a competitor's products, its methods of doing business, or its financial standing and reliability. It is also illegal for a marketer to cut off a competitor's source of supply, whether by individual effort or through collusion with others.

DECISIONS ON PRODUCTS

There are several reasons why legal restraints have been imposed on product decisions. Some resulted from legislative efforts to preserve and maintain competition. Others trace to the legal protection afforded individual companies against having their products duplicated by competitors. Still others stem from the desire of lawmakers and governmental agencies to protect consumers' interests.

New Product Additions Decisions on new products may be equivalent to those on expansion discussed earlier. If a new product decision is tied to one on a merger with or an acquisition of another firm, it is illegal if it may tend to "substantially lessen competition or tend to create a monopoly." Similarly, if a new product decision involves buying certain assets from another firm, antitrust prosecution may result on the grounds that competition may be affected adversely. Therefore, from a legal standpoint, the safest way for a company to secure new products is through its own research and development efforts.

Design Patents

Product Design Patent law imposes certain restraints on product design decisions. Holders of *design patents* are protected against others using their designs during the term the patent is in force—which may be for three and one half, seven, or fourteen years. During the time a design patent is in force, its holder has what, in effect, is a

[7] A basing point is a geographical location from which F.O.B. prices are quoted.

monopoly over its use. The holder may, if it wishes, license others to use the patent but, except in rare instances, the law does not compel it to do so. Thus, the law forbids a marketer to sell a product that is too similar to one patented and made by a competitor. (The courts declare a product as being "too similar" if consumers regard its design or outward appearance as identical to that of a competitor's product.)

Fairly recently, there has been a trend toward national legislation regulating other aspects of product design. The Child Protection and Toy Safety Act of 1969, for instance, empowers the U.S. Secretary of Health, Education, and Welfare to order dangerous toys to be taken off the market. Another example is that of the U.S. Department of Transportation which has the power to develop and enforce motor vehicle safety standards—recently, auto producers have used "increases in required product safety standards" as their reasons in attempting to justify price increases. With the growing concern of society about environmental pollution, the federal government set up the Environmental Protection Agency which has the power to establish and enforce environmental protection standards. Marketers are well advised to keep the existence of such restraints in mind in making decisions on product design. It is safe to predict that more comprehensive legal restrictions on product design will exist in the future.

Product Quality In some product areas, the law limits the marketer's discretion in making decisions on product quality. The Food, Drug, and Cosmetics Act—enacted by Congress in 1938—authorizes the establishment of mandatory minimum quality standards for food products. It also gives the Food and Drug Administration the power to fix standard grades for specific kinds of food products on a permissive basis (packers may accept the standards or not at their own option). This act also prohibits the adulteration and sale of any food, drug, therapeutic device, or cosmetic that may endanger public health. There are also numerous state and local laws relating to the quality of individual products, such as milk, cheese, and cream.

Product Packaging and Labeling The Fair Packaging and Labeling Act (1967) provides that the package label must disclose product identity, name and location of manufacturer, packer or distributor, net quantity of contents (weight, measure, numerical count, and net quantity of a serving or application when represented). This net quantity statement must appear on the main display panel in adequate type size and near the main printing of the trade name.[8]

Special laws, applicable to some industries, further regulate the

[8] "Federal Trade Commission Proposed Regulations Under the Fair Packaging and Labeling Act," CCH 50, 173, July 1967, *CCH Newsletter 313* (extra edition), June 28, 1967.

type and content of the information that the product label must carry. Among these are laws requiring different marketers to include label information on fabric flammability, fiber content, type of fur, nature and percentages of wool and other components, identification of synthetic fabrics by generic names, and prescribed warnings on products adjudged in some way to be dangerous. Various state and local laws also regulate the labeling of specific products.

In all industries not covered by special laws, the Federal Trade Commission maintains a constant watch for instances of misbranding which generally means some form of misrepresentation on a label as to the composition, properties, or origin of the product. To comply with the law, a label must be accurate and complete in all essential details.

PRICE DECISIONS

No class of marketing decisions is more hedged in by legal restraints than price decisions. Federal antitrust laws (the Clayton Act and Robinson-Patman Act) have implications for pricing, inasmuch as the "power to control prices" is one of the tests courts apply in determining the existence of monopoly power. Among state laws affecting pricing decisions are those permitting resale price maintenance and forbidding sales below cost.

Price Discrimination The Clayton Act, as amended by the Robinson-Patman Act, prohibits any direct or indirect price discrimination by a seller among different purchasers of commodities of like grade and quality, where the effect is to injure competition. The law prohibits price discrimination, but it does permit certain differentials in price; the seller must be prepared to justify any price differences it grants if it is charged with price discrimination. Proving that price differentials are justified (in terms of differences in costs in serving different customers) is extraordinarily difficult.

Price discriminations resulting from the attempts of sellers to meet competitors' prices were apparently legalized under the Robinson-Patman Act, although different court decisions in cases of this sort have been inconsistent.

Quantity Discounts

The marketer, if it grants *quantity discounts,* must make them equally available to all its customers. Thus, a noncumulative quantity discount (i.e., one based on the size of a single order and shipment) is fairly easy to justify legally. Cumulative quantity discounts (i.e., those based on how much a customer buys over an extended period) are extremely difficult to justify legally, as there is no way a marketer can make such a discount equally available to all its customers.

Functional Discounts

A functional discount is a type of price differential that is evidently legal. A *functional discount,* by definition, is one based on difference in function—for instance, one given to a wholesaler but not to a retailer. Consider, for example, the paper products manufacturer who sells part of its output through wholesalers and the rest directly to retailers—ordinarily, the manufacturer must sell to the wholesalers at a lower price than it uses in selling to retailers. Under the law, if a wholesaler and a retailer do not compete directly with each other, a marketer can legally charge the wholesaler a lower price.

Fair Trade

Resale Price Maintenance Resale price maintenance or *fair trade* is the legal process by which a marketer sets the resale prices at which middlemen must sell its brand. Forty-six of the fifty states have at one time or another had such laws. Since resale price-fixing was illegal under existing federal antimonopoly laws, the U.S. Congress passed special laws (the Miller-Tydings Act and the McGuire Act) which legalized this exception. The state acts make it lawful for a marketer of a branded product to force a wholesaler to enter into a resale price agreement with the latter's retailer customers. Furthermore, in most states, a single resale price maintenance agreement with one wholesaler and/or retailer in the state is binding on all of the others providing the marketer informs them of the agreement's existence.[9]

Unfair Trade Practices Acts

Restrictions on Minimum Prices Many states have legislation regulating minimum resale prices. More than half have *unfair trade practices acts* which forbid sales below cost. These are laws that apply to all goods sold by wholesalers and retailers and they do not require, as the fair trade laws do, that the goods be branded or that formal price-fixing agreements be signed. The laws of the various states differ with respect to what "cost" means, with cost being interpreted to mean all the way from invoice cost to invoice cost plus freight and handling charges plus a fixed markup percentage. In addition, over twenty states have laws outlawing below-cost sales of specific products, such as liquor, beer, and cigarettes.

At the federal level, one restraint on below-cost sales exists. The Federal Trade Commission prosecutes marketers who sell their products below cost with the intention of driving competitors out of the market. Such below-cost pricing is regarded as an unfair competitive practice.

MARKETING CHANNEL DECISIONS

With comparatively few exceptions (e.g., the liquor industry in certain states), the law does not interfere with the marketer's freedom to determine its own marketing channels, or to "pick and choose"

[9] However, as mentioned earlier, fair trade has met with increasingly vocal opposition. As this book went to press, it seemed apparent that fair trade had only a short life remaining.

from among the available middlemen those whom it wants to represent it. But once the marketer establishes buying-selling relationships with its middlemen, the law is concerned with the nature of these relationships.

Exclusive Dealing

Exclusive Dealing *Exclusive dealing* is an arrangement by which a marketer agrees to permit dealers to handle its product only if the dealers agree to buy all their requirements for this type of product from the manufacturer and none whatever from competing suppliers. Generally speaking, any contract with buyers requiring them to buy all their needs from one supplier is illegal. But a necessary condition for illegality is that competition be impaired or threatened. This condition is practically always present and relatively easy to prove.

Tying Contract

Tying Contracts The Clayton Act outlaws the *tying contract,* a device closely related to exclusive dealing. A tying contract involves the sale or lease of products on condition that the buyer or lessee buy or use certain other items that the seller or lessor offers to supply. For a marketer to make effective use of either exclusive dealing or tying contracts, it must possess powerful leverage with respect to at least some of the products offered for sale—for instance, when a manufacturer markets a brand so strongly preferred by consumers that dealers do not dare refuse to stock it.

Automobile Dealers Franchise Act This act relates specifically to certain aspects of manufacturer-dealer relations in the automobile industry. Its stated purpose is "to balance the powers now heavily weighted in favor of automobile manufacturers, by enabling franchised automobile dealers to bring suits in the district courts of the United States to recover damages sustained by reason of the failure of automobile manufacturers to act in good faith in complying with terms of franchises or in terminating or not renewing franchises with their dealers." *Good faith* is defined as the duty to act in a fair and equitable manner to guarantee freedom from coercion, intimidation, or threats of coercion or intimidation. Although this act applies only to the automobile industry, it may be a forerunner of legal controls over manufacturer-dealer relations in other industries.

Good Faith

Maintaining Resale Prices in Absence of Fair Trade Manufacturers sometimes get into legal difficulties when they attempt to "police" resale prices of their products in areas where they do not have lawful resale price maintenance agreements in effect. The courts have held that it is illegal for a company to refuse to deal with wholesalers as a method of persuading them not to supply the company's products to retailers who depart from suggested prices. Thus, marketers should not take any action to force middlemen to adhere to suggested prices in the absence of legal fair trade agreements.

PROMOTION DECISIONS

Of all the promotion decisions, those on advertising are most affected by legal restraints. Advertising has received more attention from lawmaking bodies and enforcement agencies than has personal selling, probably because advertising exposes itself to large audiences whereas personal selling generally does not. Furthermore, advertising, whether printed or spoken, is recorded in publications and the logs of television and radio stations, where it may be inspected later by public authorities.

False Advertising The Wheeler-Lea Act, a 1938 amendment to the Federal Trade Commission Act of 1914, expanded the earlier law's prohibition against "unfair methods of competition" to prohibit "unfair or deceptive acts or practices." Under both pieces of legislation, the FTC is responsible for preventing false and deceptive advertising. The Wheeler-Lea Act specifically outlaws the dissemination of any false advertisement to induce the purchase of foods, drugs, devices, or cosmetics. This act also strengthened the FTC's enforcement procedures.

Bait Advertising Bait advertising, simply defined, is advertising under false pretenses. The FTC considers bait advertising "an alluring but insincere offer to sell a product or service which the advertiser in truth does not intend or want to sell." Its purpose is to attract consumers interested in buying the advertised product in order to sell them a substitute product, usually at a higher price or on terms more advantageous to the advertiser. Thus, the chief aim of a bait advertisement is to obtain leads on persons interested in buying merchandise of the general type advertised. The FTC prosecutes bait advertisers as engaged in "deceptive acts."

Deceptive Price Advertising The FTC has been especially active in seeking to prevent the advertising of deceptive prices. While the commission has prosecuted dishonest price advertisers at an ever increasing rate, it has provided marketers with enough of the basic ground rules to encourage wide-spread voluntary avoidance of deceptive price advertising. According to the FTC, the law is violated whenever the term "list price" means anything but the usual price at which the product is sold at retail. The same applies to other terms such as "manufacturer's suggested retail price," "catalog price," and "nationally advertised price."

Promotional Allowances and Services The Robinson-Patman Act provides that if a customer is offered an allowance, a discount, or some other form of compensation for displaying, handling, advertising, or otherwise promoting a product, then that same payment or consideration must be made available on proportionally equal terms to all other customers competing in the product's distribution. Thus, if a manufacturer offers to share the cost of newspaper advertising with a particular retailer on a 50–50 basis to comply with the law, it must find some way to make the same offer available on proportionally equal terms to all other customers who compete with that particular retailer.

Summary

You should now understand why modern marketers, in formulating and implementing marketing strategies, must recognize that they are both influencing and being influenced by society. Marketers must keep their responsibilities to society clearly in mind as they plan the manipulation of the controllables, since marketing activities have important influences not only on buyer behavior but on general economic well-being and the quality of the environment. Society, in general, expects marketers to serve its members' consumption needs efficiently, honestly, and responsibly. The reactions of society to various marketing activities are expressed not only daily at the nation's checkout counters and cash registers but also over the long run through public opinion, political pressure, and legislative action. The marketing strategist, therefore, not only must know what society expects but must anticipate its reactions to various marketing moves. If you have gained this understanding of the important interactions of marketing and society, you are ready to move on to Chapter 21 (Overall Marketing Strategy), which focuses more specifically on the formulation and implementation of overall marketing strategy.

QUESTIONS AND PROBLEMS

1. What are marketing's social responsibilities? Does marketing fulfill its social responsibilities?
2. Does marketing cost too much? Justify your position.
3. In what ways does marketing "add value" to a product?
4. Identify as many criticisms of marketing as you can and provide solutions as to how marketing might correct these shortcomings.
5. "Marketing induces frivolous and excessive buying and it makes people materialistic." Agree or disagree? Explain.

6. In what ways does marketing contribute to environmental pollution? What can marketing do to help preserve the environment?
7. When the weight of public opinion fails to bring about results desired by society, the next step often involves applying political pressure on the offending marketer. Discuss.
8. "Business competition serves as a sort of natural protector of the public interest." If this is so, why have legal restraints on marketing decisions been imposed?
9. Explain the significance of the "market share" concept in legal actions involving corporate mergers. What are the implications, if any, of the legal aspects of this concept with respect to a company's marketing research activities?
10. Do you favor or oppose George Romney's proposal that when one firm in a basic industry gains more than a certain percentage of total industry sales, it should be required to file a plan of divestiture bringing its market share below some specified level? Why?
11. Explain the meaning of the following terms:
    a. monopoly power
    b. basing-point system
    c. generic name
    d. functional discount
12. One part of the policy manual of a large corporation reads as follows: "It is the policy of the company to comply strictly in all respects with the antitrust laws. There shall be no exception to this policy nor shall it be compromised or qualified by anyone acting for or on behalf of the company. No employee shall enter into any understanding, agreement, plan or scheme, expressed or implied, formal or informal, with any competitor, in regard to prices, terms or conditions of sale, production, distribution, territories or customers; nor exchange or discuss with a competitor prices, terms or conditions of sale or any other competitive information; nor engage in any other conduct which in the opinion of the company's counsel violates any of the antitrust laws."

    Should such a formal written statement of policy on compliance with the law be necessary? Why or why not?
13. "The law prohibits price discrimination, but it does permit certain differentials in price." Explain.
14. Distinguish between noncumulative and cumulative quantity discounts. If a company wants to minimize the risk of being charged with price discrimination, which type of quantity discount should it use? Why?
15. Under what conditions are functional discounts likely to be held legal? Illegal?

16. Why should it be illegal (as it is) for buyers to induce or knowingly receive the benefits of price discrimination?
17. The resale price maintenance laws are often called the "fair trade" laws. What is "fair" about them?
18. The most controversial feature of the state fair trade acts has been the nonsigners' clause. This clause permits a brand owner to sign a resale price maintenance contract with any dealer or distributor and, upon giving notice to all dealers or distributors involved in the particular state, the contract becomes binding on all parties selling the brand. Do you favor such a "nonsigners' clause" permitted by many state fair trade laws? Why or why not?
19. Compare and contrast the fair trade laws with the unfair trade practices acts.
20. What is meant by exclusive dealing? Tying contracts? Under what circumstances is it legal for a manufacturer to use such devices?
21. Analyze the extent to which the law imposes restraints upon a manufacturer's choice of marketing channels and the conduct of its relationships with middlemen.
22. Can a manufacturer legally refuse to deal with middlemen who do not agree to maintain resale prices? Under what circumstances?
23. Legal restraints appear to affect advertising decisions more than they do personal selling decisions. Why?
24. Differentiate among the following: false advertising, bait advertising, deceptive price advertising.
25. Under what circumstances may a manufacturer pay promotional allowances or provide promotional services to dealers?
26. The Food and Drug Administration has published official grade definitions for most canned fruits and vegetables, but packers are not required to affix the official grade designation to their products. Would you favor making it compulsory for all packers to affix these official grades to their products? Why or why not?
27. What is the extent to which the different types of legal restraints on marketing strengthen or weaken the position of consumers as participants in the economic process?

CASE PROBLEM

Big Deal City, a large regional discount operation consisting of six stores in and around one of the country's major cities, had recently begun a rather intensive newspaper advertising campaign designed to inform the buying public not only that it was against "fair trade," but also that it was doing something about it and would sell normally fair-traded items at prices up to 40 percent below fair trade prices. The advertisements also called for consumers to support a proposed bill that would eliminate the state's fair trade law.

Each of the full-page advertisements concentrated on four or five brands of various products that were fair-traded, with a specific price quotation for each and, next to it, a statement as to what percentage below the fair trade price the Big Deal City price was. Included were well-known brands of power tools, pen and pencil sets, radio and television equipment, and kitchenware.

The advertisements contended that fair trade prices forced consumers to pay higher prices and that adherence to the state's fair trade law prevented the Big Deal City discount stores from granting lower prices. In other words, Big Deal City had the opinion that fair trade was actually "unfair" to consumers and it was doing something about it in the best interests of the consuming public.

Is Big Deal City guilty of fraudulent, misleading, or deceptive advertising?

Is the discounter acting illegally with regard to the resale price maintenance law?

When you have mastered the contents of this chapter, you should be able to:

1. Contrast the relative importance of, and need for, formalized overall marketing strategies under conditions of: (a) no direct competition, (b) pure competition, (c) monopolistic competition, and (d) oligopolistic competition.
2. Analyze how a marketer in an industry characterized by monopolistic or oligopolistic competition should go about making decisions on: products, distribution, promotion, price, and the timing of marketing actions.
3. Explain the three main factors involved in selecting inputs to overall marketing strategy.
4. Explain how a marketer should go about achieving an optimum combination of inputs to its overall marketing strategy.
5. Outline the several problems that confront marketers in implementing and timing their marketing strategies.
6. Explain the nature and purpose of a marketing audit.

CHAPTER 21

OVERALL MARKETING STRATEGY

Basically, a company's overall marketing strategy is its competitive posture in the market place. Management shapes various aspects of this posture as it formulates strategies for each controllable (product, distribution, promotion, and pricing). Management's mission under the marketing concept is to manipulate the controllables in terms of the uncontrollables in ways that both meet the target market's needs and wants and facilitate achievement of the company's overall goals. To accomplish this mission, management must unify the company's product-market, distribution, promotion, and pricing strategies into an appropriate overall marketing strategy (i.e., into a deliberately planned competitive posture). Discussion and analysis in this chapter are aimed to help you integrate your previous knowledge of marketing and to gain added insights on (1) overall marketing strategies and decisions in different competitive settings, (2) the formulation of overall marketing strategy, (3) the implementation of marketing strategy and timing, and (4) the evaluation of overall marketing strategy.

Throughout this book the emphasis has been on a systems approach to managing marketing operations. In managing marketing, many decisions must be made—each seemingly independent, all in fact interrelated. Thus, if a marketer decides to change its product's price by some substantial amount, it must also reevaluate other parts of its overall marketing strategy. But, of course, if the price change is small, the need for reevaluation is not so great though the marketer should still consider the possible need for making changes in the other controllables. Significant change in any of the controllables definitely influences the effectiveness of the other controllables. The ultimate success of changes in price (or other controllables) in meeting desired objectives depends on the marketer's skill (and luck) in maintaining an optimum combination of strategies—that is, in keeping the company's overall marketing strategy in balance.

Management, in formulating and implementing overall marketing strategy, concerns itself primarily with identifying opportunities to serve target markets profitably and serving them so effectively that it is difficult for competitors to take business away on a profitable basis. But competitive postures can be either aggressive or defensive. When a marketer's products are already firmly established in the market, there is strong temptation for it to adopt a defensive posture—that is, to maintain a holding action. But the danger in defending the *status quo* is that it means yielding the initiative to competitors who may, for example, develop product innovations, which might be successfully marketed, breaking established customer loyalties and buying patterns in the process.

Seven-Up, for instance, first broke into the soft drink market not by introducing another cola, root beer, or other standard flavor, but by developing and marketing an entirely new flavor—lemon-lime. As Seven-Up succeeded in carving out a market segment for itself, certain other bottlers, such as Coca-Cola and Pepsi-Cola, dropped their predominantly defensive overall marketing strategies, introduced new flavors of their own, and took the offensive. Had Coca-Cola, for example, continued its defensive strategy, it would merely have tried to retain or increase its share of the market for cola drinks. With Seven-Up's introduction of the lemon-lime flavor, the total market for soft drinks expanded, and the competitor restricting itself to the traditional flavors found itself with a shrinking share of the total market.

Competitive Settings

The importance of (and need for) formalized overall marketing strategies (i.e., deliberately planned competitive postures) varies with the competitive setting. There are four basic kinds of competitive setting: (1) no direct competition, (2) pure competition, (3) monopolistic competition, and (4) oligopolistic competition.

NO DIRECT COMPETITION

There are no direct competitors for either the monopolist or the marketer of a radically new and different product in its market pioneering life cycle stage. But both need formalized overall marketing strategies—the monopolist because it has indirect competitors (such as the deBeers Consolidated diamond monopoly has) contending for the same prospects' interest and buying decisions, and the innovating marketer because it has only a limited period free from direct competition. Both the monopolist and the innovating marketer must initiate and stimulate primary demand—that is, demand for the product category—through promotional strategies designed to influence final buyers and middlemen. Both need distribution strategies providing for marketing channels, middlemen's cooperation, and systems for the product's physical distribution. Both require a pricing strategy; the monopolist (at least in theory) being free to maximize profits through "charging what the traffic will bear"; the innovating marketer generally choosing either a price-skimming or a penetration-pricing strategy, depending mainly upon how soon it expects direct competitors to enter the market. And, most important, both the monopolist and the innovating marketer need to integrate their individual product-market, distribution, promotion, and pricing strategies into overall marketing strategies consistent with the long-term goals of each. Such consistency is obtained only when all the elements of the strategy are in balance. Therefore, the marketer of a product which has no close substitutes must take care in choosing its target market, in distributing it, in promoting it, in pricing it, and in integrating all of these into an overall marketing strategy suitable for achieving the organization's long-term goals.

PURE COMPETITION

Economists define pure competition as a market situation with large numbers of buyers and sellers, none of whom is powerful enough to control or to influence the prevailing market price. The economist assumes, among other things, that (1) no single buyer or seller is so large that he can appreciably affect the product's total demand or supply, (2) all sellers' products are identical in every respect (i.e., each sells homogeneous units of the product), so buyers are indifferent as to which sellers they buy from, (3) no artificial restraints on prices of any kind exist (i.e., no governmental price-fixing, nor any administering of prices by individual companies, trade associations, labor unions, or others), and (4) all buyers are fully informed of all sellers' prices.

If these assumptions held true, no marketer would ever have to concern itself with formulating overall marketing strategy. Each seller would be too small to gain business through price-cutting at the expense of its competitors and, if it did cut the price, they would immediately match it. No marketer could compete by offering a better product, because product differentiation is ruled out. It would be futile for a marketer to advertise or otherwise promote its product, inasmuch as all potential buyers are already fully informed and buy solely on the basis of price. Because the economist also implicitly assumes that sellers and buyers are in direct contact, no marketer would need to worry about marketing channels or physical distribution. Under pure competition there are no marketing controllables, and there is no need for individual or overall marketing strategies.

Probably the nearest thing to pure competition is found in the distribution of certain agricultural commodities, such as the crops of truck farms.[1] For the sellers of such commodities, the critical marketing decisions (besides that of deciding on which crop to grow) relate to physical distribution: moving the commodities in time and space. A New Jersey truck farmer, for instance, has the choice of shipping each day's pick of the string bean crop to wholesale produce markets in Philadelphia or New York, or to delay sending them to market for a day or two hoping for a rise in price. But if a truck farmer is shipping a highly perishable commodity, such as strawberries or mushrooms, there may not even be the option of storing the output a short time in the hope of a higher price.

MONOPOLISTIC COMPETITION

Most modern marketers operate under conditions that approximate monopolistic competition, which means that some or all of the assumptions of pure competition do not hold. Specifically, *monopolistic competition* exists when there are many sellers of a generic kind of product but each seller's brand is in some way differentiated from every other seller's brand. The number of sellers is sufficiently large that the actions of any one have no perceptible effect upon others, and their actions have no perceptible effect upon that seller.[2] Furthermore, under monopolistic competition, it is comparatively easy for additional competitors to enter the market, such as for retailers to enter as private label competitors. This competitive setting describes many products during late phases of their market growth and during much of their market maturity life cycle stages.

Monopolistic Competition

Nearly every seller's brand of product, whether it be peanut butter or lipstick, can be differentiated (at least in final buyers' minds) from competing brands. Most ultimate consumers appear convinced that different brands of even such "identical" products as aspirin, coffee, and vinegar are not exactly alike, providing individual marketers with opportunities to build brand preferences among buyers and, hence, to control some share of the market. Of even greater significance, however, is the fact that most ultimate consumers (and even many industrial buyers) are not really fully informed—often not even adequately informed—about the offerings

[1] Some economists claim that stock transactions on the New York Stock Exchange approximate the conditions of pure competition. See R. H. Leftwich, *The Price System and Resource Allocation* (New York: Holt, Rinehart & Winston, Inc., 1966), p. 24.

[2] *Ibid.*, p. 243.

of competing sellers. Thus, for instance, it is common to find two competing (and even neighboring) supermarkets selling identical, branded items at different prices. Ultimate consumers, in fact, in making many buying decisions, particularly for low-priced items, are often overwhelmed by the sheer variety of products and brands from which to choose.

Competitive settings characterized by monopolistic competition not only provide marketing opportunities for the marketer but also clearly demand marketing skill. If a seller (producer or middleman) can differentiate its product, it has a market message to relate through its promotional strategy, which provides it with some control over its product's distribution and price. Such a seller needs skill both in formulating an appropriate overall marketing strategy and in implementing it in the competitive struggle for survival and success.

OLIGOPOLISTIC COMPETITION

Oligopolistic Competition

Many modern marketers operate under conditions approximating *oligopolistic competition.* This kind of competitive setting exists when the number of competitors is small enough that they are individually identified and known to each other and it is difficult for new competitors to enter the market. Each competitor is of sufficient importance (i.e., it is a large enough organization and has a large enough market share) that changes in its overall marketing strategy have direct repercussions on the others. Thus, each marketer in an oligopolistic industry must weigh the possible reactions of each of its competitors in formulating and implementing its own overall marketing strategy.[3] Oligopolistic competition tends to develop in the marketing of many products either during a late phase of their market growth or an early phase of their marketing maturity.

In the United States, there are oligopolies in such industries as automobiles, appliances, soap and detergents, and shoes in the consumer goods field and in steel, aluminum, textile machinery, and machine tools in the industrial goods field. A strong trend exists for the more successful firms to continue growing, and for the less successful to fail or disappear (through merger). The soap and auto industries provide dramatic examples, both having been reduced from numerous competitors to a very small group in fairly recent times. Probably, this trend will continue—indications are that there will be more, not fewer, oligopolistic industries in the future. Governmental agencies and congressional committees try continually to

[3] For an excellent analysis of four interesting competitive situations in which a firm might find itself, and the strategies appropriate for each case, see Philip Kotler, *Marketing Management: Analysis, Planning, and Control,* 2nd ed. (Englewood Cliffs, N.J.: Prentice-Hall, Inc., 1972), pp. 257–269. The situations involve strategies for (1) the smaller firm, (2) the dominant firm, (3) two firms of equal size, and (4) the many-firm situation.

discourage the merger movement as a threat to "free competition." Proposed mergers are denied and completed mergers are declared illegal when they are proved in conflict with the antimonopoly laws. However, the drift toward oligopoly is clearly continuing but through the slower process of expansion by the successful and failure or withdrawal by the others.

Oligopoly produces the most aggressive kind of competition. When a few large producers completely dominate an industry, the competitive moves of any one can have a significant effect on the entire market: when one of the large soap companies introduces a new kind of liquid detergent or a low-phosphate detergent, its competitors risk a rapid loss of market share if they do not respond appropriately and almost immediately. For this reason, competitors' actions are watched closely, and marketing changes by one firm are almost certain to be matched or countered in some way by its competitors. Changes in one competitor's product, in its distribution, in its promotion—if they hold some promise of increasing its market share—are imitated, improved upon, or otherwise countered by its competitors as rapidly as they can launch their counteroffensives. Price changes by individual industry members can be and often are matched by others almost immediately. Industry-wide price adjustments are often made so quickly that they appear to result from collusion when, in fact, there has been none whatever. Thus, even in rather small towns, when one petroleum marketer cuts the price of gasoline by a few cents per gallon, other petroleun marketers follow almost immediately. The other marketers cannot afford to wait very long to reduce prices—they know that, to retain their market shares, they must meet their competitors' prices.

However, there are times when companies in oligopolistic industries are guilty of collusion. In fact, when collusive action is attempted, the small number of competitors makes it particularly easy. As a case in point, in the early 1960s five large makers of power switch gear assemblies were found guilty of having conspired to fix prices on bids for government contracts. Collusive arrangements are rather common among small companies participating in local oligopolistic situations (e.g., local bakeries and dairies), but they are unusual (perhaps because they are not easy to hide from federal law enforcement agencies) among large national competitors.

Marketing Decisions in a Competitive Setting

In any industry characterized by monopolistic or oligopolistic competition, an individual marketer skilled in planning and applying the marketing controllables has an opportunity to win the buying preferences of certain market segments on a more or less permanent basis. Under monopolistic competition, the number of competitors is large enough that the actions of any one have no perceptible effect upon the others and their actions have no perceptible effect upon that competitor; but this does not mean that any one marketer can afford wholly to ignore its competitors' marketing activities. Especially in the long run, but sometimes even in the short run, skill (and/or luck) in such matters as product innovation, distribution, and promotion makes some companies major contenders in their industries, while others with little marketing skill (and/or luck) fall by the wayside. In other words, the potential for monopolistic competition to evolve into oligopolistic competition is almost always present. Thus, nearly every marketer has cause to carefully consider both its competitors' marketing moves and their possible reactions to its own marketing decisions. Every area of marketing decision is influenced to some extent by competitors' actions and likely reactions.

THE PRODUCT

Whether a marketer is an innovator or a follower, its product decisions (if they are to prove successful) must take into account the probable timing of competitors' actions. For example, much of the research and testing that goes into the development of a new product may be wasted if a competitor manages to introduce a similar new product to the market earlier. The competitor, then, gets not only credit for the innovation but also first "crack" at the market. In attempting to prevent such occurrences, manufacturers sometimes feel compelled to market new products that are not fully perfected. Furthermore, when one marketer introduces a new or greatly improved product, its competitors must be prepared to develop and introduce competitive substitutes as soon as they can determine that the innovation is a marketing success; this, too, may cause some to sacrifice extensive testing for earlier market introduction.

Business history is full of examples of companies that slipped from positions of industry leadership to much lower status (or even that disappeared entirely) following their competitors' introduction of new products that these companies were unwilling or unable to imitate, or which they delayed too long in matching. Consider, for example, what happened in the washing machine industry after the mass introduction of fully automatic washers. The total number of washing machine manufacturers shrank greatly, as manufacturers who failed to introduce automatic washers or who were too long in doing so withdrew from the industry. The Maytag Company, which had been the industry's sales leader for nearly 30 years, dropped to second place, while the Whirlpool Corporation took over first position. Several trade magazines attributed this status change to Whirlpool's fairly early introduction of an automatic washer and Maytag's failure to do so. However, the introduction of automatics did not guarantee success, since many companies that later left the industry had tried to market automatics. Nevertheless, the decision not to introduce an automatic evidently did guarantee failure for many who left the industry.

DISTRIBUTION

Marketing Channels Decisions on marketing channels are comparable to the military commander's choice of battlefield. Products, if they are to compete successfully, must be on sale in places where target buyers expect to buy them. If most ultimate consumers, for instance, expect to find photographic film in drugstores and at drive-up film processing booths (in shopping centers) and customarily buy their film in such places, it is difficult for a film producer to sell its product through hardware stores or service stations. Some film, to be sure, is sold through unconventional outlets but, assuming other marketing circumstances to be equal, it is easier to sell a product through outlets where target customers expect to find it. Ultimate consumers, seeing film in a hardware store, might buy it on impulse when they remember that they need film, but when they start out with the primary purpose of buying film, they usually go to stores that always carry film. Similar generalizations hold for other levels of distribution. Retailers seeking to buy a supply of some particular product ordinarily contact suppliers who they know handle such products.

However, sometimes a marketer finds it cannot use the customary channel. Retail druggists, for example, may already stock two makes of film and, hence, may refuse to stock a third (and perhaps less well-known) brand which, from their standpoint, might result in larger inventories with no increase in sales volume and therefore lower rates of stockturn. Thus, the marketer of a new film may find that its most feasible alternative is to persuade other types of retailers, such as grocers, to stock its brand, trying to overcome the unconventional outlet handicap through offering a better product, a lower price, a more effective promotional program, or some combination of these or other factors.

Physical Distribution Decisions on physical distribution are similar to those the military commander makes on logistics. Both the marketer and the military strategist want to have the right resource at the right place at the right time; but, while the military strategist looks upon cost as a minor consideration, the marketer regards the obtaining of physical distribution at a reasonable cost as highly important. In managing physical distribution, the marketer seeks to maximize the utility or economic value of its products by getting and having them where they are wanted and at the time wanted, at reasonable cost.[4]

[4] J. F. Magee, *Physical Distribution Systems* (New York: McGraw-Hill Book Company, 1967), p. 1.

Competitors' actions and operations strongly influence physical distribution decisions. If, for example, a Chicago luggage manufacturer has no competitors with plants or warehouses in the Pacific Northwest, it may serve that area directly from its Chicago factory by ordinary truck or rail shipments. Suppose, however, that a competitor opens a new plant in Seattle; the Chicago manufacturer then may find it must either use a faster transportation method, such as air freight, or change its storage method, perhaps by setting up its own warehouse in Seattle, or both. The manufacturer's decision should depend upon which alternative will provide the necessary level of service demanded by customers at a reasonable total expenditure on shipping, on storage, and on investment in inventories. If it continues with its previous physical distribution arrangement unchanged, the Seattle-based competitor may gain a strong competitive edge through its ability to provide faster delivery service to customers in that area—enabling them to reduce their own inventory investments because of quick delivery. However, the Chicago manufacturer also has other alternatives: it can improve its product, make it more attractive price-wise (to dealers, consumers, or both), or support it with heavier and/or more effective promotion—or it can put together some combination of these and other factors. No matter how the manufacturer chooses to counter the change in the competitive situation, if it makes any move at all its overall marketing strategy is revised.

TIMING MARKETING ACTIONS

A marketer's decisions on whether to lead or follow its competitors are critical to its success. Not every marketer should (or can) be a leader or innovator. While the innovator may gain an important competitive edge from "leading the pack" or because it is first with something new, it must also assume substantial risks. If its competitors are prepared to follow quickly, the innovator may gain very little, if anything, and, in fact, may actually be worse off from having been first.

Consider the risks that a marketer must accept when it decides to lead in introducing a radically new product—that is, a true product innovation. One risk is that the first marketer of a new product stands more chance of failing than those who follow—for example, the first marketer of ballpoint pens met failure, whereas those entering the market later scored great successes. A second risk is that the innovation may flop—Procter & Gamble, for example, once tried to market a liquid dentifrice, Teel, nationally; consumers would not accept it and Procter & Gamble had to withdraw it from the market. Then there are risks in just trying to get to the market first; a marketer may invest heavily in R & D, find what it thinks is an innovation, decide to test-market it, learn there that the innovation has little chance for success, and drop the innovation at this point—General Foods had this type of experience with both frozen baby foods and "instant frozen ice cream sodas."

But the marketer who decides to leave the innovations to its competitors also takes risks. The greatest hazards are those of being caught by surprise by competitors' marketing moves and of losing a substantial market share before it can launch an effective countermove. The marketer who prefers to let its competitors do the innovating must be prepared to counter their successful innovations (products or otherwise) quickly and effectively.

Formulating Overall Marketing Strategy

Formulating overall marketing strategy requires careful integration of all dimensions of the marketing effort. Ideally, the marketer should have some foolproof system for determining whether or not the combination of inputs going into the overall marketing strategy is optimal and, therefore, whether or not the resulting profit (and other desired outputs, in terms of the company's goals) is also optimal. Unfortunately, no such foolproof system has yet been devised, but some experimental work has been done in the building of mathematical models for determining marketing strategies. However, few companies rely at all on mathematical models for strategy determination.[5] Until such models become a great deal more sophisticated, the best that can be done is to apply a systematic approach to strategy formulation.[6]

What is a systematic approach to strategy formulation? It is an approach that involves evaluation of the possible inputs to the overall marketing strategy in terms of the likely outputs. Each aspect of each major input (i.e., product-market, distribution, promotion, and pricing strategies) should be analyzed and evaluated for its probable impact on the desired output (i.e., achievement of the marketer's objectives). Then the marketer should make its selections from the various inputs (product, distribution, promotion, and pricing variables) in such a way that the combination (i.e., the overall marketing strategy) is the best it can devise for achieving the desired outputs.

Factors in Selecting Marketing Inputs

Competitors' Countermoves The relative effectiveness of possible countermoves by competitors varies with different marketing inputs, and the marketer must take this into account in selecting inputs. Most competitors can easily and quickly match or otherwise

[5] On this matter, see D. J. Luck and A. E. Prell, *Market Strategy* (New York: Appleton-Century-Crofts, 1968), pp. 55–57.

[6] H. Igor Ansoff, in *Corporate Strategy* (New York: McGraw-Hill Book Co., 1965), pp. 103–121, presents an interesting discussion of two concepts—"the firm's business" and "the common thread"—that should provide guidance in the formulation of marketing strategy.

adjust to price changes; however, they often find it difficult (and sometimes impossible) to follow or retaliate against product innovations. This explains why many marketers seek to gain differential advantage over their competitors by varying product characteristics or by altering promotion rather than prices. Retail price wars often develop because some retailers fail to evaluate alternative strategies intelligently. Anxious or even desperate to increase volume, an individual retailer unobtrusively lowers prices, hoping that competitors will not notice this action or will not copy it. Of course they do, and the result is the start of a price war. If, instead, the retailer emphasizes superior customer service as its chief competitive weapon, it may not be copied, and the retailer will gain a competitive advantage. A marketer desiring to improve the "hitting power" of its overall marketing strategy should give first consideration to those moves involving inputs that are least subject to effective retaliatory actions by competitors.

Synergistic Potential

Synergistic Potential Some marketing inputs have *synergistic potential* (i.e., are capable of being mutually reinforcing), and the marketer should consider this in working toward an optimum overall marketing strategy. For example, an investment in point-of-purchase displays carefully designed to tie in with a national advertising campaign often increases the total impact of a promotional effort far more than an equal investment in additional advertising. Displays and advertisements can be made mutually reinforcing, since the display repeats the advertising message at a time when the consumer is in an outlet where the product is on sale.

Similarly, product inputs and marketing channel inputs can be mutually reinforcing or not, depending on the effectiveness with which they are integrated. For instance, when a marketer distributes its product through self-service retailers, potential buyers should be able to readily identify the product from its package and to obtain from it information that clerks would otherwise have to provide. When bed sheets are sold in full-service retail stores, they are frequently not packaged. Sales clerks inform the customers as to brand name, thread count, and shrink resistance. But when sheets are sold in self-service stores, where the help of sales clerks is not available, individual packaging provides a way of communicating product information to the consumer.

Substitutability The selection of marketing inputs is also affected by their degree of substitutability. It is important to know the extent to which one type of input can substitute for another type, inasmuch as the nature of marketing objectives (such as that of returning a certain level of profit) prevents a decision maker from making unlimited use of all inputs. Marketing strategists must ask themselves such questions as these: Will product quality higher than that found in competitive brands serve as a substitute for a promotional budget smaller than those of competitors? Will a larger promotional budget substitute for shortcomings in dealer cooperation? Will a price lower than those of competitors substitute for sparse distribution? Consideration of such substitutables helps in determining which input(s) to include and which to emphasize in the overall marketing strategy.

PROMOTION

The promotional strategies chosen by a marketer—that is, the methods it chooses to use in its efforts to stimulate market demand—are closely related to its sales expectations. If, for example, a marketer believes that a 5 percent sales increase is possible during the coming year, it may plan an advertising program and/or increase the strength and effectiveness of its sales force to the extent it thinks necessary to achieve the higher sales volume. However, in making a change in promotional strategy, the marketer should not assume that its competitors will continue their present promotional efforts. If a leading firm in an industry decides to increase its annual advertising budget from, say, $10 million to $15 million, its main competitors may decide they have to either plan similar increases or risk losing market share. If market demand for the product is expansible, all or most firms in the industry may benefit from the increased advertising—that is, if industry sales increase enough to more than cover the increased advertising costs. If, however, market demand is not expansible, total industry sales will not increase and the added advertising reduces most firms' gross margins and net profits. As with other components of overall marketing strategy, a competitor's increased promotional efforts can be countered in more ways than by simply matching or exceeding the increased promotion. Faced with a competitor's increased promotion, for example, a marketer might decide to launch a new or improved product, strengthen its distribution system (perhaps by offering special incentives to dealers to get them to push the product more), or make its product more attractive price-wise.

Promotional effort provides a major means whereby a marketer can gain a competitive edge. Both the number of dollars invested in promotion and the effectiveness with which they are used are important. Two competitors may match each other's promotional expenditures dollar for dollar, but one may get back many more sales dollars in return than the other. Two advertising campaigns may cost the same number of dollars but one, because it uses more powerful selling appeals, reaches a larger or more receptive audience, or for some other reason produces considerably more sales volume. Two otherwise identical advertising campaigns may differ in effectiveness because one fits in more appropriately with its sponsor's overall marketing strategy than the other. Similar generalizations hold for the productivity of the sales forces of different companies. The company with the more effective sales force management gets back more sales dollars per dollar spent on its sales force than one with less effective management.

PRICE

The price a marketer places on its brand must generally be "in the same ball park" as those on competing items. Although some brands of superior quality or prestige may be marketed successfully at higher-than-average prices, it is poor strategy to allow a price to get too far out of line with prices on directly competitive items. So, when competitive prices drop, the marketer of the quality brand should seriously consider cutting its price as well. And, when competitive prices go up, the marketer of the quality brand may consider raising its price.

Most marketers pursuing aggressive marketing strategies prefer not to rely on price as the main competitive weapon. They seek differential advantages over their competitors by stressing other elements in their marketing strategies—for example, products, distribution methods and systems, or promotion. Therefore, when prices in an industry are more or less uniform, this often indicates not only industry members' keen awareness of each other's prices but also their common desire to avoid using price as a main basis for competition.

Despite the general reluctance of marketers to use pricing as a competitive weapon, there are times when price competition provides the only or the most appropriate course of action. Retailers opening new stores often offer sweeping price reductions for a short time to overcome consumers' established shopping patterns and to attract them into the store. The same is true when a marketer finds it desirable to use penetration pricing in introducing a new product or in entering a new market. Furthermore, if a competitor introduces a new product, comes up with an effective new promotional gimmick, or the like, a price reduction may be a necessary competitive move to hold market share or to minimize its loss. Then, too, at all distribution levels, price reductions are regularly used for clearing out last year's models and seasonal merchandise.

A few marketers use price regularly as the main competitive weapon. To do so successfully, they must combine high efficiency (resulting in large sales volumes and low dollar unit costs) with willingness to accept low profits per sales dollar. Many discount department stores, such as the K-Mart and Zayre's operations, consistently strive to sell at prices under those of competitors. However, even in these cases, price is only one element in overall marketing strategy:

customarily, the discount department store also emphasizes "known" brands or equivalent brands of its own, shopping convenience, ease of parking, and heavy promotion.

Optimum Combination Of Marketing Inputs

Productivity In formulating overall marketing strategy, the marketer should recognize that not all inputs have equal productivity. Some inputs require a minimum level of use before they begin to have measurable effects—for example, an advertising message must often be repeated several times before consumers become aware of it. A single spot television commercial may have almost no effect on viewers, but after it has been repeated several times, viewers begin to hear, see, and remember it. In such instances, if the marketer cannot afford a sufficient number of TV spots to succeed in passing the threshold of consumers' awareness, it may be better off concentrating on some other advertising input, where the cost of crossing the threshold of awareness is lower. The lower cost per consumer contact of radio, magazines, and billboards often makes it possible, with a limited budget, to provide a much stronger impact on consumers than with TV.

Economies of Scale The choice of a combination of marketing inputs is also affected by economies of scale—that is, by efficiencies resulting from operating above a minimum level of activity. For instance, a direct-to-retailer marketing channel may offer a producer some strong advantages in terms of communications and promotional effort and, in areas where its retail outlets are geographically concentrated, the cost per salesman's call may be low enough for direct-to-retailer distribution to be economical. Yet in other areas, where the retail outlets handling its product are widely scattered, the costs of using the direct channel may be out of line with the costs of using alternative channels. In this instance, economies of scale dictate different marketing channels in the two areas. Similar economies of scale apply in using many marketing inputs, such as those involving advertising media, adding new items to the product line, servicing products directly or through middlemen, and so on. When possible economies of scale are involved, inputs already at an economical volume usually represent the most productive investment of resources.

Input Elasticity Different marketing inputs vary in their effects on demand, and the marketer needs to consider this in selecting the best combination of marketing inputs. A marketer may have to make several pricing decisions for a single product, and the choice of the best combination depends partly on an analysis of price elasticity of demand. For example, when distributors and dealers generally follow suggested prices, the marketer, in effect, establishes selling prices at all three distribution levels. An understanding of variations in price elasticity at each level helps the marketer determine whether increasing wholesalers' and retailers' margins is likely to be more or less effective than decreasing the prices consumers are asked to pay. If the consumer demand for a product is relatively price inelastic, a 5 percent increase in dealer and/or wholesaler margins may be more effective, because of the resulting increase in promotional efforts by these middlemen, than a 5 percent decrease in prices to consumers. Actually, such decisions are much more complex than the above example implies, since not only must price elasticities be taken into account, but also simultaneous comparisons need to be made of promotional and product elasticities. Although estimating price, promotional, and product elasticities is not easy, it should be tried, for even crude results are better than pure intuition.

Implementation of Marketing Strategy and Timing

Marketing inputs require different amounts of time to implement; therefore, they must be prepared and introduced in some planned sequence aimed toward making the chosen overall marketing strategy effective at some given target date. Thus, a marketer who decides to increase the size of its sales force substantially must allow from several months to a year or more for recruiting and training new recruits to the point where they become productive salesmen. If a marketer wants to open a new marketing channel, it may find even more time is needed to effect the change. Likewise, in implementing advertising strategy, the marketer finds that TV advertising schedules are generally booked a year in advance. The marketer also learns that it is often necessary to repeat advertising messages over weeks or even months before they begin to have an impact on sales. Clearly, then, the marketer must skillfully coordinate all such inputs if it is to succeed in putting its overall marketing strategy into effect.

In addition, all inputs to the overall marketing strategy do not retain their previously achieved levels of effectiveness for the same lengths of time. A marketer's new product or package will probably continue to attract buyers up to the time some competitor introduces a better product or more attractive package, and such competitive innovations can occur at almost any time. One advertising theme may lose its effectiveness after a single season of use, while another may continue to attract new buyers for years. Consequently, in planning the inputs to overall marketing strategy, the marketer must also consider each input's relative rate of decay in effectiveness.

Figure 21–1 shows how one marketer developed a sequence for the introduction and continued application of each input in his over-

Figure 21–1
Time schedule for introduction of a new product

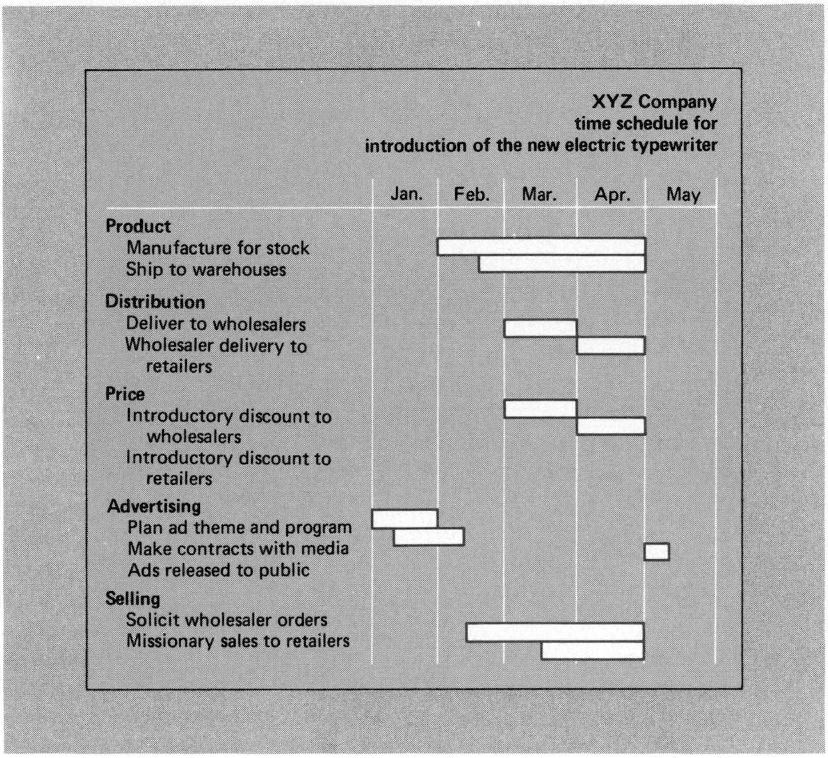

all marketing strategy. Working back (in time) from the target date for introducing the product to final buyers, the marketer scheduled each input with sufficient lead time for it to be fully effective at the target date. Since the target introduction date was May 1, wholesalers had to solicit dealers' orders thirty to sixty days before that, and salesmen had to get wholesalers' orders still earlier, so that the offering could be retailed by May 1. The marketer planned the advertising program and scheduled it for release in media on and following May 1. Previous experience had taught a valuable lesson: If advertisements reach prospective final buyers before dealers have the advertised item in stock, much of the advertising expenditure may be wasted, and if dealers stock the new item much before appearance of the advertising, they have initial difficulty in selling it, lose interest in it, and fail to give it their best efforts when the advertising does appear. Thus, at least in this case, the marketer believed it highly important to have the dates of product availability and appearance of promotion very close together in order to obtain the desired results in terms of advertising effectiveness and dealer effort. Timing is an extremely important factor in putting an overall marketing strategy into effect.

Evaluating Overall Marketing Strategy

Overall marketing strategy is a composite—built up, or put together, by blending various inputs (products, marketing channels and physical distribution systems, advertising, personal selling, other promotion, and prices) in different combinations to achieve desired outputs (i.e., objectives, such as some targeted return on investment, market share, and brand image). Overall marketing strategy is also dynamic, not unchanging; its nature, both its specific inputs and the desired outputs, must change with changes in the company, its competitive situation, its markets, and the economic climate. The marketer must monitor the overall marketing strategy continually, as the tendency is always present for the mix of inputs to get out of balance, thus reducing their effectiveness in achieving the desired outputs, which also change from time to time. Therefore, the marketer needs some systematic basis for evaluating overall marketing strategy.

THE MARKETING AUDIT

Marketing Audit

Marketing experts recommend *marketing audits* to evaluate overall marketing strategy. One writer defines a marketing audit as "a systematic, critical, and unbiased review and appraisal of the basic objectives and policies of the marketing function and of the organization, methods, procedures, and personnel employed to implement those policies and achieve those objectives."[7]

Proponents of the marketing audit stress the importance of focusing on the overall marketing strategy and the methods used in implementing it. Thus, not every evaluation of marketing personnel, organization, or individual inputs of marketing strategy is a marketing audit—most such evaluations are only parts of an audit. A true marketing audit, then, is a systematic and comprehensive appraisal of a company's total marketing operation.[8]

There are no standardized formats for making marketing audits. Each firm's management (or its consultants) should design the type of marketing audit most appropriate to fit that firm's needs. However, as the definition suggests, each audit should cover at least six main aspects of marketing operations:

1. *Objectives:* Each marketing input should have clearly stated objectives (in terms of specific desired outputs).
2. *Policies:* Both explicit and implicit policies should be appraised from the standpoint of their consistency in achieving the marketing objectives.

[7] A. R. Oxenfeldt, *Executive Action in Marketing* (Belmont, Calif.: Wadsworth Publishing Co., Inc., 1966), p. 746.

[8] E. J. Kelley, *Marketing Planning and Competitive Strategy* (Englewood Cliffs, N.J.: Prentice-Hall, Inc., 1972), p. 121

3. *Organization:* Does the organization possess the necessary capabilities for achieving the marketing objectives? Are planning and control systems appropriate for the organization?
4. *Methods:* Are the individual strategies used for carrying out the stated policies appropriate? What opportunities are there for improvement?
5. *Procedures:* Are the specific steps (who does what and how) in implementing individual strategies logical? Are they well designed? Are those chosen the ones best fitted to the situation?
6. *Personnel:* All executives playing key roles in planning marketing operations and strategy, as well as those responsible for implementation of marketing programs, should be evaluated in terms of their effectiveness relative to stated objectives, policies, and other aspects of marketing operations.

In making a marketing audit, too, it is important for a company to examine both its market and its products. Fundamentally, in examining the market, the auditors should try to answer four key questions:

1. Who is buying what, and how?
2. Who is selling what, and how?
3. How is the competition doing?
4. How are we doing?

In appraising the product line, there are two big questions:

1. Does the product line meet the demands of the market?
2. Does the product line have the proper breadth and length?

The main purpose of a marketing audit, therefore, is to uncover opportunities for improving the effectiveness of the total marketing operation. The marketing audit is in addition to the normal procedure for controlling the progress of the annual marketing plan; it is designed to reveal something about the long-run optimality of the company's total marketing program.[9] In carrying out a marketing audit, management should seek to identify strengths as well as weaknesses—areas of marketing strength are ones which may have potentials for further exploitation, areas of marketing weakness are ones requiring correction and improvement. In addition, even though the word "audit" implies an after-the-fact evaluation (a carryover from financial jargon), a true marketing audit should help management not only in evaluating past performance but in formulating overall marketing strategy for the future.

[9] Philip Kotler and Richard S. Lopata, "The Marketing Audit," in *Marketing Manager's Handbook*, ed. Steuart H. Britt (Chicago: The Dartnell Corp., 1973), p. 1074.

Summary

You should now have a good "feel" for the entire field of marketing. From your study of this chapter, which reviewed much of the content of the first twenty chapters, you should have found yourself fitting together most of what you had learned previously about the many aspects of the subject into an integrated and comprehensive understanding of marketing. You should also have gained important additional insights on overall marketing strategy: you should understand why and how the nature and composition of overall marketing strategies vary with, and are influenced by, different competitive settings. You should understand why and how in formulating overall marketing strategy the marketer seeks a combination of inputs that is optimal in terms of the desired outputs. You should understand why and how in implementing overall marketing strategy the marketer coordinates the various inputs, paying particular attention to the timing aspects of their application. And you should understand why in evaluating overall marketing strategy the marketer should systematically and comprehensively appraise the total marketing operation with an eye toward future improvements. If you have this feel and know these "whys and hows," you know basically what marketing is all about.

QUESTIONS AND PROBLEMS

1. Do you believe that the marketing concept is a myth and given only superficial attention or do you feel that it is a reality in that marketing management makes a conscious, determined effort to put the marketing concept into practice? Do marketing policies, strategies, and total programs reflect an adherence to the marketing concept?
2. Do you feel that the "systems" approach to the management of marketing activities has resulted in better, more logical development of total marketing programs?
3. Clearly distinguish among the following:
   a. pure competition
   b. monopolistic competition
   c. oligopolistic competition
4. "After all is said and done, it makes little difference how you 'mix the ingredients' of your total marketing program as long as you do what your competitors do because competition literally dictates what you can and cannot do." Agree or disagree? Justify your position.
5. A systematic approach to the formulation of overall marketing strategy involves evaluating the probable impact of each major decision (on product, distribution, promotion, price, and the like) on the company's competitive situation and on its markets. Explain this statement in detail.

6. What is meant when it is said that some marketing inputs have "synergistic" potential?
7. In what way is the selection of marketing inputs affected by their "degree of substitutability"?
8. In the development of marketing strategy, how important is timing?
9. What is a marketing audit? What should be the scope of the audit? Is a marketing audit necessary to have a successful marketing program?
10. Critically evaluate marketing's role in society and in the economy. Are marketing's activities justified from the point of view of society? Is marketing essential to the smooth functioning of our economy?

CASE PROBLEMS

Case (a): Charlestown Enterprises, Inc., was a small manufacturer of sporting goods equipment whose products were distributed to consumers primarily through department stores, discount houses, and hardware stores. Three years ago, Charlestown Enterprises had been one of the first companies to crack the "street hockey" market. Currently, street hockey equipment (sticks, pucks, and nets) accounts for 16 percent of Charlestown's sales.

Street hockey is a game essentially similar to ice hockey, except that it is played on the street or any paved or smooth surface, with a few modifications of the standard ice hockey rules. The game had been played for years in both Canada and the United States, but its popularity had really boomed during the past three years. Street hockey was played during all twelve months of the year and was enjoyed by children and adults alike.

Because of the necessity to have special equipment for street hockey, several companies recognized the need and developed products to fit that need. Competition had become quite intense, but Charlestown Enterprises had managed to gain and hold a solid share of the market. However, its market position was being jeopardized by a new competitor who had just introduced an unbreakable street hockey stick. Replacement of hockey sticks represented the consumer's largest expenditure.

The new stick looked like a regular hockey stick, except that it was of a synthetic composition. The unbreakable synthetic stick served to eliminate a nagging problem of the standard wooden hockey sticks, which were vulnerable to breakage.

Charlestown Enterprises had no competitive product and its management acknowledged that it was very likely that the innovation would catch on with street hockey enthusiasts, although there would always be a market comprised of those who wanted to play with the "real thing." Charlestown's management was undecided as to whether it should go to work in developing a competitive substitute for the new hockey stick or stay with the standard wooden stick.

What should Charlestown Enterprises do?

Case (b): Walpole Tool Company was a small manufacturer of a limited line of power tools for home use. The company had been started only a few years ago by a man who had been employed by a leading home power tool producer and who decided to establish his own business with capital he had accumulated over a long period.

Mr. Todd Upshaw, owner and president of Walpole Tool Company, took a very active part in the technical development of his tools, using the experience he had gained over many years dealing with power tools. Mr. Upshaw had developed a complicated set of attachments that would allow a standard drill to be converted into a jig saw or a mini-circular saw. Many competitive drill kits were on the market—drills that could be used not only for drilling, but also for sanding, buffing, mixing paint, and as power screwdrivers. To Mr. Upshaw's knowledge, there was no drill attachment that could convert the basic unit into a jig saw or a circular saw. He did know, however, that one industry leader was in the process of developing a jig saw attachment.

While the new attachments were rather complicated, Mr. Upshaw felt that there was a need for this type of product and that the new product was technically sound, reliable, and safe to use. He recognized that an elaborate set of instructions would have to accompany the product, since it was not a simple matter to convert the drill into either a jig saw or a circular saw.

Walpole Tool Company had always operated "close to the vest," in that it did not have enough capital to venture into new areas. Consequently, Walpole had been a follower to industry leaders, waiting until a product idea had proven successful before it got into the market. Walpole was content to follow this policy and it was not surprising that its market share was quite small.

Mr. Upshaw was considering whether or not to abandon his policy of being a follower and, with his new product, become a leader in the industry.

Should Walpole Tool Company introduce the new product?

What are the risks that must be accepted when introducing a new product?

Case (c): Pellegrino's, Inc., was a regional marketer of a wide line of Italian meats and other foods. Pellegrino products were distributed intensively in a three-state area in the northeastern part of the United States. Pellegrino brand products could be found in a variety of stores, including supermarkets, delicatessens, sandwich and pizza shops, and restaurants. Consumer demand for Pellegrino products had steadily climbed to the point where it was the most asked-for brand of Italian food in each of the three states in which it was distributed. Pellegrino had recently introduced its own pizza mix and it, too, met with immediate success. The company was progressive and continually made an effort to supply consumers and users with the best product possible at reasonable prices.

Mr. Joe Pellegrino, president of the company and grandson of its founder, was instrumental to the great success of the company. He had displayed a keen sense of management, and the result was easily seen in the outstanding reputation enjoyed by the company. His overall marketing strategy was obviously succeeding.

Mr. Pellegrino was discussing a company matter with Mr. Ed Primavera, assistant marketing manager, when the subject of a marketing audit came up. Mr. Primavera felt that, despite the marketing success of the company, a marketing audit should be undertaken in light of the fact that Pellegrino's had never had any kind of systematic evaluation of its overall marketing strategy. Mr. Pellegrino felt adamantly that there was no need for any evaluation since things had been going along so well for so long and, further, with its hold on the market it was most unlikely that Pellegrino's, Inc., could be doing anything wrong. Besides, Mr. Pellegrino reasoned, doing a marketing audit would consume a great deal of his time—time that could be better spent managing the shop.

Should Pellegrino's, Inc., have a marketing audit?

What are the purposes of a marketing audit?

Does an obviously successful overall marketing strategy preclude the necessity for a marketing audit?

INDEXES

Name Index

Subject Index